AutoCAD 2017:
A Power Guide for Beginners and Intermediate Users

CADArtifex

The premium provider of learning products and solutions
www.cadartifex.com

AutoCAD 2017: A Power Guide for Beginners and Intermediate Users

Published by
CADArtifex
www.cadartifex.com

ISBN-13: 978-1537407548
ISBN-10: 1537407546

NOTICE TO THE READER

The publisher and the author make no representations or warranties with respect to the accuracy or completeness of the contents of this work/text and specifically disclaim all warranties, including without limitation warranties of fitness for a particular purpose. Publisher does not guarantee any of the products described in the text or perform any independent analysis in connection with any of the product information contained in the text. No warranty may be created or extended by sales or promotional materials. This work is sold with the understanding that the publisher is not engaged in rendering legal, accounting, or other professional services. Neither the publisher nor the author shall be liable for damages arising herefrom. Further, readers should be aware that Internet Websites listed in this work may have changed or disappeared between when this work was written and when it is read.

Examination Copies

Textbooks received as examination copies in any form such as paperback and eBook are for review only and may not be made available for the use of the student. These files may not be transferred to any other party. Resale of examination copies is prohibited.

Electronic Files

The electronic file/eBook in any form of this textbook is licensed to the original user only and may not be transferred to any other party.

Disclaimer

The author has made sincere efforts to ensure the accuracy of the material described herein, however the author makes no warranty, expressed or implied, with respect to the quality, correctness, accuracy, or freedom from error of this document or the products it describes.

www.cadartifex.com

Dedication

First and foremost, I would like to thank my parents for standing by my side throughout my career and while writing this book.

Heartfelt thanks go to my wife and my sisters for their patience and support in taking this challenge, and letting me spare time for it.

I would also like to acknowledge the efforts of the employees at CADArtifex for their dedication in editing the content of this textbook.

Content at a Glance

Table of Contents

Chapter 7. Editing Dimensions and Adding Text .... 341 - 370

Chapter 8. Modifying and Editing Drawings - II .... 371 - 386

12   Table of Contents

Preface

AutoCAD, the product of Autodesk Inc., is one of the biggest technology provider to engineering, architecture, construction, manufacturing, media, and entertainment industries. It offers complete design, engineering, and entertainment software that let you design, visualize, simulate, and publish your ideas before they are built or created. Moreover, Autodesk continues to develop the comprehensive portfolio of state-of-art 3D software for global markets.

AutoCAD delivers a rich set of productivity tools/commands that allow you to create stunning designs, speed up the documentation work, and add precision to your engineering and architectural drawings. AutoCAD is very comprehensive in its ability to create 2D and 3D drawings. With AutoCAD you can share your designs with your clients, sub-contractors and colleagues in smart new ways.

AutoCAD 2017: A Power Guide for Beginners and Intermediate Users textbook is designed for instructor-led courses as well as for self-paced learning. This textbook is intended to help engineers, designers, and CAD operators interested in learning AutoCAD for creating engineering and architectural 2D drawings. Taken together, this textbook can be a great starting point for new AutoCAD users and a great teaching aid in classroom training. This textbook consists of 12 chapters, covering Drafting & Annotation environment of AutoCAD, which teaches you how to use AutoCAD software to create, edit, plot, and manage real world engineering and architectural drawings.

This textbook not only focuses on the usage of the tools/commands of AutoCAD but also on the concept of design. Every chapter of this textbook contains tutorials, intended to help users to experience how things can be done in AutoCAD step-by-step. Moreover, every chapter ends with hands-on test drives that allow the users of this textbook to experience themselves the ease-of-use and powerful capabilities of AutoCAD.

Who Should Read This Book

This book is written with a wide range of AutoCAD users in mind, varying from beginners to advanced users and AutoCAD instructors. The easy-to-follow chapters of this book allow you to easily understand different design techniques and AutoCAD tools/commands.

What Is Covered in This Textbook

AutoCAD 2017: A Power Guide for Beginners and Intermediate Users textbook is designed to help you learn everything you need to know to start using AutoCAD 2017 with easy to understand, step-by-step tutorials. This textbook covers the following:

Chapter 1, "Introduction to AutoCAD," introduces system requirements for installing AutoCAD and explains how to start a new drawing file. It also introduces screen components, workspaces, and sheet sets of AutoCAD. Additionally, it explains how to change the color scheme, background color, and open and save drawing files in AutoCAD.

Chapter 2, "Creating Drawings - I," explains how to set drawing units, drawing limits, and grid and snap settings. It also introduces various coordinate systems used in AutoCAD and explains how to create line, circle, and arc entities in AutoCAD. Additionally, it introduces how to cancel, erase, undo, and navigating 2D drawing.

Chapter 3, "Using Drawing Aids and Selection Methods," introduces Ortho mode, Polar Tracking, Object Snap, and Object Snap Tracking. It also explains how to specify grids and snaps settings. Additionally, it explains how to work with layers and assigning objects to layers.

Chapter 4, "Creating Drawings - II," explains how to create rectangles, polygons, polylines, ellipses, elliptical arcs, splines, donuts, construction lines, ray lines, and points. It also introduces how to define point style/size.

Chapter 5, "Modifying and Editing Drawings - I," explains various object selection methods and how to trim and extend drawing entities. It also explains how to create arrays, mirror, fillet, chamfer, offset, move, copy, rotate, scale, stretch, and lengthen drawing entities.

Chapter 6, "Working with Dimensions and Dimensions Style," explains various components of a dimension, how to create a new dimension style, modify the existing dimension style, and override dimension style. It also explains how to apply various types of dimensions such as linear dimension, aligned dimension, angular dimension, diameter dimension, radius dimension, jogged dimension, ordinate dimension, and baseline dimension.

Chapter 7, "Editing Dimensions and Adding Text," explains how to edit dimensions by using the DIMEDIT command, DIMTEDIT command, DDEDIT command, dimension grips, Properties palette, and editing tools such as Trim, Extend, and Stretch. It also introduces adding text/notes to drawings, creating and modifying text Style, and adding text by using the Single Line and Multiline Text tools. Moreover, it also introduces editing single line and multiline texts, and how to convert single line text to multiline text.

Chapter 8, "Modifying and Editing Drawings - II," explains how to edit drawing entities by using the grips and the Properties palette. It also introduces matching the properties of an object with the other drawing objects. Moreover, it also explains how to identify the coordinates of a point in a drawing.

Chapter 9, "Hatching and Gradients," explains how to create different types of hatch patterns and gradients in enclosed areas of a drawing.

Chapter 10, "Working with Blocks and Xrefs," explains how to create and insert Block and WBlock in a drawing. It also explains how to edit Blocks and make dynamic Blocks. Moreover, it also explains how to work with external reference files (Xrefs).

Chapter 11, "**Working with Layouts**," explains how to get started with a Paper space/layout and introduces different components of a layout (Paper space). It also explains how to set up sheet/paper size of a layout, how to add, rename, and delete a layout. Moreover, it also explains how to work with viewports, access Model space within a viewport, clip an existing viewport, lock the object scale in a viewport, control the display of objects in a viewport, and control layer properties of a viewport. Additionally, it explains how to switch between Model space and layout, and how to create viewports in the Model space.

Chapter 12, "**Printing and Plotting**," explains how to configure plotter (output) device in AutoCAD. It also explains how to create a plot style and set up default plot style for plotting/printing. Additionally, it explains how to plot/print drawings in AutoCAD.

Icons/Terms used in this Textbook

The following icons and terms are used in this textbook:

Note

Note: Notes highlight information requiring special attention.

Tip

Tip: Tips provide additional advice, which increases the efficiency of the users.

Flyout

A Flyout is a pop-up in which a set of tools is grouped together, see Figure 1.

Drop-down List

A drop-down list is a pop-up in which a set of options/methods is grouped together to perform a task, see Figure 2.

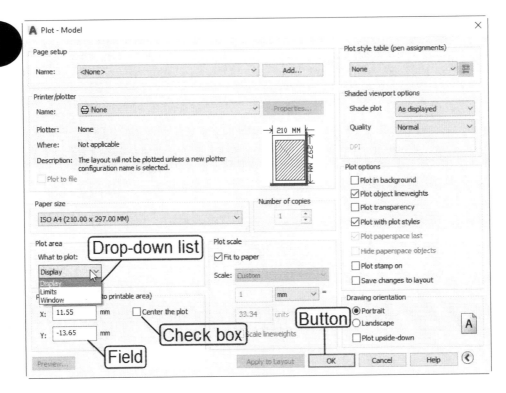

Field

A Field allows you to enter new value, or modify the existing value, as per your requirement, see Figure 2.

Check box

A Check box allows you to turn on or off the use of a particular option. A check box is used to select a particular option to turn it on, see Figure 2.

Button

A Button appears as a 3D icon and is used to confirm or discard an action. It is also used to turn on or off the uses of a particular option or command.

How to Contact the Author

We welcome your valuable feedback and suggestions. Please email us at *cadartifex@gmail.com* or *info@cadartifex.com*. You can also login to our web site *www.cadartifex.com* and write your feedback about the textbook.

Thank you very much for purchasing AutoCAD **2017: A Power Guide for Beginners and Intermediate Users** textbook. We hope that the information and concepts introduced in this textbook will help you to accomplish your professional goals.

Introduction to AutoCAD

In this chapter, you will learn the following:

- Installing AutoCAD
- Getting started with AutoCAD
- Starting a new drawing
- Working with various components of a drawing
- Starting a drawing file by using the Create New Drawing dialog box
- Changing the color scheme
- Changing the background color
- Working with workspaces
- Understanding sheet sets
- Opening a drawing file
- Saving a drawing file

Welcome to the world of Computer Added Design (CAD) with AutoCAD. AutoCAD, the product of Autodesk Inc., is one of the biggest technology provider to engineering, architecture, construction, manufacturing, media, and entertainment industries. It offers complete 3D design, engineering, and entertainment software that let you design, visualize, simulate, and publish your ideas before they are built or created. Moreover, Autodesk continues to develop the comprehensive portfolio of state-of-art 3D software for global markets.

AutoCAD delivers a rich set of productivity tools/commands that allow you to create stunning designs, speed up the documentation work, and add precision to your engineering and architectural drawings. AutoCAD is very comprehensive in its ability to create 2D and 3D drawings. With AutoCAD you can share your designs with your clients, sub-contractors and colleagues in smart new ways.

Due to the capabilities available with AutoCAD to create 2D and 3D drawings, AutoCAD is used across a wide range of industries by engineers, architects, project managers, graphic designers, and other professionals.

Installing AutoCAD

If AutoCAD is not installed in your system, you need to get it installed. However, before you start installing AutoCAD, you need to first check the system requirements and make sure that you have a system capable of running AutoCAD adequately. Below are the system requirements for installing AutoCAD 2017.

1. **Operating Systems:** Microsoft® Windows® 10 (desktop OS), Microsoft Windows 8.1 with Update KB2919355, and Microsoft Windows 7 SP1.
2. **CPU Type:** 1 gigahertz (GHz) or faster 32-bit (x86) or 64-bit (x64) processor.
3. **RAM:** For 32-bit AutoCAD 2017 - Minimum 2 GB and 3 GB or more recommended. For 64-bit AutoCAD 2017 - minimum 4 GB and 8 GB or more recommended
4. **Disk Space:** Installation 6.0 GB.
5. **Display Card:** Windows display adapter capable of 1360x768 with True Color capabilities and DirectX® 9 [1]. DirectX 11 compliant card recommended.

For more information about the system requirement for AutoCAD, visit *AutoCAD website at https://knowledge.autodesk.com/support/autocad/troubleshooting/caas/sfdcarticles/sfdcarticles/ System-requirements-for-AutoCAD-2017.html.*

Once the system is ready, install AutoCAD using the AutoCAD DVD or the downloaded AutoCAD data.

Getting Started with AutoCAD

Once the AutoCAD 2017 is installed on your system, start it by double-clicking on the **AutoCAD 2017** icon available on the desktop of your system. As soon as you double-click on the **AutoCAD 2017** icon, the system prepares for starting AutoCAD by loading all required files. Once all the required files have been loaded, the initial screen of AutoCAD 2017 appears, see Figure 1.1.

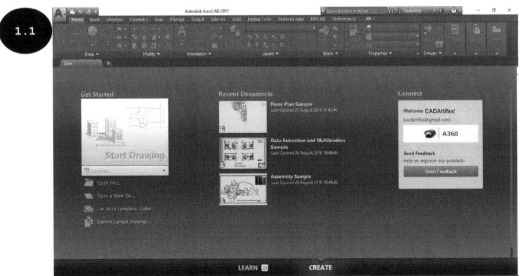

1.1

If you are starting AutoCAD for the first time after installing the software, the **Sign in** window appears, see Figure 1.2. In this window, enter your email or user name and then click on the **NEXT** button. The **Welcome** page of the **Sign in** window appears, see Figure 1.3. In this **Welcome** window, enter your password and then click on the **SIGN IN** button. The initial screen of AutoCAD 2017 appears, refer to Figure 1.1.

The initial screen of AutoCAD allows you to start new drawing, open an existing drawing, learn about various featured topics, and so on. The initial screen of AutoCAD is provided with **CREATE** and **LEARN** pages, see Figure 1.4. By default, the **CREATE** page is activated, see Figure 1.4. As a result, the initial screen of AutoCAD allows you to create a new drawing, open an existing drawing, and also displays a list of recently opened documents, see Figure 1.4. To activate the **LEARN** page, click on the **LEARN** option at the bottom of the initial screen of AutoCAD. The **LEARN** page provides access to learning resources such as What's New, Getting Started videos, Learning tips, and Online Resources, see Figure 1.5.

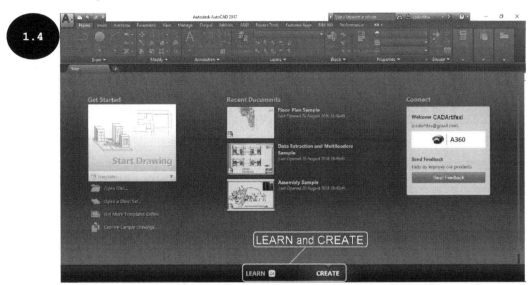

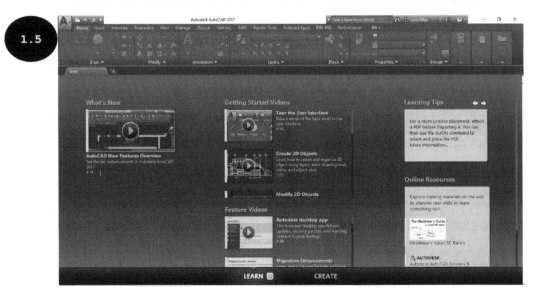

The various components of the **CREATE** page in the initial screen of AutoCAD are as follows:

Get Started

The options in the **Get Started** session are used to start a new drawing file and open an existing drawing file. The options are as follows:

Start Drawing

The **Start Drawing** option/icon of the **Get Started** session in the **CREATE** page is used to start a new drawing file with a default drawing template (*acad.dwt*). To start a new drawing file with a default template, click on the **Start Drawing** option/icon in the **Get Started** session. A new drawing file with default template (*acad.dwt*) gets started and appears in a different tab with the default name 'Drawing 1', as shown in Figure 1.6. Note that in this figure, the background color of the drawing area has been changed to white and the display of grids has been turned off for better clarity. You will learn about changing background color and grid settings later in this chapter. Also, the various components of a new drawing file are discussed later in this chapter.

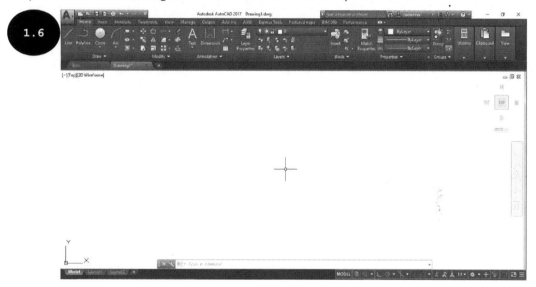

Templates

The **Templates** drop-down list of the **Get Started** session displays list of all the available drawing templates, see Figure 1.7. To invoke this drop-down list, click on **Templates** in the **Get Started** session. By default, the **acad.dwt** drawing template is selected in the **Templates** drop-down list. As a result, on clicking **Start Drawing** in the **Get Started** session. A new drawing file with *acad.dwt* drawing template (default template) gets started. Click on the required template in the **Templates** drop-down list to start a new drawing file with the specified drawing template.

The **Create New Sheet Set** option in the **Templates** drop-down list is used to create a new sheet set. A sheet set file is used to manage multiple drawings (sheets) of a project in a tree view, see Figure 1.8. In a sheet set, you can create multiple drawings and subsets under the main sheet set, see Figure 1.8. It helps in plotting, publishing, opening, e-transmiting, and zipping multiple drawings files easier and faster. To create a new sheet set, click on the **Create New Sheet Set** option in the **Templates** drop-down list. The **Create Sheet Set** dialog box appears. The options in this dialog box are used to create a new sheet set either by using an example sheet set file or the existing drawing files. You will learn more about creating a sheet set later in this chapter.

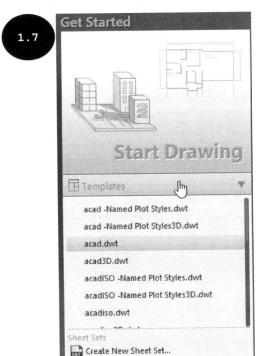

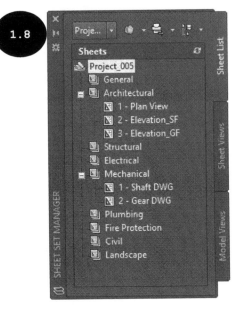

Open Files
The **Open Files** option in the **Get Started** session is used to open an existing drawing file. To open an existing drawing file, click on the **Open Files** option. The **Select File** dialog box appears. In this dialog box, browse to the location where the existing drawing file is saved. Next, select the drawing file and then click on the **Open** button in the **Select File** dialog box. The selected drawing file is opened in AutoCAD.

Open a Sheet Set
The **Open a Sheet Set** option in the **Get Started** session is used to open an existing sheet set file. To open an existing sheet set file, click on the **Open a Sheet Set** option. The **Open Sheet Set** dialog box appears. This dialog box displays the list of all the existing created sheet sets. Select the required sheet set and then click on the **Open** button.

Get More Templates Online
The **Get More Templates Online** option in **Get Started** session is used to download additional template files.

Explore Sample Drawings
The **Explore Sample Drawings** option is used to open already installed sample drawing files.

Recent Documents

The **Recent Documents** session of the **CREATE** page in the initial screen of AutoCAD displays the list of recently opened drawing files. You can click on any recently opened drawing file in the list to open it again.

Connect

The **Connect** session of the initial screen is used to sign in to **A360** account to access the online services. Also, you can access the online form to provide feedback.

Starting a New Drawing

As discussed earlier, to start a new drawing file, click on the **Start Drawing** option/icon in the **Get Started** session of the **CREATE** page in the initial screen of AutoCAD, see Figure 1.9. Alternatively, click on the **+sign**, next to the **Start** tab in the initial screen to AutoCAD, to start a new drawing file with default template, see Figure 1.10. In addition, click on the **New** tool in the **Quick Access Toolbar**, see Figure 1.11. The **Select template** dialog box appears, see Figure 1.12. By default, the *acad.dwt* drawing template is selected in this dialog box. The *acad.dwt* drawing template is used to start the 2D drawing environment whereas the *acad3D.dwt* drawing template is used to start the 3D modeling environment. Select the required drawing template and then click on the **Open** button in the dialog box. The new drawing gets started depending upon the drawing template selected.

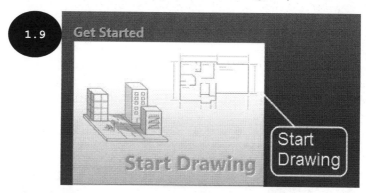

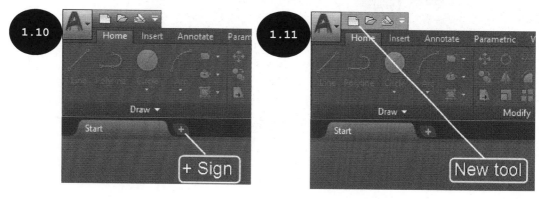

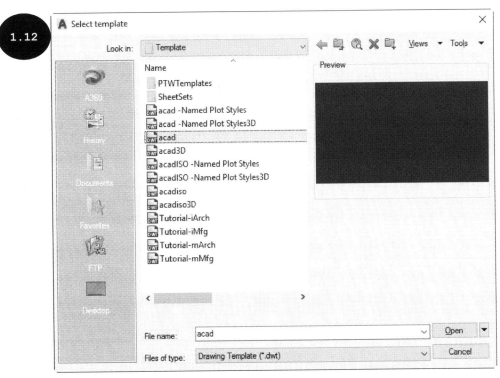

You can also start a new drawing without a drawing template either in metric or imperial unit system by using the **Select template** dialog box. To start a new drawing without using any drawing template, click on the down arrow, next to the **Open** button in the **Select template** dialog box, see Figure 1.13. A drop-down list appears, see Figure 1.13. In this drop-down list, the **Open with on Template - Imperial** and **Open with no Template - Metric** options are available. You can click on the required option.

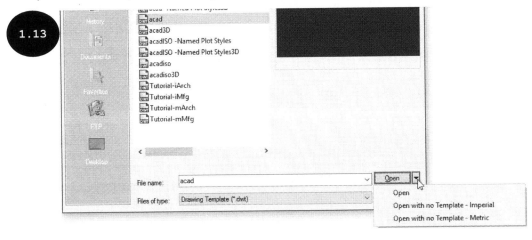

Note: As discussed, when you click on the **New** tool in the **Quick Access Toolbar**, the **Select template** dialog box appears for starting a new drawing file, by default. This is because the system variable for STARTUP is set to 3. If you set it to 1 then on clicking the **New** tool, the **Create New Drawing** dialog box appears, see Figure 1.14. You can also start a new drawing by using this **Create New Drawing** dialog box. You will learn about setting system variable and starting a new drawing file by using the **Create New Drawing** dialog box later in this chapter.

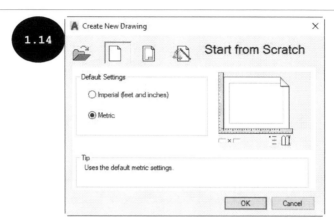

Figure 1.15 shows various components of a new drawing file such as **Application menu, Quick Access Toolbar, Ribbon, ViewCube, Command Window, Navigation Bar**, and **Status Bar**. Note that the initial screen of a new drawing, shown in the Figure 1.15 displayed using the default *acad.dwt* template (2D drawing environment). Also, the background color of the drawing area has been changed to white and the display of grids is turned off for better clarity in this figure. You will learn about changing the background color of the drawing area and controlling the display of grids later in this chapter.

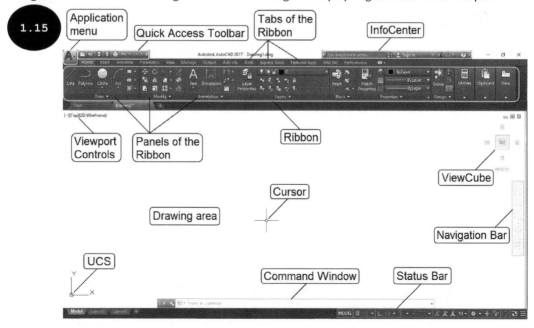

Figure 1.16 shows the initial screen of a new drawing displayed using the *acad3D.dwt* template (3D drawing environment). Note that the tools available in the **Ribbon** depend upon the activated workspace. By default, the **Drafting and Annotation** workspace is the active workbench of a new drawing. As a result, the tools related to drafting and annotation are available in the **Ribbon**. You can switch among the **Drafting and Annotation**, **3D Basics**, or **3D Modeling** workspace by using the **Workspace Switching** flyout, see Figure 1.17. In this figure, the **3D Modeling** workspace is the activated workspace for the drawing. You will learn more about workspace later in this chapter.

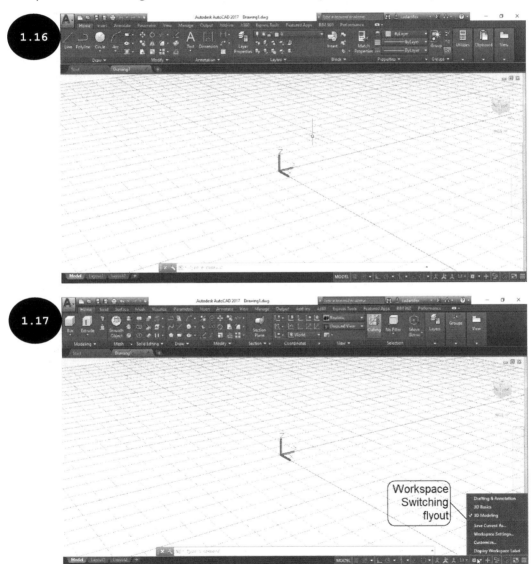

Working with Various Components of a Drawing

The various components of a new drawing such as **Application menu**, **Quick Access Toolbar**, **Ribbon**, **ViewCube**, **Command Window**, **Navigation Bar**, and **Status Bar** are as follows:

Application Menu

The **Application menu** is used to access the commonly used tools to start, open, save, export, print/publish, and so on a drawing file. To invoke the **Application menu**, click on the **Application** button (red AutoCAD icon) at the upper left corner of the screen, see Figure 1.18.

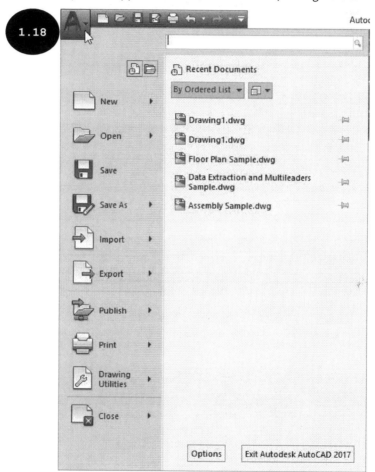

Quick Access Toolbar

The **Quick Access Toolbar** is provided with frequently used tools such as **New**, **Open**, **Save**, **Save As**, **Plot**, and **Undo**, see Figure 1.19. This tool is available at the upper left corner of the screen. In addition to the default tools, you can customize to add or remove tools in the **Quick Access Toolbar**, as per the requirement.

To add more tools in the **Quick Access Toolbar**, right-click on a tool in the **Quick Access Toolbar**. A flyout appears, see Figure 1.20. In this flyout, click on the **Customize Quick Access Toolbar** option. The **Customize User Interface** editor window appears. This editor window displays the list of all the available tools/command in AutoCAD. Move the cursor over the tool/command to be added in the **Quick Access Toolbar** and then press and hold the left mouse button. Next, drag the cursor where you want to add this tool/command in the **Quick Access Toolbar** and then release the left mouse button. The selected tool gets added in the specified location in the **Quick Access Toolbar**. Similarly, you can add multiple tools by dragging the required tools/commands one by one from the **Customize User Interface** editor window to the **Quick Access Toolbar**. You can also drag and drop multiple tools at a time in the **Quick Access Toolbar** from the **Customize User Interface** editor window by pressing the CTRL key. After adding the required tools in the **Quick Access Toolbar**, click on the OK button to exit the **Customize User Interface** editor window.

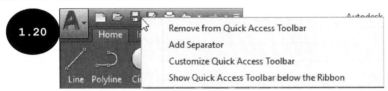

To remove tools from the **Quick Access Toolbar**, move the cursor over the tool to be removed and then right-click. A flyout appears, see Figure 1.20. In this flyout, click on the **Remove from Quick Access Toolbar** option. The selected tool is removed.

Ribbon

The **Ribbon** is composed of a series of tabs such as **Home**, **Insert**, and **Annotate** in which set of similar tools are grouped in different panels, see Figure 1.21. For example, the tools used to create drawing objects are grouped in the **Draw** panel and the tools used to modify or edit objects are grouped in the **Modify** panel, see Figure 1.21. Note that the availability of tools, panels, and tabs in the **Ribbon** depends upon the activated workspace.

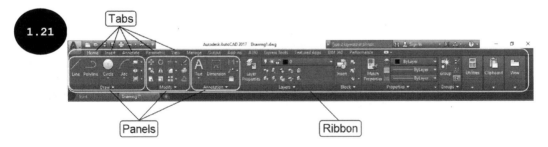

By default, the **Ribbon** is docked horizontally at the top of the drawing area. You can dock the **Ribbon** vertically to the right or left of the drawing area. You can also undock the **Ribbon** such that it can float within the drawing area. To dock the **Ribbon** vertically to the right or left of the drawing area, right-click on a tab in the **Ribbon**. A shortcut menu appears, see Figure 1.22. In this shortcut menu, click on the **Undock** option. The **Ribbon** gets undocked and appears in floating state in the drawing area. Next, right-click on the title bar of the undocked **Ribbon**. A shortcut menu appears. In this shortcut menu, click on either the **Anchor Left** < or the **Anchor Right** > option. To dock the **Ribbon** back to the default position (horizontally at the top of the drawing area), press and hold the left mouse button on the title bar of the **Ribbon** and then drag the Ribbon toward the top of the drawing area. Next, release the left mouse button when the outline of a window appears at the top of the drawing area.

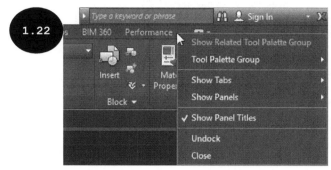

You can also change the default display state of the **Ribbon (Full Ribbon)** to three minimized states: **Minimize to Tabs, Minimize to Panel Titles**, and **Minimize to Panel Buttons**. To change the display state of the **Ribbon**, click on the down arrow available at the end of the last tab in the title bar of the **Ribbon**, see Figure 1.23. A flyout appears, see Figure 1.23. In this flyout, click on the required display state. In the **Minimize to Tabs** display state, the **Ribbon** gets minimized such that only tab titles appear in the **Ribbon**. In the **Minimize to Panel Titles** display state, only the tab and panel titles appear in the **Ribbon**. In the **Minimize to Panel Buttons** display state, only the tab titles and panel buttons appear in the **Ribbon**.

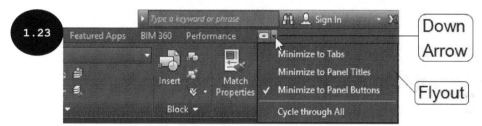

You can also cycle through the different states of **Ribbon** by clicking on the small rectangular button with a black arrow in it, located at the end of the last tab in the **Ribbon**, see Figure 1.24. On clicking this rectangular button, you can cycle through all four display states of the **Ribbon** in an order, **Full Ribbon, Minimize to Panel Buttons, Minimize to Panel Titles, Minimize to Tabs**.

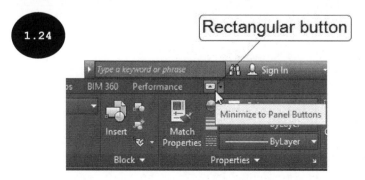

InfoCenter

The **InfoCenter** is available at the upper right corner of the AutoCAD window, see Figure 1.25. It is used to access help document for finding the information related to a topic, a tool/command, and so on. Also, it provides tools to access the Autodesk A360 account, Autodesk Exchange Apps, Autodesk YouTube/Facebook/Twitter channels, and so on. The various components of the **InfoCenter** are as follows:

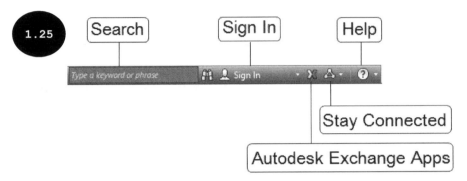

Search

The **Search** field is used to enter a keyword of a topic or command/tool to find the information related to it in the help document.

Sign In

The **Sign In** tool is used to provide information about the Autodesk A360 and to login/sign in to the Autodesk A360 account. When you click on **Sign In** tool in the **InfoCenter**, a flyout appears, see Figure 1.26. In this flyout, click on the **Sign In to A360** tool to sign in to the Autodesk A360 account. To know more about Autodesk A360, click on the **About A360** tool in this flyout.

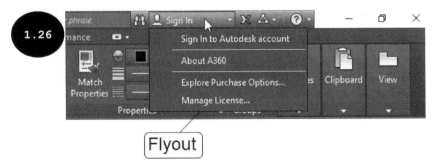

Autodesk Exchange Apps

The **Autodesk Exchange Apps** tool is used to access the Autodesk APP STORE web page for downloading the plug-ins and standlone applications.

Stay Connected

The **Stay Connected** tool is used to stay connected with the Autodesk online community. When you click on **Stay Connected** in the **InfoCenter**, a flyout appears, see Figure 1.27. This flyout provides various tools to stay connected with Autodesk.

Help

The **Help** tool is used to access online help document. When you click on the **Help** tool in the **InfoCenter**, the online **Help** document gets opened. If you click on the down arrow next to the **Help** tool in the **InfoCenter**, a flyout appears, see Figure 1.28. By using the tools in this flyout, you can access the online help document, download offline help, send feedback, get product information, and so on.

Command Window

A small horizontal window provided at the bottom of the drawing area is known as the Command Window, see Figure 1.29.

The Command Window is used to enter commands and displays subsequent command prompt sequence. By default, the Command Window displays one line of text (command prompt), which provides the information about the action to be taken and various options based on the currently active command/tool. Notice that as you continue working through a command/tool, the earlier command prompts get scrolled up and appear in faded background just above the Command Window, see Figure 1.30. Note that, by default, only last three command prompt lines appear above the Command Window, see Figure 1.30. To display all the previous command prompt lines, press the F2 key [Fn (function key) + F2]. You can also increase or decrease the display area of the Command Window to display previous command prompts. To increase or decrease the display area of the Command Window, move the cursor over the top edge of the Command Window and then drag it by pressing and holding the left mouse button.

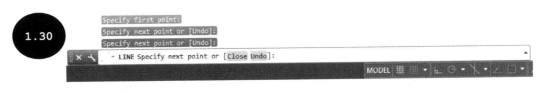

1.30

Tip: It is recommended for new users to pay attention to the command prompt as through it AutoCAD communicates with you and inform you about the action to be taken.

ViewCube

The **ViewCube** is provided at the upper right corner of the drawing area, see Figure 1.31.

1.31

It is used to change the view/orientation of a drawing/model. You can switch between standard and isometric views by using the **ViewCube**. It is primarily used for 3D modeling where you can view the 3D model in different standard and isometric views. By default, it is in an inactive state. When you move the cursor over the **ViewCube**, it becomes active and works as a navigation tool. You can navigate the drawing by using the **ViewCube** components, see Figure 1.32. The various **ViewCube** components are as follows:

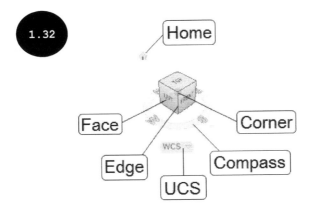

1.32

Home

The **Home** icon of the **ViewCube** is used to bring the current view of the drawing to the default home position.

Corner

A corner of the **ViewCube** is used to get an isometric view or to rotate the view freely in all directions. To get an isometric view, click on a corner of the **ViewCube** and to rotate the view freely in all directions, drag a corner of the **ViewCube** by pressing and holding the left mouse button.

Compass

The **Compass** is used to rotate the view. To rotate the view by using the **Compass**, press and hold the left mouse button on the **Compass** ring and then drag the cursor.

Edge

An edge of the **ViewCube** is used to get an edge-on view or to rotate the view freely in all directions. To get an edge-on view, click on an edge of the **ViewCube** and to rotate the view freely in all directions, drag an edge by pressing and holding the left mouse button.

Face

A face of the **ViewCube** is used to get an orthogonal view such as a top, front, or right. For example, to get a top view of the drawing/model, click on the top face of the **ViewCube**.

UCS

When you click on the down arrow available in the **UCS** option of the **ViewCube**, the **UCS** drop-down list appears, see Figure 1.33. By using the options in this drop-down list, you can select an existing UCS or create a new UCS, see Figure 1.33. The term UCS stands for User Coordinate System, which is used to define the coordinate system in 2D and 3D environments. By default, AutoCAD is provided with World Coordinate System (WCS), which is a global system. You will learn more about coordinate systems in later chapters.

Note: If the **ViewCube** is not displayed on the right corner of the drawing area, click on the **View Cube** tool in the **Viewport Tools** panel of the **View** tab in the **Ribbon**, see Figure 1.34.

Navigation Bar

The **Navigation Bar** is used to access navigation tools such as **Zoom** and **Pan**, see Figure 1.35. It is available at the right of the drawing area. You can turn on or off the display of **Navigation Bar** by clicking on the **Navigation Bar** tool in the **Viewport Tools** panel of the **View** tab in the **Ribbon**, see Figure 1.36. The various navigation tools in the **Navigation Bar** are discussed in Chapter 2.

Status Bar

The **Status Bar** provides quick access to some of the commonly used drawing tools, which allow you to toggle settings such as grid, snap, dynamic input mode, ortho mode, polar tracking, and object snap, see Figure 1.37. In addition to the default tools in the **Status Bar**, you can customize to add or remove tools in the **Status Bar**, as per the requirement. To customize the **Status Bar**, click on the **Customization** tool in the **Status Bar**, see Figure 1.37. The **Customization** menu appears, see Figure 1.38.

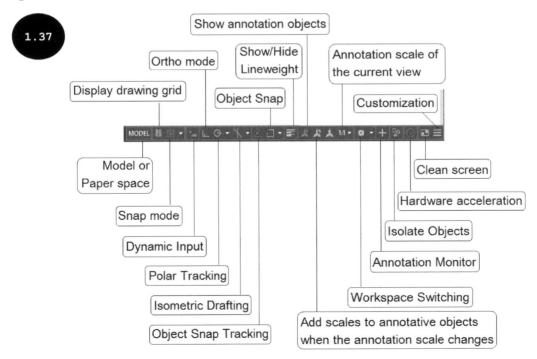

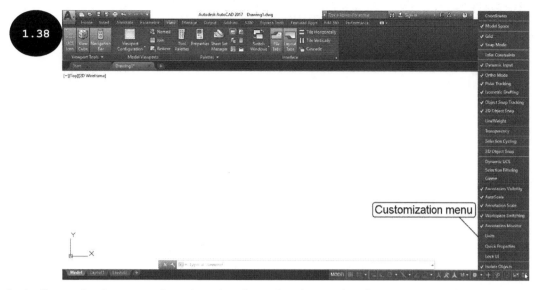

In the **Customization** menu, the tick mark in the tools indicates that the respective tools are currently available in the **Status Bar**. Click on the tools in the **Customization** menu to be added or removed in the **Status Bar**. Some of the tools in the **Status Bar** are as follows:

Model or Paper space

MODEL The **Model or Paper space** tool is used to toggle between Model space and Paper space environments of AutoCAD. When you start AutoCAD, the Model space is the default activated environment for creating drawings. You can create drawings in the Model space, whereas the Paper space is generally used for plotting drawings and generating different drawing views. You will learn more about Model space and Paper space in Chapter 11.

Display drawing grid

The **Display drawing grid** tool is used to turn on or off the display of grids in the drawing area. To turn on or off the display of grids, click on the **Display drawing grid** tool in the **Status Bar** or press F7 function key. Moreover, you can change the grid settings by using this tool. To change the grid settings, right-click on the **Display drawing grid** tool in the **Status Bar**. The **Grid Settings** option appears. Click on the **Grid Settings** option. The **Drafting Settings** dialog box appears. By using the options in the **Snap and Grid** tab of this dialog box, you can change the grid settings as required. You will learn more about specifying the grid settings in Chapter 2.

Snap Mode

The **Snap mode** tool is used to turn on or off the snap mode. You can also press F9 key to turn on or off the snap mode. The snap mode allows the cursor to move in a fixed specified incremental distance in the drawing area. For example, if the snap mode setting is specified to 1 unit in X and Y directions then the cursor will move 1 unit incremental distance in X and Y directions. To specify the snap mode settings, right-click on the **Snap mode** tool in the **Status Bar** and then click on the **Snap Settings** option in the shortcut menu that is displayed. The **Drafting Settings** dialog box appears. By using the options in the **Snap and Grid** tab of this dialog box, you can specify the snap settings as required. You will learn more about specifying the snap settings in Chapter 2.

Dynamic Input

The **Dynamic Input** tool is used to turn on or off the Dynamic Input mode. If the Dynamic Input mode is turned on, you can enter inputs such as commands and coordinates near the cursor in the drawing area instead of entering in the Command Window. It acts as an alternative method of entering commands in AutoCAD. When a command is in progress, the Dynamic Input boxes appear near the cursor tip which allows you to enter coordinates and specify options, see Figure 1.39. You will learn more about entering coordinates and commands by using the Dynamic Input boxes and Command Window in later chapters.

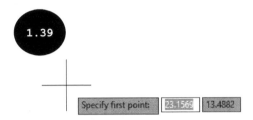

Ortho Mode

The **Ortho Mode** tool is used to turn on or off the Ortho mode. You can also press F8 function key to turn on or off the Ortho mode. When the Ortho mode is turned on, the movement of the cursor gets restricted to horizontal and vertical only. As a result, you can only draw straight line at right angles.

Polar Tracking

The **Polar Tracking** tool is used to turn on or off the Polar tracking mode. When the Polar tracking mode is turned on, the movement of the cursor gets snapped at a specified angle increment in the drawing area. To specify the angle incremental value, right-click on the **Polar Tracking** button in the **Status Bar**. A flyout appears, see Figure 1.40. This flyout displays a list of pre-defined incremental angles. You can select the required increment angle from this flyout. You can also specify a new increment angle other than the increment angles listed in the flyout. To specify a new increment angle, click on the **Tracking Settings** option in the flyout. The **Drafting Settings** dialog box appears. In this dialog box, specify the increment angle in the **Increment angle** field of the **Polar Tracking** tab and then click on the **OK** button. The new increment angle for polar tracking has been specified.

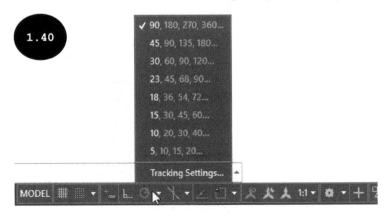

Isometric Drafting

The **Isometric Drafting** tool is used to turn on or off the Isometric Drafting mode. When the Isometric Drafting mode is turned on, you can easily create 2D isometric representation of a 3D model. You can select the **isoplane Left**, **isoplane Top**, or **isoplane Right** as the current 2D isometric drafting plane for creating 2D isometric drawing. By default, the **isoplane Left** drafting plane is selected as the current 2D isometric drafting plane. To select the required 2D isometric drafting plane, click on the down arrow next to the **Isometric Drafting** tool in the **Status Bar**. A flyout appears, see Figure 1.41. In this flyout, click on the required 2D isometric drafting plane for creating isometric drawing.

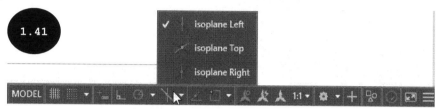

Object Snap Tracking

The **Object Snap Tracking** tool is used to turn on or off the Object Snap Tracking mode. The Object Snap Tracking mode works in conjunction with Object Snap mode and is used to align new points with respect to existing points or locations in a drawing. For example, to draw a circle at the center of a rectangle, move the cursor over the midpoint the horizontal line 'A' (see Figure 1.42) and then move the cursor vertically downward when the cursor snaps to the midpoint of the horizontal line. A vertical tracking line appears, see Figure 1.42. Next, move the cursor over the midpoint of the vertical line 'B' and then move the cursor horizontally toward the right. A horizontal tracking line appears, see Figure 1.43. Next, move the cursor at the intersection of both the tracking lines and then click to specify the midpoint of circle, see Figure 1.44.

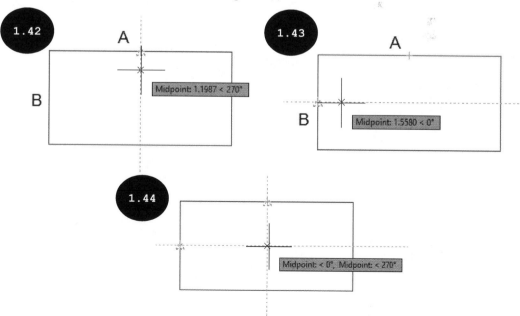

Object Snap

The **Object Snap** tool is used to turn on or off the Object Snap mode. The Object Snap mode is used to snap the cursor over the existing objects of the drawing such as midpoint, endpoint, and intersection. It is very useful method of specifying exact points in the drawing area. When the Object Snap mode is turned on, the cursor snaps to the existing objects of the drawing as per the specified object snap settings. To specify or control the object snap settings, right-click on the **Object Snap** tool in the **Status Bar**. A flyout appears, see Figure 1.45. This flyout displays a list of all object snaps. Note that a tick mark in front of object snaps in the flyout indicates that the respective object snaps are activated. You can click on the required object snaps to activate or deactivate them in the flyout. Note that the cursor snaps to the objects in the drawing area depending upon the active object snaps. For example, if only the **Endpoint** object snap is activated then the cursor will only snap to the end points of existing objects in the drawing area, see Figure 1.46.

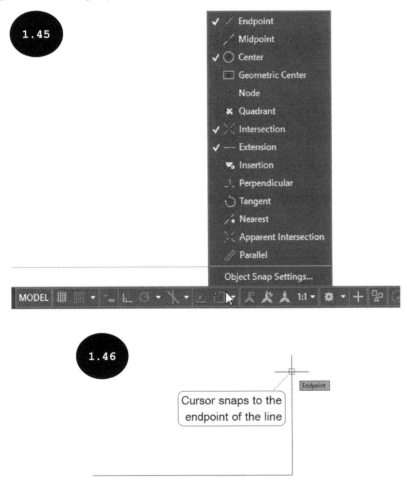

1.45

✓ Endpoint
  Midpoint
✓ Center
  Geometric Center
  Node
  Quadrant
✓ Intersection
✓ Extension
  Insertion
  Perpendicular
  Tangent
  Nearest
  Apparent Intersection
  Parallel
Object Snap Settings...

MODEL

1.46

Endpoint

Cursor snaps to the
endpoint of the line

You can also invoke the **Drafting Settings** dialog box by clicking on the **Object Snap Settings** option in the flyout to control the object snap setting, see Figure 1.47. In the **Object Snap** tab of the dialog box, select the required object snap check boxes to activate them. For example, on selecting the **Endpoint** check box, the endpoint object snap is activated and the cursor snaps to the endpoints of the existing drawing objects in the drawing area. Similarly, on selecting the **Midpoint** check box, the midpoint object snap is activated and the cursor snaps to the midpoints of existing drawing objects in the drawing area. To select all the object snap check boxes, click on the **Select All** button in the dialog box. Similarly, to uncheck all the object snap check boxes, click on the **Clear All** button in the dialog box. After selecting the required object snap check boxes in the dialog box, click on the **OK** button. The object snap settings are specified and the cursor snaps to the existing objects in the drawing area depending upon the specified object snap settings in the dialog box.

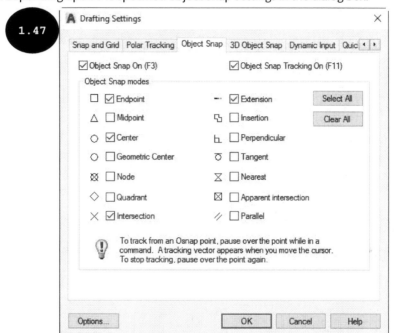

Show/Hide Lineweight

The **Show/Hide Lineweight** tool is used to turn on or off the display of the object lineweight in the drawing area. You will learn more about specifying lineweight to drawing objects in later chapters.

Show annotation objects

The **Show annotation objects** tool is used to turn on or off the display of annotation objects in the drawing area.

Annotation scale of the current view

The **Annotation scale of the current view** flyout is used to select the annotation scale for the annotative objects in the Model space. To invoke this flyout, click on the down arrow next to the **Annotation scale of the current view** button in the **Status Bar**.

Workspace Switching

The **Workspace Switching** flyout is used to switch among the AutoCAD workspaces: **Drafting & Annotation**, **3D Basics**, and **3D Modeling**. To invoke the **Workspace Switching** flyout, click on the down arrow next to the **Workspace Switching** button in the **Status Bar**, see Figure 1.48. Note that the availability of tools in the **Ribbon** depends upon the current active workspace.

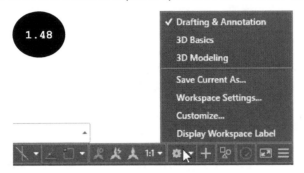

Isolate Objects

The **Isolate Objects** tool is used to isolate and display objects in the drawing area. You can isolate an object or a set of objects in the drawing area. To isolate objects, click on the **Isolate Objects** tool in the **Status Bar**. A flyout appears, see Figure 1.49. In this flyout, click on the **Isolate Objects** tool. You are prompted to select objects to be isolated in the drawing area. Select the objects to be isolated and then right-click or press ENTER. The selected objects get isolated such that the remaining drawing objects are hidden. You can also hide an object or a set of objects in the drawing area by using the **Hide Objects** tool of the flyout. To hide objects in the drawing area, click on the **Hide Objects** tool in the flyout, see Figure 1.49. You are prompted to select objects to be hidden. Select the objects to be hidden and then right-click or press ENTER. The selected objects get hidden in the drawing area. To display all the drawing objects back in the drawing area or end the object isolation, click on the **End Object Isolation** tool in the flyout, see Figure 1.50.

Clean Screen

The **Clean screen** tool in the **Status Bar** is used to expand the drawing display area by hiding the **Ribbon** and all the available toolbars except the Command Window, **Status Bar**, and **Quick Access Toolbar**.

Customization

The **Customization** tool is used to customize the **Status Bar**. To customize the **Status Bar**, click on the **Customization** tool in the **Status Bar**. The **Customization** menu appears, which displays a list of all the tools that can be added to the **Status Bar**. Note that a tick mark in front of tools in the **Customization** menu indicates that the respective tools are currently available in the **Status Bar**. You can click on the tools in the **Customization** menu to add or remove them in the **Status Bar**.

Starting a Drawing File by using the Create New Drawing dialog box

As discussed, when you click on the **New** tool in the **Quick Access Toolbar** for stating a new drawing file, the **Select template** dialog box appears, by default. To invoke the **Create New Drawing** dialog box on clicking the **New** tool in the **Quick Access Toolbar**, enter STARTUP in the Command Window and then press ENTER. You are prompted to enter new value for STARTUP.

```
Enter new value for STARTUP <3>:
```

Enter 1 in the Command Window and then press ENTER. The new system variable for the STARTUP is set to 1. Now, when you click on the **New** tool in the **Quick Access Toolbar** for stating a new drawing file, **the Create New Drawing** dialog box appears, see Figure 1.51. By using the **Create New Drawing** dialog box, you can start a new drawing file from scratch, use a template, or a wizard to start a new drawing file. The methods of starting a new drawing file by using the **Create New Drawing** dialog box are as follows:

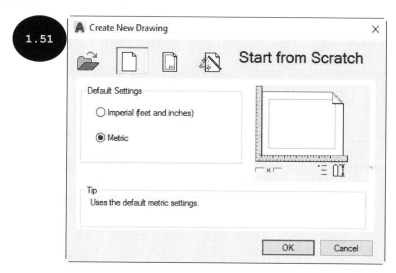

Starting a Drawing file from Scratch

To start a new drawing file from scratch by using the **Create New Drawing** dialog box, make sure that the **Start from Scratch** button is activated in the dialog box, see Figure 1.51. You can start a new drawing file from scratch either with the default imperial (*acad.dwt*) or metric (*acadiso.dwt*) settings. By default, the **Metric** radio button is selected in the dialog box. As a result, on clicking the **OK** button, a new drawing file with default metric settings is invoked. To start a new drawing file with default imperial settings, select the **Imperial (feet and inches)** radio button in the dialog box and then click on the **OK** button.

Starting a Drawing file by using a Template

To start a new drawing file by using a standard drawing template, click on the **Use a Template** button in the **Create New Drawing** dialog box. A list of drawing templates appears in the dialog box, see Figure 1.52. By default, the *Acad.dwt* drawing template is selected in the dialog box. Note that the selection of default template depends upon the settings specified while installing AutoCAD. Select a required template in this dialog box to start a new drawing file. Note that the new drawing file has the same settings as of the selected drawing template. A drawing template contains drawing settings such as units, limits, text height, and scale factor. After selecting a required drawing template, click on the **OK** button. The new drawing file gets started.

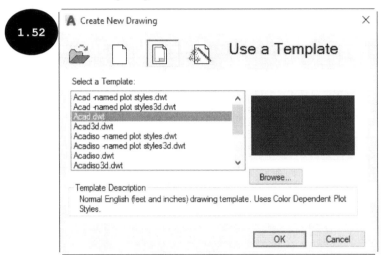

Starting a Drawing file by using a Wizard

In AutoCAD, you can also start a new drawing with **Advanced Setup** and **Quick Setup** wizards which allow you to specify settings such as unit, angle, angle measurement, angle direction, and area for the new drawing. To start a new drawing file by using a wizard, click on the **Use a Wizard** button in the **Create New Drawing** dialog box, see Figure 1.53. The **Advanced Setup** and **Quick Setup** options appear in the **Select a Wizard** area of the dialog box, see Figure 1.53.

The **Advanced Setup** option allows you to specify unit, angle, angle measurement, angle direction, and so on for the new drawing, whereas the **Quick Setup** option only allows you to specify unit and area settings for the drawing.

To start a new drawing with **Advanced Setup** wizard, select the **Advanced Setup** option in the **Select a Wizard** area of the dialog box and then click on the **OK** button. The **Advanced Setup** dialog box displays **Units** page in it, see Figure 1.54. The options in the **Units** page of the **Advanced Setup** dialog box are used to set the units for measurement in the drawing. Select the required unit of measurement: Decimal, Engineering, Architectural, Fractional, or Scientific by selecting the respective radio button. You can also specify the precision for the measurement by using the **Precision** drop-down list of the **Units** page. After selecting the unit and precision for the drawing, click on the **Next** button. The **Angle** page of the **Advanced Setup** dialog box appears, see Figure 1.55.

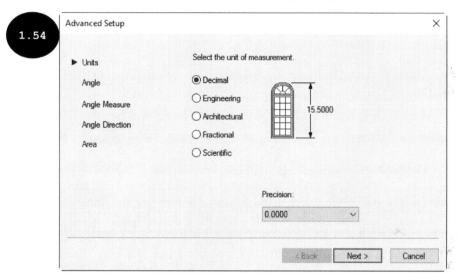

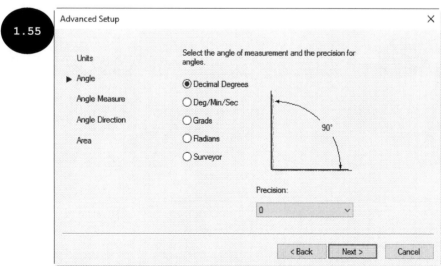

The options in the **Angle** page of the **Advanced Setup** dialog box are used to set the angle of measurement and the precision for angle measurement for the drawing. Select the required angle of measurement: Decimal Degrees, Deg/Min/Sec, Grads, Radians, or Surveyor by selecting the respective radio button. Also, select the precision for angle measurement by using the **Precision** drop-down list of the **Angle** page. After selecting the angle and precision for angle measurement, click on the **Next** button. The **Angle Measure** page of the **Advanced Setup** dialog box appears, see Figure 1.56.

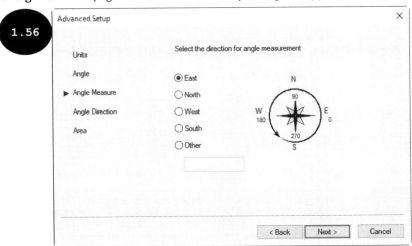

The options in the **Angle Measure** page are used to select the direction for angle measurement: East, North, West, or South by selecting the respective radio button. You can also set your own direction for angle measurement as per the requirement by using the **Other** radio button in this page. On selecting the **Other** radio button, the field below the **Other** radio button gets enabled. In this field, you can specify your own direction for angle measurement. Note that by default, the **East** radio button is selected in this page. As a result, the angle measures from east (0-degree) in the counter-clockwise orientation. You can set the orientation (clockwise or counter-clockwise) for angle measurement in the **Angle Direction** page which appears on clicking the **Next** button in the **Angle Measure** page, see Figure 1.57.

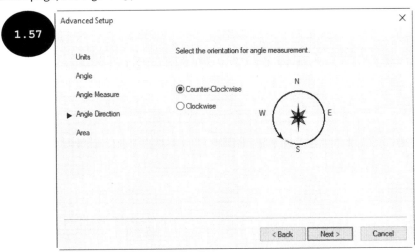

The **Angle Direction** page of the **Advanced Setup** dialog box is used to specify the orientation for the angle measurement. You can select either the counter-clockwise or clockwise orientation for angle measurement by selecting the respective radio button in this page. After selecting the orientation for angle measurement, click on the **Next** button. The **Area** page of the **Advanced Setup** dialog box appears, see Figure, 1.58.

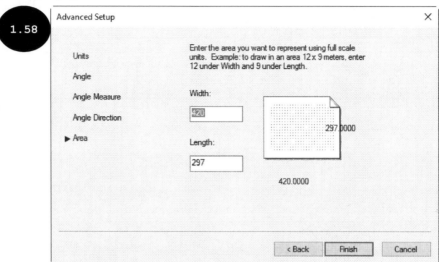

The **Area** page of the **Advanced Setup** dialog box is used to specify the drawing area for creating the drawing. You can specify the drawing area by entering the width and length in the **Width** and **Length** fields of the page, respectively. After specifying all the drawing settings, click on the **Finish** button. A new drawing with the specified settings gets started.

Similar to **Advanced Setup** wizard, you can also start a new drawing with **Quick Setup** wizard of the **Create New Drawing** dialog box. The only difference is that the **Quick Setup** wizard allows you to specify only unit and area settings in the respective pages of the dialog box, see Figure 1.59.

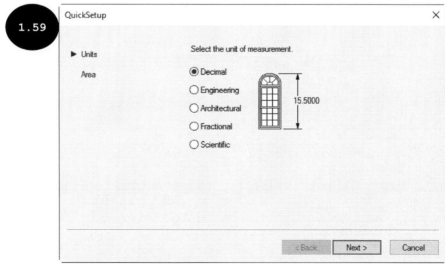

Changing the Color Scheme

AutoCAD is provided with two color schemes: dark color scheme and light color scheme. The dark color scheme is the default color scheme of AutoCAD. As a result, the **Ribbon**, **Palettes**, and several other interface components of AutoCAD appear in the dark color scheme, see Figure 1.60. You can change the color scheme by using the **Options** dialog box. To invoke the **Options** dialog box, enter OP in the Command Window and then press ENTER. Figure 1.61 shows the **Options** dialog box.

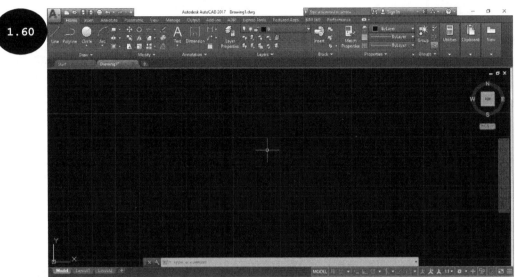

1.60

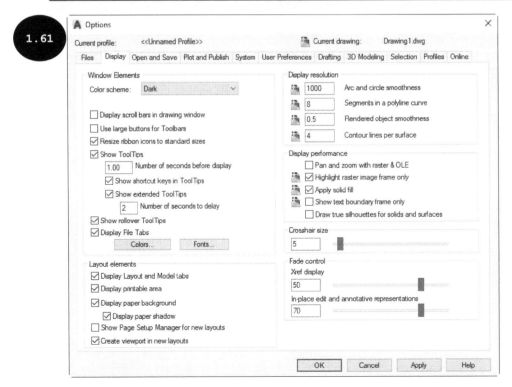

1.61

In the **Options** dialog box, click on the **Display** tab. The options related to display settings of AutoCAD appear in the dialog box, see Figure 1.61. Next, select either the **Light** or **Dark** option in the **Color scheme** drop-down list of the **Window Elements** area in the dialog box to display the AutoCAD elements/components in light color scheme or dark color scheme, respectively.

Changing the Background Color

In AutoCAD, you can change the background color of drawing area/screen, sheet/layout, command window, plot preview, and so on by using the **Options** dialog box. To change the background color of drawing area/screen, enter **OP** in the Command Window and then press ENTER. The **Options** dialog box appears. In the **Options** dialog box, click on the **Display** tab. The options related to display settings of AutoCAD appear in the dialog box. Next, click on the **Colors** button in the **Window Elements** area of the dialog box. The **Drawing Window Colors** dialog box appears, see Figure 1.62.

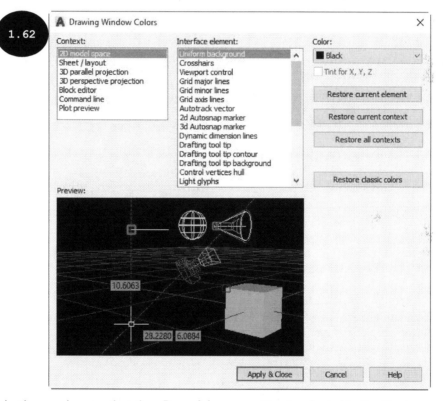

In this dialog box, make sure that the **2D model space** option is selected in the **Context** area and the **Uniform background** option is selected in the **Interface element** area of the dialog box, see Figure 1.62. Next, select the color to be assigned to the drawing area/screen background in the **Color** drop-down list. Similarly, you can change the background color of other drawing contexts such as sheet/layout, command window/line, and plot preview by using the **Drawing Window Colors** dialog box. After selecting the color to be assigned to the background, click on the **Apply & Close** button in the dialog box. The selected color is assigned and the dialog box gets closed.

Working with Workspaces

A workspace is defined as a task-oriented drawing environment in which you can control or organize the display of sets of user interface elements such as **Ribbon**, toolbars, menus, and palettes as per the requirement for accomplishing the tasks. By default, AutoCAD has three predefined workspaces: **Drafting & Annotation**, **3D Basics**, and **3D Modeling**. When you start a new drawing file in AutoCAD, the **Drafting & Annotation** workspace is the default active workspace for creating drawing. The **Drafting & Annotation** workspace display the necessary tools, menus, and palettes that are used for creating and annotating 2D drawings. The **3D Basics** and **3D Modeling** workspaces provide necessary tools, menus, and palettes which are used for creating 3D drawings. You can switch between the predefined workspaces and create a new workspace as per the requirement. The methods of switching between workspaces and creating a new workspace are as follows:

Switching between Workspaces

To switch between workspaces, click on the **Workspace Switching** button in the **Status Bar**. The **Workspace Switching** flyout appears, see Figure 1.63. It displays a list of all the available workspaces. You can click on the required workspace in this flyout to make it the current active workspace for the drawing.

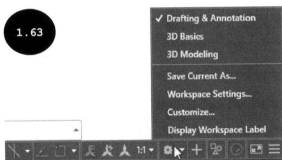

Creating a Workspace

In addition to the predefined workspaces, you can create your own workspace in which you can customize the arrangement of sets of user interface elements such as **Ribbon**, toolbars, menus, and palettes as per the requirement. To create a new workspace, first of all customize the arrangement of tools in the **Ribbon**, toolbars, menus, and palettes. Next, click on the **Workspace Switching** button in the **Status Bar**. The **Workspace Switching** flyout appears, see Figure 1.63. In this flyout, click on the **Save Current As** option. The **Save Workspace** window appears, see Figure 1.64. In this window, enter the name for the workspace and then click on the **Save** button. The new workspace is created and added to the list of workspaces in the **Workspace Switching** flyout as the current active workspace.

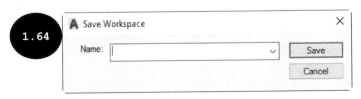

Understanding Sheet Sets

Most of the real world projects require multiple drawing sheets, sometimes more than hundreds in number. The cross-referencing between multiple drawing sheets of a project is a very time consuming process. Also, plotting, publishing, and opening multiple drawing sheets of a project require considerable time. To help managing multiple drawing sheets of a project easily and efficiently, AutoCAD provides the sheet set feature. A sheet set is very powerful feature of AutoCAD, which is used to manage or organize a set of multiple drawings (sheets) of a project in a proper order. All drawings in a sheet set act as a single unit and are displayed in a tree view. In AutoCAD, you can create two types of sheet sets: Example sheet set and Existing Drawings sheet set. An Example sheet set uses an example sheet set with default settings to create a new sheet set in a well organized structure, whereas the Existing Drawings sheet set is used to create a new sheet set to organize existing drawings. You can create both these types of sheet sets by using the SHEET SET MANAGER palette. The methods of creating different types of sheet sets are as follows:

Creating Example Sheet Set

To create an Example sheet set, click on the **Sheet Set Manager** tool in the **Palettes** panel of the **View** tab in the **Ribbon**. The SHEET SET MANAGER palette appears, see Figure 1.65. Alternatively, enter **SHEETSET** in the Command Window and then press ENTER to invoke the SHEET SET MANAGER palette. In the SHEET SET MANAGER palette, make sure that the **Sheet List** tab is activated, see Figure 1.65. Next, click on the down arrow next to the **Open** button in the SHEET SET MANAGER palette. A drop-down list appears, see Figure 1.66. In this drop-down list, click on the **New Sheet Set** option. The **Create Sheet Set** dialog box appears with the display of **Begin** page in it, see Figure 1.67.

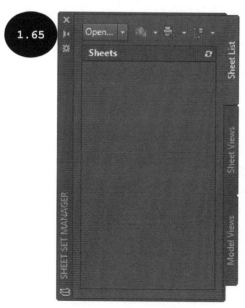
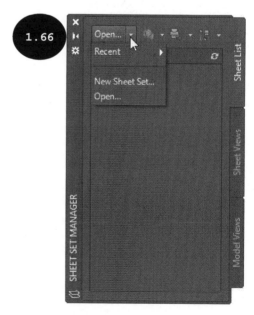

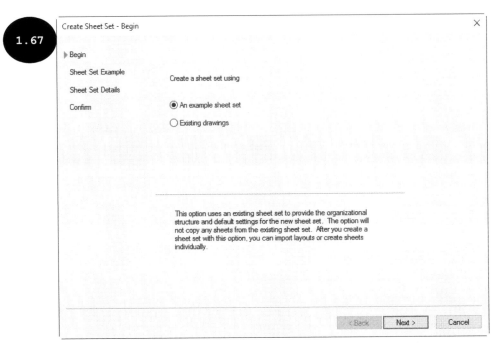

In the **Begin** page of the **Create Sheet Set** dialog box, make sure that the **An example sheet set** radio button is selected and then click on the **Next** button. The **Sheet Set Example** page of the **Create Sheet Set** dialog box appears, see Figure 1.68. In this page, the **Select a sheet set to use as an example** radio button is selected, by default. As a result, a list of all the available example sheet sets is displayed below this radio button, see Figure 1.68. Select a required example sheet set in this field for creating new sheet set.

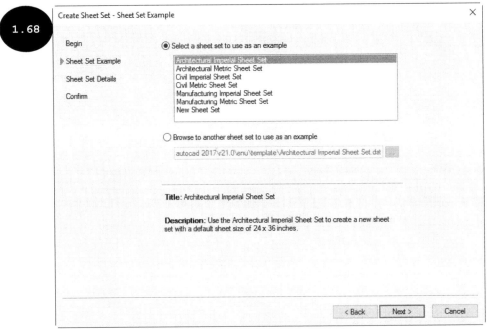

You can also select a sheet set which is in a different location and not available in the list of example sheet set. To select it, select the **Browse to another sheet set to use as an example** radio button and then click on the **Browse** button [...] in the **Sheet Set Example** page of the dialog box, see Figure 1.68. The **Browse for Sheet Set** dialog box appears. In this dialog box, browse to the location where the required sheet set is saved and then select it. Next, click on the **Open** button. After selecting the required example sheet set for creating a new sheet set in this page, click on the **Next** button. The **Sheet Set Details** page of the dialog box appears. In this page, enter the name of the new sheet set, description, and location to save the file by using the **Name of new sheet set**, **Description**, and **Store sheet set data file (.dst) here** fields, respectively. Next, click on the **Next** button. The **Confirm** page of the dialog box appears, see Figure 1.69. This page displays the structure of the sheet set and details of the sheet set properties. Review all the sheet set properties and then click on the **Finish** button. A new sheet set is created with the specified properties and displays the sheet set structure in the **SHEET SET MANAGER** palette, see Figure 1.70.

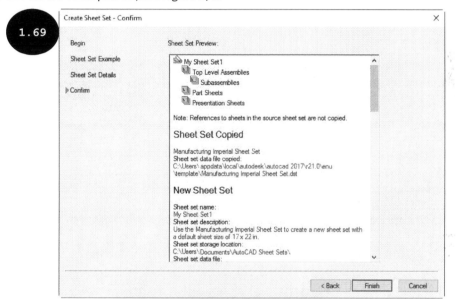

Now, you can add multiple drawing sheets in different subsets of the newly created sheet set and then create drawings in it. To add a new drawing sheet in a subset, right-click on a subset and then click on the **New Sheet** option in the shortcut menu appeared, see Figure 1.71. The **New Sheet** window appears. In this window, specify the sheet number, title, and file name and then click on the **OK** button. A new drawing sheet is added under the selected subset, see Figure 1.72. Similarly, you can add multiple drawing sheets under different subsets. You can also add new subsets in the main sheet set. To add subsets in the main sheet set, right-click on the name of the sheet set in the **SHEET SET MANAGER** palette and then click on the **New Subset** option in the shortcut menu appeared. The **Subset Properties** window appears. In this window, specify the subset name and other properties and then click on the **OK** button. A new subset with the specified name and properties gets added in the sheet set. After adding the required drawing sheets and subsets, you can open the drawing sheet and create the drawings. To open a drawing sheet for creating the drawing, right-click on the drawing sheet in the **SHEET SET MANAGER** palette and then click on the **Open** option in the shortcut menu appeared. The drawing sheet gets opened in a separate window with default drawing template. Now, you can create the drawing in this sheet by using the drawing tools. You will learn about creating drawings by using the drawing tools in later chapters.

Creating Existing Drawings Sheet Set
An Existing Drawing sheet set is created by using the existing drawings of a project. To create a sheet set by using the existing drawing sheets, invoke the **SHEET SET MANAGER** palette and then click on the down arrow next to the **Open** button in it. A drop-down list appears. In this drop-down list, click on the **New Sheet Set** option. The **Create Sheet Set** dialog box appears with the display of **Begin** page, see Figure 1.73.

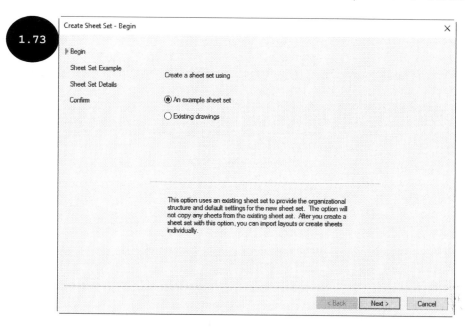

In the **Begin** page of the **Create Sheet Set** dialog box, select the **Existing drawings** radio button and then click on the **Next** button. The **Sheet Set Details** page of the dialog box appears. In this page, enter the sheet set details such as name, description, and location to save the file. Next, click on the **Next** button. The **Choose Layouts** page of the dialog box appears, see Figure 1.74. Click on the **Browse** button in this page. The **Browse for Folder** window appears. In this widow, browse to the folder in which all drawing files to be added in the sheet set are saved and then click **OK**. All the drawing files of the selected folder with their initial layouts get listed in the box available in the **Choose Layouts** page. You can browse to multiple folders one by one to add the respective drawing files.

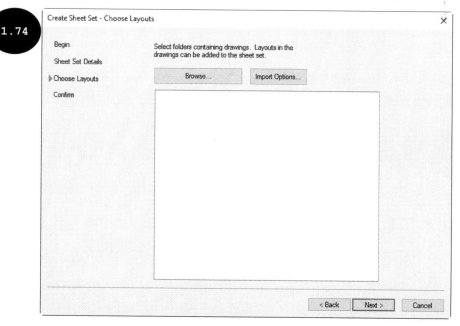

Note that the drawing files and their initial layouts listed in the box of the **Choose Layout** page have a tick mark in the front. You can uncheck the drawing files and layouts which you do not want to be included in the sheet set. After selecting the drawing files and layouts to be included in the sheet set, click on the **Next** button. The **Confirm** page of the dialog box appears. This page displays the information about the layouts included in the sheet set. Next, click on the **Finish** button. A sheet set is created by using the existing drawing files.

Opening a Drawing File

To open an existing drawing, click on the **Open** tool in the **Quick Access Toolbar**, see Figure 1.75. The **Select File** dialog box appears. You can also enter **OPEN** in the Command Window and then press ENTER to invoke the **Select File** dialog box. In this dialog box, browse to the location where the file to be opened is saved. Note that by default, the **Drawing (*.dwg)** file extension is selected in the **Files of type** drop-down list in the dialog box. As a result, the drawing files having *.dwg* file extension appear in the dialog box. Select the drawing file to be opened and then click on the **Open** button. The selected drawing gets opened in AutoCAD. You can also open the *.dxf* files and *.dwt* (template) files by selecting the **DXF (*.dxf)** and **Drawing Template (*.dwt)** file extensions in the **Files of type** drop-down list, respectively.

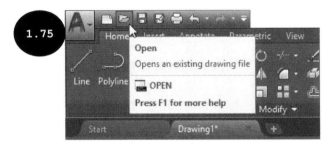

You can also open a drawing file as a read only which protects the drawing from change and it is used for review only. Note that AutoCAD does not restrict you to make a change in the read only file but at the same time it does not allow you to save the changes made in the read only file. To open a drawing as a read only, select the drawing to be opened and then click on the down arrow next to the **Open** button in the **Select File** dialog box. The **Open** drop-down list appears, see Figure 1.76. In this drop-down list, select the **Open Read-Only** option. The selected drawing gets opened as a read only file.

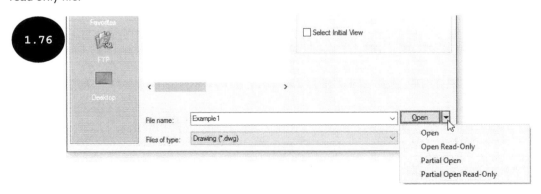

Note: When you try to save the read only file after making some modifications or changes, the **AutoCAD Message** window appears, which inform you that the current drawing file is write protected. However, you can save the modified read only file with a different name by using the **Save As** tool.

In AutoCAD, you can also open a partial view or a small portion of a drawing instead of opening the complete drawing by using the **Partial Open** option of the **Open** drop-down list, see Figure 1.76. This option is very useful if you want to modify a small portion of a big complex drawing. To open a partial view of a drawing, select the drawing in the **Select File** dialog box and then invoke the **Open** drop-down list, see Figure 1.76. Next, click on the **Partial Open** option. The **Partial Open** dialog box appears, which displays different views and layers of the selected drawing. Select the check boxes corresponding to the layers whose geometries are to be opened. Next, click on the **Open** button in the dialog box. The geometries/objects associated to the selected layers get displayed in the drawing area.

Saving a Drawing File

While creating a drawing or editing an existing drawing, it is very important to save your work periodically in order to avoid any data loss. To save a drawing file, click on the **Save** tool in the **Quick Access Toolbar**, see Figure 1.77. Alternatively, press CTRL + S or enter SAVE in the Command Window. Note that if you are saving a drawing first time then on clicking the **Save** tool, the **Save Drawing As** dialog box appears. In this dialog box, browse to the location where you want to save the drawing file and then enter the name of the drawing file in the **File name** field of the dialog box. Next, click on the **Save** button. The drawing file gets saved in the specified location of your computer with the specified name in the *.dwg* file extension. The *.dwg* is the file extension of AutoCAD. Note that if the drawing is already saved with a specific name in your computer and you have made modifications in it then on clicking the **Save** tool, the drawing gets saved directly without the display of **Save Drawing As** dialog box.

You can also save an already saved drawing file with a different name. To save an already saved drawing file with different name, click on the **Save As** tool in the **Quick Assess Toolbar**, see Figure 1.78. Alternatively, enter SAVEAS in the Command Window and then press ENTER. The **Save Drawing As** dialog box appears. In this dialog box, enter a new name for the drawing file in the **File name** field and then click on the **Save** button. The drawing file gets saved with the new specified name without effecting the original drawing file.

Note: AutoCAD allows you to save your drawing file in previous versions of AutoCAD. You can select the required version of AutoCAD in which you want to save your drawing from the **Files of type** drop-down list in the **Save Drawing As** dialog box, see Figure 1.79.

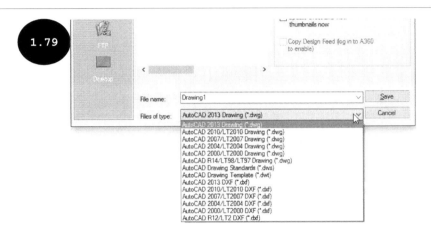

In addition to saving a drawing file by using the **Save** or **Save As** tools, AutoCAD automatically save your drawing file after every 10 minutes, by default. You can change the default time interval for automatically saving drawing files by using the **Options** dialog box. To change the default time interval for saving drawing, enter **OP** in the Command Window and the press ENTER. The **Options** dialog box appears. In this dialog box, click on the **Open and Save** tab to display the options related to open and save drawing files. Next, enter the time interval in the **Minutes between saves** field of the **File Safety Precautions** area in the dialog box. Next, click **OK** button to accept the change and exit the dialog box.

Summary

In this chapter, you have learned about system requirements for installing AutoCAD and how to start a new drawing file. You have also learned about various screen components of AutoCAD, how to change color scheme and background color, different workspaces of AutoCAD, and sheet set. In addition, you have learned how to open and save drawing files in AutoCAD.

Questions

- The _____ is used to enter commands and displays command prompt sequence.

- The _____ tool is used to turn on or off the display of grids in the drawing area.

- If the _____ mode is turned on, the cursor snaps over the existing objects of the drawing.

- AutoCAD is provided with two color schemes: _____ and _____ .

- By default, AutoCAD has three predefined workspaces: _____ , _____, and _____ .

Creating Drawings - I

In this chapter, you will learn the following:

- Setting up drawing units
- Setting drawing limits
- Specifying grid and snap settings
- Understanding coordinate systems
- Creating drawing
- Drawing lines
- Drawing circles
- Drawing arc
- Canceling, erasing, and undoing objects
- Navigating 2D drawing

Before you start creating drawings in AutoCAD, it is important to first specify drawing units, limits, and grid and snap settings. Also, you should be familiar with the coordinate systems used in AutoCAD.

Setting up Drawing Units

The first and foremost step to create a drawing is to set up the units of measurement for the drawing. As discussed in Chapter 1, while starting a new drawing in AutoCAD, you can define different format for the units of measurement: Architectural, Decimal, Engineering, Fractional, or Scientific. You can also change or modify the units settings at any point during the process of creating drawing by using the UNITS command.

To set up a drawing unit format for the current drawing, type **UNITS** in the Command Window and then press ENTER, see Figure 2.1. The **Drawing Units** dialog box appears, see Figure 2.2.

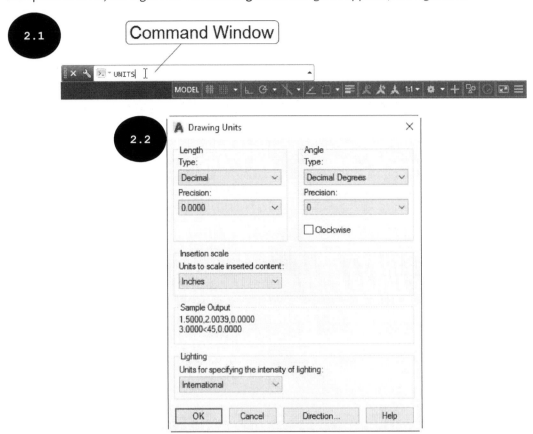

You can also type **UN** instead of **UNITS** in the Command Window for invoking the **Drawing Units** dialog box. **UN** is the shortcut for the **UNITS** command.

Once the **Drawing Units** dialog box has been invoked, you can set the required unit format for the measurement of length and angle. The options in the **Drawing Units** dialog box are as follows:

Length

The options in the **Length** area of the **Drawing Units** dialog box are used to set the required unit format and precision for the measurement of length. The options of the **Length** area are as follows:

Type

The **Type** drop-down list of the **Length** area is used to select the required unit format. You can select the architectural, decimal, engineering, fractional, or scientific unit format for the measurement of length from this drop-down list. Different unit formats of this drop-down list are as follows:

Architecture

The **Architectural** unit format is used to specify/measure units in feet and inches. As the name suggests, this unit format is mostly used by the architects to enter/measure units in feet and inches. In this unit format, inches are represented in fraction.

> **Note:** The **Sample Output** area of the dialog box displays sample output or example of the current units format selected in the **Type** drop-down list of the dialog box.

Decimal

The **Decimal** unit format is used to specify/measure units in the metric units system. This unit format is mostly used by users to work with the metric unit system for measurement.

Engineering

Similar to the **Architectural** unit format, the **Engineering** unit format is used to specify/measure units in feet and inches. The only difference between these two unit formats is that inches in the **Engineering** unit format are represented in decimal form.

Fractional

The **Fractional** unit format is used to specify/measure units in the fractional unit system. For example, 5 feet, 6½ inches is read as 66-1/2 inches in the fractional unit system.

Scientific

The **Scientific** unit format is used to specify/measure units in the scientific units system. For example, 10 million parsecs is read as 10E+06 in the scientific units system, where 10 represents 10 accurate and E+06 represents exponential function to the sixth power.

Precision

The **Precision** drop-down list of the **Length** area is used to set precision for the measurement of units. The availability of options in the **Precision** drop-down list depends on the type of unit format selected in the **Type** drop-down list.

Angle

The options of the **Angle** area of the dialog box are used to specify unit format and precision for the measurement of angle. You can select the **Decimal Degrees**, **Deg/Min/Sec**, **Grads**, **Radians**, or **Surveyor's Units** format for the measurement of angle by using the **Type** drop-down list of the **Angle** area. The **Precision** drop-down list of the **Angle** area is used to specify precision for the angle measurements.

If you have selected the **Decimal Degrees**, **Deg/Min/Sec**, **Grads**, or **Radians** unit format for the measurement of angle, you can specify angle in decimal, degrees/minutes/seconds, grads, or radians, respectively. Whereas, if you have selected the **Surveyor's Units** format, you can specify angle with respect to the deviation of north and south, see Figure 2.3. The surveyor unit is also known as bearings in civil engineering. Note that the angle value used in a surveyor unit is not greater than 90-degree. For example, to set an angle which measured 40-degree from north and 30 minutes toward east, you need to specify **N40d30'E**.

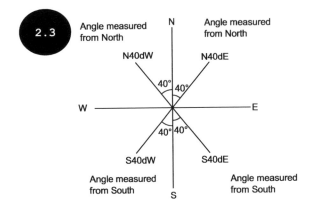

Clockwise

By default, the **Clockwise** check box is unchecked in the **Angle** area of the dialog box. As a result, direction for positive angle is measured in counterclockwise direction, see Figure 2.4. To measure positive angle in clockwise direction, select the **Clockwise** check box, see Figure 2.5.

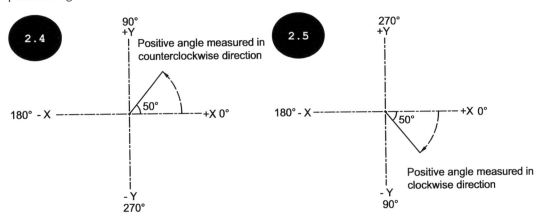

Note: It is evident from Figures 2.4 and 2.5 that the position of zero degree (0 degree) is set at East position, by default. You can change the position of zero degree from East (which is set as default) to other position, such as north, south, or west by using the **Direction** button in the **Drawing Units** dialog box. To set the position of zero degree, click on the **Direction** button in the **Drawing Units** dialog box. The **Direction Control** dialog box appears, see Figure 2.6. Using this dialog box, you can set base angle (zero degree) at any position by selecting the appropriate radio button. You can also specify an angle value other than 0 (zero) by selecting the **Other** radio button and then entering the required angle value in the **Angle** field.

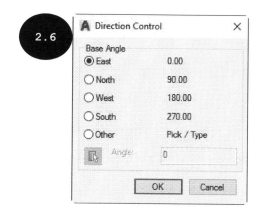

Insertion scale

The **Units to scale inserted content** drop-down list of the **Insertion Scale** area is used to set units for the blocks and drawings inserted in the current drawing. Note that the unit selected in this drop-down list is applied automatically to the blocks or drawings inserted in the current drawing. If the blocks and drawings inserted in the current drawing have different units then AutoCAD may scale them in order to correct the mismatch and set the unit specified in the **Units to scale inserted content** drop-down list.

Sample Output

The **Sample Output** area of the **Drawing Units** dialog box is used to display the sample output or example of the current length and angle units settings specified in the dialog box.

Lighting

The **Units for specifying the intensity of lighting** drop-down list of the **Lighting** area is used to set the unit of measurement for the intensity of photometric light in the current drawing.

After specifying the desired settings for measurement of units in the **Drawing Units** dialog box, click OK to accept the settings and close the dialog box.

Setting Drawing Limits

After defining drawing units, it is important to set drawing limits (work area) in the drawing area. Drawing limit is an invisible and imaginary rectangular boundary in the drawing area, which defines the size of the work area. Defining drawing limit helps in limiting the grid display within the drawing limit, zooming drawing within the drawing limit, and plotting drawing. You can define drawing limit for a drawing depending upon the overall size of the drawing. For example, if you are drawing a plan view of a building that is roughly around 28 x 36 feet then you can define drawing limit around 36 x 44 feet. Note that drawing limit is the size of your work area that accommodates the entire drawing and dimensions with some extra space, see Figure 2.7.

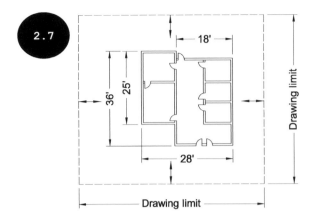

To define drawing limit for a drawing, enter **LIMITS** in the Command Window and then press ENTER. The command prompt for setting drawing limit is as follows:

Command: **LIMITS**
Reset Model space limits:
Specify lower left corner or [ON/OFF] <0.0000,0.0000>: **0,0**
Specify upper right corner <12.0000,9.0000>: **70,80**

Note: If the display of grids is turned on, the grids are displayed in the entire drawing area, by default. To display grids within the drawing limit, enter **GRIDDISPLAY** in the Command Window and then type **0** in the command prompt. Next, press ENTER. You will learn more about grid settings later in this chapter.

Specifying Grid and Snap Settings

Grid is a rectangular pattern of lines or dots, which is intended to speed up the creation of drawing by aligning objects and visualizing the distance between drawing entities. Grid lines can be used as reference lines for creating drawings. Also, grid lines appear similar to the sheet of graph paper for creating drawing, see Figure 2.8.

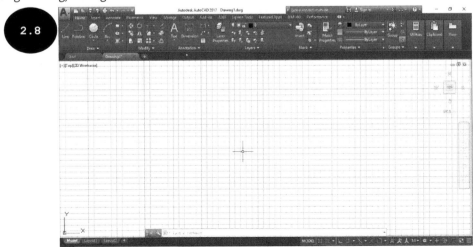

Note: The background color of the drawing area shown in Figure 2.8 has been changed to white for clear visualization. The method of changing background color has been discussed in Chapter 1.

You can control the spacing, angle, and alignment of grid lines. Also, you can restrict the movement of the cursor over grid lines by specifying the grid and snap settings.

To specify the grid and snap settings in AutoCAD, right-click on the **Display drawing grid** button in the **Status Bar**, see Figure 2.9. The **Grid Settings** option appears, see Figure 2.9. Next, click on the **Grid Settings** option. The **Drafting Settings** dialog box appears, see Figure 2.10.

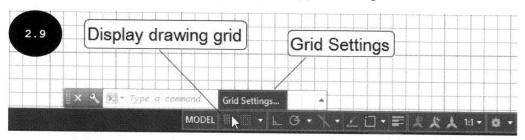

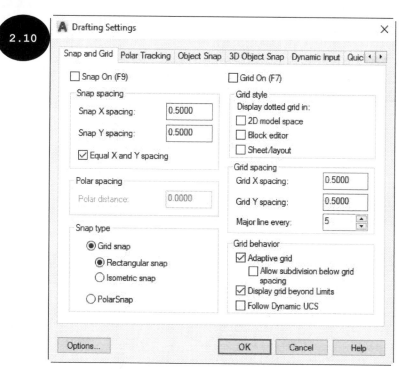

Make sure that the **Snap and Grid** tab is activated in the **Drafting Settings** dialog box, see Figure 2.10. The options in the **Snap and Grid** tab of the dialog box are used to specify the snap and grid settings. Some of these options are as follows:

Grid On (F7)

The **Grid On** check box of this dialog box is used to toggle the display of grid lines in the drawing area. Alternatively, you can click on the **Display drawing grid** button in the **Status Bar** or press the F7 key to toggle the display of grid lines.

Grid style

The options in the **Grid style** area of the dialog box are used to specify grid styles in 2D context. These options are as follows:

2D model space

The **2D model space** check box of the **Grid style** area is used to set grid style to dotted grid lines in the 2D model space (drawing area).

Block editor

The **Block editor** check box is used to set grid style to dotted grid lines in the Block editor. You will learn more about the Block editor in later chapters.

Sheet/layout

The **Sheet/layout** check box is used to set grid style to dotted grid lines in sheet and layout. You will learn more about sheet and layout in later chapters.

Grid spacing

The options in the **Grid spacing** area of the dialog box are used to specify spacing between grid lines. These options are as follows:

Grid X spacing

The **Grid X spacing** field of the **Grid spacing** area is used to specify the spacing between grid lines along the X direction.

Grid Y spacing

The **Grid Y spacing** field of this area is used to specify the spacing between grid lines along the Y direction.

Major line every

The **Major line every** field is used to specify the display of major grid lines with respect to minor grid lines. For example, if you enter 5 in this field, the major grid lines will appear on every 5 counts of minor grid lines. Grid lines are of two types: major grid lines and minor grid lines. The major grid lines appear darker than the minor grid lines.

Snap On (F9)

The **Snap On** check box of the dialog box is used to toggle the snap mode on or off. Alternatively, you can click on the **Snap mode** button in the **Status Bar** or press the F9 key to turn the snap mode on or off. Note that by turning the snap mode on, the movement of the cursor gets restricted in the specified X and Y intervals, that are specified in the **Snap spacing** area of this dialog box.

Snap spacing

The options of the **Snap spacing** area are used to snap the movement of the cursor in the specified X and Y intervals along the X and Y directions, respectively. These options are as follows:

Snap X spacing

The **Snap X spacing** field is used to specify the snap spacing along the X direction. For example, if you enter 5 in this field then the cursor will snap after every 5 units along the X direction.

Snap Y spacing

The **Snap Y spacing** field is used to specify the snap spacing along the Y direction. For example, if you enter 5 in this field then the cursor will snap after every 5 units along the Y direction.

Equal X and Y spacing

The **Equal X and Y spacing** check box is used to make the snap spacing same along the X and Y directions.

Once you have specified the grid and snap settings in the **Drafting Settings** dialog box, click on the OK button to accept changes and exit from the dialog box.

> **Tip:** In AutoCAD, you are provided with shortcuts to toggle the display of grids and snap settings. To toggle the display of grids in the drawing area, you can click on the **Display drawing grid** button ▓ in the **Status Bar** or press the F7 key. Similarly, to toggle the snap settings on and off, you can click on the **Snap mode** button ▓ in the **Status Bar** or press the F9 key.

Understanding Coordinate Systems

In AutoCAD, the Cartesian and Polar coordinate systems are used for specifying points in the drawing area. Cartesian coordinate system is also known as rectangular coordinate system and it consists of two perpendicular lines (x-axis and y-axis) that intersect at a point called origin, see Figure 2.11. The origin has coordinate values of X = 0, Y = 0. In Cartesian coordinate system, the location of every point is specified with respect to the X and Y coordinates values that are measured from perpendicular lines (x-axis and y-axis), see Figure 2.11. Note that in two-dimensional space (2D plane), the Cartesian coordinate system has two perpendicular axes. Whereas, in three-dimensional space (3D), the system has three perpendicular axes (x-axis, y-axis, and z-axis).

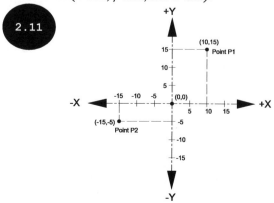

2.11

It is evident from Figure 2.11 that in Cartesian coordinate system, you need to specify the X and Y coordinates with respect to the X and Y axes to define a point.

In Polar coordinate system, to define the position of a point, you need to specify distance and angle rather than the X and Y coordinates, see Figure 2.12. Note that in Polar coordinate system, the distance is measured from the origin and the angle is measured with respect to an axis representing zero degree, see Figure 2.12. In AutoCAD, the +X axis (East) represents zero degree for measuring the angle, by default. You can change the position of zero degree other then the +X axis (East) as discussed earlier in this Chapter.

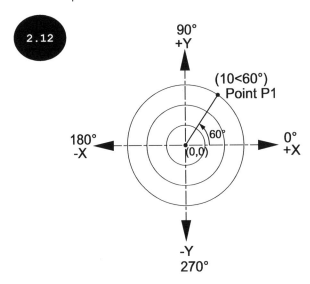

The Cartesian and Polar coordinate systems are following two types:

Cartesian coordinate system
1. Absolute Cartesian coordinate system
2. Relative Cartesian coordinate system

Polar coordinate system
1. Absolute Polar coordinate system
2. Relative Polar coordinate system

Different types of Cartesian and Polar coordinate systems are as follows:

Absolute Cartesian Coordinate System

In Absolute Cartesian coordinate system, every point you specify in the drawing area is measured from the origin (0,0) and the location of a point is specified with respect to the X and Y coordinates, see Figure 2.13. Note that the X and Y coordinates you specify for locating a point should be separated by a comma. In Figure 2.13, the Point P1 has coordinates (X=10, Y=15) which are measured 10 units along the X axis and 15 units along the Y axis from the origin. Similarly, the Point P2 coordinates (X=25, Y=20) are measured 25 units along the X axis and 20 units along the Y axis from the origin.

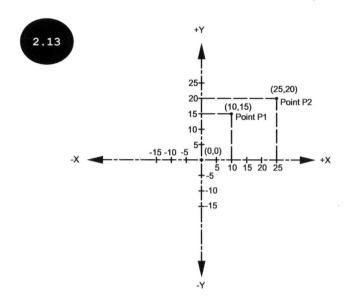

2.13

Note: In AutoCAD, you can specify coordinates either by using the Command Window or by using the Dynamic Input boxes. As discussed, the Command Window is available at the bottom of the drawing area, see Figure 2.14. The Dynamic Input boxes appear near the cursor in the drawing area, in case the Dynamic Input mode is turned on, see Figure 2.15. To turn on or off the Dynamic Input mode, click on the **Dynamic Input** button in the **Status Bar**. If the **Dynamic Input** button is not available in the Status Bar by default, click on the **Customization** button in the **Status Bar**. A flyout appears. In this flyout, click on the **Dynamic Input** option. The **Dynamic Input** button becomes available in the **Status Bar**.

In Absolute Cartesian coordinate system, the method of specifying the X and Y coordinates of a point in the Command Window as well as in the Dynamic Input boxes are as follows:

Specifying Coordinates in the Command Window - Absolute Coordinate

To specify a point, according to Absolute Cartesian coordinate system in the Command Window, enter the X and Y coordinates, separated by a comma, see Figure 2.14. In this figure, the coordinates (**25, 20**) specified in the Command Window are measured 25 units along the X axis and 20 units along the Y axis from the origin for defining the start point of a line.

2.14

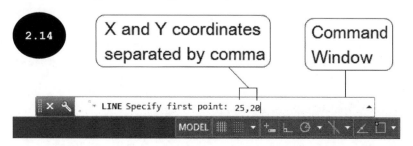

Specifying Coordinates in the Dynamic Input boxes - Absolute Coordinate

To specify a point, according to Absolute Cartesian coordinate system in the Dynamic Input boxes, enter # as prefix to the X coordinate and then followed by the Y coordinate, see Figure 2.15. In this figure, the coordinates (#25, 20) specified in the Dynamic Input boxes are measured 25 units along the X axis and 20 units along the Y axis from the origin for defining the start point of a line.

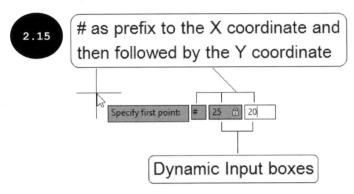

Tip: To switch between the Dynamic Input boxes for specifying the coordinates (X and Y), you need to press the TAB key. Alternatively, press the COMMA (,) key after specifying the X coordinate to switch to the next Dynamic Input box for specifying the Y coordinate.

Note: In Absolute coordinate system, whether you specify coordinates in the Command Window or in the Dynamic Input boxes, the coordinates are measured from the origin.

Relative Cartesian Coordinate System

In Relative Cartesian coordinate system, every point you specify in the drawing area is measured from the last specified point in the drawing area and whose location is specified with respect to the X and Y coordinates, see Figure 2.16. In Figure 2.16, the coordinates (X=10, Y=15) of the point 'P2' are measured 10 units along the X axis and 15 units along the Y axis from the last specified point (point P1).

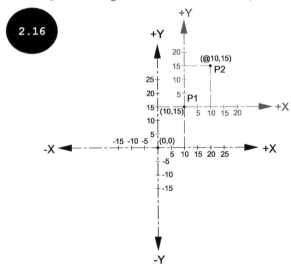

In Relative coordinate system, the method of specifying the X and Y coordinates of a point in the Command Window as well as in the Dynamic Input boxes are as follows:

Specifying Coordinates in the Command Window - Relative Coordinate

To specify a point, according to Relative coordinate system in the Command Window, enter @ as prefix to the X coordinate and then followed by the Y coordinate separated by a comma, see Figure 2.17. Note that the coordinates (@10, 15) of a point specified in the Command Window are measured from the last specified point, refer to Figure 2.16.

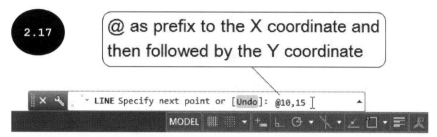

Specifying Coordinates in the Dynamic Input boxes - Relative Coordinate

To specify a point, according to Relative coordinate system in the Dynamic Input boxes, enter the coordinates (X and Y) of the point directly in the Dynamic Input boxes with respect to the last specified point in the drawing area.

Note: As discussed, in Relative coordinate system, whether you specify coordinates in the Command Window or in the Dynamic Input boxes, coordinates are measured with respect to the last specified point in the drawing area.

Absolute Polar Coordinate System

In Absolute Polar coordinate system, to define a point, you need to specify the distance and angle values separated by an angle bracket (<). Note that in Absolute Polar coordinate system, the distance value is measured from the origin and the angle value is measured from an axis which represents zero degree, see Figure 2.18.

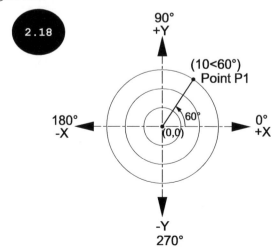

In Absolute Polar coordinate system, the method of specifying a point in the Command Window as well as in the Dynamic Input boxes is as follows:

Specifying Angle and Distance Values in the Command Window - Absolute Polar Coordinate

To specify a point, according to Absolute Polar coordinate system in the Command Window, enter the distance and angle values separated by an angle bracket (<), see Figure 2.19. In this figure, the distance and angle (10<60) values specified are measured 10 units distance from the origin and 60-degree angle from the X axis, refer to Figure 2.18.

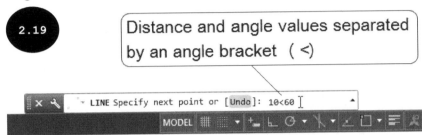

Specifying Angle and Distance Values in the Dynamic Input boxes - Absolute Polar Coordinate

To specify a point, according to Absolute Polar coordinate system in the Dynamic Input boxes, enter # as prefix to the distance value and then followed by the angle value, see Figure 2.20. In this figure, the coordinates (#10<60) specified in the Dynamic Input boxes are measured 10 units distance from the origin and 60-degree angle from the X axis, which represents zero degree.

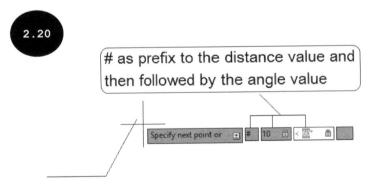

Relative Polar Coordinate System

In Relative Polar coordinate system, every point you specify in the drawing area is measured from the last specified point in the drawing area and whose location is defined by specifying the distance and angle values separated by an angle bracket (<), see Figure 2.21. In Figure 2.21, the distance and angle values (10<25°) of the point 'P2" are measured from the last specified point (P1).

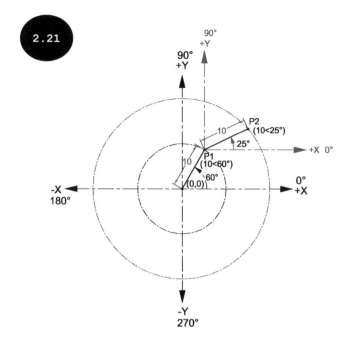

In Relative Polar coordinate system, the method of specifying the distance and angle values of a point in the Command Window as well as in the Dynamic Input boxes are as follows:

Specifying Angle and Distance Values in the Command Window - Relative Polar Coordinate

To specify a point, according to Relative Polar coordinate system in the Command Window, enter @ as prefix to the distance value and then followed by the angle value separated by an angle bracket (<), see Figure 2.22. In this figure, the distance and angle values (@25<60) of a point are measured 25 units distance from the last specified point and 60-degree angle from the X axis originating from the last specified point.

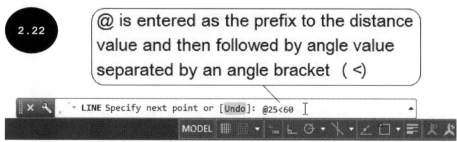

Specifying Angle and Distance Values in the Dynamic Input boxes - Relative Polar Coordinate

To specify a point, according to Relative Polar coordinate system in the Dynamic Input boxes, enter distance and angle values directly in the Dynamic Input boxes, see Figure 2.23.

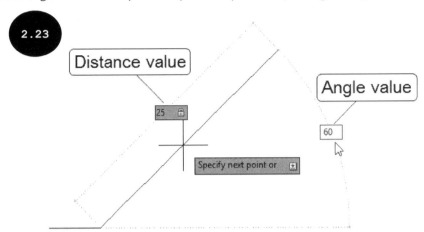

The following table summarizes information about different coordinate systems discussed earlier:

Coordinate System		Command Window	Dynamic Input
Cartesian Coordinate System	Absolute cartesian coordinate system	X,Y *For example: 10,25*	# X,Y *For example: #10,25*
	Relative cartesian coordinate system	@X,Y *For example: @10,25*	X,Y *For example: 10,25*
Polar coordinate system	Absolute polar coordinate system	distance<angle *For example: 25<60*	#distance<angle *For example: #25<60*
	Relative polar coordinate system	@distance<angle *For example: @25<60*	distance<angle *For example: 25<60*

Creating Drawing

Once you have setup drawing units, limits, grid and snap settings, and understand about different coordinate systems, you can start creating drawing in AutoCAD. In AutoCAD, the tools used for creating drawings are grouped together in the **Draw** panel of the **Home** tab, see Figure 2.24. The tools of this Draw panel can be invoked by clicking on the required tool. Alternatively, you can enter the shortcut key/command of the tool to be invoked in the Command Window. For example, to invoke the **Line** tool, click on the **Line** tool in the **Draw** panel or enter **L** in the Command Window and then press ENTER.

Drawing Lines

A line defines the shortest distance between two points. You can draw a line by defining its start point and endpoint. To draw a line, click on the **Line** tool in the **Draw** panel of the **Home** tab or enter **L** in the Command Window and then press ENTER. The **Line** tool gets activated and you are prompted to specify the first point of the line. You can specify the coordinates (X and Y) of the first point of the line in the Command Window or in the Dynamic Input boxes. You can also click in the drawing area to specify points.

Note: As discussed, you can specify points by entering their coordinates according to Absolute coordinate system, Relative coordinate system, or Polar coordinate system in the Command Window or in the Dynamic Input boxes. You can also pick points directly in the drawing area by clicking the left mouse button.

Procedure for Drawing Line

1. Click on the **Line** tool in the **Draw** panel or enter **L** in the Command Window and then press ENTER. You are prompted to specify the first point of the line.

   ```
   Specify first point:
   ```

2. Specify the coordinates (X and Y) of the first point in the Command Window or in the Dynamic Input boxes. As soon as you specify the coordinates of the first point, you are prompted to specify the next (second) point of the line.

   ```
   Specify next point or [Undo]:
   ```

Note: To specify coordinates in the Command Window, you may need to turn off the Dynamic Input mode. To turn off the Dynamic Input mode, click on the **Dynamic Input** button in the **Status Bar**.

3. Specify the coordinates (X and Y) of the second point in the Command Window or in the Dynamic Input boxes. A line is drawn between the two specified points in the drawing area, see Figure 2.25. Also, a rubber band line is attached with the cursor and you are prompted to specify the next (third) point of the line.

   ```
   Specify next point or [Undo]:
   ```

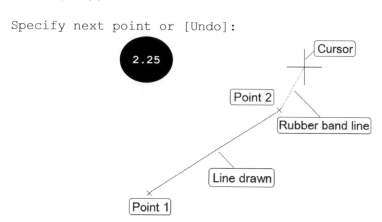

4. Similarly, you can continue specifying points in the drawing area for creating a chain of lines.

> **Note:** After specifying the third point of the line, the command sequence appears as "Specify next point or [Close Undo]:" By using the options (Close and Undo) of the command sequence, you can create the close loop of the line entities and undo the last specified point.
>
> To undo or remove the last specified point, click on the **Undo** option in the Command Window. Alternatively, you can enter U in the Command Window and then press ENTER to undo or remove the last specified point. You can undo or remove multiple points one after another by continuously using this option.
>
> To create a close loop of the line entities where the last point join to the first specified point, click on the **Close** option in the Command Window or enter C in the Command Window and then press ENTER, see Figure 2.26.

5. Once all the line entities have been drawn, exit from the **Line** tool by pressing the ENTER key. You can also press the **ESC** or **SPACEBAR** key to exit from the **Line** tool. Alternatively, right-click in the drawing area and then click on the **Enter** or **Cancel** option in the shortcut menu appeared to exit from the **Line** tool, see Figure 2.27.

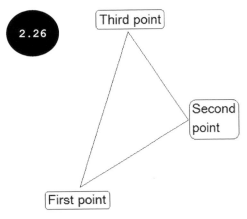

Command Sequence for Drawing Line

```
Tool/Command: Line or L (ENTER)
Specify first point: (Specify X, Y coordinates)
Specify next point or [Undo]: (Specify X, Y coordinates)
Specify next point or [Undo]: (Specify X, Y coordinates)
Specify next point or [Close Undo]: ENTER
```

> **Note:** While creating a drawing, it does not important which coordinate system to be followed for specifying points in the drawing area. You can use any of the coordinate systems or in combination of coordinate systems to specify points in the drawing area as per your convenience.

Example 1

Create the drawing shown in Figure 2.28 by using Absolute Cartesian coordinate system. Also, specify the coordinates of the points by using the Command Window.

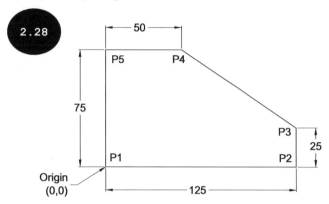

Section 1: Starting AutoCAD

1. Double-click on the AutoCAD icon on your desktop. The initial screen of AutoCAD appears with the **Start** tab, see Figure 2.29.

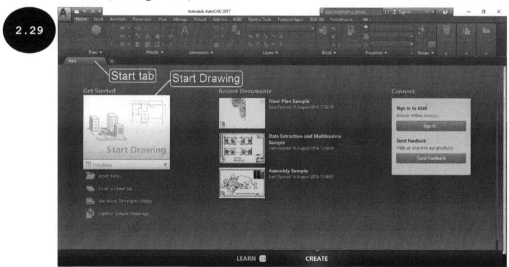

2. In the **Get Started** section of the **Start** tab, click on **Start Drawing**, see Figure 2.29. The new drawing file with the default drawing template gets invoked.

Alternatively, invoke a new drawing file by clicking on the **New** tool in the **Quick Access Toolbar**, which is at the top left corner of AutoCAD. On doing so, the **Select template** dialog box appears. In this dialog box, select the *acad.dwt* template and then click on the **Open** button. A new drawing file with *acad.dwt* template is invoked. You can also right-click on the **Start** tab and then click on the **New** option in the shortcut menu appeared to invoke a new drawing file. Additionally, you can click on the + sign available next to the **Start** tab to invoke a new drawing file.

Section 2: Selecting Workspace for Creating Drawing

1.   Click on the **Workspace Switching**  button in the **Status Bar**. A flyout appears, see Figure 2.30.

2.30

✓ Drafting & Annotation

3D Basics

3D Modeling

Save Current As...

Workspace Settings...

Customize...

Display Workspace Label

2.   In this flyout, make sure that the **Drafting & Annotation** option is tick-marked to create drawings in the Drafting & Annotation workspace.

> **Note:**   A tick mark next to a workspace indicates that it is selected as the current workspace for creating drawings. By default, the Drafting & Annotation workspace is selected as the current workspace for creating drawings. You can click on any workspace to make it current for creating drawings.

Section 3: Defining Limits for Drawing

1.   Follow the command sequence given below for defining the limits of the drawing.

```
Command: LIMITS (ENTER)
Specify lower left corner or [ON/OFF]<0.0000,0.0000>: 0,0 (ENTER)
Specify upper right corner <12.0000,9.0000>: 250,150 (ENTER)
```

Section 4: Creating Drawing by using Absolute Coordinate System

As stated in the description of the example, you need to enter coordinates in the Command Window according to Absolute coordinate system for specifying points. To enter coordinates in the Command Window, it is recommended to turn off the Dynamic Input mode.

1.   Click on the **Dynamic Input** button ▆ in the **Status Bar** to turn off the Dynamic Input mode.

2.   Click on the **Line** tool in the **Draw** panel of the **Home** tab. The **Line** tool is invoked and you are prompted to specify the first point of the line. You can also enter **L** in the Command Window and then press ENTER to invoke the **Line** tool.

3.   Follow the command sequence given below for creating the drawing.

```
Specify first point: 0,0 (ENTER)
Specify next point or [Undo]: 125,0 (ENTER)
Specify next point or [Undo]: 125,25 (ENTER)
Specify next point or [Undo]: 50,75 (ENTER)
```

```
Specify next point or [Undo]: 0,75 (ENTER)
Specify next point or [Close Undo]: C or Close
```

Tip: To specify points in the Dynamic Input boxes according to Absolute coordinate system, you need to enter # as prefix to the X coordinate and then followed by the Y coordinate in the Dynamic Input boxes.

Note: To fit the drawing complete in the drawing area, enter ZOOM in the Command Window and then press ENTER. Next, enter All in the Command Window and then press ENTER. The drawing is fit completely inside the drawing area.

Hands-on Test Drive 1

Create the same drawing created in Example 1 by using Relative Cartesian coordinate system, see Figure 2.31. Also, specify the coordinates of the points by using the Command Window.

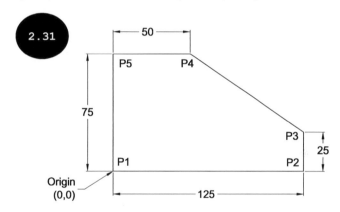

Hint: In Relative Cartesian coordinate system, every point you specify in the drawing area is measured from the last specified point in the drawing area.

Command sequence for creating drawing with some of the coordinates of the points are as follows:

```
Tool/Command: Line or L (ENTER)
Specify first point: 0,0 (ENTER)
Specify next point or [Undo]: @125,0 (ENTER)
Specify next point or [Undo]: @0,25 (ENTER)
Specify next point or [Undo]: _____ (ENTER)
Specify next point or [Undo]: _____ (ENTER)
Specify next point or [Close Undo]: C or Close
```

Example 2

Create the drawing shown in Figure 2.32 by using Relative Polar coordinate system. Also, specify the coordinates of the points by using the Command Window.

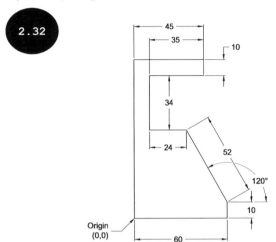

Section 1: Starting AutoCAD

1. Start AutoCAD by double-clicking on the AutoCAD icon on your desktop, if not already started.

2. In the **Get Started** section of the initial screen, click on **Start Drawing**. The new drawing file with the default drawing template gets invoked.

Section 2: Selecting Workspace for Creating Drawing

1. Click on the **Workspace Switching** ⚙ button in the Status Bar. A flyout appears, see Figure 2.33.

2. Make sure that the **Drafting & Annotation** option is tick-marked in this flyout.

Section 3: Defining Limits for Drawing

1. Follow the command sequence given below for defining the limits of the drawing.

```
Command: LIMITS (ENTER)
Specify lower left corner or [ON/OFF]<0.0000,0.0000>: 0,0 (ENTER)
Specify upper right corner <12.0000,9.0000>: 120,200 (ENTER)
```

Section 4: Creating Drawing by using Relative Polar Coordinate System

As stated in the description of the example, you need to enter coordinates in the Command Window according to Relative Polar coordinate system for specifying points. To enter coordinates in the Command Window, it is recommended to turn off the Dynamic Input mode.

1. Click on the **Dynamic Input** button ▦ in the **Status Bar** to turn off the Dynamic Input mode.

2. Click on the **Line** tool in the **Draw** panel of the **Home** tab. The **Line** tool is invoked and you are prompted to specify the first point of the line. Alternatively, you can enter L in the Command Window and then press ENTER to invoke the **Line** tool.

Note: In Relative Polar coordinate system, you need to enter @ as prefix to the distance value and then followed by the angle value separated by an angle bracket (<) in the Command Window. Note that in Relative Polar coordinate system, every point you specify in the drawing area by defining its distance and angle values is measured from the last specified point in the drawing area.

3. Follow the command sequence given below for creating the drawing.

```
Specify first point: 0,0 (ENTER)
Specify next point or [Undo]: @60<0 (ENTER)
Specify next point or [Undo]: @10<90 (ENTER)
Specify next point or [Undo]: @52<120 (ENTER)
Specify next point or [Undo]: @24<180 (ENTER)
Specify next point or [Undo]: @34<90 (ENTER)
Specify next point or [Undo]: @35<0 (ENTER)
Specify next point or [Undo]: @10<90 (ENTER)
Specify next point or [Undo]: @45<180 (ENTER)
Specify next point or [Close Undo]: C or Close
```

Hands-on Test Drive 2

Create the same drawing created in Example 2, by using Relative Polar coordinate system, see Figure 2.34. You need to specify the coordinates of the points by using the Dynamic Input boxes.

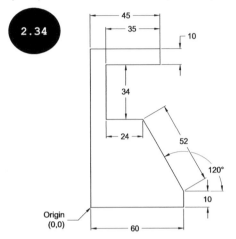

Hint: For specifying points by using Relative Polar coordinate system in the Dynamic Input boxes, you first need to turn on the Dynamic Input mode by clicking on the Dynamic Input button in the Status Bar. Next, you can directly enter the distance and angle values without any prefix in their respective Dynamic Input boxes, which appear near the cursor tip.

Drawing Circles

In AutoCAD, you can draw circles by using the following methods:

- Drawing circles by defining center point and radius
- Drawing circles by defining center point and diameter
- Drawing circles by defining two points on the circumference of a circle
- Drawing circles by defining three points on the circumference of a circle
- Drawing circles by defining two tangent points and radius
- Drawing circles by defining three tangent points

In AutoCAD, the tools for creating circles are grouped together in the **Circle** flyout of the **Draw** panel in the **Home** tab, see Figure 2.35. Alternatively, you can invoke the **Circle** command for creating circles by entering **CIRCLE** or **C** in the Command Window and then pressing ENTER. Different methods of creating circles are as follows:

Drawing Circles by Defining Center Point and Radius

You can draw a circle by defining its center point and radius by using the **Center, Radius** tool of the **Circle** flyout. To draw a circle by defining its center point and radius, click on the down arrow in the active circle tool of the **Draw** panel. The **Circle** flyout appears, see Figure 2.35. In this flyout, click on the **Center, Radius** tool. The **Center, Radius** tool gets activated and you are prompted to specify the center point of the circle. Alternatively, you can enter **C** or **CIRCLE** in the Command Window and then press ENTER to activate this tool. Once the **Center, Radius** tool has been activated, you can specify the coordinates (X , Y) of the center point of the circle either in the Command Window or in the Dynamic Input boxes. Additionally, you can click in the drawing area to specify the center point of the circle. The procedure for drawing a circle by defining center point and radius is as follows:

Procedure for Drawing a Circle by Defining Center Point and Radius

1. Invoke the **Circle** flyout and then click on the **Center, Radius** tool. You are prompted to specify the center point of the circle. Alternatively, you can enter **C** in the Command Window and then press ENTER to invoke the tool.

    ```
    Specify center point for circle or [3P 2P Ttr (tan tan radius)]:
    ```

2. Specify the coordinates (X , Y) of the center point either in the Command Window or in the Dynamic Input boxes. You are prompted to specify the radius of the circle.

    ```
    Specify radius of circle or [Diameter]:
    ```

Tip: To create a circle by defining its diameter, click on the **Diameter** option in the command prompt or enter **D** in the Command Window and then press ENTER. Next, specify the diameter of the circle in the Command Window.

3. Enter the radius value of the circle and then press ENTER. The circle of specified radius is created in the drawing area, see Figure 2.36.

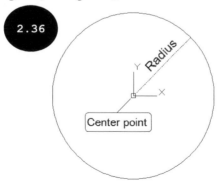

2.36

Drawing Circles by Defining Center Point and Diameter

You can draw a circle by defining its center point and diameter by using the **Center, Diameter** tool of the **Circle** flyout, see Figure 2.37. Alternatively, you can invoke the tool by entering C or CIRCLE in the Command Window and then pressing ENTER.

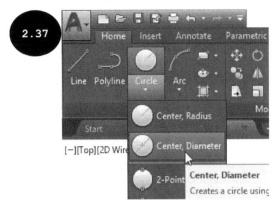

2.37

Procedure for Drawing a Circle by Defining Center Point and Diameter

1. Invoke the **Circle** flyout and then click on the **Center, Diameter** tool. You are prompted to specify the center point of the circle. Alternatively, you can enter C in the Command Window and then press ENTER to invoke the tool.

   ```
   Specify center point for circle or [3P 2P Ttr (tan tan radius)]:
   ```

2. Specify the coordinates (X , Y) of the center point either in the Command Window or in the Dynamic input boxes. You are prompted to specify the diameter of the circle.

   ```
   Specify radius of circle or [Diameter] <20.0000>:_d Specify
   diameter of circle:
   ```

Note: If you invoke the tool for creating a circle by entering the C or CIRCLE in the Command Window, then after specifying the center point of the circle, you need to click on the **Diameter** option in the command prompt for specifying the diameter of the circle.

3. Enter diameter of the circle and then press ENTER. The circle of specified diameter is created, see Figure 2.38.

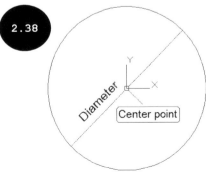

2.38

Drawing Circles by Defining 2 Points

You can draw a circle by defining two points on the circumference of the circle by using the **2 Point** tool, see Figure 2.39. You can also enter C or **CIRCLE** in the Command Window and then click on the **2P** option in the command prompt appeared for creating the circle by defining two points on the circumference of the circle.

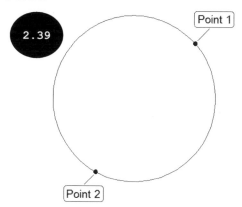

Procedure for Drawing Circle by Defining 2 Points

1.   Invoke the **Circle** flyout and then click on the **2 Point** tool. You are prompted to specify the first point on the circumference of the circle. Alternatively, enter C in the Command Window and then press ENTER. Next, click on the **2P** option in the command prompt appeared.

```
Specify center point for circle or [3P 2P Ttr (tan tan radius)]:_2p
Specify first end point of circle's diameter:
```

2.   Enter the coordinate (X , Y) of the first point either in the Command Window or in the Dynamic Input boxes and then press ENTER. Alternatively, click in the drawing area to define the first point on the circumference of the circle. As soon as you specify the first point, you are prompted to specify the second point of the circle.

```
Specify second end point of circle's diameter:
```

3.   Enter the coordinate (X , Y) of the second point on the circumference of the circle either in the Command Window or in the Dynamic Input boxes and then press ENTER. The circle is drawn, see Figure 2.39. You can also click directly in the drawing area to define the second point on the circumference of the circle.

Drawing Circles by Defining 3 Points

In AutoCAD, you can draw a circle by defining three points on the circumference of the circle, see Figure 2.40. To draw a circle by defining 3 points on its circumference, invoke the **Circle** flyout of the **Draw** panel and then click on the **3 Point** tool. Alternatively, enter C or **CIRCLE** in the Command Window and then press ENTER. Next, click on the **3P** option in the command prompt or enter **3P** in the Command Window.

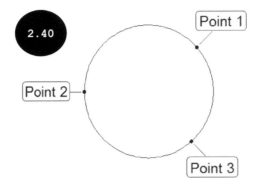

Procedure for Drawing Circle by Defining 3 Points

1. Invoke the **Circle** flyout and then click on the **3 Point** tool. You are prompted to specify the center point of the circle.

   ```
   Specify center point for circle or [3P 2P Ttr (tan tan radius)]:_3p
   Specify first point on circle:
   ```

2. Enter the coordinate (X , Y) of the first point either in the Command Window or in the Dynamic Input boxes. Alternatively, you can click directly in the drawing area to define the first point. As soon as you specify the first point, you are prompted to specify the second point of the circle.

   ```
   Specify second point on circle:
   ```

3. Enter the coordinate (X , Y) of the second point. You are prompted to specify the third point. Also, the preview of the circle appears such that it has passed through the two specified points.

   ```
   Specify third point on circle:
   ```

4. Enter the coordinate (X , Y) of the third point. The circle is drawn, see Figure 2.40.

Drawing Circles by Defining Tangent, Tangent, Radius

In AutoCAD, you can draw a circle that is tangent to two objects/entities. To draw a circle tangent to two objects/entities, you need to define two tangent objects and the radius of the circle by using the **Tan, Tan, Radius** tool, see Figure 2.41.

Procedure for Drawing Circle by Defining Tangent, Tangent, Radius

1. Invoke the **Circle** flyout and then click on the **Tan, Tan, Radius** tool. You are prompted to specify the first tangent object. Alternatively, enter **C** in the Command Window and then press ENTER. Next, click on the **Ttr (tan tan radius)** option in the command prompt or enter **ttr** in the Command Window.

   ```
   Specify point on object for first tangent of circle:
   ```

2. Click on the first tangent object in the drawing area, see Figure 2.41. You are prompted to specify the second tangent object.

```
Specify point on object for second tangent of circle:
```

3. Click on the second tangent object in the drawing area, see Figure 2.41. You are prompted to specify the radius of the circle.

```
Specify radius of circle:
```

4. Enter the radius value of the circle either in the Command Window or in the Dynamic Input boxes and then press ENTER. The circle tangent to the two selected objects is drawn, see Figure 2.41.

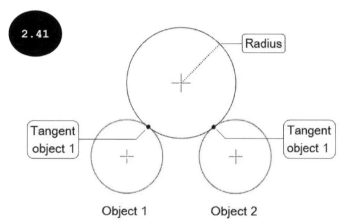

2.41

Radius

Tangent object 1

Tangent object 1

Object 1   Object 2

Drawing Circles by Defining Tangent, Tangent, Tangent

In AutoCAD, you can draw a circle that is tangent to three objects/entities. To draw a circle tangent to three objects/entities, you need to define three tangent objects one after another by using the Tan, Tan, Tan tool, see Figure 2.42.

Procedure for Drawing Circle by Defining Tangent, Tangent, Tangent

1. Invoke the Circle flyout and then click on the Tan, Tan, Tan tool. You are prompted to specify the first tangent object.

```
Specify center point for circle or [3P 2P Ttr (tan tan radius)]:_3p
Specify first point on circle:_tan to
```

2. Click on the first tangent object in the drawing area, see Figure 2.42. You are prompted to specify the second tangent object.

```
Specify second point on circle:_tan to
```

3. Click on the second tangent object in the drawing area, see Figure 2.42. You are prompted to specify the third tangent object.

```
Specify third point on circle:_tan to
```

4. Click on the third tangent object, see Figure 2.45. The circle tangent to three selected objects is drawn, see Figure 2.42.

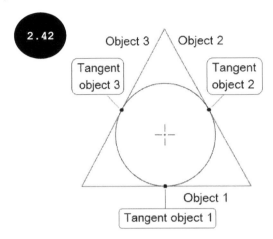

Drawing Arc

In AutoCAD, you can draw arcs by using different methods. The tools for drawing arcs are grouped together in the **Arc** flyout of the **Draw** panel in the **Home** tab, see Figure 2.43. Alternatively, you can invoke the **Arc** command for creating arcs by entering **ARC** or **A** in the Command Window and then pressing ENTER. Different methods to create arcs are as follows:

Drawing Arc by Defining 3 Points

You can draw an arc by defining three points on the circumference of the arc by using the **3-Point** tool, see Figure 2.44. To draw an arc by defining three points on the circumference of the arc, click on the down arrow in the active arc tool of the **Draw** panel. The **Arc** flyout appears, see Figure 2.43. Next, click on the **3-Point** tool in the flyout. The **3-Point** tool is activated. Alternatively, you can enter **A** or **ARC** in the Command Window and then press ENTER to invoke the **3-Point** tool. Once the **3-Point** tool has been activated, you are prompted to specify the start point of the arc. You can specify the coordinate (X , Y) of the start point of the arc either in the Command Window or in the Dynamic Input boxes. You can also click the left mouse button directly in the drawing area to specify the point.

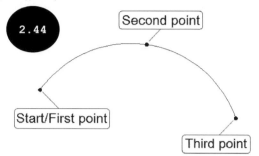

Procedure for Drawing Arc by Defining 3 Points

1. Click on the down arrow in the active arc tool of the **Draw** panel to invoke the **Arc** flyout and then click on the **3-Point** tool. You are prompted to specify the start point of the arc. Alternatively, enter **A** in the Command Window and then press ENTER.

   ```
   Specify start point of arc or [Center]:
   ```

2. Enter the coordinate (X , Y) of the start point and then press ENTER. You are prompted to specify the second point of the arc. You can also click directly in the drawing area to specify the start point of the arc.

   ```
   Specify second point of arc or [Center End]:
   ```

3. Move the cursor counter-clockwise or clockwise in the drawing area and then click the left mouse button to specify the second point of the arc on the circumference of the arc. You can also specify the second point of the arc by entering its coordinate (X , Y). As soon as you specify the second point, you are prompted to specify the end point of the arc. Also, the preview of the arc appears such that it has passed through the first and second points specified in the drawing area.

   ```
   Specify end point of arc:
   ```

4. Specify the end point of the arc on the circumference of the arc by clicking the left mouse button in the drawing area. The arc is drawn such that it has passed through the three specified points, see Figure 2.45.

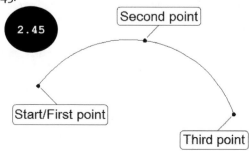

Drawing Arc by Defining Start, Center, and End Points

You can draw an arc by defining the start, center, and end points using the **Start, Center, End** tool of the **Arc** flyout, see Figure 2.46.

Procedure for Drawing Arc by Defining Start, Center, and End Points

1. Invoke the **Arc** flyout and then click on the **Start, Center, End** tool. You are prompted to specify the start point of the arc. Alternatively, enter **A** in the Command Window and then press ENTER.

    ```
    Specify start point of arc or [Center]:
    ```

2. Enter the coordinate (X , Y) of the start point and then press ENTER. You are prompted to specify the center point of the arc. You can also click the left mouse button in the drawing area to specify the start point of the arc.

    ```
    Specify second point of arc or [Center End]:_c Specify center
    point of arc:
    ```

    Note: If you invoke the tool for creating an arc by entering **A** or **ARC** in the Command Window then after specifying the start point of the arc, you need to click on the **Center** option in the command prompt for specifying the center point of the arc.

3. Move the cursor to the required location in the drawing area and then click to specify the center point of the arc. You can also enter the coordinate (X , Y) for specifying the center point of the arc. As soon as you specify the center point, you are prompted to specify the end point of the arc. Also, the preview of the arc appears in the counter-clockwise direction in the drawing area.

    ```
    Specify end point of arc or [Angle chord Length]:
    ```

    Note: By default, an arc is created in the counter-clockwise direction. To change the direction of creating arc from counter-clockwise direction to clockwise direction, press and hold the CTRL key and then specify the end point of the arc.

4. Specify the end point of the arc by clicking the left mouse button in the drawing area. The arc is drawn, see Figure 2.46.

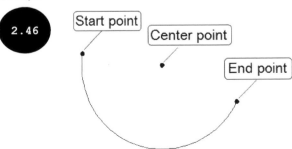

Drawing Arc by Defining Start Point, Center Point, and Angle

You can draw an arc by defining start point, center point, and angle using the **Start, Center, Angle** tool of the **Arc** flyout, see Figure 2.47. Below is the command sequence for drawing an arc by specifying start point, center point, and angle.

Tool/Command: *Click on the **Start, Center, Angle** tool in the **Arc** flyout*
Specify start point of arc or [Center]: *Specify the start point of the arc*
Specify center point of arc: *Specify the center point of the arc*
Specify included angle (hold Ctrl to switch direction): *Specify the angle of the arc (see Figure 2.47)*

Tip: As discussed, you can specify coordinates (X, Y) either in the Command Window or in the Dynamic Input boxes for specifying points in the drawing area. Alternatively, you can click the left mouse button directly in the drawing area for specifying points.

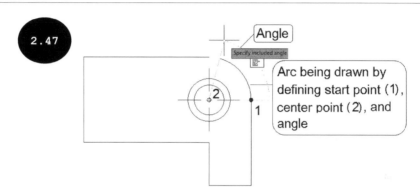

2.47

Arc being drawn by defining start point (1), center point (2), and angle

Drawing Arc by Defining Start Point, Center Point, and Length

You can draw an arc by defining start point, center point, and length using the **Start, Center, Length** tool of the **Arc** flyout, see Figure 2.48. Below is the command sequence for drawing an arc by specifying start point, center point, and length.

Tool/Command: *Click on the **Start, Center, Length** tool in the **Arc** flyout*
Specify start point of arc or [Center]: *Specify the start point of the arc*
Specify center point of arc: *Specify the center point of the arc*
Specify length of chord (hold Ctrl to switch direction): *Specify the length of the arc (see Figure 2.48)*

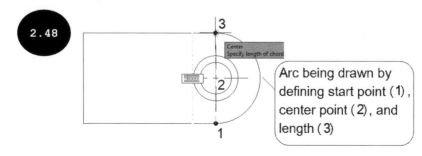

2.48

Arc being drawn by defining start point (1), center point (2), and length (3)

Drawing Arc by Defining Start Point, End Point, and Angle

You can draw an arc by defining start point, end point, and angle using the **Start, End, Angle** tool of the **Arc** flyout, see Figure 2.49. Below is the command sequence for drawing an arc by specifying start point, end point, and angle.

```
Command/Tool:  Click on the Start, End, Angle tool in the Arc flyout
Specify start point of arc or [Center]:  Specify the start point of the arc
Specify end point of arc:  Specify the end point of the arc
Specify center point of arc or [Angle Direction Radius]:_a Specify
included angle:  Specify the angle of the arc (see Figure 2.49)
```

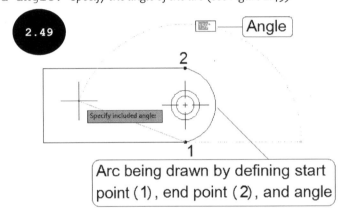

Arc being drawn by defining start point (1), end point (2), and angle

Drawing Arc by Defining Start Point, End Point, and Direction

You can draw an arc by defining start point, end point, and direction using the **Start, End, Direction** tool of the **Arc** flyout, see Figure 2.50. Below is the command sequence for drawing an arc by specifying start point, end point, and direction.

```
Tool/Command:  Click on the Start, End, Direction tool in the Arc flyout
Specify start point of arc or [Center]:  Specify the start point of the arc
Specify end point of arc:  Specify the end point of the arc
Specify center point of arc or [Angle Direction Radius]:_d Specify
tangent direction for the start point of arc:  Specify the direction of the arc
(see Figure 2.50)
```

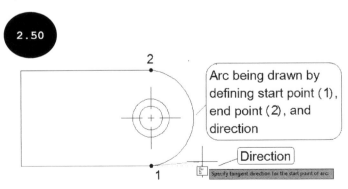

Arc being drawn by defining start point (1), end point (2), and direction

Drawing Arc by Defining Start Point, End Point, and Radius

You can draw an arc by defining start point, end point, and radius using the **Start, End, Radius** tool of the **Arc** flyout, see Figure 2.51. Below is the command sequence for drawing an arc by specifying start point, end point, and radius.

> Tool/Command: *Click on the Start, End, Radius tool in the Arc flyout*
> Specify start point of arc or [Center]: *Specify the start point of the arc*
> Specify end point of arc: *Specify the end point of the arc*
> Specify radius of arc: *Specify the radius of the arc (see Figure 2.51)*

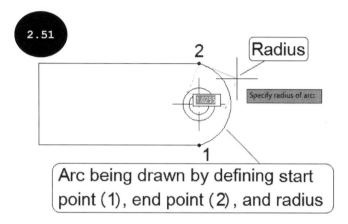

Arc being drawn by defining start point (1), end point (2), and radius

Drawing Arc by Defining Center Point, Start Point, and End Point

You can draw an arc by defining center point, start point, and end point using the **Center, Start, End** tool of the **Arc** flyout, see Figure 2.52. Below is the command sequence for drawing an arc by specifying center point, start point, and end point.

> Tool/Command: *Click on the Center, Start, End tool in the Arc flyout*
> Specify start point of arc or [Center]: _c Specify center point of arc: *Specify the center point of the arc (see Figure 2.52)*
> Specify start point of arc: *Specify the start point of the arc (see Figure 2.52)*
> Specify end point of arc or [Angle chord Length]: *Specify the end point of the arc (see Figure 2.52)*

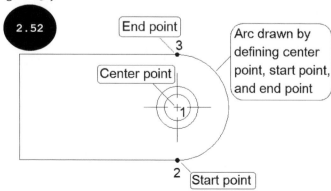

Arc drawn by defining center point, start point, and end point

Drawing Arc by Defining Center Point, Start Point, and Angle

You can draw an arc by defining center point, start point, and angle using the **Center, Start, Angle** tool of the **Arc** flyout, see Figure 2.53. Below is the command sequence for drawing an arc by specifying center point, start point, and angle.

```
Tool/Command:  Click on the Center, Start, Angle tool in the Arc flyout
Specify start point of arc or [Center]:_c Specify center point of
arc:  Specify the center point of the arc (see Figure 2.53)
Specify start point of arc:  Specify the start point of the arc (see Figure 2.53)
Specify included angle:  Specify the angle of the arc (see Figure 2.53)
```

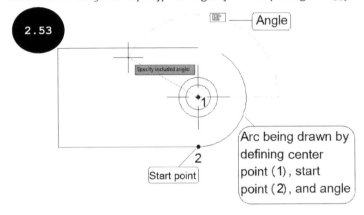

2.53

Start point

Arc being drawn by defining center point (1), start point (2), and angle

Drawing Arc by Defining Center Point, Start Point, and Length

You can draw an arc by defining center point, start point, and length using the **Center, Start, Length** tool of the **Arc** flyout, see Figure 2.54. Below is the command sequence for drawing an arc by specifying center point, start point, and length.

```
Command/Tool:  Click on the Center, Start, Length tool of the Arc flyout
Specify start point of arc or [Center]:_c Specify center point of
arc:  Specify the center point of the arc
Specify start point of arc:  Specify the start point of the arc
Specify end point of arc or [Angle chord Length]:_1 Specify length
of chord:  Specify length to draw an arc (see Figure 2.54)
```

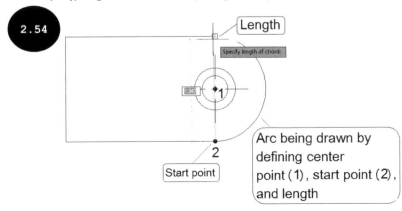

2.54

Length

Start point

Arc being drawn by defining center point (1), start point (2), and length

Drawing Arc by using the Continue Tool

You can draw an arc tangent to the last drawn line or arc entity by using the **Continue** tool of the **Arc** flyout. Below is the command sequence for drawing an arc tangent to the last drawn line or arc entity.

> Tool/Command: *Click on the **Continue** tool in the **Arc** flyout. The preview of an tangent arc appears such that its start point is fixed with the end point of the last drawn entity*
> Specify end point of arc: *Click to specify the end point of the arc*

Canceling, Erasing and Restore Objects

In AutoCAD, you can cancel or exit the current active command/tool, erase or delete unwanted entities, and restore the erased or deleted entities in the drawing area. To cancel or exit the current active command/tool, press the ESC or ENTER key. Alternatively, right-click in the drawing area and then click on the **Cancel** or **Enter** option in the shortcut menu displayed. For example, if you are creating line entities by using the **Line** tool then press the ESC or ENTER key to terminate the creation of lines and exit from the **Line** tool. Refer to the command sequence given below:

> Tool/Command: *Line or L* (***ENTER***)
> Specify first point: *Specify X, Y coordinates*
> Specify next point or [Undo]: *Specify X, Y coordinates*
> Specify next point or [Undo]: *ESC or ENTER*

To erase the drawing entities those are drawn by mistake or drawn wrongly, enter E or **ERASE** in the Command Window and then press ENTER. The erase command gets invoked and you are prompted to select the objects to be erased. Click on the objects to be erased from the drawing. You can click on multiple objects one by one for erasing them. Next, press the ENTER key or right-click in the drawing area. The selected objects are erased from the drawing. Refer to the command sequence given below:

> Command: *ERASE or E* (***ENTER***)
> Select objects: *Click to select the first object to be erased*
> Select objects: *Click to select the second object to be erased*
> Select objects: ***ENTER***

Tip: You can also click on the ERASE tool ▨ in the **Modify** panel of the **Home** tab to erase the drawing entities.

To erase all objects/entities of a drawing at a time, invoke the **ERASE** tool/command and then enter **All** in the Command Window.

If you have erased/deleted an object by mistake or accidentally and want to restore it, enter **Undo** or **U** in the Command Window and then press ENTER. The undo command gets invoked and the previously erased/deleted object gets restored in the drawing area. You can use the undo command multiple times to restore the previously erased/deleted objects one by one. Alternatively, press the CTRL plus Z key to restore or undo the previously erased/deleted objects.

Navigating 2D Drawing

In AutoCAD, you can navigate drawing by using the navigating tools. The navigating tools such as **Zoom** and **Pan** can be accessed from the **Navigation Bar**, which is on the right of the drawing area, see Figure 2.55. Different navigating tools are as follows:

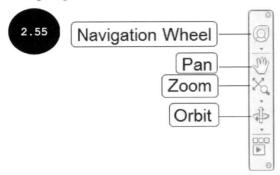

Zoom

AutoCAD has a number of powerful tools to zoom in or zoom out drawing for better control over drawing. The tools to zoom in or zoom out the drawing are in the **Zoom** flyout of the **Navigation Bar**. To invoke the **Zoom** flyout, click on the down arrow in the active zoom tool of the **Navigation Bar**, see Figure 2.56. Some of the zoom tools are as follows:

Zoom Realtime

The **Zoom Realtime** tool is used to zoom in or zoom out the drawing area, dynamically. In other words, you can dynamically enlarge or reduce the view of the drawing area by using the **Zoom Realtime** tool. To invoke the **Zoom Realtime** tool, click on the down arrow in the active zoom tool of the Navigation Bar. The **Zoom** flyout appears, see Figure 2.56. In this flyout, click on the **Zoom Realtime** tool, see Figure 2.57. Alternatively, to invoke the **Zoom Realtime** tool, enter Z or ZOOM in the Command Window and then press ENTER twice. Refer to the command sequence given below:

```
Tool/Command: Zoom or Z (ENTER)
Specify corner of window, enter a scale factor (nX or nXP), or
[All/Center/Dynamic/Extents/Previous/Scale/Window/Object]<real
time>: ENTER
```

Once the **Zoom Realtime** tool has been invoked, press and hold the left mouse button in the drawing area and then drag the cursor upward or downward in the drawing area. On dragging the cursor upward, the drawing view starts enlarging and on dragging the cursor downward, the drawing view starts reducing. Note that in the process of enlarging or reducing (zooming in or zooming out) the drawing view, the scale of the drawing remains the same; only the viewing distance changes in order to enlarge or reduce the view.

Zoom All

The **Zoom All** tool is used to zoom the entire drawing or drawing limit to fit inside the drawing area. If the drawing is large and goes outside the drawing limit then the entire drawing fits inside the drawing area on using the **Zoom All** tool, see Figure 2.58. However, if the drawing is smaller than the drawing limit then the drawing limit fits inside the drawing area on using the **Zoom All** tool, see Figure 2.59. To invoke the **Zoom All** tool, click on the down arrow in the active zoom tool of the **Navigation Bar**. The **Zoom** flyout appears. In this flyout, click on the **Zoom All** tool. Alternatively, enter Z or ZOOM in the Command Window and then press ENTER. Next, enter **A** or **ALL** in the Command Widow to invoke **Zoom All** tool. Refer to the command sequence given below:

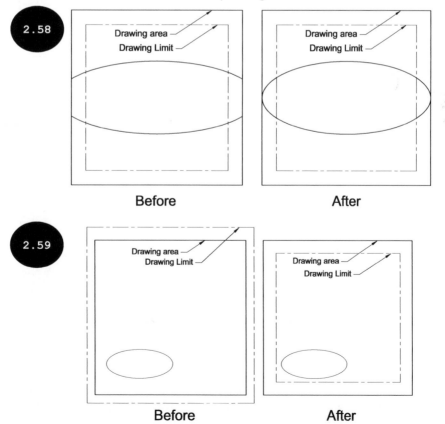

```
Command: Z or Zoom (ENTER)
Specify corner of window, enter a scale factor (nX or nXP), or
[All/Center/Dynamic/Extents/Previous/Scale/Window/Object]<real
time>: A or ALL (ENTER)
```

As soon as you invoke the **Zoom All** tool/command, the entire drawing or drawing limit fits inside the drawing area.

Zoom Window

The **Zoom Window** tool is used to zoom in an area of a drawing. You can specify an area of a drawing to be zoomed in by drawing a rectangular window around it. To invoke the **Zoom Window** tool, invoke the **Zoom** flyout of the Navigation Bar and then click on the **Zoom Window** tool. Alternatively, enter **Z** or ZOOM in the Command Window and then press ENTER. Next, enter **W** in the Command Widow to invoke the **Zoom Window** tool. Refer to the command sequence given below:

```
Command: Z or Zoom (ENTER)
Specify corner of window, enter a scale factor (nX or nXP), or
[All/Center/Dynamic/Extents/Previous/Scale/Window/Object]<real
time>: W (ENTER)
Specify first corner:  Click to specify the first corner of the rectangular window in the
drawing area (ENTER)
Specify first corner: Specify opposite corner:  Click to specify the second/
opposite corner of the rectangular window
```

Once the **Zoom Window** tool/command has been invoked, specify an area of a drawing to be zoomed in by drawing a rectangular window around it. The specified area that lies inside the window drawn magnifies and fits inside the drawing area.

Zoom Previous

The **Zoom Previous** tool is used to display the previously zoomed view of a drawing. To invoke the **Zoom Previous** tool, invoke the **Zoom** flyout of the Navigation Bar and then click on the **Zoom Preview** tool. Alternatively, enter **Z** or **Zoom** in the Command Window and then press ENTER. Next, enter **P** in the Command Widow to invoke the **Zoom Previous** tool. Refer to the command sequence given below:

```
Command: Z or Zoom (ENTER)
Specify corner of window, enter a scale factor (nX or nXP), or
[All/Center/Dynamic/Extents/Previous/Scale/Window/Object]<real
time>: P (ENTER)
```

As soon as the **Zoom Preview** tool/command has been invoked, the previously zoomed view gets displayed in the drawing area.

Zoom Extents

The **Zoom Extents** tool is used to fit a drawing completely inside the drawing area by expanding or shrinking the drawing. By using this tool, all the entities in the drawing get magnified to their largest possibilities in the drawing area. To invoke the **Zoom Extents** tool, invoke the **Zoom** flyout of the Navigation Bar and then click on the **Zoom Extents** tool. Alternatively, enter **Z** or **ZOOM** in the Command Window and then press ENTER. Next, enter **E** in the Command Widow to invoke this tool. Refer to the command sequence given below:

```
Command: Z or Zoom (ENTER)
Specify corner of window, enter a scale factor (nX or nXP), or
[All/Center/Dynamic/Extents/Previous/Scale/Window/Object]<real
time>: E (ENTER)
```

Zoom In

The **Zoom In** tool is used to zoom in a drawing by doubling its size in the drawing area. To invoke the **Zoom In** tool, invoke the **Zoom** flyout of the **Navigation Bar** and then click on the **Zoom In** tool. Alternatively, enter **Z** or **ZOOM** in the Command Window and then press ENTER. Next, enter **2X** in the Command Widow to invoke this tool. Refer to the command sequence given below:

```
Command: Z or Zoom (ENTER)
Specify corner of window, enter a scale factor (nX or nXP), or
[All/Center/Dynamic/Extents/Previous/Scale/Window/Object]<real
time>: 2X (ENTER)
```

Zoom Out

The **Zoom Out** tool is used to zoom out the drawing by decreasing its size to half of the original size of the drawing. To invoke the **Zoom Out** tool, invoke the **Zoom** flyout of the Navigation Bar and then click on the **Zoom Out** tool. Alternatively, enter **Z** or **ZOOM** in the Command Window and then press ENTER. Next, enter **.5X** in the Command Widow to invoke this tool. Refer to the command sequence given below:

```
Command: Z or Zoom (ENTER)
Specify corner of window, enter a scale factor (nX or nXP), or
[All/Center/Dynamic/Extents/Previous/Scale/Window/Object]<real
time>: .5X (ENTER)
```

Note: You can turn on or off the display of the Navigation Bar in the drawing area by using the **Navigation Bar** tool in the **Viewport Tools** panel of the **View** tab in the **Ribbon**, see Figure 2.60. By default, this tool is activated in the **Viewport Tools** panel of the **View** tab. As a result, the display of **Navigation Bar** is turned on in the drawing area.

2.60

Pan

The **Pan** tool is used to pan/move a drawing in the drawing area. To invoke the **Pan** tool, click on the **Pan** tool in the **Navigation Bar**, see Figure 2.61. Once the **Pan** tool has been invoked, you can pan the drawing by pressing and holding the left mouse button and then dragging the cursor.

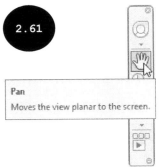

Tutorial 1

Draw the drawing shown in Figure 2.62 by specifying points using the Absolute Cartesian coordinate system. Also, use the Dynamic Input boxes for specifying coordinates. The dimensions shown in this figure are for your reference only. You will learn about applying dimensions in the later chapters.

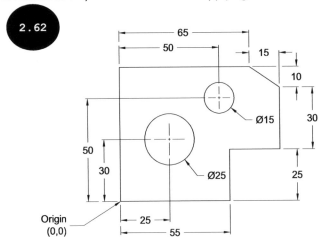

Section 1: Starting AutoCAD

1. Double-click on the AutoCAD icon on your desktop. The initial screen of AutoCAD appears with the **Start** tab, see Figure 2.63.

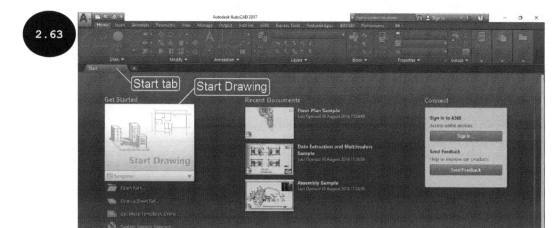

2. In the **Get Started** section of the **Start** tab, click on **Start Drawing**, see Figure 2.63. The new drawing file with the default drawing template gets invoked.

Note: Alternatively, to invoke a new drawing file, click on the **New** tool in the **Quick Access Toolbar**, which is at the top left corner of AutoCAD. The **Select template** dialog box appears. In this dialog box, select the *acad.dwt* template and then click on the **Open** button. A new drawing file with the *acad.dwt* template is invoked. You can also right-click on the **Start** tab and then click on the **New** option in the shortcut menu appeared. Additionally, you can click on the + sign available next to the **Start** tab to invoke a new drawing file.

Section 2: Selecting Workspace for Creating Drawing

1. Click on the **Workspace Switching** ⚙ button in the **Status Bar**. A flyout appears, see Figure 2.64.

2. In this flyout, make sure that the **Drafting & Annotation** option is tick-marked to create drawings in the Drafting & Annotation workspace.

Note: A tick-mark next to a workspace indicates that it is selected as the current workspace for creating drawings. By default, the Drafting & Annotation workspace is selected as the current workspace for creating drawings. You can click on any workspace to make it current for crating drawings.

Section 3: Defining Limits for the Drawing

1. Follow the command sequence given below for defining limits for the drawing.

```
Command: LIMITS (ENTER)
Specify lower left corner or [ON/OFF]<0.0000,0.0000>: 0,0 (ENTER)
Specify upper right corner <12.0000,9.0000>: 160,130  (ENTER)
```

Section 4: Creating Drawing by Using Absolute Coordinate System

As stated in the tutorial description, you need to enter coordinates in the Dynamic Input boxes according to the Absolute Cartesian coordinate system for specifying points. To enter coordinates in the Dynamic Input boxes, you need to make sure that the Dynamic Input mode is turned on.

1. Make sure that the Dynamic Input mode is turned on. You can turn on or off the Dynamic Input mode by clicking on the **Dynamic Input** button ▦ in the **Status Bar**. It is a toggle button.

2. Click on the **Line** tool in the **Draw** panel of the **Home** tab. The **Line** tool is activated and you are prompted to specify the first point of the line. Alternatively, you can enter L in the Command Window and then press ENTER to invoke the **Line** tool.

Note: In the Absolute coordinate system, the coordinate values are measured from the origin. To specify coordinates in the Dynamic Input boxes according to the Absolute coordinate system, you need to enter # as prefix to the X coordinate and then followed by the Y coordinate.

3. Follow the command sequence given below for creating the drawing.

```
Specify first point: 0,0 (ENTER)
Specify next point or [Undo]: #55,0 (ENTER)
Specify next point or [Undo]: #25,0 (ENTER)
Specify next point or [Undo]: #80,25 (ENTER)
Specify next point or [Undo]: #80,55 (ENTER)
Specify next point or [Close Undo]: #65,65 (ENTER)
Specify next point or [Close Undo]: #0,65 (ENTER)
Specify next point or [Close Undo]: C or Close (See Figure 2.65)

Command: Z or Zoom (ENTER)
Specify corner of window, enter a scale factor (nX or nXP), or
[All/Center/Dynamic/Extents/Previous/Scale/Window/Object]<real
time>: A or ALL (ENTER)
```

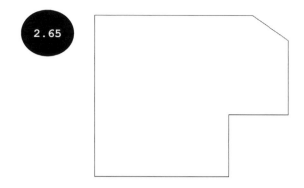

Command: *C or Circle* (**ENTER**)
Specify center point for circle or [3P 2P Ttr (tan tan radius)]:
25,30 (**ENTER**)
Specify radius of circle or [Diameter] <7.6802>: *D* (**ENTER**)
Specify diameter of circle <15.3603>: *25* (**ENTER**) *(See Figure 2.66)*

Command: *C or Circle* (**ENTER**)
Specify center point for circle or [3P 2P Ttr (tan tan radius)]:
50,50 (**ENTER**)
Specify radius of circle or [Diameter] <7.6802>: *D* (**ENTER**)
Specify diameter of circle <15.3603>: *15* (**ENTER**) *(See Figure 2.67)*

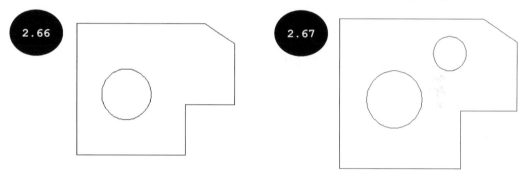

Section 5: Saving the Drawing

After creating the drawing, you need to save it.

1. Click on the **Save** tool in the **Quick Access Toolbar**. The **Save Drawing As** dialog box appears.

2. Browse to a local drive of your system and then create a folder with the name *AutoCAD*.

3. Create another folder with the name *Chapter 2* inside the *AutoCAD* folder. Next, enter **Tutorial 1** in the **File name** field of the dialog box.

4. Click on the **Save** button in the dialog box. The drawing is saved with the name Tutorial 1.

Tutorial 2

Draw the drawing shown in Figure 2.68 by using Relative Polar coordinate system. Also, use the Dynamic Input mode for specifying coordinate points. The dimensions shown in this figure are for your reference only. You will learn about applying dimensions in the later chapters.

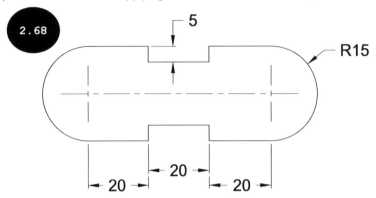

Section 1: Starting AutoCAD

1. Start AutoCAD and then click on the **New** tool in the **Quick Access Toolbar**, which is at the top left corner of the screen, see Figure 2.69. The **Select template** dialog box appears, see Figure 2.70.

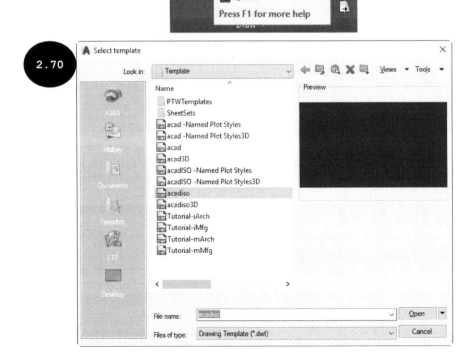

2. In the dialog box, click on the *acad.dwt* template and then click on the **Open** button. A new drawing file with the *acad.dwt* template is invoked.

3. Make sure that the Drafting & Annotation workspace is selected as the current workspace for creating the drawing.

Section 2: Drawing Line Entities

As stated in the tutorial description, you need to enter coordinates in the Dynamic Input boxes as per the Relative Polar coordinate system for specifying points.

1. Make sure that the Dynamic Input mode is turned on. You can turn on or off the Dynamic Input mode by clicking on the **Dynamic Input** button █ in the **Status Bar**. It is a toggle button.

2. Click on the **Ortho Mode** button in the **Status Bar** or press the **F8** key to turn on the Ortho mode. By activating the Ortho mode, you can create horizontal or vertical straight lines only.

3. Click on the **Line** tool in the **Draw** panel of the **Home** tab. The **Line** tool is invoked and you are prompted to specify the first point of the line.

Note: In Relative Polar coordinate system, the distance and angle values are measured from the last specified point in the drawing area.

4. Follow the command sequence given below for creating the drawing.

Specify first point: *Click the left mouse button in the drawing area to specify the first point*
Specify next point or [Undo]: *Move the cursor horizontally toward the right and then enter* **20** *in the Dynamic Input box* (**ENTER**) *(See Figure 2.71)*
Specify next point or [Undo]: *Move the cursor vertically upward and then enter* **5** (**ENTER**)
Specify next point or [Undo]: *Move the cursor horizontally toward the right and then enter* **20** (**ENTER**)
Specify next point or [Undo]: *Move the cursor vertically downward and then enter* **5** (**ENTER**)
Specify next point or [Close Undo]: *Move the cursor horizontally toward the right and then enter* **20** (**ENTER**)
Specify next point or [Close Undo]: *Move the cursor vertically upward and then enter* **30** (**ENTER**) *(See Figure 2.72)*

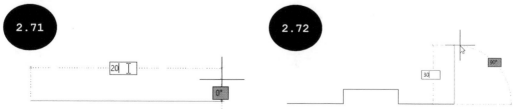

```
Specify next point or [Close Undo]:
```
Move the cursor horizontally toward the left and then enter **20**   (***ENTER***)
```
Specify next point or [Close Undo]:
```
Move the cursor vertically downward and then enter **5**   (***ENTER***)
```
Specify next point or [Close Undo]:
```
Move the cursor horizontally toward the left and then enter **20**   (***ENTER***)
```
Specify next point or [Close Undo]:
```
Move the cursor vertically upward and then enter **5**   (***ENTER***)
```
Specify next point or [Close Undo]:
```
Move the cursor horizontally toward the left and then enter **20**   (***ENTER***)
```
Specify next point or [Close Undo]:
```
C *or* **Close**   *(See Figure 2.73)*

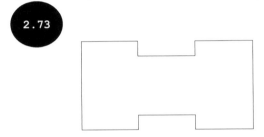

2.73

```
Command: Z or Zoom  (ENTER)
Specify corner of window, enter a scale factor (nX or nXP), or
[All/Center/Dynamic/Extents/Previous/Scale/Window/Object]<real
time>: A or ALL  (ENTER)
```

Section 3: Erasing the Unwanted Entities of the Drawing

1. Click on the **Erase** tool of the **Modify** panel of the **Home** tab or enter **E** in the Command Window. The **Erase** tool is activated and you are prompted to select the objects to be erased,

```
Select objects:
```

2. Click on the right and left most vertical entities one after another as the entities to be erased, see Figure 2.74. Next, press ENTER. The selected entities are erased, see Figure 2.75.

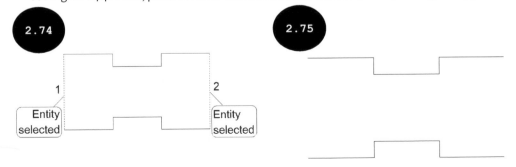

2.74

2.75

Section 4: Drawing Arcs

1. Click on the down arrow at the bottom of the active arc tool. The **Arc** flyout appears, see Figure 2.76.

2. In this flyout, click on the **Start, End, Radius** tool, see Figure 2.76. The **Start, End, Radius** tool is activated and you are prompted to specify the start point of the arc.

   ```
   Specify start point of arc or [Center]:
   ```

3. Click on the **Object Snap** button 🔲 in the **Status Bar** to activate the Object Snap mode. You will learn more about Object Snap mode in later chapters.

4. Move the cursor over the end point of the lower right most horizontal line and then click to specify the start point of the arc when the cursor snaps to the end point of line, see Figure 2.77.

   ```
   Specify end point of arc:
   ```

5. Move the cursor over the end point of the upper right most horizontal line and then click to specify the end point of the arc when the cursor snaps to it, see Figure 2.78.

```
Specify center point of arc or [Angle Direction Radius]:_r Specify
radius of arc:
```

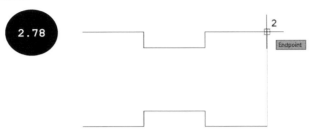

6. Move the cursor horizontally toward the right and then enter **15** as the radius of arc in the **Dynamic Input** box, which appears near the cursor in the drawing area. The arc is drawn, see Figure 2.79.

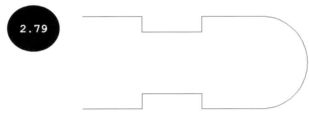

7. Similarly, draw an arc on the left side of the drawing by using the **Start, End, Radius** tool, see Figure 2.80.

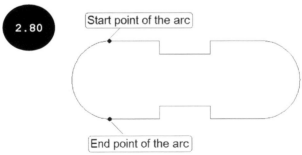

Section 5: Saving the Drawing

After creating the drawing, you need to save it.

1. Click on the **Save** tool in the **Quick Access Toolbar**. The **Save Drawing As** dialog box appears.

2. Browse to the *Chapter 2* folder, inside the *AutoCAD* folder. If the folders have not been created in Tutorial 1 of this chapter then you need to first create these folders in a local drive of your system.

3. Enter **Tutorial 2** in the **File name** field of the dialog box and then click on the **Save** button. The drawing is saved with the name Tutorial 2.

Hands-on Test Drive 3

Draw the drawing shown in Figure 2.81 by using the Relative Cartesian coordinate system. Also, use the Dynamic Input boxes for specifying coordinate points. The dimensions shown in this figure are for your reference only. You will learn about applying dimensions in the later chapters.

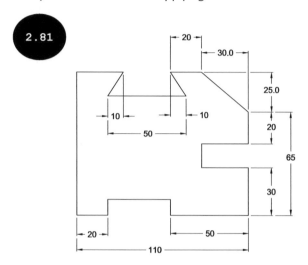

Hands-on Test Drive 4

Draw the drawing shown in Figure 2.82 by using the Relative Cartesian coordinate system. Also, use the Dynamic Input boxes for specifying coordinate points.

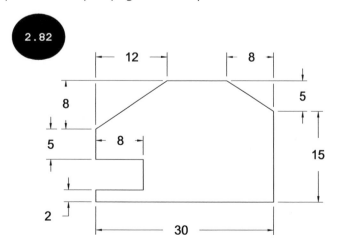

Summary

In this chapter, you have learned how to set drawing units, drawing limits, and grid and snap settings. You have also learned about various coordinate systems used in AutoCAD and how to create line, circle, and arc entities in AutoCAD. In addition, you have learned how to cancel, erase, undo, and navigating 2D drawing.

Questions

- The _____ is the shortcut for the UNITS command.

- In _____ coordinate system, every point you specify in the drawing area is measured from the origin (0,0) and their location is specified with respect to X and Y coordinates.

- In AutoCAD, you can specify coordinates either by using the _____ or _____ .

- In _____ coordinate system, every point you specify in the drawing area is measured from the last specified point in the drawing area and their location is specified with respect to X and Y coordinates.

- In _____ coordinate system, to define a point you need to specify distance and angle values separated by an angle bracket (<).

- The _____ tool is used to draw a circle by defining two points on the circumference of the circle.

- The _____ tool is used to draw an arc by defining the start, center and end points.

- The _____ tool is used to display the previously zoomed view of a drawing.

Using Drawing Aids and Selection Methods

In this chapter, you will learn the following:

- Working with Ortho mode
- Working with Polar Tracking
- Working with Object Snap
- Working with Object Snap Tracking
- Specifying grids and snaps settings
- Working with layers
- Assigning objects to layers

Drawing aids such as grid and snap, Ortho, Polar Tracking, and Object Snap Tracking are highly essential for creating drawings accurately and quickly, in AutoCAD. Of all these drawing aids, the grid and snap settings has already been discussed in the Chapter 2. The remaining drawing aids are discussed next.

Working with Ortho Mode

The Ortho mode is used to create horizontal or vertical straight lines. You can turn on the Ortho mode to create horizontal or vertical lines (lines at an incremental angle of 90-degree). By turning on the Ortho mode, you can easily and accurately draw the horizontal or vertical line entities of a drawing. To turn on the Ortho mode, click on the **Ortho Mode** button in the **Status Bar**, see Figure 3.1. Note that it is a toggle button. You can also press F8 key to turn on or off the Ortho mode to create horizontal or vertical lines.

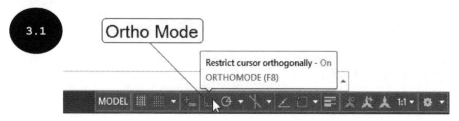

Example 1

Draw the drawing shown in Figure 3.2 by turning on the Ortho mode.

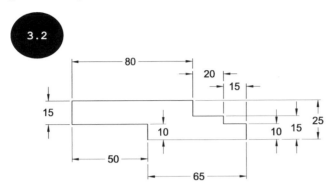

Section 1: Starting AutoCAD

1. Double-click on the AutoCAD icon on your desktop to start AutoCAD. The initial screen of AutoCAD appears with the **Start** tab, see Figure 3.3.

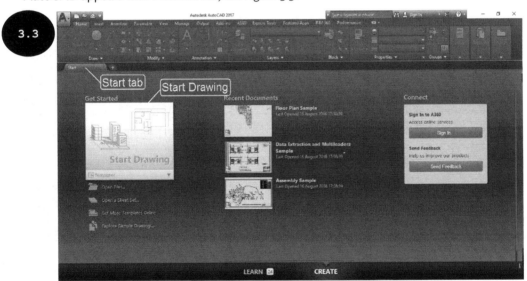

2. In the **Get Started** section of the **Start** tab, click on **Start Drawing**, see Figure 3.3. The new drawing file with the default drawing template gets invoked. Alternatively, click on the **New** tool in the **Quick Access Toolbar**, which is at the top left corner of AutoCAD screen. The **Select template** dialog box appears. In this dialog box, select the **acad.dwt** template and then click on the **Open** button. A new drawing file with the **acad.dwt** template is invoked.

Section 2: Creating Drawing by Using Ortho Mode

As stated in the description of the example, you need to create the drawing of this example by turning on the Ortho mode.

1. Click on the **Ortho Mode** button in the **Status Bar** to turn on the Ortho mode, see Figure 3.4. Alternatively, press the F8 key to turn on the Ortho mode.

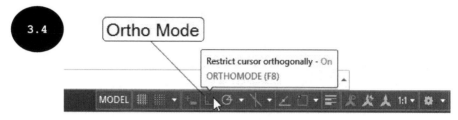

2. Make sure that the Dynamic Input mode is activated. You can turn on the Dynamic Input mode by clicking on the **Dynamic Input** button in the **Status Bar**.

Note: If the **Dynamic Input** button is not available in the **Status Bar** by default then click on the **Customization** button in the **Status Bar**. A flyout appears. In this flyout, click on the **Dynamic Input** option. The **Dynamic Input** button becomes available in the **Status Bar**.

3. Click on the **Line** tool in the **Draw** panel of the **Home** tab. The **Line** tool is activated and you are prompted to specify the first point of the line. Alternatively, enter L in the Command Window and then press ENTER to activate the **Line** tool.

```
Specify first point:
```

4. Follow the command sequence given below for creating the drawing:

Specify first point: *Click in the drawing area to specify the first point of the line*
Specify next point or [Undo]: *Move the cursor horizontally toward the right and then enter 65 in the Dynamic Input box* (***ENTER***) *(See Figure 3.5)*
Specify next point or [Undo]: *Move the cursor vertically upward and then enter 10* (***ENTER***)
Specify next point or [Undo]: *Move the cursor horizontally toward the left and then enter 15* (***ENTER***)
Specify next point or [Undo]: *Move the cursor vertically upward and then enter 5* (***ENTER***)
Specify next point or [Close Undo]: *Move the cursor horizontally toward the left and then enter 20* (***ENTER***)
Specify next point or [Undo]: *Move the cursor vertically upward and then enter 10* (***ENTER***)
Specify next point or [Close Undo]: *Move the cursor horizontally toward the left and then enter 80* (***ENTER***)

Specify next point or [Undo]: *Move the cursor vertically downward and then enter* **15** (***ENTER***)

Specify next point or [Close Undo]: *Move the cursor horizontally toward the right and then enter* **50** (***ENTER***)

Specify next point or [Close Undo]: *C or Close* (***ENTER***) *(See Figure 3.6)*

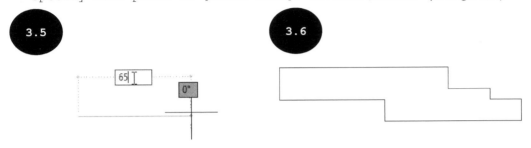

Tip: If the drawing has horizontal/vertical lines as well as inclined line entities then you can create horizontal/vertical lines by turning on the Ortho mode. For creating inclined lines, you need to turn off the Ortho mode. You can turn on or off the Ortho mode at any point of creating drawing.

Working with Polar Tracking

The Polar Tracking mode is used to create line entities at an increment of set angle. To create line entity at an increment of set angle, turn on the Polar Tracking mode by clicking on the **Polar Tracking** button in the **Status Bar**, see Figure 3.7. Alternatively, press the F10 key. Once the Polar Tracking mode has been turned on, the cursor snaps at the set incremental angle for creating line, see Figure 3.8. For example, if the incremental angle is set to 45-degree then the cursor snaps at 0-degree, 45-degree, 90-degree, 135-degree, 180-degree, and so on for creating line entities. Figure 3.8 shows a line being created at 45-degree angle, which is set as the incremental angle.

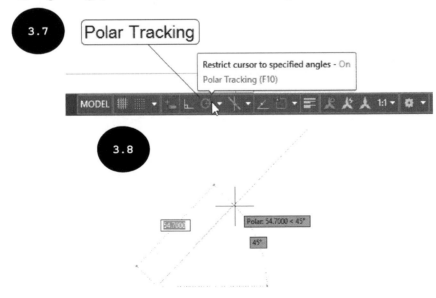

You can set incremental angle for creating line entities as required by using the **Drafting Settings** dialog box. To invoke the **Drafting Settings** dialog box, right-click on the **Polar Tracking** button in the **Status Bar**. A flyout appears, see Figure 3.9. In this flyout, click on the **Tracking Settings** option. The **Drafting Settings** dialog box appears with the **Polar Tracking** tab activated in it, see Figure 3.10. In the **Increment angle** field of the **Drafting Settings** dialog box, you can enter incremental angle value for polar tracking, as required.

Note: In addition to specifying incremental angle for polar tracking in the **Drafting Settings** dialog box, you can also select the predefined incremental angle directly from the flyout, see Figure 3.9. The flyout shows a list of commonly used increment angles, such as **90,180, 270, 360** and **45, 90, 135, 180**.

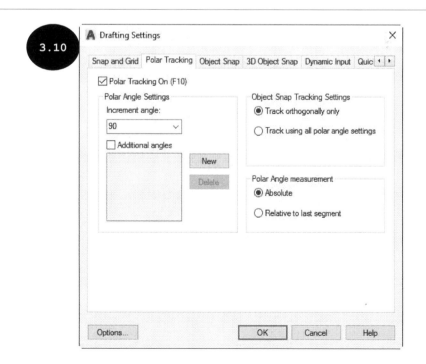

Note: Among the Ortho and Polar Tracking modes, only one mode can be activated at a time. If you turn on the Ortho mode, the Polar Tracking mode will automatically be deactivated, and vice-versa.

Example 2

Draw the drawing shown in Figure 3.11 by using the Polar Tracking mode.

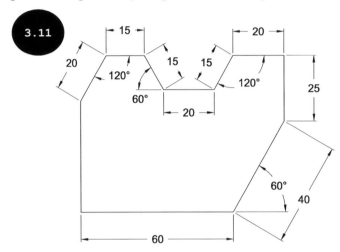

Section 1: Starting AutoCAD
1.   Start a new AutoCAD drawing file.

Section 2: Creating Drawing by Using the Polar Tracking Method
1.   Click on the **Line** tool in the **Draw** panel of the **Home** tab. The **Line** tool is activated and you are prompted to specify the first point of the line. Alternatively, enter **L** in the Command Window and then press ENTER to activate the **Line** tool.

```
Specify first point:
```

It is cleared from the drawing of this exercise that the inclined line entities have an increment angle of 60-degree. Therefore, you need to set increment angle for Polar Tracking to 60-degree for creating these inclined line entities quickly and easily.

2.   Move the cursor over the **Polar Tracking** button in the **Status Bar** and then right-click to display a flyout, see Figure 3.12.

3.   Click on the **30, 60, 90, 120** option in the flyout. The 30-degree is set as the increment angle for polar tracking.

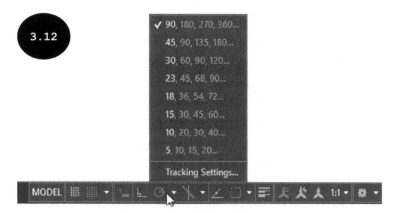

4. Make sure that the Dynamic Input mode is activated. If not activated, click on the **Dynamic Input** button ⬛ in the **Status Bar** to activate the Dynamic Input mode.

5. Follow the command sequence given below for creating the drawing:

Specify first point: *Click in the drawing area to specify the first point of the line*
Specify next point or [Undo]: *Move the cursor horizontally toward the right and then enter 60 in the Dynamic Input box (**ENTER**) (See Figure 3.13)*
Specify next point or [Undo]: *Move the cursor counter-clockwise and then enter 40 when the cursor snaps at an angle of 60-degree (**ENTER**) (See Figure 3.14)*

Specify next point or [Undo]: *Move the cursor vertically upward and then enter 25 (**ENTER**) (See Figure 3.15)*
Specify next point or [Undo]: *Move the cursor horizontally toward the left and then enter 20 (**ENTER**)*
Specify next point or [Close Undo]: *Move the cursor clockwise and then enter 15 when the cursor snaps at the angle of 120-degree (**ENTER**) (See Figure 3.16)*

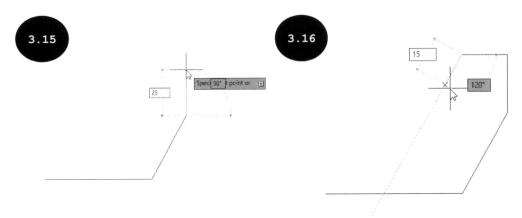

Specify next point or [Close Undo]: *Move the cursor horizontally toward the left and then enter 20* (**ENTER**)

Specify next point or [Close Undo]: *Move the cursor counter-clockwise and then enter 15 when the cursor snaps at the angle of 120-degree* (**ENTER**) *(See Figure 3.17)*

Specify next point or [Close Undo]: *Move the cursor horizontally toward the left and then enter 15* (**ENTER**)

Specify next point or [Close Undo]: *Move the cursor clockwise and then enter 20 when the cursor snaps at the angle of 120-degree* (**ENTER**) *(See Figure 3.18)*

Specify next point or [Close Undo]: *C or Close* (**ENTER**) *(See Figure 3.19)*

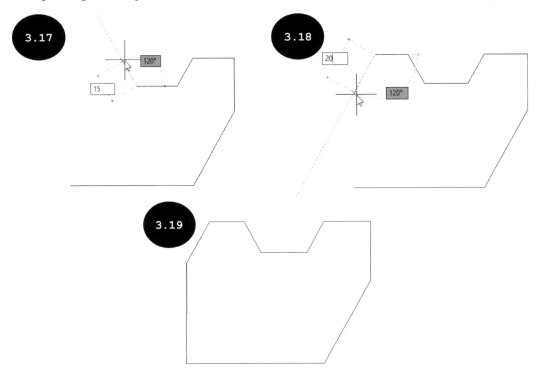

Working with Object Snap

The Object Snap mode is used to specify the points relative to an existing geometry of a drawing. To specify points relative to an existing geometry, it is recommended to turn on the Object Snap mode, so that points can be specified easily and accurately on the existing geometry of the drawing. The Object Snap mode is one of the very important features of AutoCAD. On turning on the Object Snap mode, the cursor snaps to the existing geometries, such as midpoint, center, node, insertion, perpendicular, and tangent, that helps in specifying exact points in the drawing area. For example, if you want to create a line starting from the end point of an existing arc then first invoke the **Line** tool and then turn on the Object Snap mode. Next, move the cursor over the end point of the arc and then click the left mouse button when the cursor snaps to the end point of arc, see Figure 3.20.

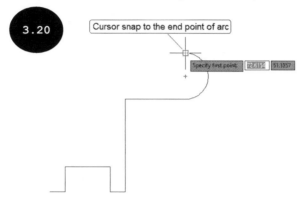

3.20 — Cursor snap to the end point of arc

To turn on or off the Object Snap mode, click on the **Object Snap** button in the **Status Bar** or press the **F3** key, see Figure 3.21.

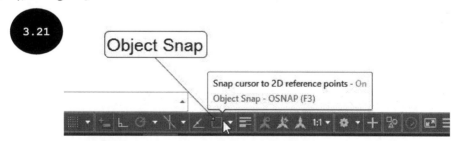

3.21 — Object Snap — Snap cursor to 2D reference points - On — Object Snap - OSNAP (F3)

In the Object Snap mode, the cursor snaps to the existing geometry depending upon the Object snap settings specified in the **Drafting Settings** dialog box. To define the Object snap settings, move the cursor over the **Object Snap** button in the **Status Bar** and then right-click. A flyout appears, see Figure 3.22. You can also click on the down arrow next to the **Object Snap** button in the **Status Bar** to display this flyout. In this flyout, click on the **Object Snap Settings** option. The **Drafting Settings** dialog box appears with the **Object Snap** tab activated in it, see Figure 3.23.

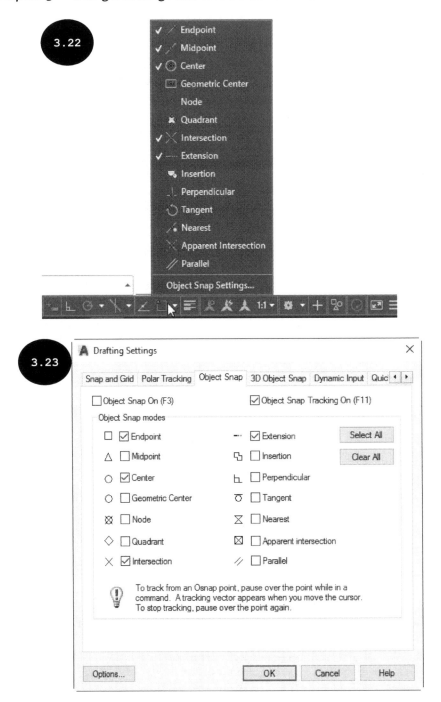

In the **Drafting Settings** dialog box, you can select the respective object snap check boxes for snapping the cursor while specifying points in the drawing area. For example, if you want to specify points on the midpoint, end point, and center point of an existing geometry then you can select their respective check boxes in this dialog box. Note that the cursor snaps only to the geometries/points that are selected in the **Drafting Settings** dialog box. Figures 3.24 through 3.27 shows geometries with different object snaps.

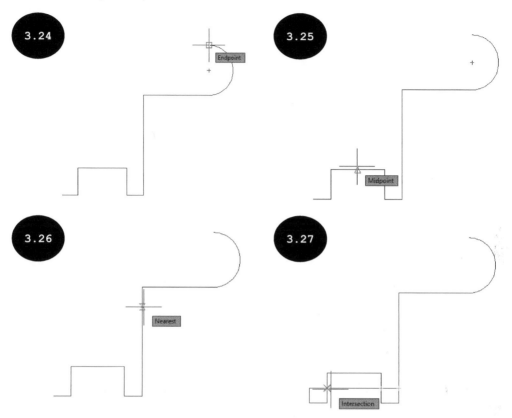

You can also select the **Select All** button in the dialog box to select all the object snap check boxes. To clear all the existing selected check boxes, click on the **Clear All** button in the **Drafting Settings** dialog box. After selecting the required object snap check boxes, click on the **OK** button in the dialog box to accept the change made as well as to exit from the dialog box.

Note: In addition to specifying Object snap settings in the **Drafting Settings** dialog box, you can also select the required object snap, such as **Endpoint**, **Midpoint**, and **Center** directly from the flyout, which appears on right-clicking on the **Object Snap** button in the **Status Bar**, refer Figure 3.22.

Working with Object Snap Tracking

The Object Snap Tracking mode is used to specify new points aligned to the existing points of a drawing, see Figure 3.28. In this figure, the center point of the circle being specified by aligning it to the end points of the inclined line entity of the drawing. Note that the Object Snap Tracking works in conjunction with the Object Snap. When the Object Snap Tracking is turned on, reference/tracking lines appear originating from the existing points of the drawing which guide the pointer of the cursor to specify a new point in the drawing area, see Figure 3.28.

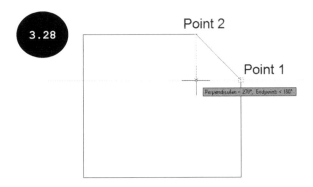

To specify points in the drawing by using the Object Snap Tracking mode, click on the **Object Snap Tracking** button in the **Status Bar** to turn it on. Alternatively, press the F11 key to turn on the Object Snap Tracking mode, see Figure 3.29. It is a toggle button.

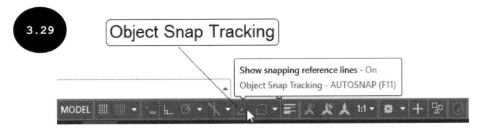

Once the Object Snap Tracking has been turned on, move the cursor to a reference point in the drawing area. When the cursor snaps to the reference point, move the cursor to a distance in the drawing area. A reference/tracking line appears, which is originated from the reference point. You can use this reference/ tracking line for specifying new points in the drawing area. For example, to draw a circle shown in Figure 3.30 whose center point is at the intersection of end points (Point 1 and Point 2), you need to first move the cursor to Point 1 and then move the cursor horizontally toward the left. A reference/tracking line appears. Next, move the cursor to Point 2 and when the cursor snaps to Point 2, move the cursor vertically downward. A reference/tracking line appears. Continue moving the cursor vertically downward untill the cursor snaps to the intersection of both the end points with the help of reference/tracking lines, see Figure 3.31. Next, click the left mouse button to specify the center point of the circle at the intersection of the end points, see Figure 3.31.

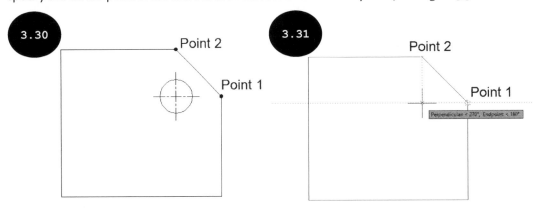

Working with Layers

In AutoCAD, you need to understand the concept of layers in order to create drawings easily and faster. With layers, you can have better control over drawing and create complex drawings faster and accurate. Layers work similar to tracing overlays on a drawing board, see Figure 3.32. You can have multiple layers in a drawing and organize your drawing by assigning different set of drawing objects to different layers. For example, all dimensions are in one layer and all hidden entities are in another layer. You can also assign different properties, such as color, linetype, and lineweight to different layers of a drawing. For example, you can assign hidden linetype to hidden layer with different lineweight. Note that in AutoCAD, all layers of a drawing give you combined look as you view the layers from the top and appear as you are working on a single sheet, see Figure 3.33. In this figure, object entities are in one layer with different lineweight; dimensions are in another layer with different color and lineweight; and centermarks are in different layer with different color and lineweight.

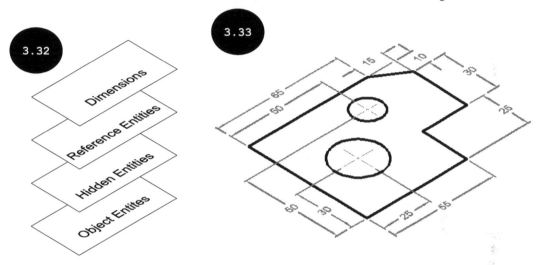

In AutoCAD, you can control the visibility, color, linetype, lineweight, and so on of layers, independently. As a result, you can work with complicated drawings very efficiently. For example, while working on a complicated drawing, you may have to create number of reference/construction lines, which you do not want to be the part of final drawing. In such case, you can create a layer with the name "Reference layer" and assign all the reference/construction lines to this layer. When the drawing is completed, you can simply turn off the "Reference layer" to hide all reference entities of the drawing. Note that you can turn on or off layers at any point of your drawing as per your requirement. It is always recommended to use layers functionally when working with AutoCAD. The good use of layers is the most important for creating drawings with good practice.

In AutoCAD, every time when you start a new drawing, only one layer is provided by default with default parameters. This default layer is named as "0" (zero) layer. The default "0" layer acts as the current layer, by default. It means anything you draw is assigned automatically to this "0" layer.

All the operations of a layer such as creating new layer, specifying layer properties, and so on can be performed by using the **LAYER PROPERTIES MANAGER**. To invoke the **LAYER PROPERTIES MANAGER**, click on the **Layer Properties** tool in the **Layers** panel of the **Home** tab, see Figure 3.34.

Alternatively, you can invoke the **LAYER PROPERTIES MANAGER** by entering **LAYER** or **LA** in the Command Window. Figure 3.35 shows the **LAYER PROPERTIES MANAGER** invoked with default "o" layer. Different operations that can be performed by using the **LAYER PROPERTIES MANAGER** are as follows:

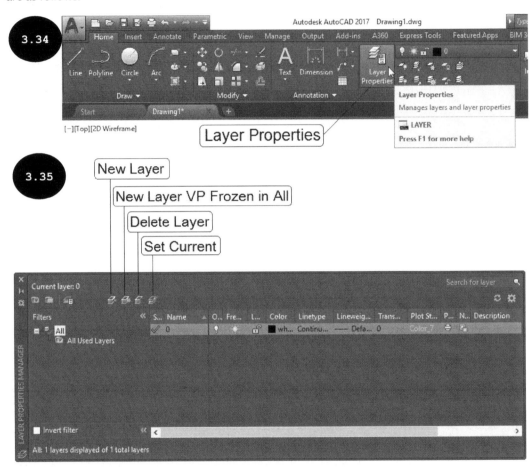

Creating New Layer

You can create a new layer by clicking on the **New Layer** button in the **LAYER PROPERTIES MANAGER**, see Figure 3.35. Alternatively, you can press the ALT + N key after invoking the **LAYER PROPERTIES MANAGER** for creating new layer. As soon as you click on the **New Layer** button, a new layer with the default name "**Layer 1**" is created with the default properties, see Figure 3.36. Note that the name of the newly created layer appears in an edit field, which indicates that the default name of the layer can be changed as per the requirement.

Note: The default properties of the newly created layer are the same as those of the existing selected layer.

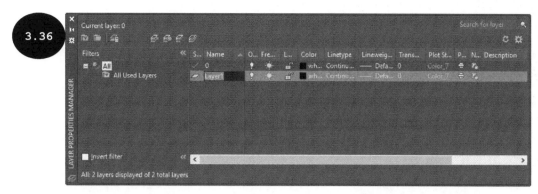

Similarly, you can create multiple layers in a drawing one by one by using the **New Layer** button of the **LAYER PROPERTIES MANAGER**. Figure 3.37 shows the **LAYER PROPERTIES MANAGER** with multiple layers.

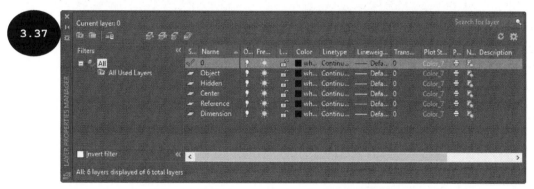

Making Current Layer

In AutoCAD, by default, the "0" layer is set as the current layer for a drawing. As a result, anything drawn in AutoCAD is assigned automatically to the "0" layer. Also, the properties such as color, linetype, and lineweight of the "0" layer get assigned to the objects drawn. Note that a green tick mark in the **Status** field of the layer, under the **Status** column indicates that the layer is set as the current layer of the drawing, see Figure 3.38.

You can set a layer as the current layer for a drawing by double-clicking either on the **Status** or **Name** field of the layer to be made current. Alternatively, you can select a layer to be made current and then click on the **Set Current** button available at the top of the **LAYER PROPERTIES MANAGER**, see Figure 3.39. You can also right-click on the layer to be made the current layer and then click on the **Set current** option in the shortcut menu appeared. Note that as discussed, the objects/entities drawn in the drawing area are automatically assigned to the current layer of the drawing, by default. However, you can further transfer the objects of one layer to another layer. The method of transferring objects from one layer to another is discussed later in this chapter.

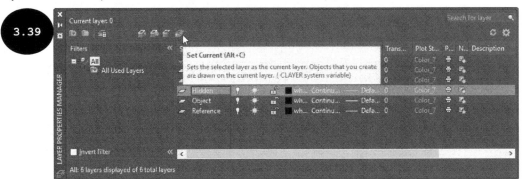

Note: You can also set a layer as the current layer without invoking the **LAYER PROPERTIES MANAGER**. To do so, move the cursor over the **Layer** drop-down list in the **Layers** panel of the **Home** tab and then click the left mouse button. The **Layer** drop-down list appears, see Figure 3.40. The **Layer** drop-down list displays the list of all the layers created in the current drawing. Next, move the cursor over the layer to be made current in the drop-down list and then click the left mouse button on it. The selected layer becomes the current layer of the drawing.

Assigning Color to Layer

You can specify/assign unique colors to different layers of a drawing. To specify a color for a layer, click on the **Color** field of the layer in the **LAYER PROPERTIES MANAGER**, see Figure 3.41. The **Select Color** dialog box appears, see Figure 3.42.

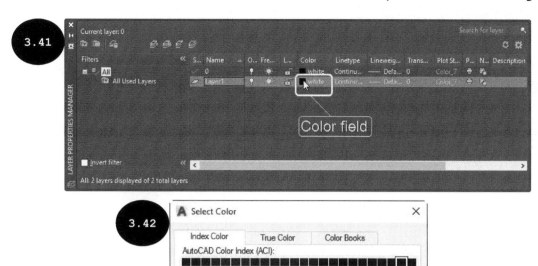

In the **Select Color** dialog box, click on the required color swatch to be assigned to the layer. Next, click on the **OK** button. The selected color is assigned to the layer. Similarly, you can assign different colors to other layers of a drawing.

Note: All entities/objects in the drawing area appear in the color, which is assigned to their respective layers.

Assigning Linetype to Layer

You can assign different linetypes to different layers of a drawing according to your requirement. For example, you can assign Center linetype to a layer that is associated with the centerlines of a drawing and Hidden linetype to a layer that is associated with hidden lines. To assign a linetype to a layer, click on the **Linetype** field of the layer in the **LAYER PROPERTIES MANAGER**, see Figure 3.43. The **Select Linetype** dialog box appears, see Figure 3.44.

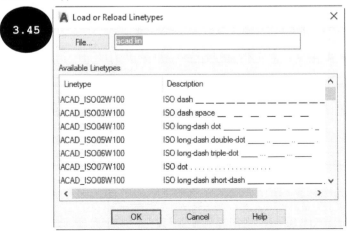

In case the **Select Linetype** dialog box appears similar to the one shown in Figure 3.44, in which only the Continuous linetype is listed, then you need to load the required linetypes into this dialog box. To load linetypes, click on the **Load** button in the **Select Linetype** dialog box. The **Load or Reload Linetypes** dialog box appears with the list of all available linetypes, see Figure 3.45. Next, click on the linetype to be loaded. You can select multiple linetypes by pressing the CTRL key. Once you have selected the linetypes to be loaded, click on the **OK** button. All the selected linetypes are listed or loaded into the **Select Linetype** dialog box. Figure 3.46 shows the **Select Linetype** dialog box with the **Center** and **Hidden** linetypes loaded.

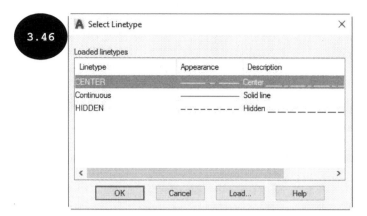

3.46

Once the required linetypes have been loaded in the **Select Linetype** dialog box, click on the linetype to be assigned to the layer. Next, click the **OK** button in the **Select Linetype** dialog box. The selected linetype is assigned to the layer. Similarly, you can assign the required linetype of another layers of the drawing.

Assigning Lineweight to Layer

Similar to assigning color and linetype to a layer, you can assign a lineweight/thickness to a layer. To assign a lineweight/thickness, click on the **Lineweight** field of the layer in the LAYER PROPERTIES MANAGER, see Figure 3.47. The **Lineweight** dialog box appears, see Figure 3.48.

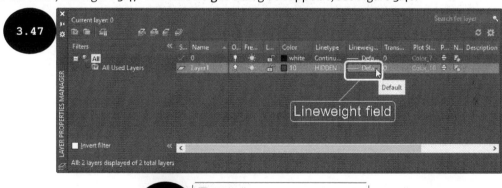

3.47

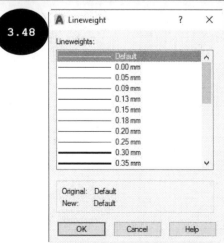

3.48

In this **Lineweight** dialog box, click on the lineweight to be assigned and then click on the **OK** button. The selected lineweight/thickness is assigned to the layer. Similarly, you can assign the required lineweight to other layers of the drawing.

> **Note:** You can turn on or off the display of the lineweight/thickness of objects in the drawing area by using the **Show/Hide Lineweight** button ▤. This is a toggle button available in the **Status Bar**.

Turning Layer On or Off

You can turn a layer on or off by clicking on the **On** field of a layer to be turned on or off, see Figure 3.49. Note that when you turn off a layer, the objects assigned to the layer become hidden or invisible in the drawing area. Also, if you plot the drawing, the objects of the hidden layer will not be plotted.

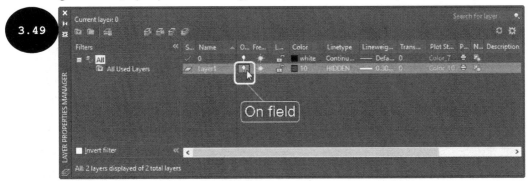

> **Note:** If you turn off a current layer by clicking on its **On** field then the **Layer – Current Layer Off** window appears, see Figure 3.50. This window confirms whether you want to turn off the current layer or keep the current layer on. Also, it informs that if you turn off the current layer then the objects drawn now will not be visible in the drawing area until you have turned on the layer.

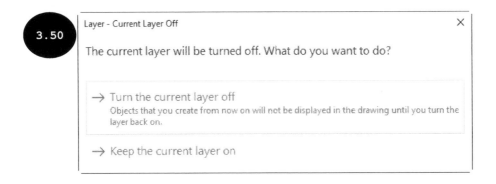

Freezing Layer

Similar to turning a layer on or off, you can also freeze or thaw a layer by clicking on the **Freeze** field of the layer to be frozen or thawed, see Figure 3.51. When you freeze a layer, the respective objects assigned to the layer get hidden in the drawing area and cannot be plotted. Note that the freezing/thawing a layer is same as turning off/on a layer with the only difference that on freezing a layer, the frozen layer is not considered while regenerating drawing. As a result, regeneration time of complex drawing is reduced. Also, it improves the overall performance of the system and speed up the zoom, pan, and other drawing operations.

Note: You cannot freeze current layer. If you click on the **Freeze** field of a current layer, the **Layer - Cannot Freeze** window appears, see Figure 3.52, which informs you that this layer cannot be frozen.

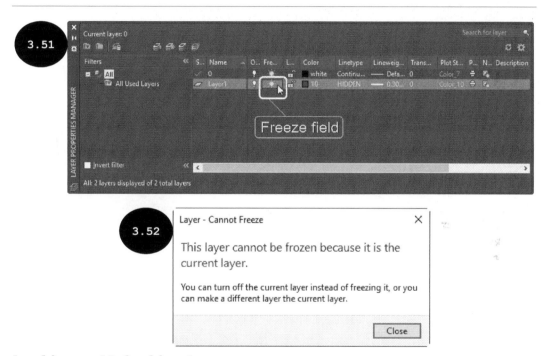

Locking or Unlocking Layer

You can lock or unlock a layer by clicking on the **Lock** field of a layer, see Figure 3.53. The objects assigned to a locked layer cannot be edited or modified. Also, the objects of the locked layer appear faded in the drawing area. Locking a layer is very useful if you do not want any editing or modification is done by mistake in the objects of a layer but still want the objects to appear in the drawing area for reference.

Deleting a Layer

You can delete an unwanted layer in a drawing. To delete an unwanted layer, select the layer to be deleted in the **LAYER PROPERTIES MANAGER** and then click on the **Delete Layer** button, see Figure 3.54. Alternatively, press ALT + D to delete the selected layer. Note that you cannot delete the default 'o' layer, defpoints layer (defpoints layer is created automatically as soon as you apply dimensions to objects in the drawing area), current layer, layers containing objects, and Xref-dependent layers.

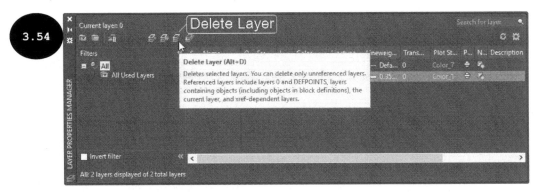

Setting Transparency of Layer

You can set transparency for the objects of a layer by using the **Transparency** field in the LAYER PROPERTIES MANAGER. On clicking the **Transparency** field of a layer, the **Layer Transparency** dialog box appears, see Figure 3.55. By using the drop-down list of this dialog box, you can select transparency for a layer from "o" to "90". The objects assigned to the layer become faded in the drawing area when the transparency of the layer is set to 10 or higher. Higher the transparency, more faded the appearance of the object in the drawing area.

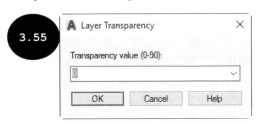

Restricting Layer from Plotting

You can restrict a layer for plotting by using the LAYER PROPERTIES MANAGER. If you do not want the objects of a layer to be plotted while plotting, then you can restrict the layer from plotting. To restrict a layer from plotting, click on the **Plot** field of the layer to be restricted from plotting, see Figure 3.56. Note that as soon as you click on the **Plot** field of a layer, a red color symbol ⊘ appears in the respective **Plot** field, which indicates that the layer has been restricted from plotting. You can click again on the **Plot** field of the layer to remove the restriction.

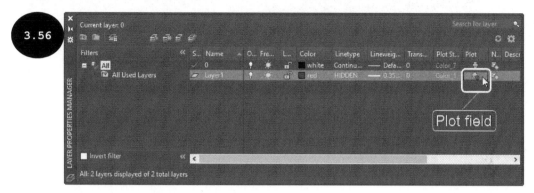

Freezing Layer in New Viewports

You can freeze a layer in the newly created viewports by using the **New VP Freeze** field of a layer in the LAYER PROPERTIES MANAGER, see Figure 3.57. On creating a new viewport, the objects of the layer which are frozen by using the **New VP Freeze** field become hidden/invisible in the newly created viewport. You can create multiple viewports of a drawing in the **Layout** tab. You will learn about the **Layout** tab and creating viewports in later chapters.

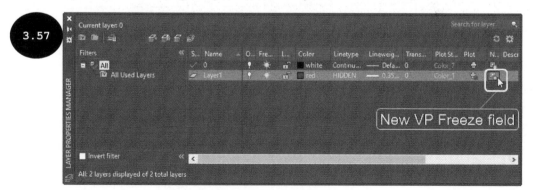

Freezing New Layer in All Layouts

In addition to freezing a layer in the newly created viewports, you can freeze the newly created layer in all viewports by using the **New Layer VP Frozen in All Viewports** button of the LAYER PROPERTIES MANAGER, Figure 3.58. When you click on the **New Layer VP Frozen in All Viewports** button, a new layer is created such that it becomes frozen in all viewports.

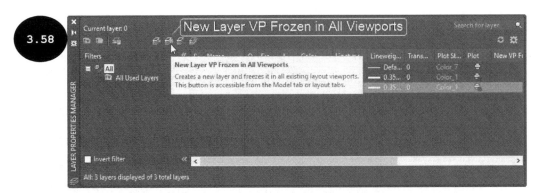

Once you have been created layers and assigned layer properties, you can close the **LAYER PROPERTIES MANAGER** by clicking on the cross mark ❌ on the title bar of the **LAYER PROPERTIES MANAGER**.

Assigning Objects to Layers

As discussed earlier, when you draw objects in the drawing area, by default, all the objects drawn get assigned automatically to the current layer. However, you can assign objects to other layers as well. To assign objects to other layer, select the objects to be assigned, see Figure 3.59 (hidden line entities are selected). Next, move the cursor over the **Layer** drop-down list in the **Layers** panel of the **Home** tab and then click on it. The **Layer** drop-down list appears, see 3.60. The **Layer** drop-down list displays all the layers created in the drawing. Next, click on the layer to assign the selected objects in the **Layer** drop-down list. The selected objects are assigned to the layer selected, see Figure 3.61. In this figure, the hidden lines of the drawing are assigned to the Hidden layer. Note that if the objects are still selected in the drawing area, press the ESC key to exit from the selected set. Similarly, you can assign different set of objects to different layers. In Figure 3.62, the hidden lines of the drawing are assigned to the Hidden layer and the centerlines are assigned to the Centerline layer.

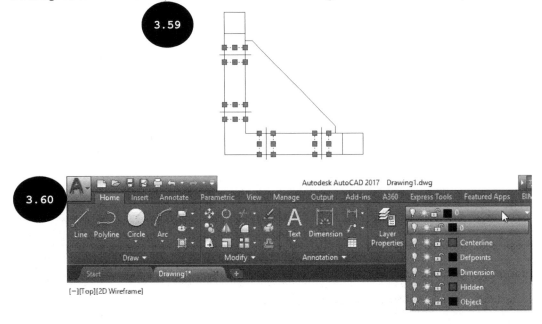

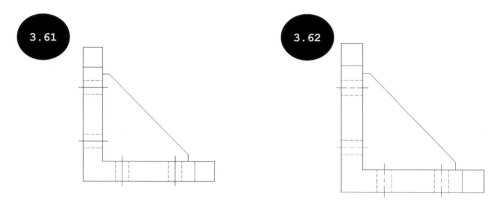

Tutorial 1

Create the drawing shown in Figure 3.63 (the dimensions shown in this figure are for your reference only. You will learn about applying dimensions in the later chapters). Also, create three layers: Object, Hidden, and Centerline with the layer properties given below.

Layer Name	Color	Linetype	Lineweight
Object	Black	Continuous	0.40 mm
Hidden	Blue	Hidden	0.30 mm
Centerline	Red	Center	0.25 mm

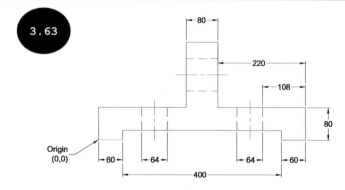

Section 1: Starting AutoCAD

1. Double-click on the AutoCAD icon on your desktop to start AutoCAD. The initial screen of AutoCAD with the **Start** tab appears, see Figure 3.64.

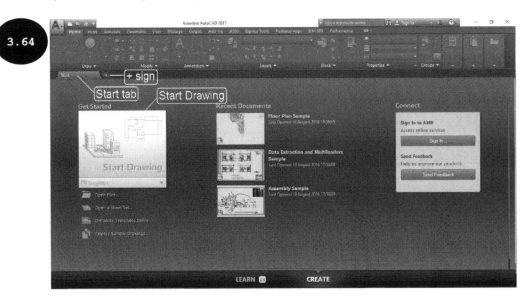

2. Click on the + sign next to the **Start** tab, see Figure 3.64. The new drawing file with the default drawing template gets invoked. Alternatively, click on **Start Drawing** in the **Get Started** section of the **Start** tab to start a new drawing file with the default drawing template. You can also start a new drawing file by using the **New** tool of the **Quick Access Toolbar**, which is at the top left corner of AutoCAD.

Section 2: Selecting Workspace for Creating Drawing

1. Click on the **Workspace Switching** ⚙ button in the **Status Bar**. A flyout appears, see Figure 3.65.

2. In this flyout, make sure that the **Drafting & Annotation** option is tick-marked in order to create drawings in the Drafting & Annotation workspace.

> **Note:** A tick-mark next to the workspace indicates that it is selected as the current workspace for creating drawings. By default, the Drafting & Annotation workspace is selected as the current workspace for creating drawings. You can click on any workspace to make it current for creating drawings.

Section 3: Creating Layer and Assigning Layer Properties

1. Click on the **Layer Properties** tool in the **Layers** panel, see Figure 3.66. The LAYER PROPERTIES MANAGER appears, see Figure 3.67. Alternatively, enter **LAYER** or **LA** in the Command Window and then press ENTER to invoke the **LAYER PROPERTIES MANAGER**.

Layer Properties

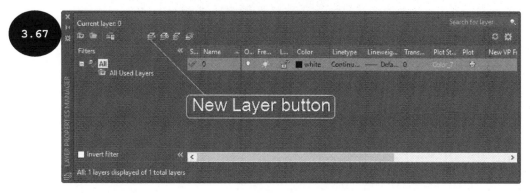

New Layer button

2. Click on the **New Layer** button in the **LAYER PROPERTIES MANAGER**. A new layer with default name "**Layer 1**" is created.

3. Enter **Object** as the name of the newly created layer in the **LAYER PROPERTIES MANAGER**.

After creating the **Object** layer, you need to define its properties such as color and lineweight. Note that the default color and linetype of the **Object** layer are the same as those mentioned in the tutorial description. Therefore, you need to only assign lineweight for the **Object** layer.

4. Click on the **Lineweight** field in the **Object** layer, see Figure 3.68. The **Lineweight** dialog box appears, see Figure 3.69.

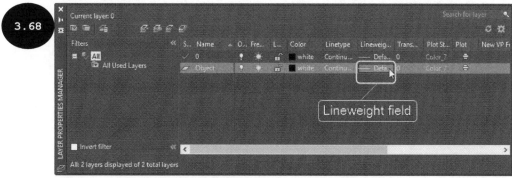

Lineweight field

5.   Click on the **0.40 mm** lineweight in the **Lineweight** dialog box, see Figure 3.69.

6.   Click on the **OK** button in the dialog box to accept the selection as well as to exit from the dialog box.

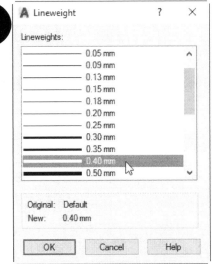

Now, you need to create the Hidden layer.

7.   Click on the **New Layer** button in the **LAYER PROPERTIES MANAGER**. A new layer with default name "**Layer 1**" is created.

8.   Enter **Hidden** as the name of the newly created layer in the **LAYER PROPERTIES MANAGER**.

After creating the Hidden layer, you need to assign color, linetype, and lineweight to it.

9.   Click on the **Color** field of the Hidden layer, see Figure 3.70. The **Select Color** dialog box appears, see Figure 3.71.

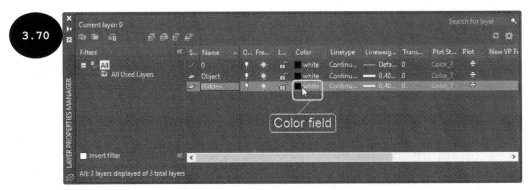

10. Click on the **Blue** color swatch in the **Select Color** dialog box, see Figure 3.71 and then click on the OK button in the **Select Color** dialog box. The blue color is assigned to the layer.

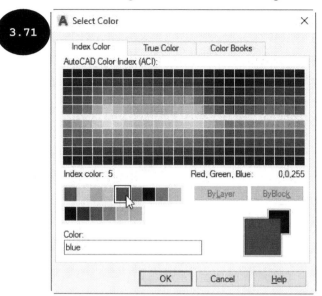

3.71

After assigning the color to the Hidden layer, you need to define Linetype and Lineweight.

11. Click on the **Linetype** field of the Hidden layer. The **Select Linetype** dialog box appears.

If the Hidden linetype, which has to be assigned to the Hidden layer, is not available in the **Select Linetype** dialog box then you need to first load it in the dialog box.

12. Click on the **Load** button in the **Select Linetype** dialog box. The **Load or Reload Linetypes** dialog box appears, see Figure 3.72.

13. Click on the **HIDDEN** linetype in the **Load or Reload Linetypes** dialog box, see Figure 3.72.

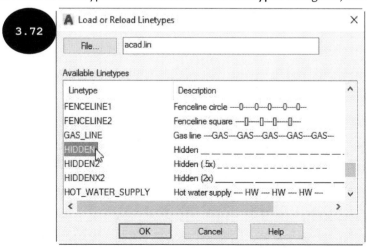

3.72

14. Click on the **OK** button in the **Load or Reload Linetypes** dialog box. The Hidden linetype is loaded in the **Select Linetype** dialog box.

15. Select the **HIDDEN** linetype in the **Select Linetype** dialog box.

16. Click on the **OK** button in the dialog box. The Hidden linetype is assigned to the layer.

Now, you need to assign Lineweight to the Hidden layer.

17. Click on the **Lineweight** field of the **Hidden** layer. The **Lineweight** dialog box appears, see Figure 3.73.

18. Click on the **0.30 mm** lineweight in the **Lineweight** dialog box, see Figure 3.73.

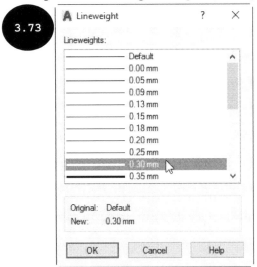

19. Click on the **OK** button in the dialog box to accept the selection as well as to exit from the dialog box.

20. Similarly, create the Centerline layer and then assign the layer properties: Color = Red, Linetype = Center, and Lineweight = 0.25 mm to it. Figure 3.74 shows the **LAYER PROPERTIES MANAGER** after creating the layers: Object, Hidden, and Centerline.

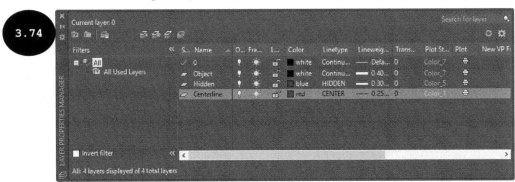

21. After creating the layers and assigning the layer properties, close the LAYER PROPERTIES MANAGER by clicking on the cross mark ☒ in the title bar of the LAYER PROPERTIES MANAGER.

Section 4: Defining Limits for Drawing

1. Follow the command sequence given below for defining limits for the drawing.

```
Command: LIMITS (ENTER)
Specify lower left corner or [ON/OFF]<0.0000,0.0000>: 0,0 (ENTER)
Specify upper right corner <12.0000,9.0000>: 820,540 (ENTER)
```

Section 5: Creating Object Entities in the Object Layer

Before creating the object entities of the drawing, you need to make the **Object** layer as the current layer so that the entities you create get assigned automatically to the **Object** layer.

1. Move the cursor over the **Layer** drop-down list in the **Layers** panel of the **Home** tab and then click the left mouse button to display the **Layer** drop-down list, see Figure 3.75.

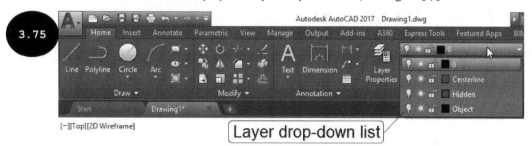

2. Click on the **Object** layer in the **Layer** drop-down list to make it current layer.

   After making the **Object** layer current, you can create the entities to be assigned to this layer.

3. Click on the **Line** tool in the **Draw** panel of the **Home** tab. You are prompted to specify the first point of the line.

```
Specify first point:
```

4. Click on the **Ortho Mode** button ⬚ in the **Status Bar** or press the F8 key to turn on the Ortho mode. Note that this is a toggle button.

5. Make sure that the Dynamic Input mode is activated. You can turn on the Dynamic Input mode by clicking on the **Dynamic Input** button ⬚ in the **Status Bar**.

6.   Follow the command sequence given below for creating the drawing entities.

```
Specify first point: 0,0 (ENTER)
Specify next point or [Undo]: Move the cursor horizontally toward the right and then
enter 60 in the Dynamic Input box  (ENTER)
Specify next point or [Undo]: Move the cursor vertically upward and then enter 24
(ENTER)
Specify next point or [Undo]: Move the cursor horizontally toward the right and then
enter 400  (ENTER)
Specify next point or [Undo]: Move the cursor vertically downward and then enter
24  (ENTER)
Specify next point or [Close Undo]: Move the cursor horizontally toward the right
and then enter 60  (ENTER)
Specify next point or [Undo]: Move the cursor vertically upward and then enter 80
(ENTER)
Specify next point or [Close Undo]: Move the cursor horizontally toward the left
and then enter 220  (ENTER)
Specify next point or [Undo]: Move the cursor vertically upward and then enter 160
(ENTER)
Specify next point or [Close Undo]: Move the cursor horizontally toward the left
and then enter 80  (ENTER)
Specify next point or [Close Undo]: Move the cursor vertically downward and
then enter 160  (ENTER)
Specify next point or [Close Undo]: Move the cursor horizontally toward the left
and then enter 220  (ENTER)
Specify next point or [Close Undo]: C or Close (ENTER)    (See Figure 3.76)
```

Tip: You may need to fit the drawing within the drawing area. To fit the drawing into the drawing area, follow the command sequence given below.

```
Command: Z or ZOOM  (ENTER)
Specify corner of window, enter a scale factor (nX or
nXP), or [All/Center/Dynamic/Extents/Previous/Scale/
Window/Object]<real time>: A or ALL  (ENTER)
```

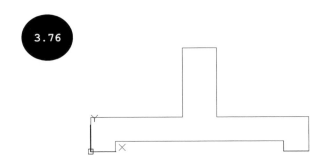

3.76

Note: To display entities in the drawing area with the lineweight/thickness assigned to the **Object** layer, click on the **Show/Hide Lineweight** button 🗏 in the **Status Bar** to activate it. This is a toggle button.

Section 6: Creating Hidden Entities in the Hidden Layer

1. Invoke the **Layer** drop-down list in the **Layers** panel of the **Home** tab and then click on the **Hidden** layer. The Hidden layer becomes current.

   After making the Hidden layer current, you can create the entities to be assigned to the Hidden layer.

2. Click on the **Line** tool in the **Draw** panel of the **Home** tab. You are prompted to specify the first point of the line.

   ```
   Specify first point:
   ```

3. Make sure that the Ortho mode is activated. You can activate/deactivate the Ortho mode by clicking on the **Ortho Mode** button 🔲 in the **Status Bar** or by pressing the F8 key.

4. Make sure that the Object Snap mode is activated. You can activate/deactivate the Object Snap mode by clicking on the **Object Snap** button 🔲 in the **Status Bar** or by pressing the F3 key.

5. Make sure that the Dynamic Input mode is activated. You can activate/deactivate the Dynamic Input mode by clicking on the **Dynamic Input** button 🔲 in the **Status Bar** or by pressing the F12 key.

6. Follow the command sequence given below for creating the hidden entities of the drawing.

   ```
   Specify first point: 108,24 (ENTER)
   Specify next point or [Undo]: Move the cursor vertically upward and then click to
   specify the end point of the line when the cursor snaps to the upper horizontal object entity (ENTER)
   (see Figure 3.77)
   ```

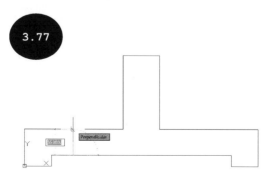

3.77

Note: If the cursor did not snap to the upper horizontal object entities as shown in Figure 3.77 then you need to change the Object Snap settings. To change the Object Snap settings, right-click on the **Object Snap** button ▓ in the **Status Bar**. A flyout appears. In this flyout, click on the **Object Snap Settings** option. The **Drafting Settings** dialog box appears. In this dialog box, make sure that the **Perpendicular** check box is selected.

Tool/Command: *Line or L* (**ENTER**)
Specify first point: **172,24** (**ENTER**)
Specify next point or [Undo]: *Move the cursor vertically upward and then click to specify the end point of the line when the cursor snaps to the upper object line* (**ENTER**) *(see Figure 3.78)*

3.78

Note: If the hidden line entities appear as continuous linetype in the drawing area then you may need to increase or decrease its linetype scale by using the **Properties** panel. To increase or decrease the linetype scale, enter **PR** in the Command Window and then press ENTER. The **Properties** panel is invoked and appears on the left of the drawing area. Next, select the hidden entity whose linetype scale has to be changed in the drawing area. The **Properties** panel displays the properties of the selected hidden entity. Next, enter **15** in the **Linetype scale** field of the **Properties** panel. If linetype scale 15 does not work, you can try any value as the linetype scale to match the display of the hidden line, as required.

Tool/Command: *Line or L* (**ENTER**)
Specify first point: **412,24** (**ENTER**)
Specify next point or [Undo]: *Move the cursor vertically upward and then click to specify the end point of the line when the cursor snaps to the upper object line* (**ENTER**) *(see Figure 3.79)*

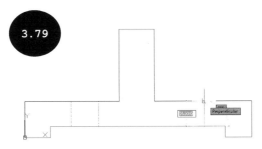

3.79

Tool/Command: *Line or L* (***ENTER***)
Specify first point: ***348,24*** (***ENTER***)
Specify next point or [Undo]: *Move the cursor vertically upward and then click to specify the end point of the line when the cursor snaps to the upper object line* (***ENTER***) *(see Figure 3.80)*

Command: *Line or L* (***ENTER***)
Specify first point: ***220,200*** (***ENTER***)
Specify next point or [Undo]: *Move the cursor horizontally toward the right and then click to specify the end point of the line when the cursor snaps to the next object line* (***ENTER***)

Command: *Line or L* (***ENTER***)
Specify first point: ***220,120*** (***ENTER***)
Specify next point or [Undo]: *Move the cursor horizontally toward the right and then click to specify the end point of the line when the cursor snaps to the next object line* (***ENTER***) *(see Figure 3.81)*

Figure 3.81 shows the drawing after creating the object and hidden line entities.

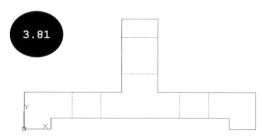

Section 7: Creating Centerlines in the Centerline Layer

1. Invoke the **Layer** drop-down list in the **Layers** panel and then click on the **Centerline** layer. The Centerline layer becomes the current layer.

   After making the Centerline layer as the current layer, you can create the centerline entities of the drawing.

2. Click on the **Line** tool in the **Draw** panel of the **Home** tab. You are prompted to specify the first point of the line.

   Specify first point:

3. Move the cursor toward the midpoint of the first drawn hidden line and then click to specify the first point of the line when the cursor snaps to its midpoint, see Figure 3.82.

4. Move the cursor horizontally toward the right and then click to specify the end point of the line when the cursor snaps to the midpoint of the next hidden line, see Figure 3.83. Next, press ENTER.

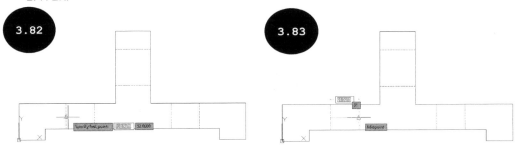

3.82

3.83

Note that the line entity drawn in the above three steps will be used as the reference line for creating the centerline.

5. Click on the **Line** tool in the **Draw** panel of the **Home** tab.

    ```
    Specify first point:
    ```

6. Move the cursor toward the midpoint of the previously drawn reference line and when the cursor snaps to its midpoint (see Figure 3.84), move the cursor vertically upward a distance outside the drawing. A reference/tracking line appears, see Figure 3.85.

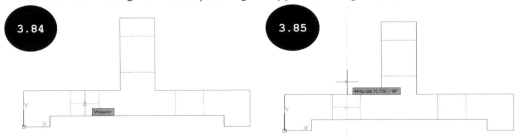

3.84

3.85

7. Click to specify the first point of the centerline somewhere near the upper horizontal line entity of the drawing, see Figure 3.85. Next, move the cursor vertically downward a distance and click to specify the end point of the centerline somewhere outside the lower horizontal line entity of the drawing, see Figure 3.86.

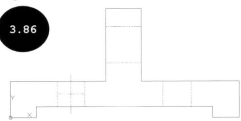

3.86

After creating the centerline, you need to delete the reference line drawn for creating the centerline.

8. Click on the reference line drawn in the drawing area. The reference line gets selected, see Figure 3.87. Next, press the DELETE key. The reference line gets deleted. Figure 3.88 shows the drawing after deleting the reference line.

9. Similarly, draw the other centerlines of the drawing, see Figure 3.89. Figure 3.89 shows the final drawing after creating all the drawing entities.

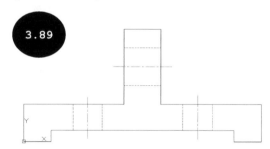

Section 8: Saving the Drawing

After creating the drawing, you need to save it.

1. Click on the **Save** tool in the **Quick Access Toolbar**. The **Save Drawing As** dialog box appears.

2. Browse to the *AutoCAD* folder and then create another folder with the name *Chapter 3* inside the *AutoCAD* folder. If the *AutoCAD* folder is not created in Chapter 2 then you need to first create this folder in a local drive of your system.

3. Enter **Tutorial 1** in the **File name** field of the dialog box and then click on the **Save** button. The drawing is saved with the name Tutorial 1 in the *Chapter 3* folder.

Tutorial 2

Create the drawing shown in Figure 3.90 (the dimensions shown in this figure are for your reference only. You will learn about applying dimensions in the later chapters). Also, create three layers: Object, Hidden, and Centerline with the layer properties given below.

Layer Name	Color	Linetype	Lineweight
Object	Black	Continuous	0.50 mm
Hidden	Blue	Hidden2	0.40 mm
Centerline	Red	Center2	0.30 mm

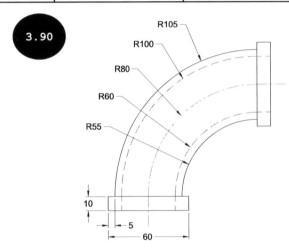

3.90

Section 1: Starting AutoCAD

1. Start AutoCAD by double-clicking on the AutoCAD icon on your desktop, if not started already.

2. Click on the **New** tool in the **Quick Access Toolbar**, which is at the top left corner of AutoCAD. The **Select template** dialog box appears. In this dialog box, select the *acad.dwt* template and then click on the **Open** button. A new drawing file with the *acad.dwt* template is invoked.

Section 2: Creating Layers and Assigning Properties to Layers

1. Click on the **Layer Properties** tool in the **Layers** panel of the **Home** tab, see Figure 3.91. The LAYER PROPERTIES MANAGER appears, see Figure 3.92.

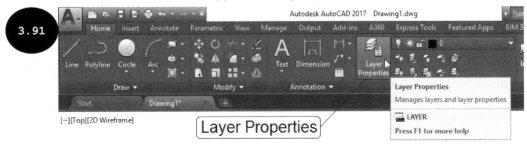

3.91

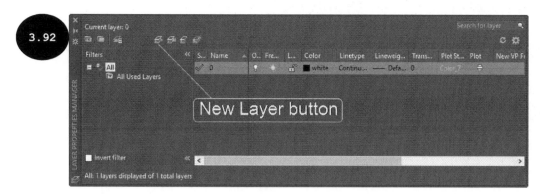

3.92

Tip: You can also enter **LAYER** or **LA** in the Command Window to invoke the **LAYER PROPERTIES MANAGER.**

2. Click on the **New Layer** button in the **LAYER PROPERTIES MANAGER.** A new layer with the default name "**Layer 1**" is created.

3. Enter **Object** as the name of the newly created layer in the **LAYER PROPERTIES MANAGER.**

   After creating the Object layer, you need to define its properties such as color and lineweight. Note that the default color and linetype assigned to the Object layer are the same as those mentioned in the tutorial description. Therefore, you need to assign only lineweight to the Object layer.

4. Click on the **Lineweight** field in the Object layer, see Figure 3.93. The **Lineweight** dialog box appears, see Figure 3.94.

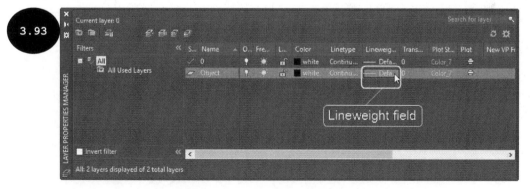

3.93

5. Click on the **0.50 mm** lineweight in the **Lineweight** dialog box, see Figure 3.94.

6. Click on the **OK** button in the dialog box to accept the selection as well as to exit from the dialog box.

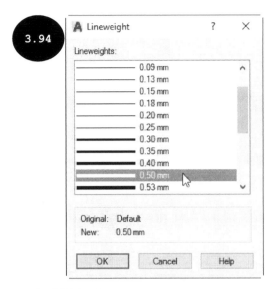

Now, you need to create the Hidden layer.

7. Click on the **New Layer** button in the **LAYER PROPERTIES MANAGER**. A new layer with the default name "**Layer 1**" is created.

8. Enter **Hidden** as the name of the newly created layer in the **LAYER PROPERTIES MANAGER**.

    After creating the Hidden layer, you need to assign color, linetype, and lineweight to it.

9. Click on the **Color** field of the Hidden layer, see Figure 3.95. The **Select Color** dialog box appears.

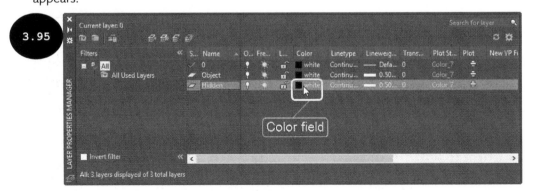

10. Click on the **Blue** color swatch in the **Select Color** dialog box and then click on the **OK** button. The selected color is assigned to the Hidden layer.

    After assigning the color to the Hidden layer, you need to define linetype and lineweight.

11. Click on the **Linetype** field of the Hidden layer. The **Select Linetype** dialog box appears.

If the Hidden2 linetype is not available in the **Select Linetype** dialog box then you need to first add/load the Hidden2 linetype in the dialog box.

12. Click on the **Load** button in the **Select Linetype** dialog box. The **Load or Reload Linetypes** dialog box appears, see Figure 3.96.

13. Click on the **HIDDEN2** linetype in the dialog box, see Figure 3.96. Next, click on the **OK** button. The Hidden2 linetype is loaded in the **Select Linetype** dialog box.

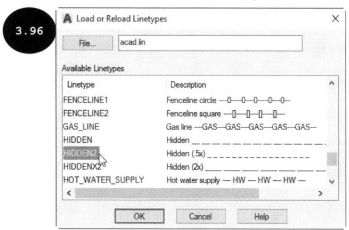

14. Click on the **HIDDEN2** linetype in the **Select Linetype** dialog box and then click on the **OK** button. The Hidden2 linetype is assigned to the Hidden layer.

15. Assign 0.40 mm lineweight to the Hidden layer.

16. Similarly, create the Centerline layer and then assign the layer properties: Color = Red, Linetype = Center2, and Lineweight = 0.3 mm, see Figure 3.97.

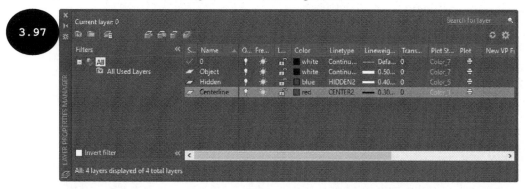

17. After creating layers and assigning properties to the layers, close the **LAYER PROPERTIES MANAGER** by clicking on the cross mark ☒ in the title bar of the **LAYER PROPERTIES MANAGER**.

Section 3: Creating Object Entities in the Object Layer

Before creating the object entities of the drawing, you need to make the Object layer as the current layer so that the entities you create get assigned automatically to the Object layer.

1.   Move the cursor over the **Layer** drop-down list in the **Layers** panel of the **Home** tab and then click the left mouse button on it to display the **Layer** drop-down list, see Figure 3.98.

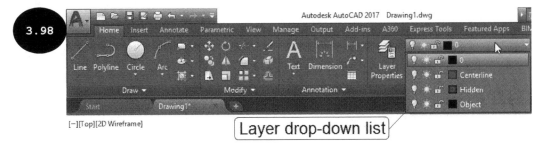

3.98

Layer drop-down list

2.   Click on the **Object** layer in the **Layer** drop-down list to make it the current layer.

After making the Object layer as the current layer, you can create the object entities of the drawing.

3.   Invoke the **Arc** flyout and then click on the **Center, Start, End** tool. You are prompted to specify the center point of the arc.

```
Specify start point of arc or [Center]:_c Specify center point of
arc:
```

4.   Click anywhere in the drawing area to specify the center point of the arc. You are prompted to specify the start point of the arc.

```
Specify start point of arc:
```

5.   Make sure that the Ortho mode and the Dynamic Input mode are activated.

6.   Move the cursor horizontally toward the left and then enter **105** in the Dynamic Input box as the radius of the arc. Next, press ENTER. You are prompted to specify the end point of the arc.

```
Specify end point of arc or [Angle chord Length]:
```

7.   Press and hold the CTRL key and then move the cursor in the clockwise direction. Next, click to specify the end point of the arc when the angle value appears 90-degree near the cursor, see Figure 3.99.

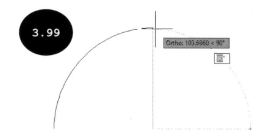

> **Note:** By default, an arc is created in the counter-clockwise direction. To change the direction of the creation of arc from counter-clockwise to clockwise direction, press and hold the CTRL key and then specify the end point of the arc.

8. Invoke the **Center, Start, End** tool again. You are prompted to specify the center point of the arc.

```
Specify start point of arc or [Center]:_c Specify center point of
arc:
```

9. Move the cursor over the arc drawn earlier in the drawing area, see Figure 3.100. The center point of the arc is highlighted in the drawing area, see Figure 3.100.

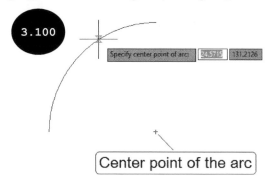

Center point of the arc

10. Move the cursor over the highlighted center point and then click the left mouse button when the cursor snaps to the center point of the arc. The center point of the arc is specified.

> **Note:** If the cursor did not snap to the existing entities, you need to specify the Object Snap settings by using the **Drafting Settings** dialog box. To specify the Object Snap settings, right-click on the **Object Snap** button ▓ in the Status Bar. A flyout appears. Next, click on the **Object Snap Settings** option in the flyout. The **Drafting Settings** dialog box appears. In this dialog box, click on the **Select All** button to select all the check boxes.

11.   Move the cursor horizontally toward the left and then enter **55** in the Dynamic Input box as the radius of the arc. You are prompted to specify the end point of the arc.

```
Specify end point of arc or [Angle chord Length]:
```

12.   Press and hold the CTRL key and then move the cursor in the clockwise direction. Next, click to specify the end point of the arc when the angle value appears 90-degree near the cursor, see Figure 3.101.

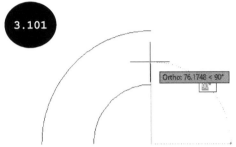

13.   Click on the **Line** tool in the **Draw** panel. You are prompted to specify the first point of the arc.

```
Specify first point:
```

14.   Move the cursor toward the start point of the first created arc and then click to specify the first point of the line when the cursor snaps to it, see Figure 3.102.

```
Specify next point or [Undo]:
```

15.   Move the cursor horizontally toward the left and then enter **5** in the Dynamic Input box as the length of the line, see Figure 3.103. Next, press ENTER.

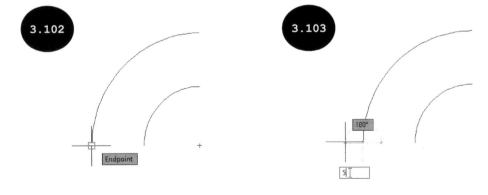

16. Follow the command sequence given below for creating the remaining line entities.

> Specify next point or [Undo]: *Move the cursor vertically downward and then enter* **10** *in the Dynamic Input box* (**ENTER**)
> Specify next point or [Undo]: *Move the cursor horizontally toward the right and then enter* **60** (**ENTER**)
> Specify next point or [Undo]: *Move the cursor vertically upward and then enter* **10** (**ENTER**)
> Specify next point or [Close Undo]: *Move the cursor horizontally toward the left and then click to specify the end point of the line when the cursor snaps to the start point of the first drawn arc* (**ENTER**) *(See Figure 3.104)*

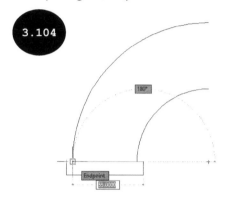

3.104

> Tool/Command: *Line or* **L** (**ENTER**)
> Specify first point: *Move the cursor toward the end point of the first drawn arc and then click to specify the first point of the line when the cursor snaps to it* *(See Figure 3.105)*
> Specify next point or [Undo]: *Move the cursor vertically upward and then enter* **5** *in the Dynamic Input box* (**ENTER**)
> Specify next point or [Undo]: *Move the cursor horizontally toward the right and then enter* **10** (**ENTER**)
> Specify next point or [Close Undo]: *Move the cursor vertically downward and then enter* **60** (**ENTER**)
> Specify next point or [Close Undo]: *Move the cursor horizontally toward the left and then enter* **10** (**ENTER**)
> Specify next point or [Close Undo]: *C or* **Close** (**ENTER**) *(See Figure 3.106)*

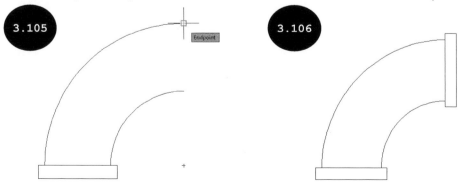

3.105

3.106

Tip: You may need to fit the drawing within the drawing area. To fit the drawing, follow the command sequence given below.

```
Command: Z or Zoom  (ENTER)
Specify corner of window, enter a scale factor (nX or
nXP), or [All/Center/Dynamic/Extents/Previous/Scale/
Window/Object]<real time>: A or ALL  (ENTER)
```

Section 4: Creating Hidden Entities in the Hidden Layer

1. Invoke the **Layer** drop-down list in the **Layers** panel of the **Home** tab and then click on the **Hidden** layer. The Hidden layer becomes the current layer of the drawing.

2. Click on the **Line** tool in the **Draw** panel. You are prompted to specify the first point of the line.

    ```
    Specify first point:
    ```

3. Make sure that the Ortho mode, Dynamic Input mode, and Object Snap mode are activated.

4. Move the cursor toward the lower left vertex of the drawing and then click to specify the first point of the line when the cursor snaps to it, see Figure 3.107.

    ```
    Specify next point or [Undo]:
    ```

5. Move the cursor horizontally toward the right and then enter **10** in the Dynamic Input box as the length of the line. Next, press ENTER.

6. Move the cursor vertically upward and then click to specify the end point of the line when the cursor snaps to the next object line entity, see Figure 3.108. Next, press ENTER.

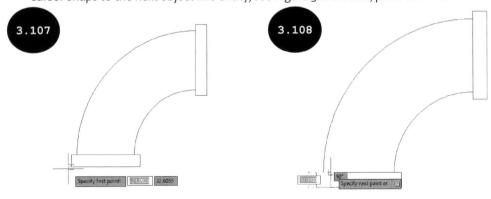

3.107

3.108

Note: If hidden line entity appears as continuous linetype in the drawing area then you may need to increase or decrease its linetype scale by using the **Properties** panel. To increase or decrease the linetype scale, enter **PR** in the Command Window and then press ENTER. The **Properties** panel is invoked and appears on the left of the drawing area. Next, select the hidden entity in the drawing area whose linetype scale has to be changed. The **Properties** panel displays the properties of the selected hidden entity. Next, enter **10** in the **Linetype scale** field of the **Properties** panel. If linetype 10 does not work, you can try any value as the scale value of the linetype to match the display of the hidden line, as required.

7. Click on the first drawn hidden line in the drawing area. The first drawn hidden line is selected, see Figure 3.109. Next, press the DELETE key. The selected line gets deleted. This line entity was drawn as a reference line for measuring 10 unit from the lower left vertex of the drawing to create the hidden line of the drawing.

8. Similarly, draw other hidden line entities by using the **Line** tool. Figure 3.110 shows the drawing after creating the hidden line entities of the drawing.

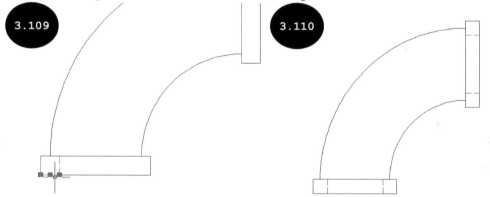

Now, you need to draw the hidden arcs of the drawing by using the **Center, Start, End** arc tool.

9. Invoke the **Arc** flyout in the **Draw** panel of the **Home** tab and then click on the **Center, Start, End** tool. You are prompted to specify the center point of the arc.

```
Specify start point of arc or [Center]: _c Specify center point of
arc:
```

10. Move the cursor over the first drawn arc in the drawing area. The center point of the first drawn arc gets highlighted in the drawing area, see Figure 3.111.

11. Move the cursor over the highlighted center point and then click the left mouse button when the cursor snaps to the highlighted center point of the arc. The center point of the hidden arc is specified.

```
Specify start point of arc:
```

12. Move the cursor over the end point of the first drawn hidden line entity and then click to specify the start point of the arc when the cursor snaps to the end point of the hidden line, see Figure 3.112.

```
Specify end point of arc or [Angle chord Length]:
```

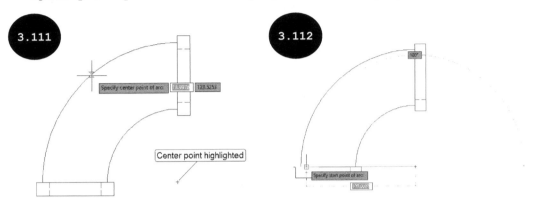

13. Press and hold the CTRL key and then move the cursor in the clockwise direction. Next, click to specify the end point of the arc when the cursor snaps to the end point of next hidden line entity, see Figure 3.113.

14. Similarly, draw the another hidden arc entity of the drawing by using the **Center, Start, End** arc tool. Figure 3.114 shows the drawing after drawing the hidden arc entities.

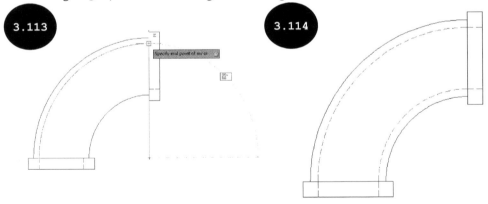

Section 5: Creating Centerlines in the Centerline Layer

1. Invoke the **Layer** drop-down list in the **Layers** panel of the **Home** tab and then click on the **Centerline** layer. The Centerline layer becomes the current layer of the drawing.

2. Invoke the **Arc** flyout in the **Draw** panel of the **Home** tab and then click on the **Center, Start, End** tool to invoke it.

```
Specify start point of arc or [Center]:_c Specify center point of
arc:
```

3. Move the cursor over the first drawn arc in the drawing area, see Figure 3.115. The center point of the arc gets highlighted in the drawing area, see Figure 3.115.

4. Move the cursor over the highlighted center point and then click to specify the center point of the arc when the cursor snaps to the highlighted center point.

```
Specify start point of arc:
```

5. Move the cursor horizontally toward the left and then enter **80** in the Dynamic Input box. Next, press ENTER.

```
Specify end point of arc or [Angle chord Length]:
```

6. Press and hold the CTRL key and then move the cursor in the clockwise direction. Next, click to specify the end point of the arc when the cursor snaps to the next intersection, see Figure 3.116.

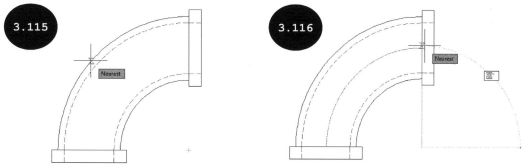

7. Click on the **Line** tool in the **Draw** panel of the **Home** tab. The **Line** tool is invoked.

```
Specify first point:
```

8. Move the cursor toward the start point of the previously drawn arc and then click to specify the start point of the line when the cursor snaps to it, see Figure 3.117.

9. Move the cursor vertically downward a small distance and then click to specify the end point of the line below the horizontal line of the drawing, see Figure 3.118.

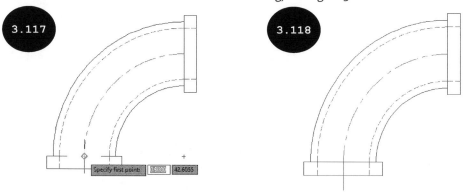

10. Similarly, draw a line on the other side of the arc. Figure 3.119 shows the final drawing.

> **Note:** To display entities in the drawing area with the lineweight/thickness assigned to the layers, click to activate the **Show/Hide Lineweight** button in the **Status Bar**. Figure 3.120 shows the drawing with the lineweight/thickness is turned on.

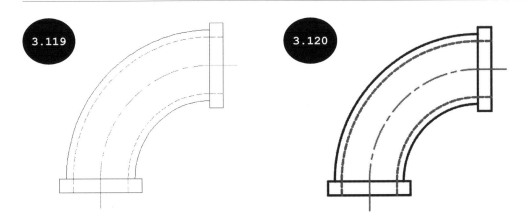

Section 6: Saving the Drawing

After creating the drawing, you need to save it.

1. Click on the **Save** tool in the **Quick Access Toolbar**. The **Save Drawing As** dialog box appears.

2. Browse to the *Chapter 3* folder, inside the *AutoCAD* folder. If these folders have not been created in Tutorial 1 of this chapter then you need to first create these folders in a local drive of your system.

3. Enter **Tutorial 2** in the **File name** field of the dialog box and then click on the **Save** button. The drawing is saved with the name Tutorial 2 in the *Chapter 3* folder.

Hands-on Test Drive 1

Create the drawing shown in Figure 3.121. Also, create three layers: Object, Hidden, and Centerline with the layer properties given below.

Layer Name	Color	Linetype	Lineweight
Object	Blue	Continuous	0.50 mm
Hidden	Green	Hidden	0.35 mm
Centerline	Red	Center	0.30 mm

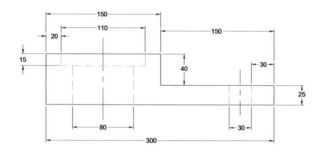

Summary

In this chapter, you have learned about Ortho mode, Polar Tracking, Object Snap, and Object Snap Tracking. You have also learned about how to specify grids and snaps settings. In addition, in this chapter, you have learned how to work with layers and assigning objects to layers.

Questions

- The _____ mode is used to create horizontal or vertical straight lines.

- The _____ mode is used to create line entities at an increment of set angle.

- When the _____ mode is turn on, the cursor snaps to the existing geometries of drawing such as midpoint, center, node, insertion, perpendicular, and tangent.

- The _____ is used to create new layers, specifying layer properties, and so on.

- The _____ tool is used to invoke the **LAYER PROPERTIES MANAGER.**

- In AutoCAD, you can not freeze the _____ layer.

- You can set the transparency for the objects of a layer by using the _____ field in the **LAYER PROPERTIES MANAGER.**

- By default, all objects drawn in the drawing get assigned automatically to the _____ layer.

Creating Drawings - II

In this chapter, you will learn the following:

- Drawing rectangle
- Drawing polygon
- Drawing polyline
- Drawing ellipse
- Drawing elliptical arc
- Drawing spline
- Drawing donuts
- Drawing construction line and ray line
- Drawing points and defining point style/size

In this chapter, you will learn about the advanced tools of AutoCAD that are used to create rectangles, polygons, ellipses, splines, donuts, and points.

Drawing Rectangle

A rectangle comprises of four line segments treated as a single object. In AutoCAD, you can draw a rectangle by different methods using the **Rectangle** tool of the **Draw** panel in the **Home** tab, see Figure 4.1. Different methods of creating a rectangle by using the **Rectangle** tool are as follows:

1.   Drawing rectangle by specifying diagonally opposite corners
2.   Drawing rectangle by specifying its area and one side
3.   Drawing rectangle by specifying its dimensions
4.   Drawing rectangle at an angle by specifying rotation angle
5.   Drawing rectangle with chamfer
6.   Drawing rectangle with fillet
7.   Drawing rectangle with elevation
8.   Drawing rectangle with thickness
9.   Drawing rectangle with width

Drawing Rectangle by Specifying Diagonally Opposite Corners

In AutoCAD, you can draw a rectangle by specifying its two diagonally opposite corners. The first specified corner defines the position of the first corner of the rectangle and the second specified corner defines the length and width of the rectangle, see Figure 4.2.

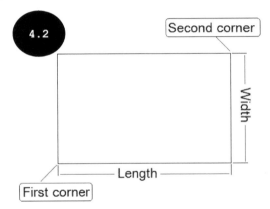

The procedure to draw a rectangle by specifying the diagonally opposite corner is as follows:

Procedure for Drawing Rectangle by Specifying Diagonally Opposite Corners

1.   Click on the **Rectangle** tool in the **Draw** panel. The **Rectangle** tool is invoked and you are prompted to specify the first corner of the rectangle. Alternatively, enter **REC** in the Command Window and then press ENTER to invoke the **Rectangle** tool.

     ```
     Specify first corner point or [Chamfer Elevation Fillet Thickness
     Width]:
     ```

2.   Click the left mouse button in the drawing area to specify the first corner of the rectangle. You are prompted to specify the second corner of the rectangle. Alternatively, you can specify coordinate (X , Y) in the Command Window to specify the first corner of the rectangle.

     ```
     Specify other corner point or [Area Dimensions Rotation]:
     ```

3.   Move the cursor diagonally to specify the second corner of the rectangle in the drawing area. The preview of the rectangle appears whose first corner is fixed at the specified location and the other corner is attached with the cursor, see Figure 4.3.

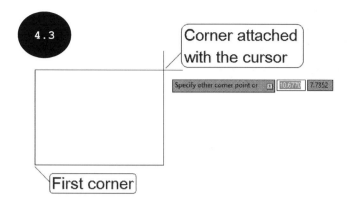

4. Enter the length and width values of the rectangle in the Dynamic Input boxes that appear near the cursor for defining the second corner of the rectangle. You can press the TAB key to switch from the one Dynamic Input box to another for specifying the length and width values of the rectangle. After entering the length and width values, press ENTER. The rectangle is drawn.

Note: If the Dynamic Input boxes do not appear near your cursor for specifying the length and width values of the rectangle, you need to turn on the Dynamic Input mode by clicking on the **Dynamic Input** button in the **Status Bar**.

Drawing Rectangle by Specifying its Area and One Side

You can draw a rectangle by specifying its area and one side (length or width) by using the **Rectangle** tool. The procedure to draw rectangle by specifying its area and one side is as follows:

Note: On specifying the area and one side (length/width) of the rectangle, AutoCAD automatically calculates the other side of the rectangle by using the formula: *Area of rectangle = Length X Width*. For example, if you specify the Area of rectangle = 500 units and length = 50 units then the *Width = 500/50*.

Procedure for Drawing Rectangle by Specifying Area and One Side

1. Click on the **Rectangle** tool in the **Draw** panel. The **Rectangle** tool is invoked and you are prompted to specify the first corner of the rectangle. Alternatively, enter **REC** in the Command Window and then press ENTER to invoke the **Rectangle** tool.

   ```
   Specify first corner point or [Chamfer Elevation Fillet Thickness
   Width]:
   ```

2. Click the left mouse button in the drawing area or enter coordinate (X , Y) to specify the first corner of the rectangle. You are prompted to specify the second corner of the rectangle.

   ```
   Specify other corner point or [Area Dimensions Rotation]:
   ```

3. Enter **A** either in the Dynamic Input box or in the Command Window and then press ENTER. You are prompted to specify the area of the rectangle. Alternatively, click on the **Area** option in the command prompt to specify the area of the rectangle.

    ```
    Enter area of rectangle in current units <10.0000>:
    ```

4. Enter the area of the rectangle and then press ENTER. You are prompted to specify either the length or width of the rectangle.

    ```
    Calculate rectangle dimensions based on [Length Width] <Length>:
    ```

5. Enter **L** and then press ENTER for defining the length of the rectangle. You are prompted to specify the length of the rectangle. Note that for defining the width of the rectangle, you need to enter **W** in the Command Window.

    ```
    Enter rectangle length <5.0000>:
    ```

6. Enter the length value of the rectangle and then press ENTER. The rectangle of the defined area and length is drawn in the drawing area, see Figure 4.4.

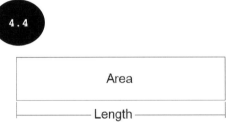

Note: The value entered inside the < > symbol in the command prompt is the last defined or default value of the command. For example, in the prompt "Calculate rectangle dimensions based on [Length Width] <Length>:", the length entered inside the <> is the default selected option of the command. If you want to go with the default selected option, you can directly press ENTER; else, specify the new option in the Command Window and then press ENTER.

Drawing Rectangle by Specifying Dimensions

You can draw a rectangle by specifying dimensions: length and width by using the **Rectangle** tool. The procedure to draw a rectangle by specifying dimensions is as follows:

Procedure for Drawing Rectangle by Specifying Dimensions

1. Click on the **Rectangle** tool or enter **REC** in the Command Window. You are prompted to specify the first corner of the rectangle.

    ```
    Specify first corner point or [Chamfer Elevation Fillet Thickness Width]:
    ```

2. Click the left mouse button in the drawing area or specify coordinates (X , Y) to specify the first corner of the rectangle. You are prompted to specify the second corner of the rectangle.

```
Specify other corner point or [Area Dimensions Rotation]:
```

3. Enter D and then press ENTER. You are prompted to specify the length of rectangle. Alternatively, click on the **Dimensions** option in the command prompt.

```
Specify length for rectangle <100.000>:
```

4. Enter the length value of the rectangle and then press ENTER. You are prompted to specify the width of the rectangle.

```
Specify width for rectangle <2.0000>:
```

5. Enter the width value of the rectangle and then press ENTER. You are prompted to specify the other corner of rectangle.

```
Specify other corner point or [Area Dimensions Rotation]:
```

6. Click to specify the other corner point of the rectangle. The rectangle of the defined length and width is drawn in the drawing area, see Figure 4.5.

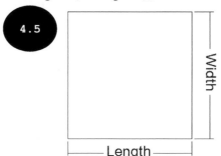

Drawing Rectangle at an Angle

You can draw a rectangle at an angle by using the **Rectangle** tool. The procedure to draw rectangle at an angle is as follows:

Procedure for Drawing Rectangle at an Angle

1. Click on the **Rectangle** tool. You are prompted to specify the first corner of the rectangle.

```
Specify first corner point or [Chamfer Elevation Fillet Thickness
Width]:
```

2. Click the left mouse button in the drawing area or enter coordinates (X , Y) to specify the first corner of the rectangle. You are prompted to specify the second corner of the rectangle.

```
Specify other corner point or [Area Dimensions Rotation]:
```

3.   Enter **R** and then press ENTER. You are prompted to specify the rotation angle of the rectangle. You can also click on the **Rotation** option in the command prompt to specify the rotation angle of the rectangle.

```
Specify rotation angle or [Pick points] <0.0000>:
```

4.   Enter the rotational angle and then press ENTER. You are prompted to specify the other corner of rectangle.

```
Specify other corner point or [Area Dimensions Rotation]:
```

5.   Move the cursor in the drawing area. The preview of the rectangle at the specified angle appears in the drawing area. Next, click the left mouse button in the drawing area to define the second corner of the rectangle. You can also enter coordinates (X , Y) to define the second corner of the rectangle. The rectangle at the specified rotational angle is drawn, see Figure 4.6.

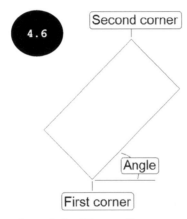

4.6

Drawing Rectangle with Chamfer
In AutoCAD, you can draw a rectangle with chamfer on its corners by using the **Rectangle** tool, see Figure 4.7. The procedure to draw a rectangle with chamfer is as follows:

4.7

Procedure for Drawing Rectangle with Chamfer

1.   Click on the **Rectangle** tool. You are prompted to specify the first corner of the rectangle.

```
Specify first corner point or [Chamfer Elevation Fillet Thickness
Width]:
```

2.   Click on the **Chamfer** option in the command prompt or enter C and then press ENTER. You are prompted to specify the first chamfer distance.

```
Specify first chamfer distance for rectangle <0.0000>:
```

3.   Enter the first chamfer distance and then press ENTER. You are prompted to specify the second chamfer distance.

```
Specify first chamfer distance for rectangle <0.0000>:
```

4.   Enter the second chamfer distance and then press ENTER. You are prompted to specify the first corner of the rectangle.

```
Specify first corner point or [Chamfer Elevation Fillet Thickness
Width]:
```

5.   Click the left mouse button in the drawing area or enter coordinates (X , Y) to specify the first corner of the rectangle. You are prompted to specify the second corner of the rectangle.

```
Specify other corner point or [Area Dimensions Rotation]:
```

6.   Click the left mouse button in the drawing area or enter coordinates (X , Y) to specify the second corner of the rectangle. The rectangle with chamfer is drawn in the drawing area.

Drawing Rectangle with Fillets

In AutoCAD, you can draw a rectangle with fillets on its corners by using the **Rectangle** tool, see Figure 4.8. The procedure to draw the rectangle with fillets is as follows:

4.8

Procedure for Drawing Rectangle with Fillets

1. Click on the **Rectangle** tool. You are prompted to specify the first corner of the rectangle.

    ```
    Specify first corner point or [Chamfer Elevation Fillet Thickness
    Width]:
    ```

2. Click on the **Fillet** option in the command prompt or enter **F** and then press ENTER. You are prompted to specify the fillet radius of the rectangle.

    ```
    Specify fillet radius for rectangle <0.0000>:
    ```

3. Enter the fillet radius of the rectangle and then press ENTER. You are prompted to specify the first corner of the rectangle.

    ```
    Specify first corner point or [Chamfer Elevation Fillet Thickness
    Width]:
    ```

4. Click the left mouse button in the drawing area or enter coordinates (X , Y) to specify the first corner of the rectangle. You are prompted to specify the second corner of the rectangle.

    ```
    Specify other corner point or [Area Dimensions Rotation]:
    ```

5. Click the left mouse button in the drawing area or enter coordinates (X , Y) to specify the second corner of the rectangle. The rectangle with fillets on its corners is drawn in the drawing area.

Drawing Rectangle with Elevation

You can draw a rectangle at a specified elevation along the Z direction from the origin (0,0,0), see Figure 4.9 by using the **Rectangle** tool. The procedure to draw rectangle with elevation is as follows:

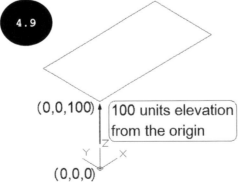

Procedure for Drawing Rectangle with Elevation

1. Click on the **Rectangle** tool. You are prompted to specify the first corner of the rectangle.

    ```
    Specify first corner point or [Chamfer Elevation Fillet Thickness
    Width]:
    ```

2. Click on the **Elevation** option in the command prompt or enter **E** and then press ENTER. You are prompted to specify the elevation of the rectangle.

```
Specify the elevation for rectangles <0.0000>:
```

3. Enter the elevation value along the Z axis with respect to the origin (0,0,0) and then press ENTER. You are prompted to specify the first corner of the rectangle.

```
Specify first corner point or [Chamfer Elevation Fillet Thickness
Width]:
```

4. Specify the first corner of the rectangle. You are prompted to specify the second corner of the rectangle.

```
Specify other corner point or [Area Dimensions Rotation]:
```

5. Specify the second corner of the rectangle. The rectangle with the specified elevation is drawn in the drawing area, see Figure 4.9.

Note: You can change the orientation of the rectangle to isometric in order to view the elevation of the rectangle drawn by clicking on the **Home** button ⚬ in the **ViewCube**, which is available at the upper right corner of the screen.

Drawing Rectangle with Thickness

You can draw a rectangle with a specified thickness along the z axis by using the **Rectangle** tool, see Figure 4.10. The procedure to draw a rectangle with a specified thickness is as follows:

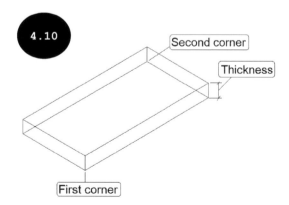

4.10

Second corner

Thickness

First corner

Procedure for Drawing Rectangle with Thickness

1. Click on the **Rectangle** tool. You are prompted to specify the first corner of the rectangle.

```
Specify first corner point or [Chamfer Elevation Fillet Thickness
Width]:
```

2.   Click on the **Thickness** option in the command prompt or enter T and then press ENTER. You
     are prompted to specify the thickness along the Z axis for the rectangle.

```
Specify thickness for rectangles <0.0000>:
```

3.   Enter thickness value along the Z axis with respect to the origin (0,0,0) and then press ENTER.
     You are prompted to specify the first corner of the rectangle.

```
Specify first corner point or [Chamfer Elevation Fillet Thickness
Width]:
```

4.   Specify the first corner of the rectangle. You are prompted to specify the second corner of the
     rectangle.

```
Specify other corner point or [Area Dimensions Rotation]:
```

5.   Specify the second corner of the rectangle. The rectangle with the specified thickness is drawn
     in the drawing area.

6.   Click on the **Home** button ⚹ in the **ViewCube**, which is available at the upper right corner of
     the screen. The orientation of the drawing is changed to isometric, see Figure 4.10.

Drawing Rectangle with Width

You can draw a rectangle with the specified width by using the **Rectangle** tool, see Figure 4.11. The
procedure to draw rectangle with width is as follows:

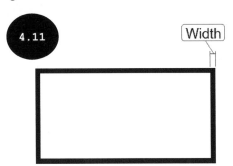

Procedure for Drawing Rectangle with Width

1.   Click on the **Rectangle** tool. You are prompted to specify the first corner of the rectangle.

```
Specify first corner point or [Chamfer Elevation Fillet Thickness
Width]:
```

2.   Click on the **Width** option in the command prompt or enter **W** and then press ENTER. You are
     prompted to specify the width of the rectangle.

```
Specify line width for rectangle <0.0000>:
```

3. Enter the width value of the rectangle and then press ENTER. You are prompted to specify the first corner of the rectangle.

```
Specify first corner point or [Chamfer Elevation Fillet Thickness
Width]:
```

4. Specify the first corner of the rectangle. You are prompted to specify the second corner of the rectangle.

```
Specify other corner point or [Area Dimensions Rotation]:
```

5. Specify the second corner of the rectangle. The rectangle with the specified width is drawn in the drawing area, see Figure 4.11.

Drawing Polygon

AutoCAD allows you to draw polygons of equal sides in the range from 3 to 1024. A polygon is a closed geometry having equal sides as well as equal angle between sides. Figure 4.12 shows a polygon having five sides. You can draw a polygon by using the **Polygon** tool of the **Draw** panel, see Figure 4.13, or by entering **POL** in the Command Window. POL is the shortcut of the POLYGON command.

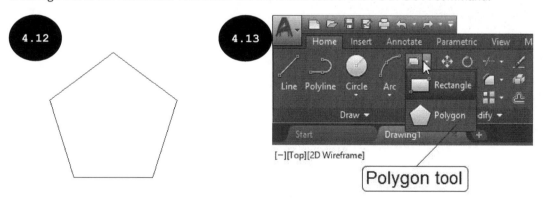

In AutoCAD, you can draw two types of polygon: Inscribed polygon and Circumscribed polygon by using the **Polygon** tool, see Figures 4.14 and 4.15. Both the types of polygon are discussed next.

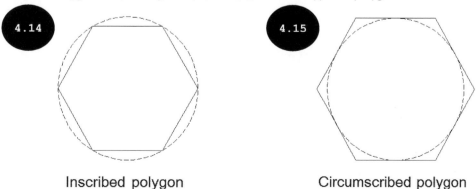

Inscribed polygon   Circumscribed polygon

Inscribed Polygon

An Inscribed polygon is drawn inside an imaginary circle such that its vertices touch the imaginary circle, see Figure 4.14.

Circumscribed Polygon

A Circumscribed polygon is drawn outside an imaginary circle such that the midpoints of the polygon sides touch the imaginary circle, see Figure 4.15.

The procedure to draw the Inscribed and Circumscribed polygons is as follows:

Procedure for Drawing Polygon (Inscribed and Circumscribed)

1. Click on the down arrow in the **Rectangle** tool of the **Draw** panel. A flyout appears, refer to Figure 4.13. In this flyout, click on the **Polygon** tool. The **Polygon** tool is invoked and you are prompted to specify the number of polygon sides. Alternatively, enter **POL** in the Command Window and then press ENTER to invoke the **Polygon** tool.

    ```
    Enter number of sides <4>:
    ```

2. Enter the number of polygon sides and then press ENTER. You are prompted to specify the center of polygon.

    ```
    Specify center of polygon or [Edge]:
    ```

3. Click the left mouse button in the drawing area or enter coordinates (X , Y) to specify the center of polygon. You are prompted to specify the type of polygon (Inscribed in circle or Circumscribed about circle).

    ```
    Enter an option [Inscribed in circle Circumscribed about circle]
    <I>:
    ```

4. Enter **I** or **C** in the Command Window for drawing Inscribed or circumscribed polygon, respectively. Next, press ENTER. You are prompted to specify the radius of an imaginary circle.

    ```
    Specify radius of circle:
    ```

5. Enter the radius value of an imaginary circle and then press ENTER. The polygon is drawn depending upon the option: **Inscribed in circle** or **Circumscribed about circle** selected.

Drawing Polyline

A Polyline consists of one or more than one line or arc segment and acts as a single object. In AutoCAD, drawing a polyline is similar to drawing a line with the only difference that the polyline consists of a series of line segments, arc segments, or the combination of line and arc segments and acts as a single object, see Figure 4.16. You can draw a polyline by using the **Polyline** tool of the **Draw** panel or by entering **PL** in the Command Window. PL is the shortcut of the POLYLINE command. The procedure to draw a polyline is as follows:

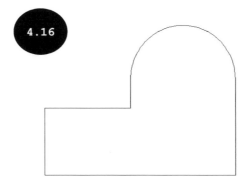

4.16

Procedure for Drawing Polyline with Line Segments

1. Click on the **Polyline** tool in the **Draw** panel of the **Home** tab or enter **PL** in the Command Window and then press ENTER. You are prompted to specify the start point of the polyline.

```
Specify start point:
```

2. Click the left mouse button in the drawing area or specify coordinates (X , Y) to specify the start point of the polyline. You are prompted to specify the next point of the polyline.

```
Specify next point or [Arc Halfwidth Length Undo Width]:
```

3. Specify the next point of the polyline. A line segment is drawn and you are prompted to specify the next point of the polyline.

```
Specify next point or [Arc Halfwidth Length Undo Width]:
```

4. Specify the next point of the polyline. The second line segment of polyline is drawn in the drawing area, see Figure 4.17. You are prompted to specify the next point of the polyline.

```
Specify next point or [Arc Halfwidth Length Undo Width]:
```

4.17

5. Similarly, you can draw a series of continuous line segments of a polyline, one after another by specifying points in the drawing area.

Procedure for Drawing Polyline with Line and Arc Segments

1. Click on the **Polyline** tool in the **Draw** panel of the **Home** tab or enter **PL** in the Command Window and then press ENTER. You are prompted to specify the start point of the polyline.

    ```
    Specify start point:
    ```

2. Specify the start point of the polyline. You are prompted to specify the next point of the polyline.

    ```
    Specify next point or [Arc Halfwidth Length Undo Width]:
    ```

3. Specify the next point of the polyline. A line segment is drawn and you are prompted to specify the next point of the polyline.

    ```
    Specify next point or [Arc Halfwidth Length Undo Width]:
    ```

    In addition to drawing line segments, you can draw arc segments in a polyline.

4. Click on the **Arc** option in the command prompt. The Arc mode for drawing arc segment is invoked and you are prompted to specify the endpoint of the arc. Alternatively, enter **A** in the Command Window and then press ENTER to invoke the Arc mode.

    ```
    Specify endpoint of arc or [Angle CEnter CLose Direction Halfwidth
    Line Radius Second pt Undo Width]:
    ```

5. Click to specify the end point of the arc. An arc segment is drawn, see Figure 4.18. Note that the Arc mode is still invoked and you are prompted to specify the endpoint of another arc .

    ```
    Specify endpoint of arc or [Angle CEnter CLose Direction Halfwidth
    Line Radius Second pt Undo Width]:
    ```

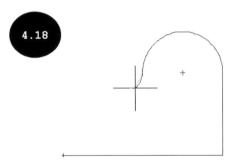
4.18

6. To draw the line segment again, enter **L** in the Command Window and then press ENTER. Alternatively, click on the **Line** option in the command prompt. You are prompted to specify the end point of the line segment.

    ```
    Specify next point or [Arc Halfwidth Length Undo Width]:
    ```

7. Similarly, you can draw a polyline with a series of line and arc segments. Once you have drawn a polyline, press the ENTER key to exit from creating polyline.

Tip: When the Arc mode is invoked while drawing a polyline and you are prompted to specify the end point of the arc segment, you are also provided with additional options such as angle, center, direction, and radius in the command prompt for drawing arc. These options are discussed next.

```
Specify endpoint of arc or [Angle CEnter CLose Direction
Halfwidth Line Radius Second pt Undo Width]:
```

Angle: By clicking on the **Angle** option in the command prompt, you can specify the angle of the arc segment from the start point, see Figure 4.19. The positive angle value creates counter-clockwise arc segment and the negative angle value creates clockwise arc segment.

Center: By clicking on the **Center** option in the command prompt, you can specify the center point of the arc segment to be drawn, see Figure 4.20.

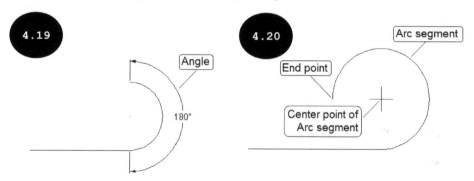

Direction: By clicking on the **Direction** option in the command prompt, you can specify the direction of tangent for the arc segment, see Figure 4.21.

Radius: By clicking on the **Radius** option in the command prompt, you can specify the radius of the arc segment, see Figure 4.22.

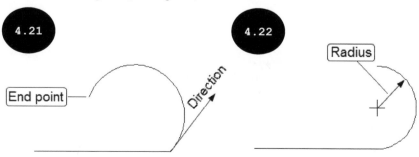

Procedure for Drawing Polyline with Width

1.   Click on the **Polyline** tool in the **Draw** panel of the **Home** tab or enter **PL** in the Command Window and then press ENTER. You are prompted to specify the start point of the polyline.

```
Specify start point:
```

2.   Specify the start point of the polyline. You are prompted to specify the next point of the polyline.

```
Specify next point or [Arc Halfwidth Length Undo Width]:
```

3.   Click on the **Width** option in the command prompt. You are prompted to specify the starting width of the polyline. Alternatively, enter **W** and then press ENTER.

```
Specify starting width <0.0000>:
```

4.   Enter the starting width value (see Figure 4.23) and then press ENTER. You are prompted to specify the ending width of the polyline.

```
Specify ending width <0.0000>:
```

5.   Enter the ending width value (see Figure 4.23) and then press ENTER. You are prompted to specify the next point of the polyline.

```
Specify next point or [Arc Halfwidth Length Undo Width]:
```

6.   Specify the next point of the polyline. A line segment with specified width is drawn and you are prompted to specify the next point of the polyline. Also, a rubber band line segment with constant width (which is specified as the ending width) appears in the drawing area whose one end is fixed at the last specified point and the other end is attached with the cursor, see Figure 4.23.

```
Specify next point or [Arc Halfwidth Length Undo Width]:
```

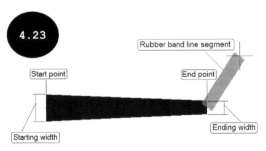

4.23

Rubber band line segment

Start point   End point

Starting width   Ending width

7.   Similarly, you can draw a continuous series of line and arc segments in a polyline with specified width. Once you have drawn polyline, press the ENTER key to exit from creating polyline.

Note: By default, the fill mode for polyline is set to 1. As a result, the polyline segments having width are drawn as solid, see Figure 4.23. However, if you set the fill mode to 0 (zero), the polyline segments having width are drawn as outlines only, see Figure 4.24. To change the fill mode, enter **FILLMODE** in the Command Window and then press ENTER. Next, enter 1 or **0** in the Command Window, as required.

The end specified width of a polyline segment becomes uniform width for other polyline segments until have changed the width again.

Tip: Similar to defining width for a line segment of a polyline, you can specify start width and end width for an arc segment of the polyline, see Figure 4.25.

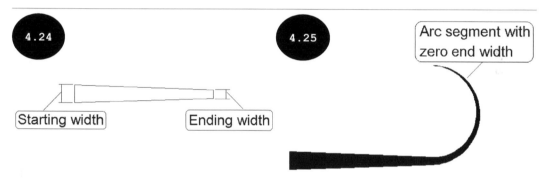

Procedure for Drawing Polyline with Halfwidth

1. Invoke the **Polyline** tool.

   ```
   Specify start point:
   ```

2. Specify the start point of the polyline.

   ```
   Specify next point or [Arc Halfwidth Length Undo Width]:
   ```

3. Click on the **Halfwidth** option in the command prompt or enter H and then press ENTER. You are prompted to specify the starting half width of polyline segment.

   ```
   Specify starting half-width <0.0000>:
   ```

Note: The half width of a polyline segment is measured from the center of the polyline segment to the one side edge of the polyline segment, see Figure 4.26.

4. Specify the starting half width of a polyline segment (see Figure 4.26) and then press ENTER. You are prompted to specify the ending half width of the polyline segment.

   ```
   Specify ending half-width <5.0000>:
   ```

5. Enter the ending half width value (see Figure 4.26) and then press ENTER. You are prompted to specify the next point of the polyline.

```
Specify next point or [Arc Halfwidth Length Undo Width]:
```

6. Specify the next point of the polyline segment. A line segment with specified half width is drawn and you are prompted to specify the next point of the polyline. Also, a rubber band line segment with constant half width (which is specified as the ending half width) appears in the drawing area whose one end is fixed at the last specified point and the other end is attached with the cursor, see Figure 4.26.

```
Specify next point or [Arc Halfwidth Length Undo Width]:
```

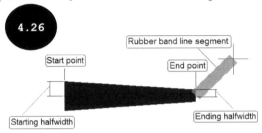

7. Similarly, you can draw a series of line and arc segments in a polyline. Once you have drawn polyline, press the ENTER key to exit from creating polyline.

Tip: To draw an arc segment in a polyline, enter **A** in the Command Window or click on the **Arc** option of the command prompt.

Drawing Ellipse

An ellipse is drawn by defining its major axis and minor axis, see Figure 4.27. In AutoCAD, you can draw ellipse by using the **Center** and **Axis, End** tools. These tools are available in the **Ellipse** flyout of the **Draw** panel, see Figure 4.28. The procedure of creating ellipse by using these tools is as follows:

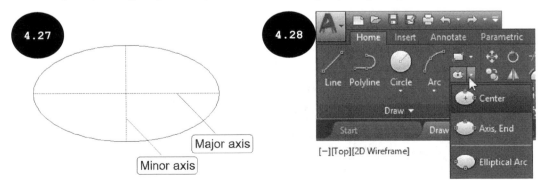

Procedure for Drawing Ellipse by Using the Axis, End Tool

1. Invoke the **Ellipse** flyout by clicking on the down arrow next to an ellipse tool in the **Draw** panel, see Figure 4.28.

2. Click on the **Axis, End** tool in the **Ellipse** flyout. The **Axis, End** tool is invoked and you are prompted to specify the first endpoint of the ellipse axis. Alternatively, enter **EL** in the Command Window and then press ENTER to invoke the **Axis, End** tool.

   ```
   Specify axis endpoint of ellipse or [Arc Center]:
   ```

3. Click the left mouse button in the drawing area or enter coordinates (X , Y) to specify the first endpoint of the ellipse axis (P1), see Figure 4.29. You are prompted to specify the second endpoint of the ellipse axis.

   ```
   Specify other endpoint of axis:
   ```

4. Click the left mouse button in the drawing area or enter coordinates (X , Y)/length of the axis to specify the second endpoint (P2), see Figure 4.29. You are prompted to specify the distance of the other ellipse axis.

   ```
   Specify distance to other axis or [Rotation]:
   ```

5. Move the cursor, clockwise or anti clockwise direction a distance. The preview of an ellipse appears in the drawing are, see Figure 4.30. Next, click the left mouse button or enter length to specify the distance of the other ellipse axis (P3), see Figure 4.29. The ellipse of specified major and minor axes is drawn.

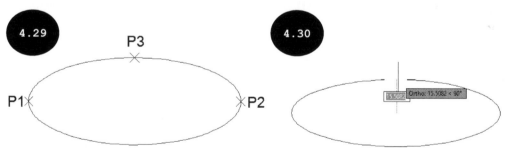

Procedure for Drawing Ellipse by Using the Center Tool

1. Invoke the **Ellipse** flyout, see Figure 4.28.

2. Click on the **Center** tool in the **Ellipse** flyout. You are prompted to specify the center point of the ellipse axis. Alternatively, enter **EL** in the Command Window and then press ENTER. Next, enter **C** and then press ENTER to invoke the **Center** tool.

   ```
   Specify center of ellipse:
   ```

3. Click the left mouse button in the drawing area or enter coordinates (X , Y) to specify the center point of the ellipse axis (P1), see Figure 4.31. You are prompted to specify the endpoint of the ellipse axis.

    ```
    Specify endpoint of axis:
    ```

4. Specify the endpoint of the ellipse axis (P2), see Figure 4.31. You are prompted to specify the distance to the other ellipse axis.

    ```
    Specify distance to other axis or [Rotation]:
    ```

5. Move the cursor, clockwise or anti clockwise direction a distance. The preview of an ellipse appears in the drawing area. Next, enter the distance of the ellipse axis and then press ENTER. The ellipse of specified major and minor axes is drawn.

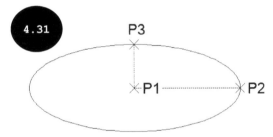

Drawing Elliptical Arc

In addition to drawing an ellipse in AutoCAD, you can also draw an elliptical arc, see Figure 4.32. You can draw an elliptical arc by using the **Elliptical Arc** tool of the **Ellipse** flyout, see Figure 4.33. You can also enter **EL** and then **A** in the Command Window to invoke this tool. The procedure to draw an elliptical arc is as follows:

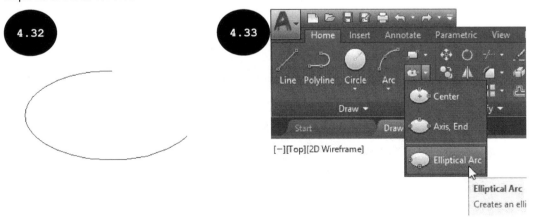

Procedure for Drawing Elliptical Arc

1. Invoke the **Ellipse** flyout and then click on the **Elliptical Arc** tool, see Figure 4.33. Alternatively, enter **EL** in the Command Window and then press ENTER. Next, enter **A** and then press ENTER to invoke the **Elliptical Arc** tool.

    ```
    Specify axis endpoint of elliptical arc or [Center]:
    ```

2. Specify the start point of the elliptical arc axis (P1), see Figure 4.34. You are prompted to specify the other endpoint of the elliptical arc axis.

    ```
    Specify other endpoint of axis:
    ```

3. Specify the endpoint of the elliptical arc axis (P2), see Figure 4.34. You are prompted to specify the distance for the other axis.

    ```
    Specify distance to other axis or [Rotation]:
    ```

4. Move the cursor clockwise or counter-clockwise to a small distance. The preview of an imaginary ellipse appears in the drawing area. Next, specify the distance of the other axis (P3), see Figure 4.34. You are prompted to specify start angle of the elliptical arc.

    ```
    Specify start angle or [Parameter]:
    ```

5. Move the cursor clockwise or counter-clockwise and then specify the start angle for the elliptical arc, see Figure 4.34. You are prompted to specify the end angle of the elliptical arc.

    ```
    Specify end angle or [Parameter Included angle]:
    ```

6. Move the cursor clockwise or counter-clockwise and then specify the end angle for the elliptical arc, see Figure 4.34. The elliptical arc is drawn.

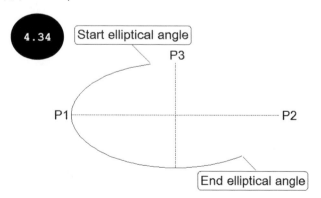

Drawing Spline

A spline is defined as a smooth curve having a high degree of smoothness and passes through or near a set of fit points or control vertices that influence the shape of the curve, see Figures 4.35 and 4.36. The smooth curves are technically known as NURBS (non-uniform rational B-splines). However, it is simply referred as spline. In AutoCAD, you can draw splines/smooth curves by using the **Spline Fit** and **Spline CV** tools. Both the tools are discussed next.

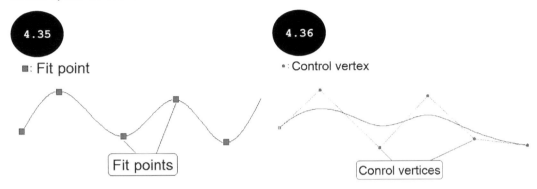

Drawing Spline by Using the Spline Fit Tool

The **Spline Fit** tool is used to create a spline such that it passes through a set of fit points that influence the shape of the spline, see Figure 4.35. The procedure to draw a spline by using the **Spline Fit** tool is as follows:

Procedure for Drawing a Spline by Using the Spline Fit Tool

1. Expand the **Draw** panel by clicking on the down arrow in the title bar of the **Draw** panel, see Figures 4.37. Figure 4.38 shows the expanded form of the **Draw** panel.

2. Click on the **Spline Fit** tool in the expanded **Draw** panel, see Figure 4.38. The **Spline Fit** tool is invoked and you are prompted to specify the first fit point of the spline. Alternatively, enter SPL in the Command Window and then press ENTER to invoke the **Spline Fit** tool.

```
Specify first point or [Method Knots Objects]:
```

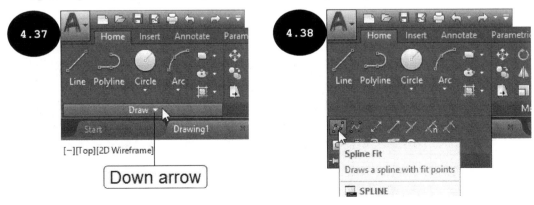

3. Click the left mouse button in the drawing area to specify the first fit point of the spline. You are prompted to specify the next fit point of the spline.

```
Enter next point or [start Tangency toLerance]:
```

Note: Before you specify the second fit point of a spline, you can define its start tangency by entering T in the Command Window or by clicking on the **start Tangency** option in the command prompt. Figure 4.39 shows a spline with start tangency point.

By default, the tolerance value for a spline is set to 0 (zero). As a result, the resultant spline passes exactly through the specified fit points. On specifying the positive tolerance value, the resultant spline deviates from the specified fit points and maintains uniform tolerance distance between the spline and fit points, see Figure 4.40. To specify tolerance for a spline, enter L in the Command Window or click on the **toLerance** option in the command prompt, which appears after specifying the first fit point of a spline. The tolerance value is applied to all fit points except the start and end fit points, see Figure 4.40.

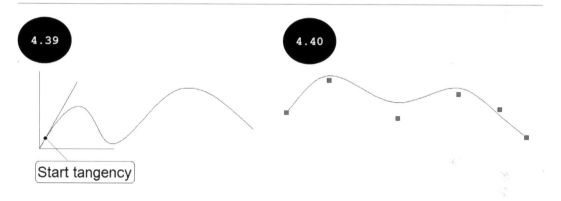

4.39

4.40

Start tangency

4. Click to specify the second fit point of the spline. You are prompted to specify the next fit point of the spline. Also, the preview of the spline appears such that it passes through the specified fit points.

```
Enter next point or [end Tangency toLerance Undo]:
```

5. Click to specify the third fit point of the spline. You are prompted to specify the next fit point of the spline. Also, the preview of the spline appears such that it passes through the specified fit points.

```
Enter next point or [end Tangency toLerance Undo Close]:
```

6. Similarly, you can continue specifying fit points for creating spline. Once you have specified all the fit points of the spline, press ENTER to exit from creating spline.

Note: Before you terminate the creation of spline, you can define its end tangency by entering the T in the Command Window or by clicking on the **end Tangency** option in the command prompt. Figure 4.41 shows a spline with end tangency point.

You can also draw a close spline. To draw a close spline whose end fit point joins to the start point, enter C in the Command Window and then press ENTER. Figure 4.42 shows a close spline. In order to draw a close spline, you need to define minimum three fit points.

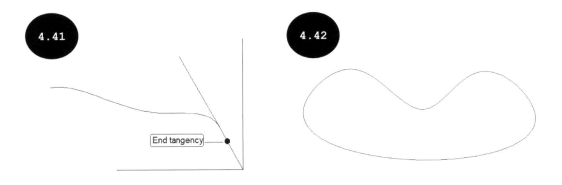

Tip: In case you have specified a fit point of a spline by mistake, you can undo/remove the last specified fit point by entering U in the command prompt and then pressing the ENTER key. You can undo multiple specified last points one after the other by using this command.

Drawing Spline by Using the Spline CV Tool

The **Spline CV** tool is used to create a spline such that it passes near a set of control vertices that influence the shape of the spline, see Figure 4.43. The procedure to draw a spline by using the **Spline CV** tool is as follows:

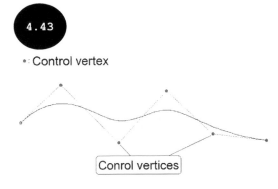

Procedure for Drawing a Spline by Using the Spline CV Tool

1. Expand the **Draw** panel by clicking on the down arrow available in the title bar of the **Draw** panel and then click on the **Spline CV** tool, see Figures 4.44. The **Spline CV** tool is invoked and you are prompted to specify the first control point for creating spline.

   ```
   Specify first point or [Method Knots Objects]:
   ```

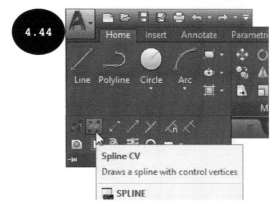

2. Click the left mouse button in the drawing area to specify the first control point of the spline. You are prompted to specify the next control point of the spline.

   ```
   Enter next point:
   ```

3. Click to specify the second control point of the spline. You are prompted to specify the next control point of the spline. Also, the preview of the spline appears such that it passes near the specified control points.

   ```
   Enter next point or [Undo]:
   ```

4. Click to specify the third control point of the spline. You are prompted to specify the next control point of the spline.

   ```
   Enter next point or [Close Undo]:
   ```

5. Similarly, you can continue specifying control points for creating spline. Once you have specified all the control points, press the ENTER key. The spline is created.

Note: You can also draw a closed spline. To draw a close spline whose end control point joins to the start control point, enter **C** in the Command Window and then press ENTER.

You can also undo/remove the last specified control point by entering **U** in the Command Window and then pressing the ENTER key.

Drawing Donuts

A donut is a filled solid ring/circle, which is made up of two end-to-end jointed polyarcs with width. The width of polyarc is defined by specifying the inside and outside diameters, see Figure 4.45. If you specify the inside diameter as 0 (zero) then the donut will be drawn as a filled circle, see Figure 4.46. In AutoCAD, you can draw donuts by using the **Donut** tool, which is available in the expanded **Draw** panel. The procedure to draw donuts is as follows:

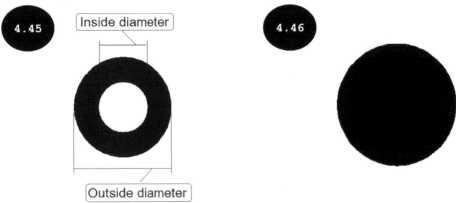

Procedure for Drawing Donuts

1. Expand the **Draw** panel of the **Home** tab and then click on the **Donut** tool, see Figures 4.47. You are prompted to specify the inside diameter of donut. Alternatively, enter **DO** in the Command Window and then press ENTER to invoke the **Donut** tool.

   `Specify inside diameter of donut <0.0000>:`

2. Enter the inside diameter value of donut and then press ENTER. You are prompted to specify the outside diameter of donut.

   `Specify outside diameter of donut <current>:`

3. Enter the outside diameter value of donut and then press ENTER. You are prompted to specify the center of donut.

   `Specify center of donut or <exit>:`

4. Click the left mouse button in the drawing area or specify coordinates (X , Y) to define the center of donut. A donut is drawn with specified parameters in the drawing area. Also, an another donut of same parameters is attached with the cursor. It means you can draw multiple donuts one after another by specifying their centers in the drawing area.

5. Press ENTER to exit from creating donuts.

Note: By default, the fill mode is set to 1. As a result, the resultant donut appears as solid ring/ circle. However, if you change the fill mode to 0 (zero), the resultant donut will not be filled and will appear similar to the one shown in Figure 4.48. To define the fill mode, enter **FILLMODE** in the Command Window and then specify the fill value (0 or 1). Next, press ENTER.

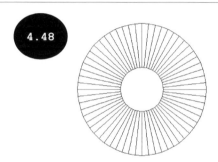

4.48

Drawing Construction and Ray lines

Construction lines and ray lines act as references lines for creating objects. A construction line is also known as XLINE. A construction line is extended to infinite length in both the directions and passes through two picked points, see Figure 4.49. Whereas, a ray line is extended to infinite length in one direction only from the first picked point, see Figure 4.49. You can create a construction line (XLINE) by using the **Construction Line** tool and a ray line by using the **Ray** tool. Both the tools are available in the expanded **Draw** panel of the **Home** tab, see Figure 4.50. The procedures to draw construction line and ray line are as follows:

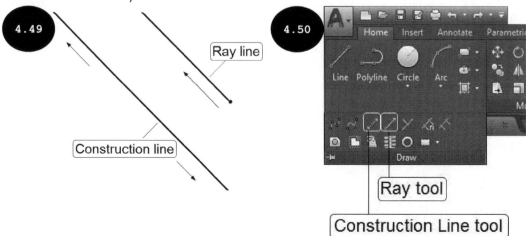

4.49

Ray line

Construction line

4.50

Ray tool

Construction Line tool

Procedure for Drawing Construction Lines

1. Expand the **Draw** panel of the **Home** tab and then click on the **Construction Line** tool, see Figures 4.50. The **Construction Line** tool is invoked and you are prompted to specify a point in the drawing area. Alternatively, enter **XLINE** in the Command Window and then press ENTER to invoke the **Construction Line** tool.

   ```
   Specify a point or [Hor Ver Ang Bisect Offset]:
   ```

2. Click to specify a point (P1) in the drawing area, see Figure 4.51. You are prompted to specify a through point.

   ```
   Specify through point:
   ```

3. Click to specify a through point (P2) in the drawing area, see Figure 4.51. A construction line of infinite length passing through the specified points (P1 and P2) is drawn in the drawing area. Also, the preview of another construction line appears in the drawing area such that it passes through the first specified point and is attached with the cursor. It means you can create multiple construction lines one after another by specifying points in the drawing area.

4. Click to specify another through point (P3) in the drawing area, see Figure 4.51. A another construction line of infinite length passing through the points (P1 and P3) is drawn in the drawing area. Also, the preview of another construction line appears in the drawing area. Similarly, you can create multiple construction lines passing through a common point.

5. Once construction lines have been created, press ENTER to exit from the tool. Figure 4.51 shows two construction lines created.

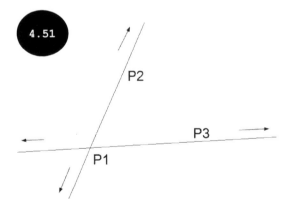

You can also create horizontal, vertical, at an angle, bisect, and offset construction lines by using the **Construction Line** tool. The procedures of creating horizontal, vertical, and other construction lines are as follows:

Procedure for Drawing Horizontal and Vertical Construction Lines

1. Expand the **Draw** panel of the **Home** tab and then click on the **Construction Line** tool. The **Construction Line** tool is invoked and you are prompted to specify a point in the drawing area. Alternatively, you can enter **XLINE** in the Command Window and then press ENTER to invoke the **Construction Line** tool.

    ```
    Specify a point or [Hor Ver Ang Bisect Offset]:
    ```

2. Enter **H** in the Command Window and then press ENTER. A horizontal construction line attached with the cursor is displayed and you are prompted to specify a through point. Alternatively, you can click on the **Hor** option in the command prompt.

    ```
    Specify through point:
    ```

3. Click to specify a through point in the drawing area. A horizontal construction line is created such that it passes through the specified point, see Figure 4.52. Note that an another horizontal construction line attached with the cursor is displayed. As a result, you can create multiple horizontal construction lines one after another by specifying points in the drawing area.

4. Once you have created horizontal construction lines, press ENTER.

5. Similarly, you can create vertical construction lines by entering **V** in the Command Window or by clicking on the **Ver** option in the command prompt, see Figure 4.52.

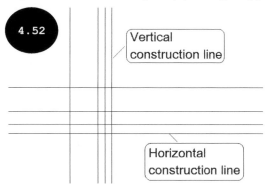

Procedure for Drawing Construction Lines at an Angle

1. Invoke the **Construction Line** tool. You are prompted to specify a point in the drawing area.

    ```
    Specify a point or [Hor Ver Ang Bisect Offset]:
    ```

2. Enter **A** in the Command Window and then press ENTER. You are prompted to specify angle value for the construction line. Alternatively, you can click on the **Ang** option of the command prompt.

    ```
    Enter angle of xline (0) or [Reference]:
    ```

3.   Enter the angle value and then press ENTER. A construction line at the specified angle is attached with the cursor. Also, you are prompted to specify another through point.

```
Specify through point:
```

4.   Click to specify a through point in the drawing area. A construction line at the specified angle is created such that it passes through the specified through point, see Figure 4.53. Also, an another construction line of specified angle is attached with the cursor. As a result, you can create multiple construction lines one after another by specifying points in the drawing area.

5.   Once you have created construction lines at the specified angle, press ENTER or right-click to exit.

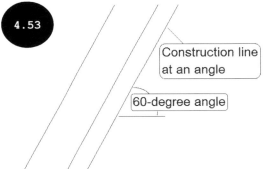

Procedure for Drawing Bisect Construction Lines

1.   Invoke the **Construction Line** tool. You are prompted to specify a point in the drawing area.

```
Specify a point or [Hor Ver Ang Bisect Offset]:
```

2.   Enter B in the Command Window and then press ENTER. You are prompted to specify vertex point. Alternatively, you can click on the **Bisect** option in the command prompt.

```
Specify angle vertex point:
```

3.   Click to specify vertex point (P1) in the drawing area, see Figure 4.54. You are prompted to specify angle start point.

```
Specify angle start point:
```

4.   Click to specify angle start point (P2) in the drawing area, see Figure 4.54. You are prompted to specify angle end point.

```
Specify angle end point:
```

5.   Click to specify angle end point (P3) in the drawing area, see Figure 4.54. A construction line is created such that it passes through the vertex (P1) and bisects to an angle created by specified points, see Figure 4.54. Next, press the ENTER key or right-click to exit.

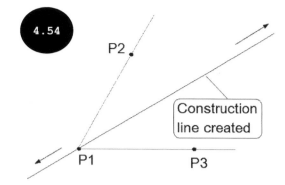

4.54

P2

Construction
line created

P1   P3

Procedure for Drawing Construction Lines at an Offset Distance

1. Invoke the **Construction Line** tool. You are prompted to specify a point in the drawing area.

   ```
   Specify a point or [Hor Ver Ang Bisect Offset]:
   ```

2. Enter O in the Command Window and then press ENTER or click on the **Offset** option of the command prompt. You are prompted to specify offset distance for construction line (xline).

   ```
   Specify offset distance or [Through] <0.0000>:
   ```

Note: The **Offset** option is used to create construction line at an offset distance to a selected line/xline.

3. Enter offset distance value and then press ENTER. You are prompted to select a line. You can select a line or a construction line as reference line for measuring the offset distance.

   ```
   Select a line object:
   ```

4. Click to select a line or a construction line. You are prompted to specify a side to offset.

   ```
   Specify side to offset:
   ```

5. Click on either side of the selected line as the side for creating construction line. The construction line is created at the specified offset distance, see Figure 4.55.

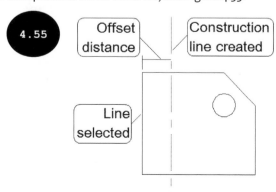

4.55

Offset
distance

Construction
line created

Line
selected

Tip: In addition to defining offset value, you can also specify a point in the drawing area for defining offset distance. To do so, click on the **Through** option in the command prompt or enter **T** in the Command Window when you are prompted to specify offset distance. Next, click on the line as a reference line and then click in the drawing area to specify offset distance. The construction line is created.

Procedure for Drawing Ray Lines

A ray line is similar to construction lines (Xlines) with the only difference that it extends to infinite length in one direction only from the first specified point.

1. Expand the **Draw** panel in the **Home** tab and then click on the **Ray** tool. Alternatively, enter **RAY** in the Command Window and then press ENTER. You are prompted to specify the start point.

   ```
   Specify start point:
   ```

2. Click to specify the start point of the ray line in the drawing area. You are prompted to specify a through point.

   ```
   Specify through point:
   ```

3. Click to specify the through point in the drawing area. A ray line of infinite length in one direction from the start point is created in the drawing area. Also, the preview of another ray line appears in the drawing area whose origin is fixed at the specified start point. You can create multiple ray lines one after another by specifying through points.

4. Once you have created ray lines, press ENTER or right-click to exit. Figure 4.56 shows two ray lines sharing the same start point created.

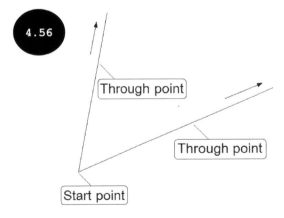

Drawing Points and Defining Point Style/Size

In AutoCAD, a point acts as reference geometry for creating other drawing objects, measuring distance, and so on. You can draw points by using the **Multiple Points** tool, which is in the expanded **Draw** panel of the **Home** tab, see Figure 4.57. Alternatively, you can use the POINT command to draw points. By default, the point style of a point is simple dot which is relatively small in size. As the default size of a point is small, it is difficult to visible on the screen. You can make the required changes in the point style and size by using the **Point Style** tool. The procedures to draw reference points, changing point style, and size are as follows:

Procedure for Drawing Reference Points

1. Expand the **Draw** panel of the **Home** tab and then click on the **Multiple Points** tool, see Figures 4.57. The **Multiple Points** tool is invoked and you are prompted to specify a point in the drawing area. Alternatively, enter PO in the Command Window and then press ENTER to invoke the **Multiple Points** tool.

    ```
    Specify a point:
    ```

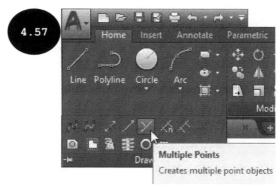

2. Click to specify a point in the drawing area. The point is created with default point style (dot). You are prompted to specify another point.

    ```
    Specify a point:
    ```

    Note: The point created with default point style and size may not be visible easily in the drawing area due to its small size. You can change the point style and size by using the **Point Style** tool. The procedure to change the point style and size is discussed later in this chapter.

    ---

3. You can continue specifying points in the drawing area and create multiple points. Once you have drawn points, press ESC to exit.

Procedure for Defining Point Style and Point Size

1. Expand the **Utilities** panel of the **Home** tab and then click on the **Point Style** tool, see Figures 4.58. The **Point Style** dialog box appears, see Figure 4.59. Alternatively, you can enter DDPTYPE in the Command Window and then press ENTER to invoke the **Point Style** dialog box.

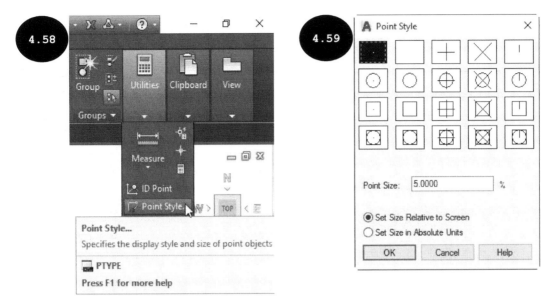

2. Click on the required point style in the **Point Style** dialog box.

   After selecting the required point style, you can define the point size by using the **Set Size Relative to Screen** and **Set Size in Absolute Units** radio buttons of the **Point Style** dialog box. By default, the **Set Size Relative to Screen** radio button is selected. As a result, you can specify percentage relative to the screen for defining the point size in the **Point Size** field of the dialog box. To define the point size in absolute unit, click to select the **Set Size in Absolute Units** radio button and then enter the absolute unit of the point size in the **Point Size** field of the dialog box, see Figure 4.60.

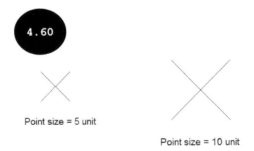

Point size = 5 unit

Point size = 10 unit

3. Click to select the required radio button: **Set Size Relative to Screen** or **Set Size in Absolute Units** in the **Point Style** dialog box for defining the point size.

4. Specify the point size in terms of percentage relative to the screen or absolute unit in the **Point Size** field of the **Point Style** dialog box, respectively.

5. Click on the **OK** button in the dialog box to accept the changes as well as to exit the dialog box.

Tutorial 1

Create the drawing shown in Figure 4.61. The dimensions shown in the figure are for your reference only.

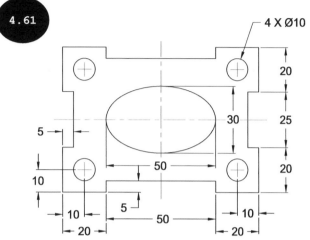

Section 1: Starting AutoCAD

1. Double-click on the AutoCAD icon on your desktop to start AutoCAD. The initial screen of AutoCAD with the **Start** tab appears, see Figure 4.62.

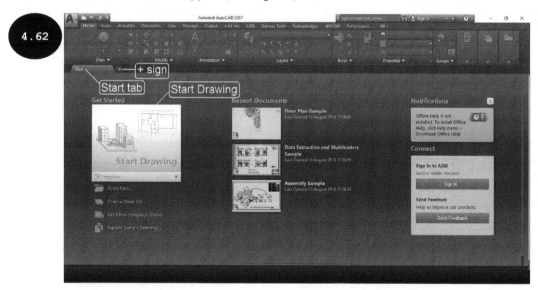

2. Click on the + sign next to the **Start** tab, see Figure 4.62. A new drawing file with the default drawing template is invoked. Alternatively, click on **Start Drawing** in the **Get Started** section of the **Start** tab to start a new drawing file with default drawing template. You can also start a new drawing file by using the **New** tool of the **Quick Access Toolbar**, which is at the top left corner of AutoCAD.

Section 2: Selecting Workspace for Creating Drawing

1. Click on the **Workspace Switching** ⚙ button in the **Status Bar**. A flyout appears, see Figure 4.63.

4 . 63

✓ **Drafting & Annotation**

3D Basics

3D Modeling

Save Current As...

Workspace Settings...

Customize...

Display Workspace Label

2. In this flyout, make sure that the **Drafting & Annotation** option is tick-marked in order to create drawing in the Drafting & Annotation workspace.

Section 3: Drawing Outer Loop of the Drawing

1. Click on the **Line** tool in the **Draw** panel of the **Home** tab. The **Line** tool is invoked and you are prompted to specify the first point of the line. Alternatively, you can enter **L** in the Command Window and then press ENTER to invoke the **Line** tool.

```
Specify first point:
```

2. Click on the **Ortho Mode** button 📐 of the **Status Bar** or press the F8 key to turn on the Ortho mode. Note that this is a toggle button.

3. Make sure that the Dynamic Input mode is activated. You can activate the Dynamic Input mode by clicking on the **Dynamic Input** button ⊞ in the **Status Bar**.

4. Follow the command sequence given below for creating the drawing.

```
Specify first point: 0,0 (ENTER)
Specify next point or [Undo]:
```
Move the cursor horizontally toward the right and then enter 20 in the Dynamic Input box (**ENTER**)
```
Specify next point or [Undo]:
```
Move the cursor vertically upward and then enter 5 (**ENTER**)
```
Specify next point or [Undo]:
```
Move the cursor horizontally toward the right and then enter 50 (**ENTER**)
```
Specify next point or [Undo]:
```
Move the cursor vertically downward and then enter 5 (**ENTER**)
```
Specify next point or [Close Undo]:
```
Move the cursor horizontally toward the right and then enter 20 (**ENTER**)
```
Specify next point or [Undo]:
```
Move the cursor vertically upward and then enter 20 (**ENTER**)
```
Specify next point or [Close Undo]:
```
Move the cursor horizontally toward the left and then enter 5 (**ENTER**)

```
Specify next point or [Undo]:
```
Move the cursor vertically upward and then enter 25 (**ENTER**)
```
Specify next point or [Close Undo]:
```
Move the cursor horizontally toward the right and then enter 5 (**ENTER**)
```
Specify next point or [Close Undo]:
```
Move the cursor vertically upward and then enter 20 (**ENTER**)
```
Specify next point or [Close Undo]:
```
Move the cursor horizontally toward the left and then enter 20 (**ENTER**)
```
Specify next point or [Close Undo]:
```
Move the cursor vertically downward and then enter 5 (**ENTER**)
```
Specify next point or [Close Undo]:
```
Move the cursor horizontally toward the left and then enter 50 (**ENTER**)
```
Specify next point or [Close Undo]:
```
Move the cursor vertically upward and then enter 5 (**ENTER**)
```
Specify next point or [Close Undo]:
```
Move the cursor horizontally toward the left and then enter 20 (**ENTER**)
```
Specify next point or [Close Undo]:
```
Move the cursor vertically downward and then enter 20 (**ENTER**)
```
Specify next point or [Close Undo]:
```
Move the cursor horizontally toward the right and then enter 5 (**ENTER**)
```
Specify next point or [Close Undo]:
```
Move the cursor vertically downward and then enter 25 (**ENTER**)
```
Specify next point or [Close Undo]:
```
Move the cursor horizontally toward the left and then enter 5 (**ENTER**)
```
Specify next point or [Close Undo]:
```
*C or **Close*** *(See Figure 4.64)*

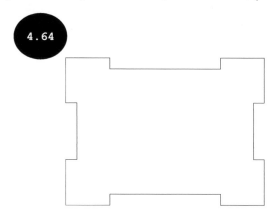

4.64

Section 4: Drawing Ellipse

1. Invoke the **Ellipse** flyout in the **Draw** panel and then click on the **Center** tool, see Figure 4.65. You are prompted to specify the center of ellipse. Alternatively, you can enter **EL** in the Command Window and then press ENTER. Next, enter **C** and then press ENTER to invoke the tool.

```
Specify center of ellipse:
```

2. Move the cursor to the midpoint of the left middle vertical line (P1) (see Figure 4.66) and then move the cursor to the midpoint of the upper middle horizontal line (P2), see Figure 4.66. Next, move the cursor vertically downward. A reference/tracking line appears.

3. Continue moving the cursor vertically downward and then click to specify the center point of the ellipse when the cursor snaps to the intersection of reference/tracking lines, which are passing through the points (P1 and P2), see Figure 4.66.

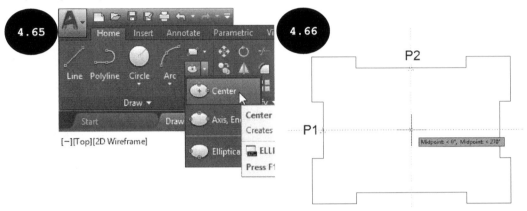

4. Move the cursor horizontally toward the right and then enter **25** in the Dynamic Input box. Next, press ENTER.

5. Move the cursor vertically upward to a small distance. Next, enter **15** in the Dynamic Input box and then press ENTER. An ellipse of major axis 50 and minor axis 30 is drawn, see Figure 4.67.

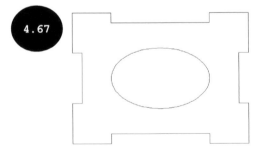

Section 5: Drawing Circles

In this section, you will draw the circles of the drawing with the help of construction lines (xlines).

1. Expand the **Draw** panel of the **Home** tab and then click on the **Construction Line** tool. You are prompted to specify the start point of the construction line (xline). Alternatively, you can enter **XLINE** in the Command Window to invoke the **Construction Line** tool.

    ```
    Specify a point or [Hor Ver Ang Bisect Offset]:
    ```

2. Click on the **Offset** option in the command prompt or enter O and then press ENTER. You are prompted to specify offset distance.

   ```
   Specify offset distance or [Through] <0.0000>:
   ```

3. Enter **10** as the offset distance value and then press ENTER. You are prompted to select a line object.

   ```
   Select a line object:
   ```

4. Click on the lower left vertical line (L1), see Figure 4.68. You are prompted to specify side to offset construction line (xline).

   ```
   Specify side to offset:
   ```

5. Click anywhere inside the outer closed loop of the drawing. A construction line (xline) at an offset distance of 10 units from the selected vertical line is created. Also, you are prompted to select a line object.

   ```
   Select a line object:
   ```

6. Click on the lower left horizontal line (L2), see Figure 4.68. You are prompted to specify side to offset construction line (xline).

   ```
   Specify side to offset:
   ```

7. Click anywhere inside the outer closed loop of the drawing. A construction line (xline) at an offset distance of 10 units from the selected horizontal line is created, see Figure 4.69. Also, you are prompted to select a line object.

   ```
   Select a line object:
   ```

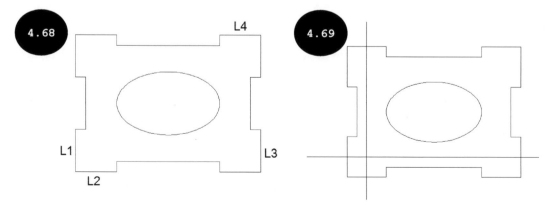

8. Similarly, select the lower right vertical line (L3) and the upper right horizontal line (L4) for creating other construction lines, refer to Figure 4.68. Figure 4.70 shows the drawing after creating all the construction lines.

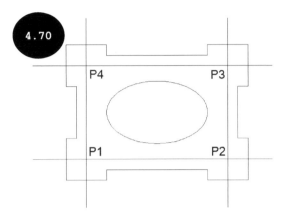

9. Press ENTER or right-click to exit from the creation of construction lines.

    After creating the construction lines (xlines), you can use the intersection of the construction lines for specifying the center point of the circles.

10. Enter C in the Command Window and then press ENTER to invoke the **Center, Radius** tool. You can also click on the **Center, Radius** tool in the **Draw** panel. You are prompted to specify the center point of the circle.

    ```
    Specify center point for circle or [3P 2P Ttr (tan tan radius)]:
    ```

11. Move the cursor over the lower left intersection of the construction lines (P1), see Figure 6.70, and then click to specify the center point of the circle when the cursor snaps to the intersection (P1). You are prompted to specify the radius of the circle.

    ```
    Specify radius of circle or [Diameter] <0.0000>:
    ```

12. Enter 5 as the radius value of the circle and then press ENTER. A circle of radius 5 units is drawn, see Figure 6.71.

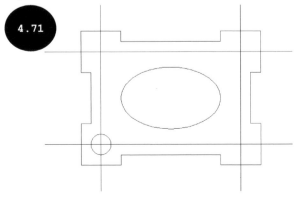

13. Similarly, draw the other three circles of radius 5 units at the intersections (P2, P3, and P4) of construction lines, see Figure 6.72.

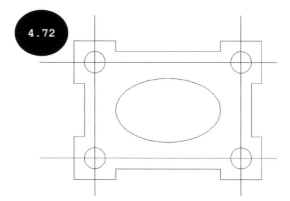

4.72

After drawing all the circles, you can delete the construction lines. However, it is recommended that you create a layer and move all the construction lines to it. Next, hide the layer. Figure 4.73 shows the final drawing after hiding the construction lines.

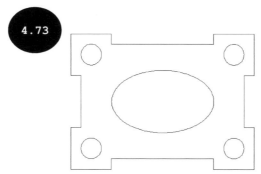

4.73

Tip: To move a set of entities to a layer, select the entities to be moved. Next, invoke the **Layer** drop-down list in the **Layers** panel of the **Home** tab and then click on the layer in the drop-down list to which you want to move the selected set of entities.

Section 6: Saving the Drawing

After creating the drawing, you need to save it.

1. Click on the **Save** tool in the **Quick Access Toolbar**. The **Save Drawing As** dialog box appears.

2. Browse to the *AutoCAD* folder and then create a folder with the name *Chapter 4* inside the *AutoCAD* folder.

3. Enter **Tutorial 1** in the **File name** field of the dialog box and then click on the **Save** button. The drawing is saved with the name Tutorial 1 in the *Chapter 4* folder.

Tutorial 2

Draw the drawing shown in Figure 4.74. The dimensions shown in the figure are for your reference only.

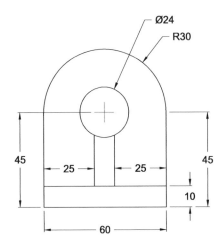

Section 1: Starting AutoCAD

1. Start AutoCAD and click on the **New** tool in the **Quick Access Toolbar**, which is at the top left corner of AutoCAD. The **Select template** dialog box appears.

2. In the **Select template** dialog box, click on the *acad.dwt* template and then click on the **Open** button. A new drawing file with the *acad.dwt* template is invoked

Section 2: Defining Drawing Limits

1. Define the drawing limits. You can define the drawing limits based on the overall drawing dimensions of the drawing and by keeping some extra space for placing dimension in the drawing area.

Section 3: Creating Drawing

1. Click on the **Rectangle** tool in the **Draw** panel of the **Home** tab. The **Rectangle** tool is invoked and you are prompted to specify the first corner of the rectangle. Alternatively, you can enter **REC** in the Command Window and then press ENTER to invoke the **Rectangle** tool.

   ```
   Specify first corner point or [Chamfer Elevation Fillet Thickness
   Width]:
   ```

2. Click in the drawing area to specify the first corner of the rectangle. You are prompted to specify the other corner of the rectangle.

   ```
   Specify other corner point or [Area Dimensions Rotation]:
   ```

You need to create a rectangle by specifying dimensions (length 60 units and width 10 units).

3. Click in the **Dimensions** option in the command prompt. You are prompted to specify the length of the rectangle. Alternatively, you can enter **D** and then press ENTER.

    ```
    Specify length for rectangles <current>:
    ```

4. Enter **60** as the length of the rectangle and then press ENTER. You are prompted to specify width of the rectangle.

    ```
    Specify width for rectangles <current>:
    ```

5. Enter **10** as the width of the rectangle and then press ENTER. You are prompted to specify other corner of the rectangle.

    ```
    Specify other corner point or [Area Dimensions Rotation]:
    ```

6. Click to specify the corner point of the rectangle in the drawing area. A rectangle of length 60 units and width 10 units is created, see Figure 4.75.

4.75

Now, you need to create the line entities of the drawing.

7. Click on the **Line** tool in the **Draw** panel. You are prompted to specify the first point of the line. Alternatively, you can enter **L** in the Command Window and then press ENTER.

    ```
    Specify first point:
    ```

8. Move the cursor over the upper left corner of the rectangle and then click to specify the start point of the line when the cursor snaps to it. You are prompted to specify the next point of the line.

    ```
    Specify next point or [Undo]:
    ```

9. Move the cursor vertically upward and then enter **35** as the length of the line. Next, press ENTER. A line of length 35 units is drawn, see Figure 4.76. Make sure that the Ortho mode and the Dynamic Input mode are activated.

10. Right-click and then select the **Enter** option from the shortcut menu appeared to exit from the **Line** tool.

11. Similarly, draw another vertical line of same length starting from the upper right corner of the rectangle, see Figure 4.77.

After creating the line entities, you need to create arc of radius 30 units.

12. Invoke the **Arc** flyout and then click on the **Start, End, Radius** tool. You are prompted to specify the start point of the arc.

    Specify start point of arc or [Center]:

13. Move the cursor over the endpoint of the right vertical line and then click to specify the start point of the arc when the cursor snaps to it. You are prompted to specify the endpoint of the arc.

    Specify end point of arc:

14. Move the cursor over the endpoint of the left vertical line and then click to specify the endpoint of the arc when the cursor snaps to it. You are prompted to specify the radius of the arc.

    Specify radius of arc:

15. Move the cursor vertically upward and then enter **30** as the radius of the arc. Next, press ENTER. An arc of radius 30 units is drawn, see Figure 4.78.

After creating the arc, you need to create a circle such that it is concentric to the arc drawn.

16. Invoke the **Center, Radius** tool in the **Draw** panel. The **Center, Radius** tool is invoked and you are prompted to specify the center point of the circle. Alternatively, you can enter **C** in the Command Window and then press ENTER.

    ```
    Specify center point for circle or [3P 2P Ttr (tan tan radius)]:
    ```

17. Move the cursor over the circumference of the previously drawn arc and then move the cursor toward its center point. Next, click to specify the center point of the circle when the cursor snaps to the center point of the arc. You are prompted to specify the radius of circle.

    ```
    Specify radius of circle or [Diameter]:
    ```

18. Enter **12** as the radius of the circle and then press ENTER. A circle of radius 12 units is drawn, see Figure 4.79.

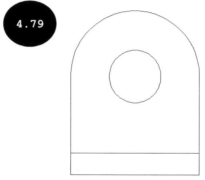

Now, you need to draw two inner vertical lines of the drawing with the help of construction lines (xlines).

19. Expand the **Draw** panel of the **Home** tab and then click on the **Construction Line** tool. You are prompted to specify the start point of the construction line (xline). Alternatively, you can enter XLINE in the Command Window to invoke the tool.

    ```
    Specify a point or [Hor Ver Ang Bisect Offset]:
    ```

20. Click on the **Offset** option of the command prompt or enter O and then press ENTER. You are prompted to specify the offset distance.

    ```
    Specify offset distance or [Through] <0.0000>:
    ```

21. Enter **25** as the offset distance and then press ENTER. You are prompted to select a line object.

    ```
    Select a line object:
    ```

22. Click on the left vertical line. You are prompted to specify side to offset the construction line.

```
Specify side to offset:
```

23. Click anywhere on the right side of the selected line. A construction line (xline) at an offset distance of 25 units from the left vertical line is created, see Figure 4.80. Also, you are prompted to select a line object.

```
Select a line object:
```

24. Click on the right vertical line. You are prompted to specify side to offset the construction line.

```
Specify side to offset:
```

25. Click anywhere on the left side of the selected line. A construction line (xline) at an offset distance of 25 units from the right vertical line is created, see Figure 4.81. Next, right-click to exit from the tool.

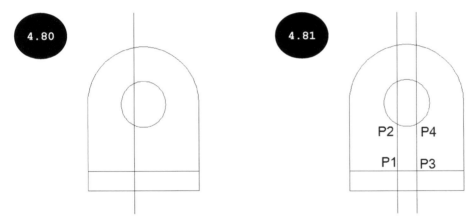

After creating the construction lines (xlines), you can use the construction lines for creating two inner vertical lines of the drawing.

26. Invoke the **Line** tool and then create a vertical line whose start point is at the intersection of P1 and end point is at the intersection of P2, refer to Figure 4.81.

27. Similarly, create another vertical line whose start point is at the intersection of P3 and end point is at the intersection of P4, refer to Figure 4.81.

After creating all the drawing entities, you can delete the construction lines. However, it is recommended that you create a layer and name it as Construction and then move the construction lines to the Construction layer. Next, hide the Construction layer. Figure 4.82 shows the final drawing after hiding the construction lines.

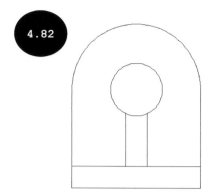

Section 4: Saving the Drawing

After creating the drawing, you need to save it.

1. Click on the **Save** tool in the **Quick Access Toolbar**. The **Save Drawing As** dialog box appears.

2. Browse to the *Chapter 4* inside the *AutoCAD* folder. If the *Chapter 4* is not created in the Tutorial 1 of this chapter then you need to first create this folder.

3. Enter **Tutorial 2** in the **File name** field of the dialog box and then click on the **Save** button. The drawing is saved with the name Tutorial 2 in the *Chapter 4* folder.

Tutorial 3

Draw the drawing shown in Figure 4.83. You need to create the drawing by using polylines and donut. The dimensions shown in the figure are for your reference only.

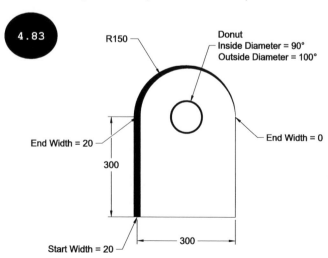

Section 1: Starting AutoCAD

1. Start a new drawing file in AutoCAD. Make sure that the Drafting & Annotation workspace is activated.

2. Define the drawing limits.

Section 2: Creating Drawing

1. Click on the **Polyline** tool in the **Draw** panel. You are prompted to specify the start point of the polyline. Alternatively, you can enter **PL** in the Command Window to invoke the **Polyline** tool.

   ```
   Specify start point:
   ```

2. Click in the drawing area to specify the start point of the polyline. You are prompted to specify the next point of the polyline.

   ```
   Specify next point or [Arc Halfwidth Length Undo Width]:
   ```

3. Click on the **Width** option in the command prompt or enter **W** and then press ENTER. You are prompted to specify the starting width of the polyline.

   ```
   Specify starting width <0.0000>:
   ```

4. Enter **20** as the starting width of the polyline and then press ENTER. You are prompted to specify the end width of the polyline.

   ```
   Specify ending width <20.0000>:
   ```

5. Enter **20** as the end width of the polyline and then press ENTER. You are prompted to specify the next point of the polyline.

   ```
   Specify next point or [Arc Halfwidth Length Undo Width]:
   ```

6. Make sure that the Ortho mode is activated. Next, move the cursor vertically upward a distance in the drawing area.

7. Enter **300** as the length of the polyline and then press ENTER. You are prompted to specify the next point of the polyline.

   ```
   Specify next point or [Arc Halfwidth Length Undo Width]:
   ```

   Now, you need to create a polyarc having starting width 20 units and end width 0.

8. Click on the **Arc** option in the command prompt or enter **A** in the Command Window and then press ENTER. You are prompted to specify the end point of the arc.

   ```
   Specify endpoint of arc or [Angle CEnter Close Direction Halfwidth
   Line Radius Second pt Undo Width]:
   ```

9. Click on the **Width** option in the command prompt or enter **W** in the Command Window and then press ENTER. You are prompted to specify the starting width of the arc.

    ```
    Specify starting width <20.0000>:
    ```

10. Enter **20** as the starting width of the arc and then press ENTER. You are prompted to specify the end width of the arc.

    ```
    Specify ending width <20.0000>:
    ```

11. Enter **0** (Zero) as the end width of the polyline and then press ENTER. You are prompted to specify the endpoint of the arc.

    ```
    Specify endpoint of arc or [Angle CEnter Close Direction Halfwidth
    Line Radius Second pt Undo Width]:
    ```

12. Move the cursor horizontally toward the right and then enter **300**. Next, press ENTER. A polyarc is created, see Figure 4.84. Also, you are prompted to specify the endpoint of the arc.

    ```
    Specify endpoint of arc or [Angle CEnter Close Direction Halfwidth
    Line Radius Second pt Undo Width]:
    ```

13. Enter **L** and then press ENTER to invoke the Line mode of the polyline. You are prompted to specify the next point of the line.

    ```
    Specify next point or [Arc Close Halfwidth Length Undo Width]:
    ```

14. Move the cursor vertically downward and then enter **300** as the length of the line. Next, press ENTER. You are prompted to specify the next point of the line.

    ```
    Specify next point or [Arc Close Halfwidth Length Undo Width]:
    ```

15. Enter **C** in the Command Window and then press ENTER or click on the **Close** option in the command prompt to close the polyline, see Figure 4.85.

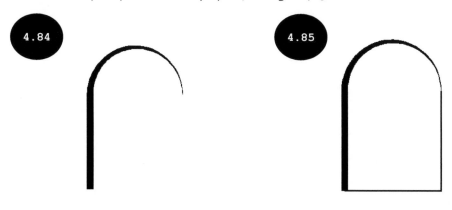

Section 3: Creating Donut

1.   Expand the **Draw** panel of the **Home** tab and then click on the **Donut** tool. You are prompted to specify the inside diameter of donut. Alternatively, enter **DO** in the Command Window and then press ENTER.

```
Specify inside diameter of donut <0.0000>:
```

2.   Enter **90** as the inside diameter of the donut and then press ENTER. You are prompted to specify the outside diameter of the donut.

```
Specify outside diameter of donut <0.0000>:
```

3.   Enter **100** as the outside diameter of the donut and then press ENTER. A donut of specified parameter is attached with the cursor. Also, you are prompted to specify the center point of the donut.

```
Specify center of donut or <exit>:
```

4.   Make sure that Object Snap mode is activated.

5.   Move the cursor over the circumference of the arc and then move the cursor toward the center point of the arc. Next, click to specify the center point of the donut when the cursor snaps to the center point of the arc. A donut is created, see Figure 4.86.

6.   Press ENTER or right-click to exit from the **Donut** tool. Figure 4.86 shows the final drawing.

4.86

Section 4: Saving the Drawing

After creating the drawing, you need to save it.

1.   Click on the **Save** tool in the **Quick Access Toolbar**. The **Save Drawing As** dialog box appears.

2.   Browse to the *Chapter 4* inside the *AutoCAD* folder.

3. Enter **Tutorial 3** in the **File name** field of the dialog box and then click on the **Save** button. The drawing is saved with the name Tutorial 3 in the *Chapter 4* folder.

Hands-on Test Drive 1

Draw the drawing shown in Figure 4.87. The dimensions shown in the figure are for your reference only. You will learn about applying dimensions in later chapters.

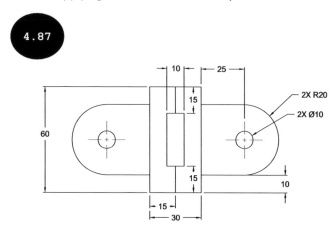

4.87

Hands-on Test Drive 2

Draw the drawing shown in Figure 4.88. The dimensions shown in the figure are for your reference only.

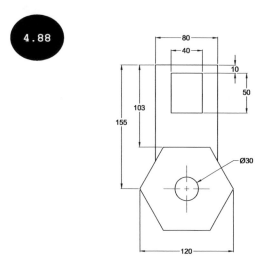

4.88

Summary

In this chapter, you have learned how to create rectangles, polygons, polylines, ellipses, elliptical arcs, splines, donuts, construction lines, ray lines, and points. You have also learned how to define point style/size.

Questions

- The _____ tool is used to draw rectangles by using different methods.

- The value enter inside the _____ symbol in the command prompt is the last defined or default value of the command.

- AutoCAD allow you to draw polygons of equal sides in the range between _____ to _____ .

- In AutoCAD, you can draw two type of polygon: _____ and _____ .

- You can draw polyline by using the _____ tool.

- A ellipse is drawn by defining its _____ and _____ axes.

- You can draw an elliptical arc by using the _____ tool.

- In AutoCAD, you can draw splines/smooth curves by using the _____ and _____ tools.

- The _____ tool is used to create a spline such that it passes through a set of fit points that influence the shape of the spline.

- A construction line is also known as _____ .

- A _____ line is extended to infinity length in both the directions and passes through two specified points.

- You can draw donuts by using the _____ tool.

Modifying and Editing Drawings - I

In this chapter, you will learn the following:

- Working with object selection methods
- Trimming drawing entities
- Extending drawing entities
- Working with array
- Mirroring drawing entities
- Filleting drawing entities
- Chamfering drawing entities
- Offsetting drawing entities
- Moving drawing objects
- Copying drawing objects
- Rotating drawing objects
- Scaling drawing objects
- Stretching drawing objects
- Lengthening drawing objects

Performing editing and modifying operations in a drawing is very important to complete the drawing as per the requirement. In AutoCAD, you can perform various editing operations such as trimming unwanted entities, extending entities, mirroring, creating array, moving, and rotating entities. The tools to perform various editing and modifying operations are in the **Modify** panel of the **Home** tab, see Figure 5.1.

Before you learn about various editing and modifying operations, it is important to understand about different object selection methods available in AutoCAD.

Working with Object Selection Methods

In AutoCAD, you can select drawing objects individually one by one by clicking the left mouse button. However, selecting objects individually one by one is very time consuming method if you have to perform the editing operation on multiple objects of a drawing. For example, if you have to move a group of objects from one location to another. Therefore, AutoCAD is provided with various selection methods such as Window selection, Cross window selection, Add, Crossing polygon, Fence, and All. Out of all these, the Window selection and Cross window selection methods are the most widely used selection methods. The different selection methods are as follows:

Window Selection Method

The Window selection method is used for selecting group of objects together by creating a rectangular window from left (P1) to right (P2) around the objects to be selected, see Figure 5.2. Note that only the objects that are completely enclosed within the rectangular window will be selected and the objects that lie partially inside the rectangular window will not be selected. Also, the boundary of the rectangular window is of solid outlines.

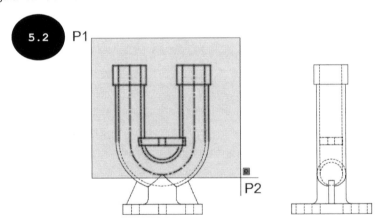

Cross Window Selection Method

The Cross window selection method is used for selecting group of objects together by creating a rectangular cross widow from right (P1) to left (P2) around the objects to be selected, see Figure 5.3. Note that all objects that are completely enclosed as well as the objects that touch the rectangular cross window will be selected. Means, the objects that lie partially inside the rectangular cross window will also be selected. Also, the boundary of the rectangular cross widow is of dashed outlines.

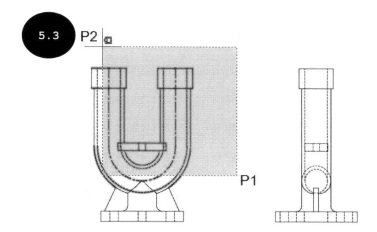

In AutoCAD, you may have noticed that on invoking some of the tools/commands, you are prompted to select objects. In this case, when you are prompted to select objects, you can invoke different selection methods, as per your requirement. Some of the selection methods are as follows:

Window Selection

When you are prompted to select objects in the command prompt, enter W in the Command Window and then press ENTER to invoke the Window selection method. The method of selecting objects by using the Window selection method has been discussed earlier.

Cross Window Selection

When you are prompted to select objects in the command prompt, enter C in the Command Window and then press ENTER to invoke the Cross window selection method. The method of selecting objects by using the Cross window selection method has been discussed earlier.

All Selection

The All selection method is used to select all drawing objects except the objects that are assigned to the frozen or locked layers. To invoke the All selection method, enter ALL in the Command Window and then press ENTER when you are prompted to select objects in the command prompt.

For example,
```
Tool/Command:  M or MOVE (ENTER)
Select objects:  ALL (ENTER)
```

Note: The **M** is the short form of the **Move** command. This command is used to move drawing objects from one location to another. You will learn more about the **Move** command later in this chapter.

Cross Polygon Selection

The Cross polygon selection method is used to select group of objects by drawing a cross polygon boundary around the objects to be selected, see Figure 5.4. Note that in Cross polygon selection method, all the objects that are completely enclosed as well as the objects that touch the cross polygon boundary will be selected. Also, the cross polygon boundary appears as dashed outline.

To invoke this selection method , enter **CP** in the Command Window and then press ENTER when you are prompted to select objects in the command prompt. Once the Cross polygon selection method has been invoked, click in the drawing area to specify the first polygon point (P1) followed by the endpoints of the polygon lines, as required, see Figure 5.4. After drawing a cross polygon boundary around the objects to be selected by specifying the endpoints of the polygon lines, press ENTER to exit. All the objects that are completely enclosed or touch the cross polygon boundary are selected.

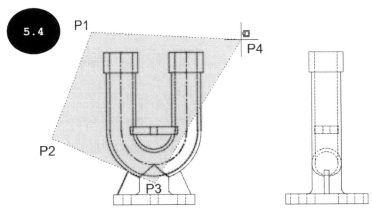

Window Polygon Selection

The Window polygon selection method is used to select group of objects by drawing a polygon boundary around the objects to be selected, see Figure 5.5. Note that in the Window polygon selection method, only the objects that are completely enclosed within the polygon boundary will be selected. Also, the polygon boundary appears as a solid outline.

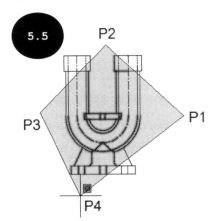

To invoke this selection method, enter **WP** in the Command Window and then press ENTER when you are prompted to select objects in the command prompt. Next, you can click in the drawing area to specify the first polygon point (P1) followed by the endpoints of the polygon lines, as required, see Figure 5.5. After drawing a polygon boundary around the objects to be selected by specifying the endpoints of the polygon lines, press ENTER to exit. All the objects that are completely enclosed within the polygon boundary are selected.

Fence Selection

The Fence selection method is used to select group of objects by drawing a series of continuous lines over the objects to be selected, see Figure 5.6. Note that in the Fence selection method, the objects which come across the lines drawn will be selected.

To invoke this selection method, enter **F** in the Command Window and then press ENTER when you are prompted to select objects in the command prompt. Next, you can click in the drawing area to specify the first point (P1) of the fence line followed by the continuous endpoints one after another, as required, see Figure 5.6. After drawing a series of continuous lines over the objects to be selected, press ENTER to exit. All the objects which come across the fence line are selected.

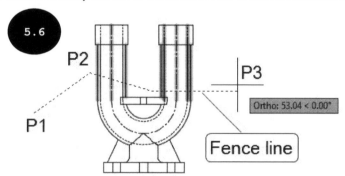

Fence line

Last Selection

The Last selection method is used to select the last drawn object in the drawing. To invoke this selection method, enter **L** in the Command Window and then press ENTER. The last drawn object gets selected.

Trimming Drawing Entities

In AutoCAD, you can trim the unwanted drawing entities of a drawing upto to their nearest intersection or the intersection with cutting edges/boundaries. You can trim the entities by using the **Trim** tool of the **Modify** panel, see Figure 5.7. You can also invoke the **Trim** tool for trimming entities by entering **TR** in the Command Window and then pressing ENTER. The procedure to trim the unwanted entities of a drawing is as follows:

Procedure for Trimming Entities

1. Click on the **Trim** tool in the **Modify** panel, see Figure 5.7. You are prompted to select cutting edges/boundaries. Alternatively, enter **TR** in the Command Window and then press ENTER.

```
Select cutting edges ...
Select objects or <select all>:
```

2. Click on the objects/entities to be used as the cutting edges/boundaries to trim entities, see Figure 5.8. You can select rectangles, lines, circles, polylines, construction lines, and so on as the cutting edges to trim entities. Next, press ENTER. You are prompted to select objects to be trimmed.

```
Select object to trim or shift-select to extend or
[Fence Crossing Project Edge eRase Undo]:
```

Note: Instead of selecting the objects/entities as the cutting edges/boundaries, you can directly select the entities to be trimmed and skip the step 2 mentioned above. To select the entities to be trimmed without selecting the cutting edges, press the ENTER key when you are prompted to select the cutting edges. Next, click on the entity to be trimmed. The portion of the selected entity is trimmed upto its nearest intersection.

3. Click on the entity to be trimmed, see Figure 5.8. The portion of the selected entity where you clicked the left mouse button is trimmed upto the intersection with the cutting edges, see Figure 5.9. Also, you are prompted to select another objects to be trimmed.

```
Select object to trim or shift-select to extend or
[Fence Crossing Project Edge eRase Undo]:
```

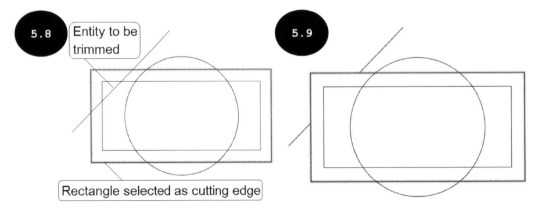

5.8 Entity to be trimmed

Rectangle selected as cutting edge

5.9

Tip: You can select the objects to be trimmed by clicking the left mouse button one by one or by using a selection method such as Window, Cross window, or Fence, as discussed earlier.

4. Similarly, click on the other entities to be trimmed one by one, see Figure 5.10. The portion of the selected entities are trimmed upto the intersection with the cutting edges, see Figure 5.11.

5. Once you have trimmed all the unwanted entities of the drawing, press ENTER to exit.

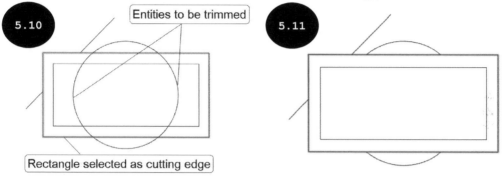

Entities to be trimmed

Rectangle selected as cutting edge

Note: You can also extend the entities upto the nearest intersection or at the intersection with cutting edges/boundaries by using the **Trim** tool. To extend the entities by using the **Trim** tool, press and hold the SHIFT key and then click on the entity to be extended. The selected entity from the side you have selected is extended upto the intersection with cutting edges.

Extending Drawing Entities

You can extend the entities upto their nearest intersection or the intersection with boundaries by using the **Extend** tool of the **Trim** flyout in the **Modify** panel, see Figure 5.12. You can also invoke the **Extend** tool by entering **EX** in the Command Window and then pressing ENTER. The procedure to extend drawing entities by using the **Extend** tool is as follows:

Procedure for Extending Entities

1. Click on the down arrow next to the **Trim** tool in the **Modify** panel. A flyout appears, see Figure 5.12. In this flyout, click on the **Extend** tool. You are prompted to select boundary edges. Alternatively, enter **EX** in the Command Window and then press ENTER to invoke the **Extend** tool.

    ```
    Select boundary edges ...
    Select objects or <select all>:
    ```

2. Click on the objects to be used as the boundary edges for extending entities, see Figure 5.13. You can select rectangles, lines, circles, polylines, construction lines, and so on as the boundary edges. Next, press ENTER. You are prompted to select objects to be extended.

    ```
    Select object to extend or shift-select to trim or
    [Fence Crossing Project Edge Undo]:
    ```

> **Note:**   If you want to extend entities upto their nearest intersection, skip the step 2 of selecting boundary edges discussed above and then press ENTER. Next, directly click on the entity to be extended. The selected entity gets extended upto their nearest intersection.

3. Click on the entity to be extended, see Figure 5.13. The portion of the selected entity is extended upto the intersection with the boundary edges, see Figure 5.14. Also, you are prompted to select another objects to be extended.

    ```
    Select object to extend or shift-select to trim or
    [Fence Crossing Project Edge Undo]:
    ```

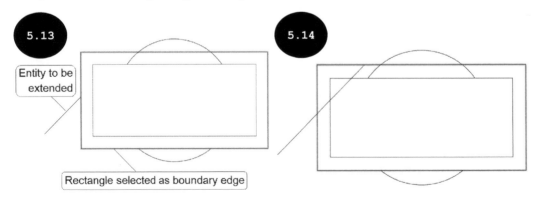

5.13

Entity to be extended

Rectangle selected as boundary edge

5.14

4. Similarly, click on the entities to be extended one by one, see Figure 5.15. The portion of the selected entities gets extended upto the intersection with the boundary edges, see Figure 5.16.

> **Tip:**   You can select the entities to be extended by clicking the left mouse button or by using a selection method such as Window, Cross window, or Fence.

5. Once you have extended the required entities of a drawing, press ENTER or right-click to exit the **Extend** tool.

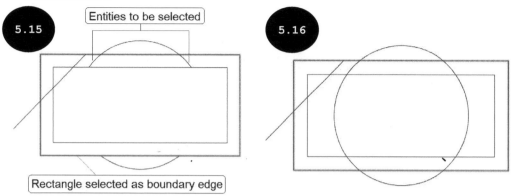

Working with Array

Array is a very powerful feature of AutoCAD for creating multiple instances/duplicate copies of an existing geometry in rectangular fashion, circular fashion, or along a path, see Figures 5.17 through 5.19.

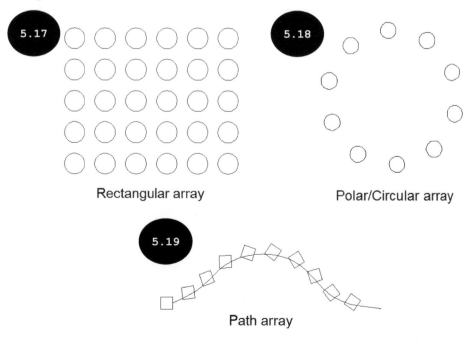

> **Note:** You can also trim entities upto the nearest intersection or at the intersection of boundaries by using the **Extend** tool. To trim the entities by using the **Extend** tool, press and hold the SHIFT key and then click on the entity to be trimmed. The selected entity from the side you have clicked is trimmed upto the intersection.

In AutoCAD, you can create rectangular array, polar/circular array, and path array by using the **Rectangular Array**, **Polar Array**, and **Path Array** tools of the **Array** flyout in the **Modify** panel, see Figure 5.20. The procedures to create arrays are as follows:

5.20

Array flyout

Procedure for Creating Rectangular Array

1.   Invoke the **Array** flyout in the **Modify** panel (see Figure 5.20) and then click on the **Rectangle Array** tool. You are prompted to select objects to be array. Alternatively, enter **AR** in the Command Window and then press ENTER to invoke the tool.

```
Select objects:
```

2.   Click on the object/objects to be array in the drawing area, see Figure 5.21. Next, press ENTER or right-click. The preview of the rectangular array appears in the drawing area with default parameters, see Figure 5.22. Also, the **Array Creation** tab appears in the **Ribbon** which is provided with different options for controlling the array parameters, see Figure 5.23. In addition, you are prompted to select array grips to edit array.

```
Select grip to edit array or [ASsociative Base point COUnt Spacing
COLumns Rows Levels eXit] <eXit>:
```

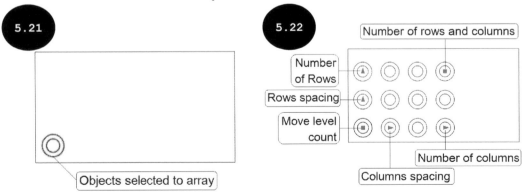

5.21

Objects selected to array

5.22

Number of rows and columns

Number of Rows

Rows spacing

Move level count

Number of columns

Columns spacing

Tip: You can select the objects to be array by clicking the left mouse button or by using a selection method such as Window, Cross window, or Fence, as discussed earlier.

Note: If you have invoked the array tool by entering AR in Command Window then after selecting the objects to be array, you are prompted to select type of array "Enter array type [Rectangular PAth POlar] <Polar>:". Click on the **Rectangular** option in the command prompt or enter **R** and then press ENTER to create rectangular array.

3. Specify the columns count, rows count, column spacing, and row spacing for the rectangular array in the respective fields in the **Columns** and **Rows** panel of the **Array Creation** tab, see Figure 5.23.

Tip: You can also use the grips that appear in the preview of rectangular array (refer to Figure 5.22) for specifying array parameters such as columns count, rows count, and column spacing. For example, to increase or decrease the number of array columns, click on the **Number of columns** grip (refer to Figure 5.22) and then move the cursor toward the right or left to change the array columns count and then click to specify the placement point.

4. Once you are done with editing the array parameters, press ENTER to exit. The rectangular array is created, see Figure 5.24.

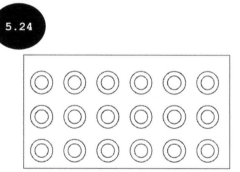

Procedure for Creating Polar/Circular Array

1. Invoke the **Array** flyout and then click on the **Polar Array** tool, see Figure 5.25. You are prompted to select objects. Alternatively, enter **AR** in the Command Window and then press ENTER.

```
Select objects:
```

2. Select objects to be array in the drawing area. The selected objects get highlighted, see Figure 5.26. You can select one or more than one object to be array by clicking the left mouse button.

3. Once you have selected the objects, press ENTER or right-click. You are also prompted to specify the center point of array.

```
Specify center point of array or [Base point Axis of rotation]:
```

Note: If you have invoked the array tool by entering **AR** in Command Window then after selecting the objects to be array, you are prompted to select type of array "Enter array type [Rectangular PAth POlar] <Polar>:". Click on the **POlar** option in the command prompt or enter **PO** in the Command Window and then press ENTER to create polar array.

4. Click to specify the center point of the array. The preview of circular/polar array appears in the drawing area with default parameters, see Figure 5.27. Also, the **Array Creation** tab appears in the **Ribbon** which is provided with different options for controlling the array parameters. In addition, you are prompted to select array grips to edit array.

```
Select grip to edit array or [ASsociative Base point Items Angle
between Fill angle ROWs Levels ROTate items eXit] <eXit>:
```

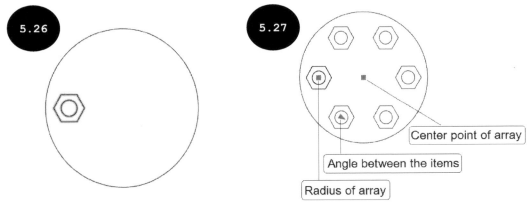

5. Specify the item count and angle between items for the circular array in the respective fields available in the **Items** panel of the **Array Creation** tab. Alternatively, use the grips, which appear in the preview of the array (refer to Figure 5.27) for specifying array parameters.

6. Once you have edited the array parameters, press ENTER to exit. The circular/polar array is created, see Figure 5.28.

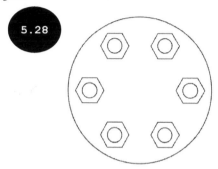

5.28

Procedure for Creating Path Array

1. Invoke the **Array** flyout and then click on the **Path Array** tool. You are prompted to select objects. Alternatively, enter **AR** in the Command Window and then press ENTER.

   ```
   Select objects:
   ```

2. Select objects to be array. The selected objects get highlighted, see Figure 5.29. For selecting multiple objects you can use Window or Cross Window selection method. After selecting the objects to be array, press ENTER or right-click. You are also prompted to select path curve.

   ```
   Select path curve:
   ```

3. Click on the path curve along which you want to pattern the selected objects, see Figure 5.29. The preview of path array appears in the drawing area with default parameters, see Figure 5.30. Also, the **Array Creation** tab appears in the **Ribbon** which is provided with different options for controlling the array parameters. You are also prompted to select grips to edit array.

   ```
   Select grip to edit array or [ASsociative Method Base point
   Tangent direction Items Rows Levels Align items Z direction eXit]
   <eXit>:
   ```

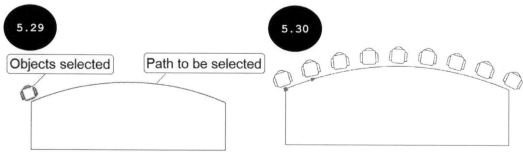

5.29

Objects selected

Path to be selected

5.30

4. Specify the item spacing for the path array in the respective field available in the **Items** panel of the **Array Creation** tab. Alternatively, use the grips which appear in the preview of path array for specifying the spacing between the items.

5. Once you have edited the array parameters, press ENTER. The path array is created, see Figure 5.31.

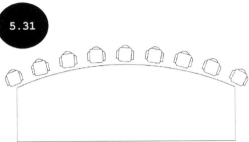

Mirroring Drawing Entities

In AutoCAD, you can create a mirror image of the drawing entities/objects about a mirroring line by using the **Mirror** tool of the **Modify** panel, see Figure 5.32. The procedure to mirror drawing entities is as follows:

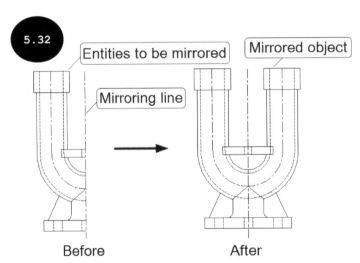

Procedure for Mirroring Entities

1. Click on the **Mirror** tool in the **Modify** panel. You are prompted to select objects. Alternatively, enter **MI** in the Command Window and then press ENTER.

   Select objects:

2. Select objects/entities to be mirrored and then press ENTER. You are prompted to select first point of the mirror line. For selecting multiple objects, you can use the Window or Cross Window selection method.

    ```
    Specify first point of mirror line:
    ```

3. Click to specify the first point of the mirror line. You are prompted to select second point of the mirror line.

    ```
    Specify first point of mirror line: Specify second point of mirror
    line:
    ```

4. Click to specify the second point of the mirror line. You are prompted to define whether to erase the source/original objects. By default, the **No** option is selected.

    ```
    Erase source objects? [Yes No] <N>:
    ```

Note: The mirroring line is an imaginary line which can be defined by specifying two points in the drawing area.

5. Press ENTER to accept the default option (**No**) for keeping the source/original objects in the resultant drawing, see Figure 5.33 (a). The mirror image is created.

Note: If you do not want to keep the source/original objects in the resultant drawing then enter Y in the Command Window and then press ENTER, see Figure 5.33 (b).

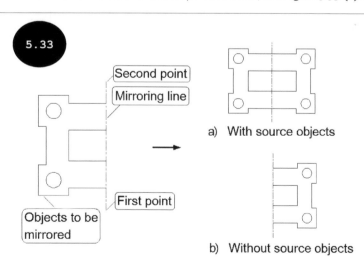

5.33

Second point
Mirroring line

a) With source objects

First point

Objects to be mirrored

b) Without source objects

Filleting Drawing Entities

A fillet is a curved edge which is used to remove or eliminate sharp edges of the model that can cause injury while handling. Also, fillet distributes the stress of the model, which makes model more durable and capable of withstanding larger loads. Figure 5.34 shows a drawing with fillets on its corners.

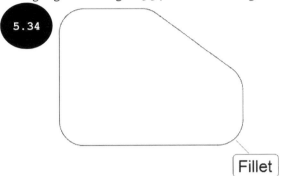

In AutoCAD, you can create fillet between two intersecting or non intersecting entities/objects by using the **Fillet** tool of the **Modify** panel, see Figure 5.35. The procedure to create fillet is as follows:

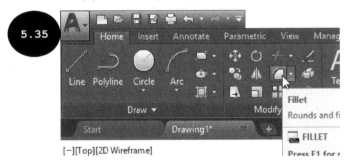

Procedure for Creating Fillet

1. Click on the **Fillet** tool in the **Modify** panel, see Figure 5.35. You are prompted to select the first object. Alternatively, enter **F** in the Command Window and then press ENTER to invoke the **Fillet** tool.

    ```
    Select first object or [Undo Polyline Radius Trim Multiple]:
    ```

    Before you select the first object for the fillet, it is recommended to specify the radius of the fillet. If you do not specify the fillet radius then the default fillet radius will be applied.

2. Click on the **Radius** option in the command prompt or enter **R** in the Command Window and then press ENTER. You are prompted to specify fillet radius.

    ```
    Specify fillet radius <current>:
    ```

3. Enter the radius value and then press ENTER. You are prompted to select first object.

    ```
    Select first object or [Undo Polyline Radius Trim Multiple]:
    ```

4. Click on the first object of the fillet, see Figure 5.36. You are prompted to select second object.

```
Select  second  object  or  shift-select  to  apply  corner  or
[Radius]:
```

5. Click on the second object of the fillet, see Figure 5.36. The fillet of specified radius is created, see Figure 5.37.

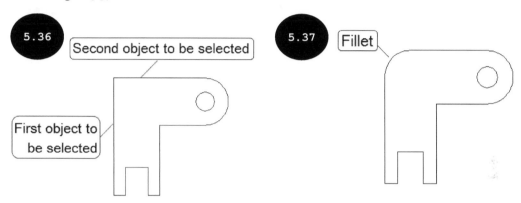

You can also fillet non intersecting parallel or non parallel entities, see Figures 5.38 and 5.39.

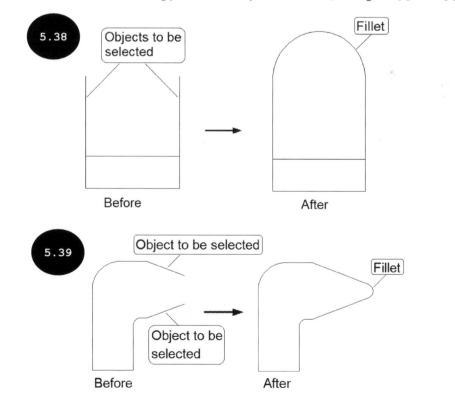

Note: You can fillet all the corners of a polyline object at a time, see Figure 5.40. To fillet all corners of a polyline object, click on the **Polyline** option in the command prompt when you are prompted to select first object "Select first object or [Undo Polyline Radius Trim Multiple]:". Alternatively, enter **P** in the Command Window and then press ENTER. Next, select the polyline object whose all corners are to be filleted.

By default, when you create a fillet at a corner, an arc/fillet is created by trimming the selected objects, see Figure 5.41 (a). This is because the trim mode is set to **Trim**. To set the trim mode to **No Trim**, click on the **Trim** option in the command prompt when you are prompted to select first object "Select first object or [Undo Polyline Radius Trim Multiple]:". Next, enter **N** in the Command Window and then press ENTER. Now, on creating a fillet at a corner, an arc/fillet is created without trimming the selected objects, see Figure 5.41 (b).

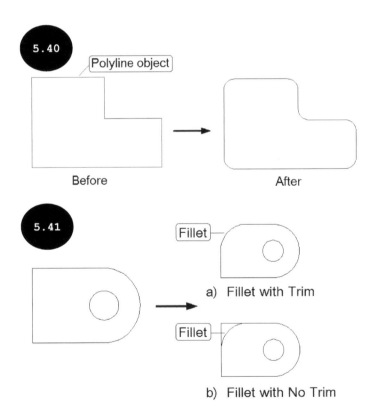

5.40

Polyline object

Before   After

5.41

Fillet

a) Fillet with Trim

Fillet

b) Fillet with No Trim

Chamfering Drawing Entities

A chamfer is a bevel edge that is non perpendicular to its adjacent edges. In AutoCAD, you can create chamfer by using the **Chamfer** tool of the **Modify** panel, see Figure 5.42. Figure 5.43 shows a drawing with chamfer at its upper left corner.

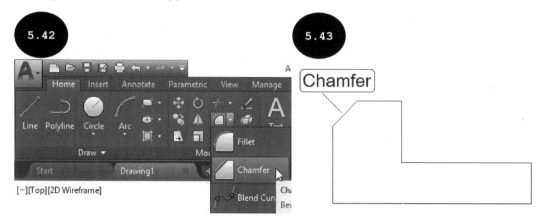

In AutoCAD, you can create chamfer by using two methods: **Distance distance** method and **Angle distance** method. The procedures to create chamfer by using these methods are as follows:

Procedure for Creating Chamfer by Distance distance Method

1. Click on the down arrow next to the **Fillet** tool in the **Modify** panel. A flyout appears. In this flyout, click on the **Chamfer** tool, see Figure 5.42. Alternatively, enter **CHA** in the Command Window and then press ENTER. You are prompted to select first line for creating chamfer.

    ```
    Select first line or [Undo Polyline Distance Angle Trim mEthod
    Multiple]:
    ```

    Before you select the first line for the chamfer, it is recommended to define the type of method for creating chamfer.

2. Click on the **Distance** option in the command prompt or enter **D** and then press ENTER to invoke the **Distance distance** method. You are prompted to specify first chamfer distance.

    ```
    Specify first chamfer distance <current>:
    ```

3. Enter the first chamfer distance value and then press ENTER. You are prompted to specify second chamfer distance.

    ```
    Specify second chamfer distance <current>:
    ```

4. Enter the second chamfer distance value and then press ENTER. You are prompted to select first line for creating chamfer.

    ```
    Select first line or [Undo Polyline Distance Angle Trim mEthod
    Multiple]:
    ```

5. Click on the first chamfer line, see Figure 5.44. You are prompted to select second chamfer line.

```
Select  second  line  or  shift-select  to  apply  corner  or  [Distance
Angle Method]:
```

6. Click on the second chamfer line, see Figure 5.44. The chamfer of specified distance is created, see Figure 5.45.

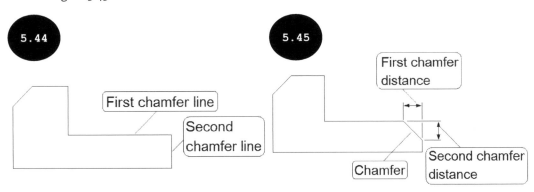

Procedure for Creating Chamfer by Angle distance Method

1. Click on the down arrow next to the **Fillet** tool in the **Modify** panel. A flyout appears. In this flyout, click on the **Chamfer** tool. Alternatively, enter **CHA** in the Command Window and then press ENTER. You are prompted to select first line for creating chamfer.

```
Select  first  line  or  [Undo  Polyline  Distance  Angle  Trim  mEthod
Multiple]:
```

2. Click on the **Angle** option in the command prompt or enter **A** and then press ENTER to invoke the **Angle distance** method. You are prompted to specify the chamfer length on the first line.

```
Specify  chamfer  length  on   the  first  line  <current>:
```

3. Enter the chamfer length value and then press ENTER. You are prompted to specify chamfer angle.

```
Specify  chamfer  angle  from  the  first  line  <0>:
```

4. Enter the chamfer angle value and then press ENTER. You are prompted to select chamfer first line.

```
Select  first  line  or  [Undo  Polyline  Distance  Angle  Trim  mEthod
Multiple]:
```

5. Click on the first chamfer line, see Figure 5.46. You are prompted to select second chamfer line.

```
Select second line or shift-select to apply corner or [Distance
Angle Method]:
```

6. Click on the second chamfer line, see Figure 5.46. The chamfer of specified angle and distance is created, see Figure 5.47.

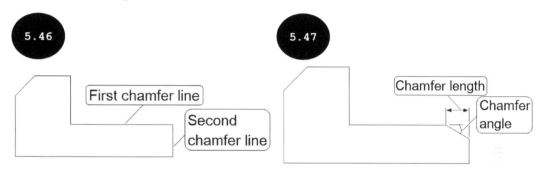

Offsetting Drawing Entities

In AutoCAD, you can offset an existing object/entity at a specified offset distance and create a new object, see Figure 5.48. Note that the shape of the newly created object is same and parallel to the object selected. You can offset an existing entity or entities by using the **Offset** tool of the **Modify** panel, see Figure 5.49. The procedure to create objects by offsetting existing entities is as follows:

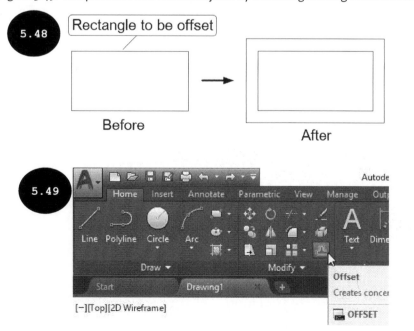

Procedure for Offsetting Objects/Entities

1. Click on the **Offset** tool in the **Modify** panel. You are prompted to specify offset distance. Alternatively, enter O in the Command Window and then press ENTER.

    ```
    Specify offset distance or [Through Erase Layer] <current>:
    ```

2. Enter offset distance value and then press ENTER. You are prompted to select object to be offset.

    ```
    Select object to offset or [Exit Undo] <Exit>:
    ```

> **Note:** In addition to specifying the offset distance value, you can specify two points in the drawing area by clicking the left mouse button for defining the offset distance.

3. Click on the object to be offset, see Figure 5.50. The preview of the offset entity is attached to the cursor, see Figure 5.50. You are prompted to specify a point for defining the offset side.

    ```
    Specify point on side to offset or [Exit Multiple Undo] <Exit>:
    ```

4. Click on either side of the selected entity for defining the offset side. The offset entity is created, see Figure 5.51. Also, you are again prompted to select object to offset.

    ```
    Select object to offset or [Exit Undo] <Exit>:
    ```

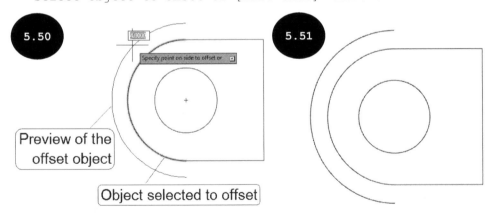

5. Similarly, you can select the other objects one by one to offset, see Figure 5.52.

6. Once you have created the offset entities, press ENTER to exit.

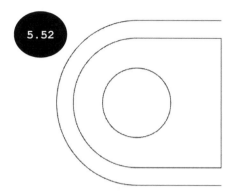

> **Note:** By default, when you offset an entity, the original selected entity remains available in the drawing area and new offset entity gets created. This is because the erase mode is turned off, by default. To turn on the erase mode, click on the **Erase** option in the command prompt when you are prompted to select first object "`Specify offset distance or [Through Erase Layer] <current>:`". Next, enter Y and then press ENTER. Now, on offsetting an object, the original object selected to be offset is erased from the drawing area and a new offset object gets created.

Moving Drawing Objects

While creating drawing in AutoCAD, sometimes you may need to move the drawing objects from their current location to the new location in the drawing area. In AutoCAD, you can move the drawing objects from one location to another by using the **Move** tool of the **Modify** panel, see Figure 5.53. The procedure to move the drawing objects is as follows:

Procedure for Moving Objects/Entities

1. Click on the **Move** tool in the **Modify** panel (refer to Figure 5.53) or enter **M** in the Command Window and then press ENTER. You are prompted to select objects to be moved.

   ```
   Select objects:
   ```

2. Click on the object to be moved in the drawing area, see Figure 5.54 (a). You can select one or more than one object to be moved. For selecting multiple objects, you can use the Window or Cross Window selection method.

3. Once you have selected objects to be moved, press ENTER. You are prompted to specify base point. Note that the base point acts as a reference point for moving the selected objects.

```
Specify base point or [Displacement] <Displacement>:
```

4. Click to specify the base point in the drawing area, see Figure 5.54 (a). You are prompted to specify second/placement point for the selected objects. Also, the preview of selected object is attached to the cursor.

```
Specify second point or <use first point as displacement>:
```

5. Click to specify second point in the drawing area as the placement point for the selected objects, see Figure 5.54 (a). The object is moved to the specified location, see Figure 5.54 (b).

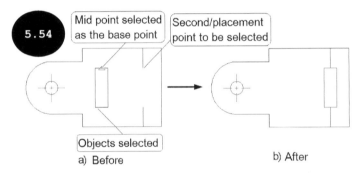

a) Before   b) After

Copying Drawing Objects

While creating drawing in AutoCAD, you may need to create duplicate copies of an object. You can create multiple copies of an object by using the **Copy** tool of the **Modify** panel, see Figure 5.55. The procedure to copy objects is as follows:

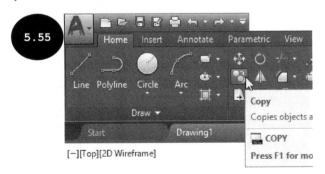

Procedure for Copying Objects/Entities

1. Click on the **Copy** tool in the **Modify** panel (refer to Figure 5.55) or enter CO in the Command Window and then press ENTER. You are prompted to select objects to be copied.

    ```
    Select objects:
    ```

2. Click on the object to be copied, see Figure 5.56 (a). You can select one or multiple objects to be copied. For selecting multiple objects, you can use the Window or Cross Window selection method.

3. Once you have selected objects, press ENTER. You are prompted to specify a base point. Note that the base point acts as a reference point for copying the selected objects.

    ```
    Specify base point or [Displacement mOde] <Displacement>:
    ```

4. Click to specify the base point in the drawing area, see Figure 5.56 (a). You are prompted to specify second/placement point for the selected objects. Also, the preview of selected object is attached to the cursor.

    ```
    Specify    second    point    or    [Array]    <use    first    point    as
    displacement>:
    ```

5. Click to specify second/placement point for the selected objects in the drawing area, see Figure 5.56 (a). The selected object is copied to the specified location, see Figure 5.56 (b). Also, you are still prompted to specify the second/placement point. Similarly, you can create multiple copies of the selected object by specifying the respective placement points one after another.

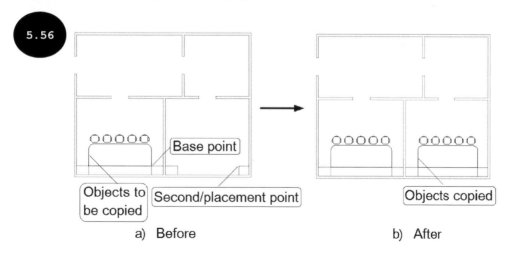

a) Before   b) After

6. Once you have copied the selected object, press the ENTER key to exit.

Rotating Drawing Objects

While creating drawing in AutoCAD, you may need to rotate objects at an angle around a point. You can rotate an object or a set of objects at an angle by using the **Rotate** tool of the **Modify** panel, see Figure 5.57. The procedure to rotate objects is as follows:

Procedure for Rotating Objects/Entities

1. Click on the **Rotate** tool in the **Modify** panel (refer to Figure 5.57) or enter **RO** in the Command Window and then press ENTER. You are prompted to select objects.

    ```
    Select objects:
    ```

2. Click on the object to be rotated, see Figure 5.58 (a). You can select one or multiple objects to be rotated. For selecting multiple objects, you can use the Window or Cross Window selection method.

3. Once you have selected objects, press ENTER. You are prompted to specify a base point. Note that the base point acts as a reference point for rotating the selected objects.

    ```
    Specify base point:
    ```

4. Click to specify the base point in the drawing area, see Figure 5.58 (a). You are prompted to specify rotational angle. Also, the preview of selected objects is attached to the cursor.

    ```
    Specify rotation angle or [Copy Reference] <current>:
    ```

5. Enter rotational angle value and then press ENTER. The selected objects are rotated at a specified angle, see Figure 5.58 (b). Note that you can also specify the rotational angle by clicking the left mouse button in the drawing area.

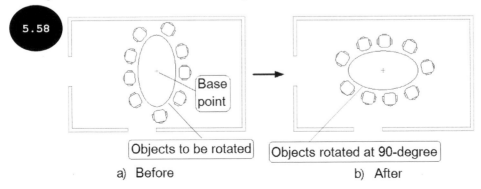

a) Before   b) After

Scaling Drawing Objects

In addition to moving, rotating, and copying drawing objects, you may need to increase or decrease the scale of the objects as well while creating or editing a drawing. With increasing/decreasing the scale of a drawing object, the size of the object is enlarged/shrunk, respectively, by maintaining the aspect ratio of the object. You can scale an object or a set of objects by using the **Scale** tool of the **Modify** panel, see Figure 5.59. The procedure to scale objects is as follows:

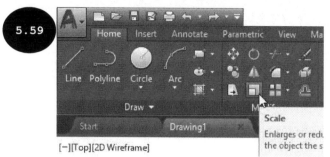

Procedure for Scaling Objects/Entities

1. Click on the **Scale** tool in the **Modify** panel or enter SC in the Command Window and then press ENTER. You are prompted to select objects.

   ```
   Select objects:
   ```

2. Click on the object to be scaled, see Figure 5.60 (a). You can select one or multiple objects to be scaled. For selecting multiple objects, you can use the Window or Cross Window selection method.

3. Once you have selected objects, press ENTER. You are prompted to specify a base point. Note that the base point acts as a reference point for scaling the selected objects.

   ```
   Specify base point:
   ```

4. Click to specify a base point in the drawing area, see Figure 5.60 (a). You are prompted to specify scale factor. Also, the preview of selected object is attached to the cursor. Note that as you move the cursor, the scale of the objects increases or decreases, accordingly.

   ```
   Specify scale factor or [Copy Reference]:
   ```

5. Enter scale factor and then press ENTER. The selected objects are scaled equally by maintaining the aspect ratio of the object with respect to the specified base point, see Figure 5.60 (b). Note that to enlarge the selected object, you need to enter scale factor greater than 1 and to shrink the selected object, you need to enter scale factor smaller than 1.

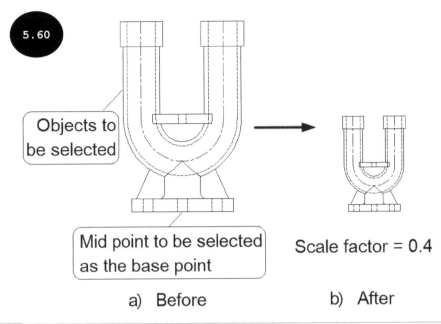

5.60

Objects to be selected

Mid point to be selected as the base point

Scale factor = 0.4

a) Before

b) After

Note: You can also scale an object by specifying the current length and the new length of the object instead of specifying the scale factor. If you do so, the object gets scaled relative to the new specified length. To scale an object by specifying the current length and the new length, click on the **Reference** option in the command prompt when you are prompted to specify scale factor "`Specify    scale    factor    or    [Copy Reference]:`". Next, specify the current length value of the object as the reference length and then press ENTER. You can also pick two points in the drawing area to specify the current/reference length of the object. After specifying the current length, enter the new length of the object and then press ENTER. The selected object gets scaled relative to the new length specified. For example, if the current length of the object is 90 unit and you want it to be 35 unit after scaling it then you need to enter 90 as the current/reference length and 35 as the new length of the object.

Stretching Drawing Objects

In AutoCAD, you can stretch an object or a group of objects in order to change its shape and size. You can stretch objects by using the **Stretch** tool of the **Modify** panel, see Figure 5.61. The procedure to stretch objects is as follows:

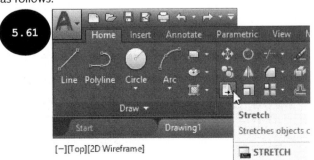

5.61

Procedure for Stretching Objects/Entities

1. Click on the **Stretch** tool in the **Modify** panel (refer to Figure 5.61) or enter S in the Command Window and then press ENTER. You are prompted to select objects to be stretched.

    ```
    Select objects:
    ```

2. Select objects by drawing a Cross Window around them such that the Cross Window partially encloses the objects to be stretched, see Figure 5.62 (a). You can select the objects to be stretched by using the Cross Window or Cross Polygon selection method.

Note: Only the objects that are partially enclosed by the Cross Window or Cross Polygon selection get stretched. The objects that are completely enclosed within the Cross Window get moved rather than being stretched.

3. Once you are done with selecting objects to be stretched, press ENTER. You are prompted to specify base point.

    ```
    Specify base point or [Displacement] <Displacement>:
    ```

4. Click to specify the base point for stretching the selected objects in the drawing area, see Figure 5.62 (a). You are prompted to specify the second point.

    ```
    Specify second point or <use first point as displacement>:
    ```

5. Click to specify the second/placement point. The portion of the objects selected get stretched by leaving the rest of the portion unchanged, see Figure 5.62 (b).

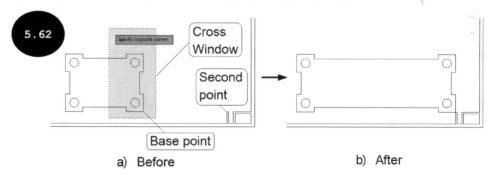

a) Before   b) After

Lengthening Drawing Objects

In AutoCAD, you can shorten or extend the line objects by using the **Lengthen** tool of the expanded **Modify** panel, see Figure 5.63. You can expand the **Modify** panel by clicking on the arrow available in the title bar of the **Modify** panel. You can shorten or extend the line object by entering the delta length, percentage, total length, or by dragging the object. The procedures to lengthen object are as follows:

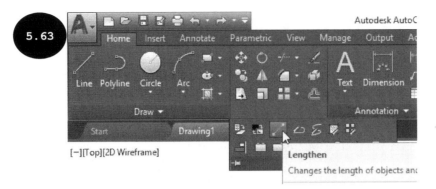

Procedure for Lengthening Object by Specifying Delta Value

1. Click on the **Lengthen** tool in the expanded **Modify** panel (see Figure 5.63) or enter **LEN** in the Command Window and then press ENTER. You are prompted to select an object.

```
Select an object or [DElta Percent Total DYnamic]:
```

2. Click on the **DElta** option in the command prompt or enter **DE** and then press ENTER. You are prompted to specify delta length of the object to be lengthened.

```
Enter delta length or [Angle]: <0.0000>:
```

> **Note:**   The delta length is the length of the object which measures the object. On entering the positive delta value, the length of the object is increased (extended) and on entering the negative delta value, the length of the object is decreased (shorten).

3. Enter delta length and then press ENTER. You are prompted to select an object.

```
Select an object to change or [Undo]:
```

4. Select the object to be lengthened, see Figure 5.64 (a). The length of the selected object is increased/decreased by the length specified, see Figure 5.64 (b). You are prompted to select the object to be lengthened again.

```
Select an object to change or [Undo]:
```

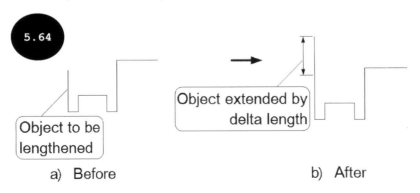

a) Before   b) After

5. You can select multiple objects one after another to be lengthened by the specified delta length. Once you have lengthen the objects, press ENTER to exit.

Procedure for Lengthening Object by Specifying Percentage

1. Click on the **Lengthen** tool in the expanded **Modify** panel or enter **LEN** in the Command Window and then press ENTER. You are prompted to select an object.

   ```
   Select an object or [DElta Percent Total DYnamic]:
   ```

2. Click on the **Percent** option in the command prompt or enter **P** and then press ENTER. You are prompted to specify percentage length of the object.

   ```
   Enter percentage length <current>:
   ```

Note: The current length of the object is taken as 100 percent. As a result, on entering the percentage value more than 100, the length of the object is increased and on entering the percentage value less than 100, the length of the object is decreased. For example, by entering percentage as 200, the length of the object becomes double of the current length.

3. Enter percentage value for increasing/decreasing the length of the object and then press ENTER. You are prompted to select an object.

   ```
   Select an object to change or [Undo]:
   ```

4. Select the object to be lengthened. The length of the object is increased/decreased with respect to the specified percentage. You are prompted to select object again.

   ```
   Select an object to change or [Undo]:
   ```

5. You can select multiple objects one after another in order to increase/decrease the length of the object as per the specified percentage value. Once you have lengthen the objects, press ENTER to exit.

Procedure for Lengthening Object by Specifying Total Length

1. Click on the **Lengthen** tool in the expanded **Modify** panel or enter **LEN** in the Command Window and then press ENTER. You are prompted to select an object.

   ```
   Select an object or [DElta Percent Total DYnamic]:
   ```

2. Click on the **Total** option in the command prompt or enter **T** and then press ENTER. You are prompted to specify the total length of the object.

   ```
   Specify total length or [Angle] <current>:
   ```

Note: The total length of a object is its overall length. You can specify total length less/greater than the current length of the object.

3.   Enter the new total length value of the object and then press ENTER. You are prompted to select an object.

```
Select an object to change or [Undo]:
```

4.   Select the object to be lengthened. The current length of the object is changed to the new specified length. You are prompted to select the object again.

```
Select an object to change or [Undo]:
```

5.   You can select objects one after another in order to increase/decrease the length of the object to the specified total length. Once you have lengthen the objects, press ENTER to exit.

Procedure for Lengthening Object by Dragging

1.   Click on the **Lengthen** tool in the expanded **Modify** panel or enter **LEN** in the Command Window and then press ENTER. You are prompted to select an object.

```
Select an object or [DElta Percent Total DYnamic]:
```

2.   Click on the **DYnamic** option in the command prompt or enter **DY** and then press ENTER. You are prompted to select an object.

```
Select an object to change or [Undo]:
```

3.   Select the object to be lengthened. The end point of the object selected is attached to the cursor. As you move the cursor, the length of the object is increased or decreased. Also, you are prompted to specify the new end point of the object.

```
Specify new end point:
```

4.   Click to specify the new end point of the object. The length of the object is increased/decreased with respect to the new end point specified. Next, press ENTER to exit.

Tutorial 1

Create the drawing shown in the Figure 5.65. The dimensions shown in the figure are for your reference only. You will learn about applying dimensions in later chapters.

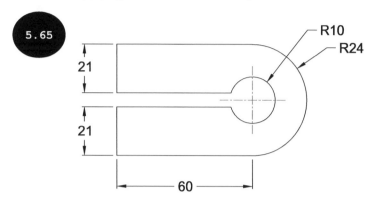

Section 1: Starting AutoCAD

1. Double-click on the AutoCAD icon on your desktop to start AutoCAD. The initial screen of AutoCAD appears with **Start** tab, see Figure 5.66.

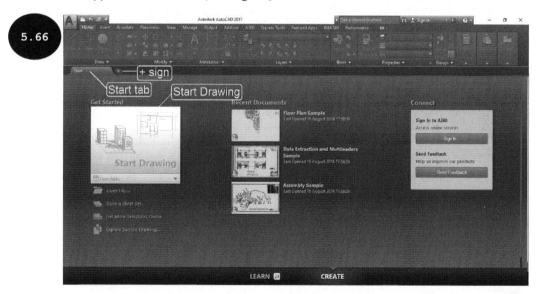

2. Click on the + sign next to the **Start** tab, see Figure 5.66. The new drawing file with the default drawing template is invoked. Alternatively, click on **Start Drawing** in the **Get Started** section of the **Start** tab to start a new drawing file with default drawing template. You can also start a new drawing file by using the **New** tool of the **Quick Access Toolbar**, which is at the top left corner of AutoCAD screen.

Section 2: Selecting Workspace for Creating Drawing

1.   Make sure that the **Drafting & Annotation** workspace is selected as the workspace for creating drawing.

Section 3: Defining the Drawing Limits

1.   Follow the command sequence given below for defining the drawing limits.

```
Command: LIMITS (ENTER)
Specify lower left corner or [ON/OFF]<0.0000,0.0000>: 0,0 (ENTER)
Specify upper right corner <12.0000,9.0000>: 150,110  (ENTER)
```

Section 4: Creating Drawing

1.   Click on the arrow next to the circle tool in the **Draw** panel. The **Circle** flyout appears. In this flyout, click on the **Center, Radius** tool. Alternatively, enter C in the Command Window and then press ENTER. You are prompted to specify the center point of the circle.

```
Specify center point for circle or [3P 2P Ttr (tan tan radius)]:
```

2.   Click in the drawing area to specify the center point of the circle. You are prompted to specify the radius of the circle.

```
Specify radius of circle or [Diameter]:
```

3.   Enter **24** and then press ENTER. The circle of radius 24 unit is created, see Figure 5.67.

4.   Invoke the **Center, Radius** tool again. You are prompted to specify the center point of the circle.

```
Specify center point for circle or [3P 2P Ttr (tan tan radius)]:
```

5.   Move the cursor toward the center point of the existing circle in the drawing area and then click to specify the center point of the circle when cursor snaps to the center point of the existing circle. You are prompted to specify radius of the circle.

```
Specify radius of circle or [Diameter]:
```

6.   Enter **10** and then press ENTER. The circle of radius 10 is created, see Figure 5.68.

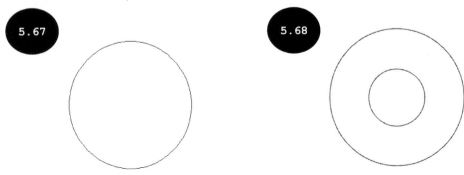

5.67

5.68

7. Click on the **Line** tool in the **Draw** panel and then move the cursor toward the top quadrant of the first drawn circle, see Figure 5.69.

8. Click to specify the first point of the line when cursor snaps to the top quadrant of the first drawn circle, see Figure 5.69. You are prompted to specify second point of the line.

```
Specify next point or [Undo]:
```

9. Make sure that the Ortho mode is turned on. Next, move the cursor horizontally toward the left and then enter **60** as the length of the line, see Figure 5.70. The line of length 60 unit is drawn. Also, you are prompted to specify next point of the line.

```
Specify next point or [Undo]:
```

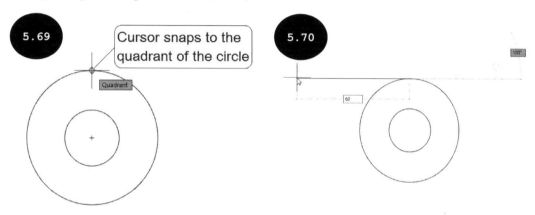

10. Move the cursor vertically downward and then enter **21** as the length of the line. Next, press ENTER. The line of length 21 unit is drawn and you are prompted to specify next point of the line.

```
Specify next point or [Undo]:
```

11. Move the cursor horizontally toward the right and then click to specify the end point of the line anywhere inside the smaller circle of diameter 20, see Figure 5.71. Next, press ENTER to exit.

12. Similarly, draw the other line entities of the drawing by using the **Line** tool, see Figure 5.72.

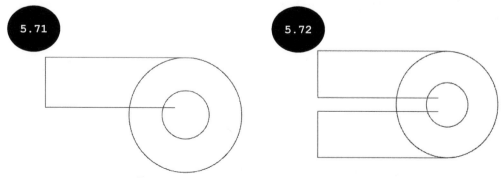

Section 5: Trimming the Drawing Entities

1. Click on the **Trim** tool in the **Modify** panel or enter **TR** in the Command Window and then press ENTER. You are prompted to select cutting edges/boundaries.

    ```
    Select cutting edges ...
    Select objects or <select all>:
    ```

2. Press ENTER to skip the selection of cutting edges/boundaries. You are prompted to select objects to be trimmed.

    ```
    Select object to trim or shift-select to extend or
    [Fence Crossing Project Edge eRase Undo]:
    ```

3. Click on the line entity (1), see Figure 5.73. The selected line entity is trimmed to its next nearest intersection, see Figure 5.74. Also, you are prompted to select objects to be trimmed again.

    ```
    Select object to trim or shift-select to extend or
    [Fence Crossing Project Edge eRase Undo]:
    ```

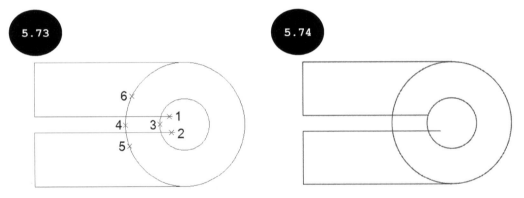

4. Similarly, click on the other entities (2, 3, 4, 5, and 6), see Figure 5.73 to trim them to their nearest intersection. Figure 5.75 shows the drawing after trimming all the unwanted entities of the drawing.

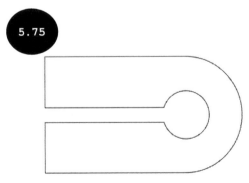

Section 6: Saving the Drawing

After creating the drawing, you need to save it.

1. Click on the **Save** tool in the **Quick Access Toolbar**. The **Save Drawing As** dialog box appears.

2. Browse to the *AutoCAD* folder and then create a folder with the name *Chapter 5* inside the *AutoCAD* folder.

3. Enter **Tutorial 1** in the **File name** field of the dialog box and then click on the **Save** button. The drawing is saved with the name Tutorial 1 in the *Chapter 5* folder.

Tutorial 2

Create the drawing shown in the Figure 5.76. The dimensions shown in the figure are for your reference only. You will learn about applying dimensions in the later chapters.

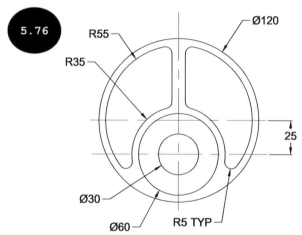

Section 1: Starting AutoCAD

1. Start AutoCAD, if not started already. Next, click on the **New** tool in the **Quick Access Toolbar**, which is at the top left corner of AutoCAD screen. The **Select template** dialog box appears.

2. In the **Select template** dialog box, click on the *acad.dwt* template and then click on the **Open** button. A new drawing file with *acad.dwt* template is invoked.

3. Specify the drawing limits.

Section 2: Creating Construction Lines

1. Click on the **Construction Line** tool in the expanded **Draw** panel of the **Home** tab. You are prompted to specify a point in the drawing area. You can also enter **XLINE** in the Command Window and then press ENTER to invoke the **Construction Line** tool.

```
Specify a point or [Hor Ver Ang Bisect Offset]:
```

2. Click on the **Hor** option in the command prompt or enter **H** and then press ENTER to create horizontal construction line. A horizontal construction line is attached to the cursor. Also, you are prompted to specify through point.

```
Specify through point:
```

3. Click in the drawing area to specify a through point. A horizontal construction line is created such that it passes through the specified point. Also, another horizontal construction line is attached to the cursor.

4. Press ENTER to exit the tool.

   Now, you need to create another horizontal construction line at an offset distance of 25 units from the existing horizontal construction line.

5. Invoke the **Construction Line** tool and then click on the **Offset** option of the command prompt or enter **O** and then press ENTER. You are prompted to specify the offset distance.

```
Specify offset distance or [Through] <Through>:
```

6. Enter **25** and then press ENTER. You are prompted to select a line object.

```
Select a line object:
```

7. Click on the existing horizontal construction line. You are prompted to specify the side to offset.

```
Specify side to offset:
```

8. Click on the bottom side of the existing horizontal construction line. The another horizontal construction line at an offset distance of 25 units is created, see Figure 5.77. Next, press ENTER to exit the tool.

9. Similarly, create two vertical construction lines at an offset distance of 5 units from each other by using the **Construction Line** tool, see Figure 5.78.

5.77

5.78

P1

P2

Section 3: Creating Drawing

1. Invoke the **Circle** flyout of the **Draw** panel and then click on the **Circle, Radius** tool. Alternatively, enter **C** in the Command Window and then press ENTER. You are prompted to specify the center point of the circle.

```
Specify center point for circle or [3P 2P Ttr (tan tan radius)]:
```

2. Move the cursor toward the intersection point (P1) created between the upper horizontal and right vertical construction lines, see Figure 5.78.

3. Click to specify the center point of the circle when cursor snaps to the intersection point (P1). You are prompted to specify the radius of the circle.

```
Specify radius of circle or [Diameter]:
```

4. Enter **60** as the radius of the circle. The circle of diameter 120 is created, see Figure 5.79.

5. Similarly, create a circle of radius 55 whose center point is at the intersection point (P1) and a circle of radius 35 whose center point is at the intersection point (P2), see Figure 5.80.

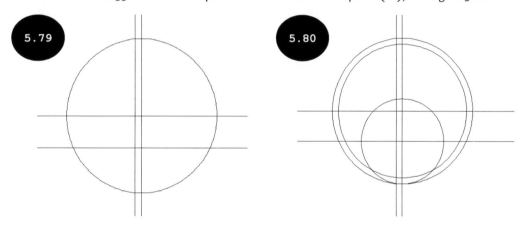

Section 4: Trimming Unwanted Drawing Entities

1. Click on the **Trim** tool in the **Modify** panel or enter **TR** in the Command Window and then press ENTER. You are prompted to select cutting edges/boundaries.

```
Select cutting edges ...
Select objects or <select all>:
```

2. Press ENTER to skip the selection of cutting edges/boundaries. You are prompted to select objects to be trimmed.

```
Select object to trim or shift-select to extend or
[Fence Crossing Project Edge eRase Undo]:
```

3. Click on line entity (1) to trim, see Figure 5.81. The selected line entity is trimmed to its next nearest intersection, see Figure 5.82. Also, you are prompted to select objects to be trimmed again.

```
Select object to trim or shift-select to extend or
[Fence Crossing Project Edge eRase Undo]:
```

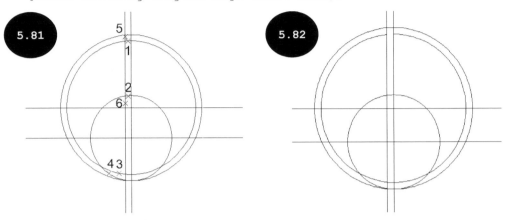

4. Similarly, click on the other entities (2, 3, 4, 5, and 6), see Figure 5.81. Figure 5.83 shows the drawing after trimming all the unwanted entities of the drawing. Next, press ENTER to exit.

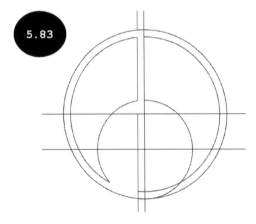

Section 5: Deleting Unwanted Drawing Entities

1. Click on the entities to be deleted (four entities), see Figure 5.84. Next, press the DELETE key. The selected entities of the drawing get deleted, see Figure 5.85.

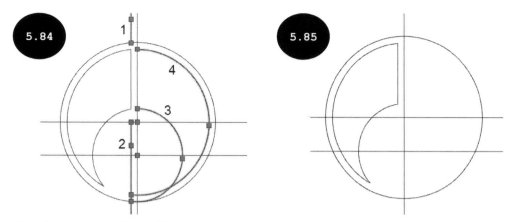

Section 6: Creating Fillets

1. Click on the **Fillet** tool in the **Modify** panel or enter **F** and then press ENTER. You are prompted to select the first object.

    ```
    Select first object or [Undo Polyline Radius Trim Multiple]:
    ```

2. Click on the **Radius** option of the command prompt or enter **R** and then press ENTER. You are prompted to specify the radius of the fillet.

    ```
    Specify fillet radius <0.0000>:
    ```

3. Enter **5** as the fillet radius and then press ENTER. You are prompted to select the first object.

    ```
    Select first object or [Undo Polyline Radius Trim Multiple]:
    ```

4. Click on the first object of the first corner, see Figure 5.86. You are prompted to select the second object.

    ```
    Select object or shift-select to apply corner or [Radius]:
    ```

5. Click on the second object of the first corner, see Figure 5.86. The fillet of radius 5 is created at the first corner of the drawing, see Figure 5.87.

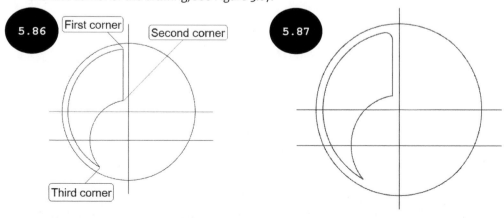

6. Similarly, create fillets of radius 5 on the second and third corners, see Figure 5.88.

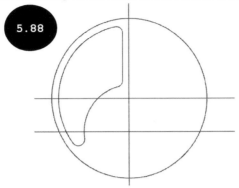

Section 7: Mirroring Drawing Entities

1. Click on the **Mirror** tool in the **Modify** panel or enter **MI** and then press ENTER. You are prompted to select objects.

   ```
   Select objects:
   ```

2. Click on the entities (6 entities) of the drawing, see Figure 5.89. The selected entities get highlighted, see Figure 5.89. Next, press ENTER. You are prompted to specify the first point of the mirror line.

   ```
   Specify first point of mirror line:
   ```

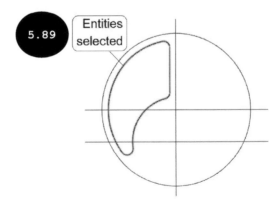

3. Click to specify the first point of the mirroring line anywhere on the vertical construction line. You are prompted to specify the second point of mirror line.

   ```
   Specify first point of mirror line: Specify second point of mirror
   line:
   ```

4. Move the cursor vertically upward and then click to specify the second point on the vertical construction line. You are prompted to specify whether you wanted to erase source objects.

   ```
   Erase source object? [Yes No] <N>:
   ```

5. Enter **N** and then press ENTER. The mirror image of the selected entities is created, see Figure 5.90.

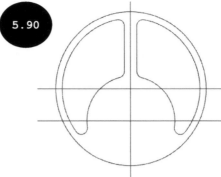

Section 8: Creating Remaining Drawing Entities

1. Create two circles of diameter 60 and diameter 30 by using the **Circle, Diameter** tool, see Figure 5.91.

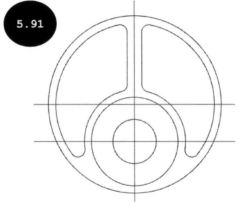

2. Create a layer named as **Construction Line** and then move the construction lines of the drawing to the **Construction Line** layer. Next, hide the **Construction Line** layer. Figure 5.92 shows the final drawing after hiding the construction lines.

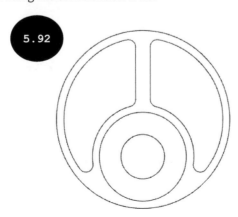

Section 9: Saving the Drawing

1.   Click on the **Save** tool in the **Quick Access Toolbar**. The **Save Drawing As** dialog box appears.

2.   Browse to the *Chapter 5* folder inside the *AutoCAD* folder.

3.   Enter **Tutorial 2** in the **File name** field of the dialog box and then click on the **Save** button. The drawing is saved with the name Tutorial 2 in the *Chapter 5* folder.

Tutorial 3

Create the drawing shown in the Figure 5.93. The dimensions shown in the figure are for your reference only. You will learn about applying dimensions in later chapters.

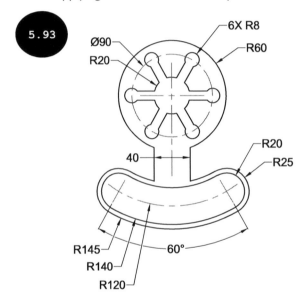

Section 1: Starting AutoCAD

1.   Start a new AutoCAD drawing file and then define the drawing limits.

Section 2: Creating Reference Entities

1.   Click on the **Construction Line** tool in the expanded **Draw** panel of the **Home** tab. You are prompted to specify a point in the drawing area. You can also enter **XLINE** in the Command Window and then press ENTER to invoke the **Construction Line** tool.

```
Specify a point or [Hor Ver Ang Bisect Offset]:
```

2.   Click on the **Ver** option in the command prompt or enter **V** and then press ENTER to create vertical construction line. A vertical construction line is attached with the cursor. Also, you are prompted to specify through point.

```
Specify through point:
```

3. Click in the drawing area to specify the through point. A vertical construction line is created such that it passes through the specified point. Next, press ENTER to exit.

4. Similarly, create a horizontal construction line by using the **Construction Line** tool.

    Now, you need to create construction lines at an angle.

5. Invoke the **Construction Line** tool and then click on the **Ang** option in the command prompt or enter **A** and then press ENTER. You are prompted to specify angle of construction line.

    ```
    Enter angle of xline (0) or [Reference]:
    ```

6. Enter **60** and then press ENTER. A construction line at the angle 60-degree, measured from the horizontal X-axis is attached to the cursor. You are prompted to specify through point.

    ```
    Specify through point:
    ```

7. Click on the intersection point created between the horizontal and vertical construction lines to specify through point. The construction line at the angle 60-degree is created, see Figure 5.94.

8. Similarly, create another construction line at the angle 120-degree from the horizontal X-axis, see Figure 5.95.

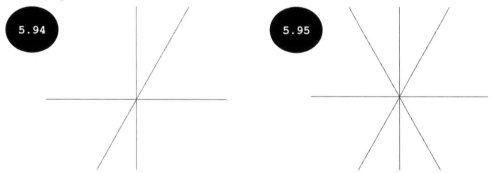

After creating the construction lines, you need to create a reference circle.

9. Invoke the **Circle, Diameter** tool in the **Draw** panel and then create a circle of diameter 90 whose center point is at the intersection of construction lines, see Figure 5.96.

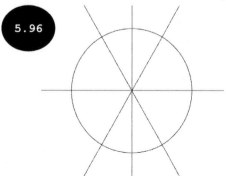

Section 3: Creating Reference Layer

1. Invoke the **LAYER PROPERTIES MANAGER** by clicking on the **Layer Properties** tool in the **Layers** panel of the **Home** tab. Alternatively, enter **LA** in the Command Window and then press ENTER to invoke the **LAYER PROPERTIES MANAGER**.

2. Create a layer named as Reference in the **LAYER PROPERTIES MANAGER** and then assign the Red color and Center linetype to it, see Figure 5.97. Next, exit the **LAYER PROPERTIES MANAGER** by clicking on the cross mark ✕.

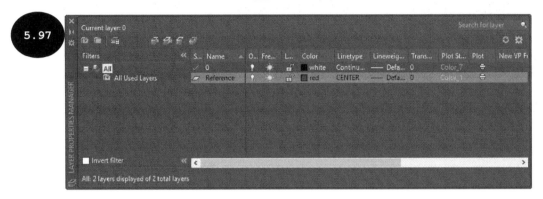

5.97

After creating the Reference layer, you need to move construction lines and the circle of diameter 90 to this Reference layer.

3. Select all construction lines and the circle of diameter 90. Next, invoke the **Layer** drop-down list of the **Layer** panel, see Figure 5.98 and then click on the **Reference** layer to assign all the selected objects to it. Figure 5.99 shows the drawing after moving the construction lines and circle to the Reference layer.

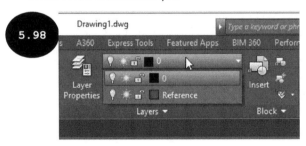

5.98

5.99

Section 4: Creating Drawing Circles

1. Click on the **Circle, Diameter** tool in the **Circle** flyout in the **Draw** panel or enter C in the Command Window and then press ENTER. You are prompted to specify the center point of the circle.

```
Specify center point for circle or [3P 2P Ttr (tan tan radius)]:
```

2. Move the cursor toward the intersection point created between the construction lines and then click to specify the center point of the circle. You are prompted to specify diameter of the circle.

```
Specify radius of circle or [Diameter]: d Specify diameter of
circle:
```

3. Enter **120** as the diameter of the circle. The circle of diameter 120 is created, see Figure 5.100.

4. Similarly, create a circle of diameter 40 at the intersection of construction lines and a circle of diameter 16 whose center point is at the intersection of horizontal construction line and the reference circle, see Figure 5.101.

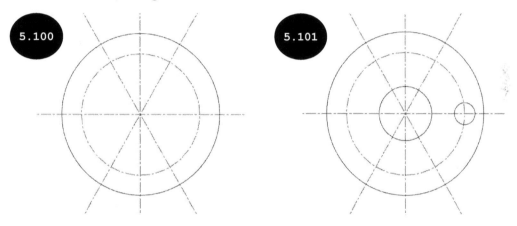

Section 5: Creating Reference Entities

1. Click on the **Offset** tool in the **Modify** panel. Alternatively, enter O and then press ENTER. You are prompted to specify the offset distance.

```
Specify offset distance or [Through Erase Layer] <Through>:
```

2. Enter **5** as the offset distance and then press ENTER. You are prompted to select object to offset.

```
Select object to offset or [Exit Undo] <Exit>:
```

3. Click on the horizontal construction line and then click to specify the placement point on the upper side of the horizontal construction line. A construction line at the offset distance of 5 units from the horizontal construction line is created. Also, you are prompted to select object to offset.

```
Select object to offset or [Exit Undo] <Exit>:
```

4. Click on the horizontal construction line again and then click to specify the placement point on the lower side of the horizontal construction line. A construction line at an offset distance of 5 units from the horizontal construction line is created, see Figure 5.102.

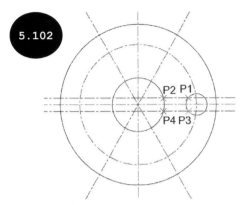

Section 6: Creating Line Entities

1. Click on the **Line** tool in the **Draw** panel. Alternatively, enter **L** and then press ENTER. You are prompted to specify the first point of the line.

    ```
    Specify first point:
    ```

2. Move the cursor to the intersection point P1, refer to Figure 5.102. Next, click to specify the first point of the line when the cursor snaps to the intersection point P1. You are prompted to specify the next point of the line.

    ```
    Specify next point or [Undo]:
    ```

3. Move the cursor horizontally toward the left and then click to specify the end point of the line when the cursor snaps to the intersection point P2, refer to Figure 5.102. Next, press ENTER to exit the **Line** tool.

4. Similarly, create another line from the intersection point P3 to intersection point P4, refer to Figure 5.102. Figure 5.103 shows the resultant drawing after creating the line entities.

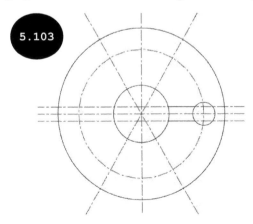

Section 7: Trimming Unwanted Entities

1. Click on the **Trim** tool in the **Modify** panel or enter **TR** in the Command Window and then press ENTER. You are prompted to select cutting edges/boundaries.

```
Select cutting edges ...
Select objects or <select all>:
```

2. Press ENTER to skip the selection of cutting edges/boundaries. You are prompted to select objects to be trimmed.

```
Select object to trim or shift-select to extend or
[Fence Crossing Project Edge eRase Undo]:
```

3. Click on the unwanted entities (four entities) to be trimmed one by one, see Figure 5.104. Figure 5.105 shows the drawing after trimming the unwanted entities.

4. Once you have trimmed the unwanted entities, press ENTER to exit the **Trim** tool.

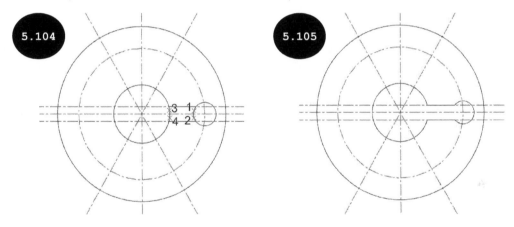

Section 8: Creating Circular/Polar Array

1. Invoke the **Array** flyout of the **Modify** panel and then click on the **Polar Array** tool, see Figure 5.106. You are prompted to select objects.

```
Select objects:
```

2. Click on the circle of diameter 16 and two horizontal lines, see Figure 5.107. The selected objects get highlighted.

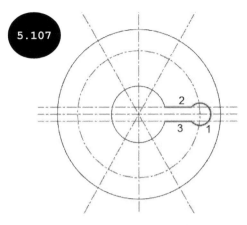

5.107

3. After selecting the objects to be array, press ENTER. You are prompted to specify the center point of array.

    Specify center point of array or [Base point Axis of rotation]:

4. Click to specify the center point of the array at the intersection of horizontal and vertical construction lines. The preview of array with default parameters appears in the drawing area. Also, you are prompted to select the grip to edit array.

    Select grip to edit array or [ASsociative Base point Items Angle between Fill angle ROWs Levels ROTate items eXits] <eXit>:

5. Make sure that **6** is entered in the **Items** field and **360** in the **Fill** field of the **Items** panel in the **Array Creation** tab. Next, press ENTER. The circular/polar array is created, see Figure 5.108.

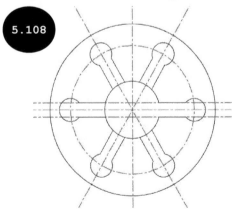

5.108

After creating the circular/polar array, you need to trim the remaining unwanted entities of the drawing by using the **Trim** tool.

6. Invoke the **Trim** tool and then trim the unwanted entities of the inner most circle of the drawing. Figure 5.109 shows the entities to be trimmed and Figure 5.110 shows the resultant drawing after trimming the entities.

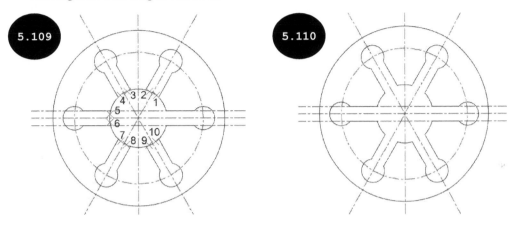

Section 9: Creating the Remaining Drawing Entities

1. Invoke the **Circle, Diameter** tool of the **Circle** flyout in the **Draw** panel and create a circle of diameter 240 whose center point is at the intersection of horizontal and vertical construction lines, see Figure 5.111. This circle will be used as the reference circle for creating drawing entities.

2. Assign the newly created circle of diameter 240 to the Reference layer. To assign the circle to the Reference layer, select the circle and then invoke the **Layer** drop-down list in the **Layers** panel. Next, click on the **Reference** layer in the **Layer** drop-down list. Figure 5.112 shows the circle after assigning it to the Reference layer.

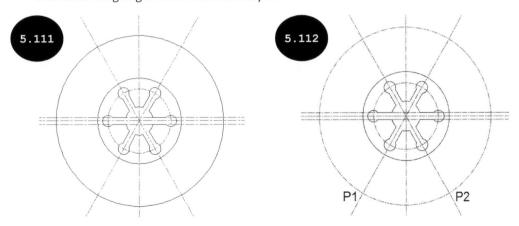

3. Invoke the **Circle, Diameter** tool again and then create two circles of diameter 40 at the intersection points 'P1' and 'P2', refer to Figure 5.112. Figure 5.113 shows the drawing after creating two circles of diameter 40.

4. Similarly, create two more circles of diameter 200 and diameter 280 at the intersection of horizontal and vertical construction lines, see Figure 5.114.

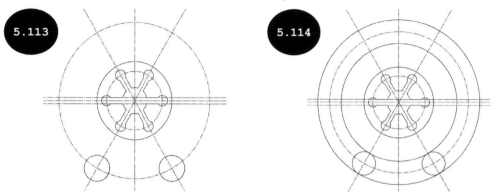

5. Click on the **Trim** tool in the **Modify** panel and then press ENTER. Next, select the unwanted entities to be trimmed. Figure 5.115 shows the entities to be trimmed and Figure 5.116 shows the drawing after trimming the entities. Next, press ENTER to exit the **Trim** tool.

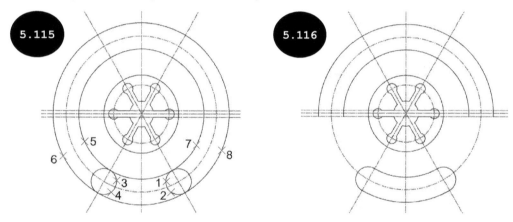

Now, you need to delete the unwanted entities of the drawing.

6. Click on the entities (two entities) to be deleted one by one, see Figure 5.117. Next, press the DELETE key. The selected entities get deleted, see Figure 5.118.

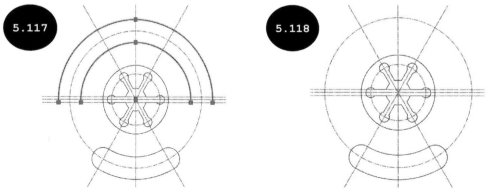

Now, you need to offset the slot entities at the offset distance of 5 units.

7.   Click on the **Offset** tool in the **Modify** panel or enter O and then press ENTER. You are prompted to specify the offset distance.

```
Specify offset distance or [Through Erase Layer] <current>:
```

8.   Enter **5** as the offset distance and then press ENTER. You are prompted to select objects.

```
Select object to offset or [Exit Undo] <Exit>:
```

9.   Click on the lower larger arc of the slot and then move the cursor outside the slot, see Figure 5.119. You are prompted to specify the point to define the offset direction.

```
Specify point on side to offset or [Exit Multiple Undo] <Exit>:
```

10.   Click outside the slot to specify the position of the offset entity. The offset entity is created, see Figure 5.120. You are prompted to select objects to offset again.

```
Select object to offset or [Exit Undo] <Exit>:
```

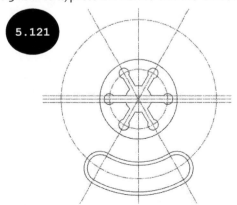

5.119

5.120

11.   Similarly, click on the other entities of the slot one by one and offset them at the offset distance of 5 units, see Figure 5.121. Next, press ENTER to exit the **Offset** tool.

5.121

Now, you need to create construction lines which help in creating other entities of the drawing.

12. Click on the **Construction Line** tool in the expanded **Draw** panel or enter **XLINE** and then press ENTER. You are prompted to specify a point in the drawing area for creating a construction line.

```
Specify a point or [Hor Ver Ang Bisect Offset]:
```

13. Click on the **Offset** option in the command prompt or enter **O** and then press ENTER. You are prompted to specify the offset distance.

```
Specify offset distance or [Through] <current>:
```

14. Enter **20** as the offset distance and then press ENTER. You are prompted to select the line object to offset.

```
Select a line object:
```

15. Click on the vertical construction line and then click on its left side to specify the placement point for creating a new vertical construction line. The vertical construction line is created, see Figure 5.122. Also, you are prompted to select the object to offset.

16. Click on the vertical construction line again and then click on its right side. The another vertical construction line is created on the right side of the existing construction line, see Figure 5.123. Next, press ENTER to exit the **Construction Line** tool.

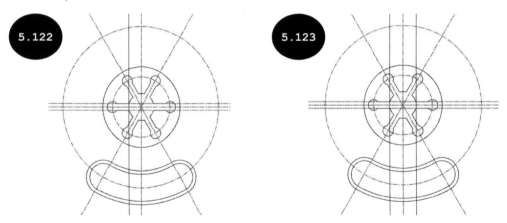

5.122   5.123

Now, you need to assign the newly created vertical construction lines to the Reference layer.

17. Click on the newly created vertical construction lines and then invoke the **Layer** drop-down list in the **Layers** panel. Next, click on the **Reference** layer in the **Layer** drop-down list. The selected objects are assigned to the Reference layer, see Figure 5.124.

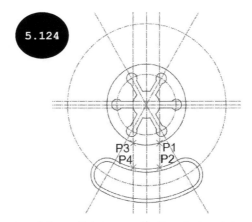

5.124

18. Invoke the **Line** tool and then click to specify the start point and end point of the line at the intersection points 'P1' and 'P2', respectively, refer to Figure 5.124. Next, press ENTER to exit the tool.

19. Similarly, create a line whose start point and end point is at the intersection points 'P3' and 'P4', respectively, refer to Figure 5.124. Figure 5.125 shows the drawing after creating the line entities at the intersection points. Next, press ENTER to exit the tool.

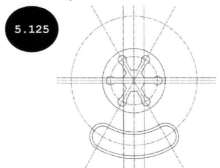

5.125

Now, you need to trim the unwanted entities of the drawing.

20. Invoke the **Trim** tool and then press ENTER. Next, trim the entities shown in Figure 5.126. Figure 5.127 shows the drawing after trimming the entities.

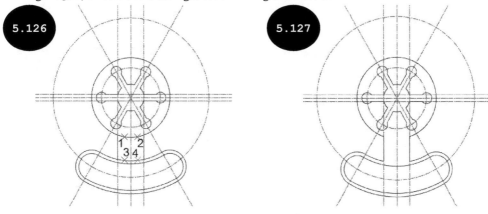

5.126

5.127

Now, you can hide the Reference layer.

21.   Invoke the **Layer** drop-down list of the **Layer** panel, see Figure 5.128. Next, click on the **Turn a layer On or Off** icon of the Reference layer, see Figure 5.128. All the construction lines assigned to the Reference layer get hidden in the drawing area. Figure 5.129 shows the final drawing.

Section 10: Saving the Drawing

After creating the drawing, you need to save it.

1.   Click on the **Save** tool in the **Quick Access Toolbar**. The **Save Drawing As** dialog box appears.

2.   Browse to the *Chapter 5* folder inside the *AutoCAD* folder.

3.   Enter **Tutorial 3** in the **File name** field of the dialog box and then click on the **Save** button. The drawing is saved with the name Tutorial 3 in the *Chapter 5* folder.

Hands-on Test Drive 1

Draw the drawing shown in the Figure 5.130. The dimensions shown in the figure are for your reference only. You will learn about applying dimensions in later chapters.

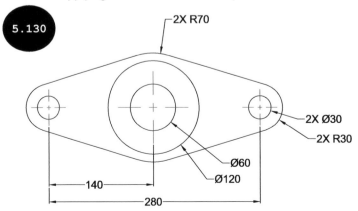

Hands-on Test Drive 2

Draw the drawing shown in the Figure 5.131.

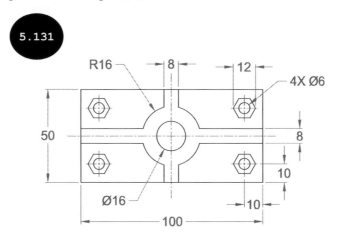

Hands-on Test Drive 3

Draw the drawing shown in the Figure 5.132.

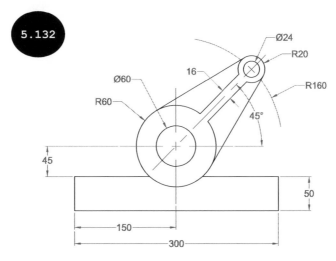

Summary

In this chapter, you have learned about various object selection methods, how to trim and extend drawing entities. You have also learned how to create array, mirror, fillet, chamfer, offset, move, copy, rotate, scale, stretch, and lengthen drawing entities.

Questions

- In the _____ selection method, only the objects that are completely enclosed within the rectangular window gets selected.

- In the _____ selection method, all objects that are completely enclosed and touch the rectangular window gets selected.

- The _____ selection method is used to select group of objects by drawing a series of continuous lines over the objects to be selected.

- In AutoCAD, you can trim the unwanted drawing entities by using the _____ tool.

- In AutoCAD, you can create different types of arrays by using the _____ , _____ , and _____ tools.

- You can create a mirror image of the drawing entities/objects about a mirroring line by using the _____ tool.

- A _____ is a curved edge which is used to remove or eliminate sharp edges of the model that can cause injury while handling the object.

- You can create chamfer by using the _____ tool.

- You can move the drawing objects from one location to another by using the _____ tool.

- You can stretch objects by using the _____ tool.

- You can rotate object or set of objects at an angle by using the _____ tool.

CHAPTER
6

Working with Dimensions and Dimensions Style

In this chapter, you will learn the following:

- Working with components of a dimension
- Creating new dimension style
- Modifying existing dimension style
- Overriding dimension style
- Applying dimensions
- Applying linear dimension
- Applying aligned dimension
- Applying angular dimension
- Applying arc length dimension
- Applying radius dimension
- Applying diameter dimension
- Applying jogged radius dimension
- Applying jogged linear dimension
- Applying ordinate dimension
- Applying baseline dimensions
- Applying continue dimensions
- Applying multiple dimensions

After creating a drawing, it is very important to dimension it. A good AutoCAD drawing with all needed dimensions conveys the complete information clearly and accurately. Note that the 2D drawings are the only source for manufacturing components. It is not only a drawing, but a language for engineers to communicate with each other. By using drawings having proper dimensions, designers/engineers communicate the information about the components to be manufactured. Therefore, it is very important to generate correct or error free drawings with all the needed dimensions and annotations for production. Any incorrect or missing information in drawings about a component can lead to the wrong production.

AutoCAD is provided with various dimensioning tools in the **Dimension** flyout of the **Annotation** panel in the **Home** tab for applying dimensions quickly and easily, see Figure 6.1.

On adding dimensions to a drawing, the dimensions appear as per the default dimension style which is the Standard dimension style. The Standard dimension style is the current dimension style of a drawing which controls the appearance of dimensions such as size of dimension text and arrows, the length of extension lines, and so on. In most of the drawings, the default dimension style may not meet your requirements therefore, AutoCAD allows you to modify the existing dimension style or create new dimension styles as per your requirement. In this chapter, you will learn about various components of dimensions that can be controlled by dimension style, creating new dimension style, and adding dimensions to a drawing.

Working with Components of a Dimension

In AutoCAD, each dimension has several components such as dimension line, dimension text, extension line, and so on, see Figure 6.2. These dimension components are controlled by dimension style. You can modify the existing dimension style or create a new dimension style as required by using the **Dimension Style Manager** dialog box. Note that each industry follows different dimension style for dimension line, dimension text, text height, text font, arrow style, and so on. Therefore it is important to become familiar with the **Dimension Style Manager** dialog box for creating your own industrial specific dimension style.

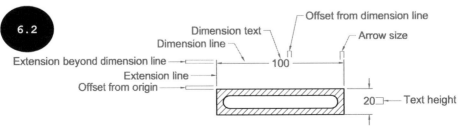

To invoke the **Dimension Style Manager** dialog box, enter **D** in the Command Window and then press ENTER. Figure 6.3 shows the **Dimension Style Manager** dialog box. You can also invoke this dialog box by clicking on the **Dimension Style** tool in the expanded **Annotation** panel of the **Home** tab, see Figure 6.4. The options of the **Dimension Style Manager** dialog box are as follows:

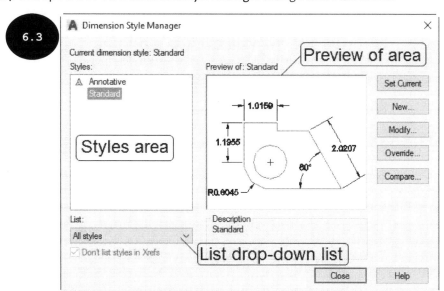

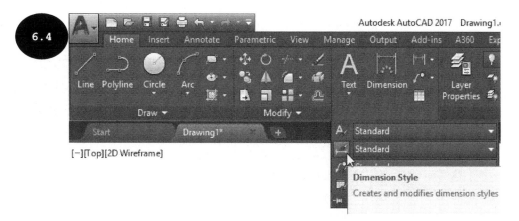

Styles

The **Styles** area is available on the left of the **Dimension Style Manager** dialog box. This area displays the list of all the available dimension styles. Note that the display of dimension styles in this area is controlled by the option selected in the **List** drop-down list of the dialog box. The options of the **List** drop-down list are discussed next.

List

The options in the **List** drop-down list control the display of dimension styles in the **Styles** area of the dialog box. By default, the **All styles** option is selected in this drop-down list. As a result, all the dimension styles available in the drawing are listed in the **Styles** area of the dialog box. If you select the **Styles in use** option, only the dimension styles that are in use get listed in the **Styles** area of the dialog box.

Don't list styles in Xrefs

On selecting the **Don't list styles in Xrefs** check box, the Xref dimension styles will not be listed in the **Styles** area of the dialog box. If you uncheck this check box, all the Xref dimension styles will be listed in the **Styles** area of the dialog box. The Xref is an external reference drawing which is attached with the current drawing as a reference file. You can attach multiple external drawings with the current drawing. You will learn more about external reference drawings in later chapters.

Preview of

The **Preview of** area of the dialog box displays the preview of the current selected dimension style in the **Style** area.

Set Current

The **Set Current** button of the dialog box is used to make the current dimension style. Note that the dimensions applied in a drawing are controlled by the current dimension style. To make a dimension style the current style, select the dimension style from the **Styles** area of the dialog box and then click on the **Set Current** button. The selected dimension style becomes the current dimension style for the drawing.

The **New**, **Modify**, and **Override** buttons of the **Dimension Style Manager** dialog box are used to create new dimension style, modify existing dimension style, and override existing dimension style, respectively. All these buttons of the dialog box are discussed next.

Creating New Dimension Style

In addition to the default dimension style, you can create new dimension styles by using the **New** button of the **Dimension Style Manager** dialog box. To create a new dimension style, invoke the **Dimension Style Manager** dialog box and then click on the **New** button. The **Create New Dimension Style** dialog box appears, see Figure 6.5.

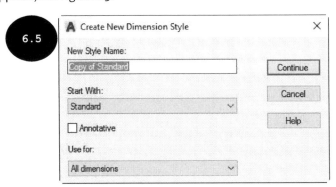

In the **New Style Name** field of the **Create New Dimension Style** dialog box, you can specify name for the dimension style. Next, select the base dimension style from the **Start With** drop-down list of the dialog box. If you want to make the annotative dimension style, select the **Annotative** check box of the dialog box. Next, select the dimension type, from the **Use for** drop-down list, to which you want to apply this dimension style. By default, the **All dimensions** option is selected in this drop-down list. As a result, the new dimension style is applied to all dimension types. If you wants to apply new dimension style only to a particular dimension type then you need to select that dimension type from this drop-down list. For example, if you want to apply the new dimension style only to the radial dimensions then select the **Radius dimensions** option from this drop-down list. Next, click on the **Continue** button in the dialog box. The **New Dimension Style** dialog box appears, see Figure 6.6. In this dialog box, you can specify dimension parameters as required by using their respective options available under the respective tabs of the dialog box. The different tabs and options of this dialog box are as follows:

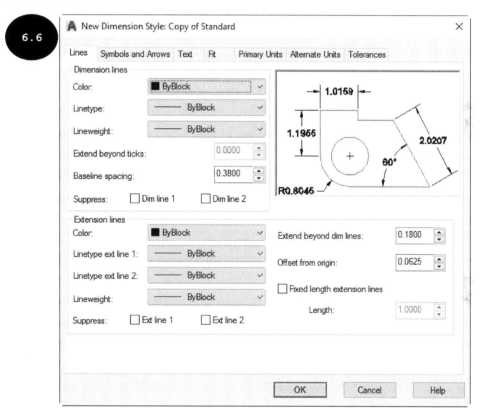

Lines Tab

The options in the **Lines** tab of the dialog box are grouped together into two areas: **Dimension lines** and **Extension lines**, refer to Figure 6.6. These options are as follows:

Dimension lines Area

The options of the **Dimension lines** area are used to control the appearance of dimension lines. The options of this area are as follows:

Color

The **Color** drop-down list is use to select the color for the dimension lines. You can assign a color to dimension lines. Figure 6.7 shows dimension lines in red color. Note that the color set for dimension lines is also applied to dimension arrowheads.

Linetype

The **Linetype** drop-down list is used to select the linetype such as continuous (solid line), center, and hidden for dimension lines. Figure 6.8 shows dimension lines with the dashed linetype.

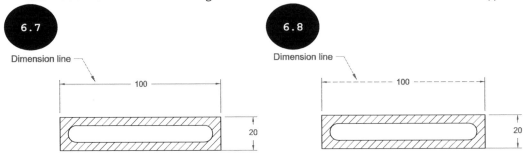

Lineweight

The **Lineweight** drop-down list is used to select the lineweight (thickness) for dimension lines. Figure 6.9 shows dimension lines with 0.80 mm lineweight.

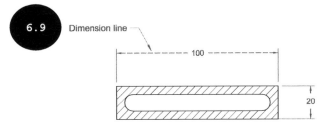

Extend beyond ticks

The **Extend beyond ticks** field is used to specify the distance for the dimension line to be extended beyond the extension lines. Figure 6.10 shows dimension lines with 0 (zero) extended distance beyond the extension lines and Figure 6.11 shows dimension lines with 3 units extended distance beyond the extension lines. By default, this field is not enabled in the dialog box. It is enabled only when the arrowhead style for dimension lines is set to architectural tick, integral, or similar in the **First** or **Second** drop-down lists of the **Arrowheads** area which is available in the **Symbols and Arrows** tab of the dialog box.

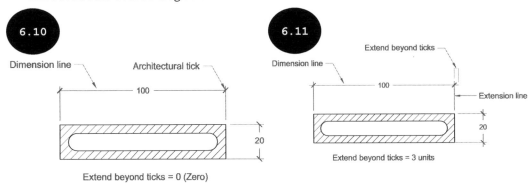

Baseline spacing

The **Baseline spacing** field is use to specify spacing between dimension lines of the baseline dimensioning, see Figure 6.12. You will learn more about applying baseline dimensioning later in this chapter.

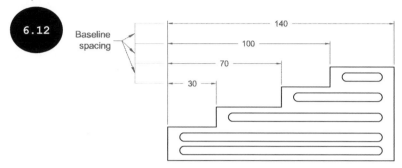

Suppress

The **Dim line 1** and **Dim line 2** suppress check boxes are used to suppress first and second dimension lines, respectively. Figure 6.13 shows dimensions with the first dimension line suppressed and Figure 6.14 shows dimensions with the second dimension line suppressed. By default, these check boxes are unchecked. As a result, both the dimension lines of a dimension appeared in a drawing.

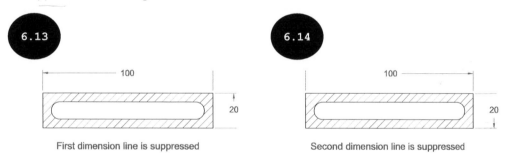

First dimension line is suppressed

Second dimension line is suppressed

Extension lines Area

The options of the **Extension lines** area are used to control the appearance of extension lines of dimensions. The options are as follows:

Color

The **Color** drop-down list of the **Extension lines** area is used to select the color for the extension lines. You can assign different color to extension lines of dimensions.

Linetype ext line 1

The **Linetype ext line 2** drop-down list of this area is used to select the linetype such as continuous (solid line), center, and hidden for the first extension lines of dimensions.

Linetype ext line 2

The **Linetype ext line 2** drop-down list of this area is used to select the linetype such as continuous (solid line), center, and hidden for the second extension lines of dimensions.

Lineweight

The **Lineweight** drop-down list of this area is used to select the lineweight (thickness) for extension lines.

Extend beyond dim lines

The **Extend beyond dim lines** field is use to specify the distance for the extension line to be extended beyond the dimension line, see Figure 6.15.

Offset from origin

The **Offset from origin** field is use to specify the offset distance for the extension line from the origin of the extension line, see Figure 6.16.

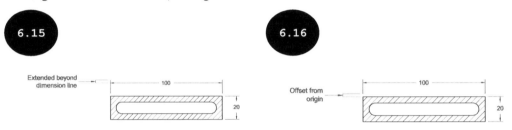

Fixed length extension lines

On selecting the **Fixed length extension lines** check box, the **Length** field which is available below this check box gets enabled. In this **Length** field, you can specify a fix distance for the extension line, starting from the dimension line, see Figures 6.17. By default, the **Fixed length extension lines** check box is unchecked. As a result, dimensions are applied with full length extension lines. Figure 6.17 shows dimensions with a specified fixed length extension lines and Figure 6.18 shows dimensions with the full length extension lines.

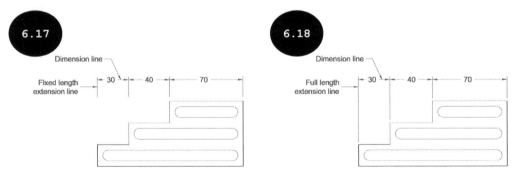

Suppress

The **Ext line 1** and **Ext line 2** suppress check boxes of the **Extension lines** area are used to suppress first and second extension lines of dimensions, respectively.

Symbols and Arrows Tab

The options in the **Symbols and Arrows** tab of the dialog box are used to specify dimension arrowheads, arrow size, center marks, dimension break, and so on in their respective fields, see Figure 6.19. The options in the **Symbols and Arrows** tab are as follows:

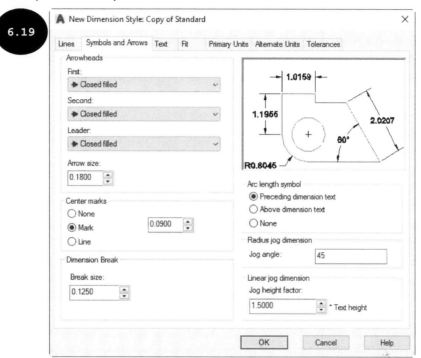

6.19

Arrowheads Area

The options in the **Arrowheads** area of the dialog box are used to control the styles and parameters for arrowheads. The options are as follows:

First and Second

The **First** and **Second** drop-down lists are used to specify the first and second arrowheads for dimension lines, respectively. By default, the same arrowhead styles (Closed filled) is applied at both ends (first and second) of the dimension lines. Also, on selecting the first arrowhead style from the **First** drop-down list, the same arrowhead style gets selected automatically for the second arrowhead style in the **Second** drop-down list. To apply different arrowhead style for the second arrowhead of the dimension lines, select the required arrowhead style from the **Second** drop-down list. Figure 6.20 shows dimensions with the **Closed filled** as the first arrowhead style and the **Architectural tick** as the second arrowhead style.

6.20

Note: In addition to selecting arrowhead styles from the **First** and **Second** drop-down lists, you can use custom/user-defined arrowhead styles for dimensions, as per your requirement. To define custom/user-defined arrowhead styles, you need to first create it as a block and then you can select the **User Arrow** option from these drop-down lists. On selecting the **User Arrow** option, the **Select Custom Arrow Block** window appears, see Figure 6.21. The **Select from Drawing Blocks** drop-down list of this window displays a list of all blocks created for the drawing. You can select the required block as the arrowhead style from this drop-down list and then click on the OK button. You will learn more about creating blocks in later chapters.

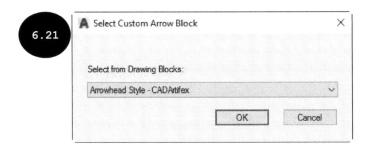

Leader

The **Leader** drop-down list is use to specify arrowhead style for leader lines.

Arrow size

The **Arrow size** field is used to specify size of dimension arrowheads.

Center marks Area

The options in the **Center marks** area are used to control the display of the center marks for the radius and diameter dimensions, see Figure 6.22. By default, the **None** radio button is selected in this area. As a result, no centermark is drawn at the center of circles or arcs on applying diameter or radius dimensions. If you select the **Mark** radio button, a cross mark will be drawn at the center of circles or arcs on applying diameter or radius dimensions, see Figure 6.23. If you select the **Line** radio button, the centerlines will be drawn at the center of circles or arcs on applying diameter or radius dimensions, see Figure 6.24. Note that as soon as you select the **Mark** or **Line** radio button, the **Size** field becomes enabled in this area. In this field, you can specify the size for the center mark or centerline to be drawn at the center of circles or arcs on applying diameter or radius dimensions.

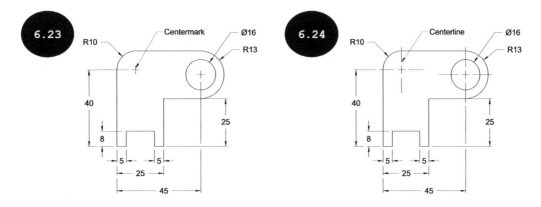

Dimension Break Area

The **Break size** field of the **Dimension Break** area (see Figure 6.25) is used to specify the default break size for the dimension lines. Note that you can break dimension lines which are intersecting with each other or drawing objects in order to avoid overlapping or confusion by using the DIMBREAK command. When you break dimension lines by using the DIMBREAK command, the break size which is specified in this **Break size** field will be applied, automatically. Figure 6.26 shows the intersecting dimension lines and Figure 6.27 shows the dimensions after breaking the dimension lines by using the DIMBREAK command.

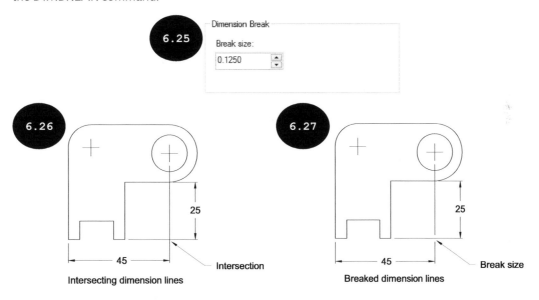

| **Tip:** | To break dimension lines which are intersecting with other dimension or drawing object, enter DIMBREAK command and then press ENTER. You are prompted to select the dimension to add/remove break. Click on the dimension to be broken and then click on object for breaking selected dimension. The object to break selected dimension can be a drawing entity or another dimension. |

Arc length symbol Area

The options in the **Arc length symbol** area (see Figure 6.28) are used to control the position of the arc length dimension symbol. By default, the **Preceding dimension text** radio button is selected in this area. As a result, on applying the arc length dimension, the arc length symbol appears before the dimension text, see Figure 6.29. On selecting the **Above dimension text** radio button, the arc length symbol appears above the dimension text. If you select the **None** radio button, the arc length symbol gets suppressed and not appears in the dimension text. You will learn about applying arc length dimension later in this chapter.

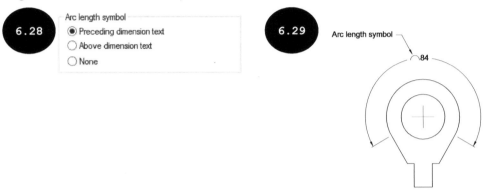

Radius jog dimension Area

The **Jog angle** field in this **Radius jog dimension** area (see Figure 6.30) is used to specify the jog angle for the jogged dimension. By default, the 45 degree jog angle is specified in this field. As a result, a jog with 45 degree angle is applied on applying the radius jog dimension to arcs or circles, see Figure 6.31. You will learn more about applying jogged dimension later in this chapter.

Linear jog dimension Area

The **Jog height factor** field of the **Linear jog dimension** area is used to specify the jog factor which controls the jog height of the linear jog dimensions. A jog height is the distance between two vertices of the jog angles that make the jog, see Figure 6.32. Note that the value entered as the jog height factor in this field gets multiplied to the text height of the dimension in order to calculate the jog height. You will learn more about applying linear jog dimensions later in this chapter.

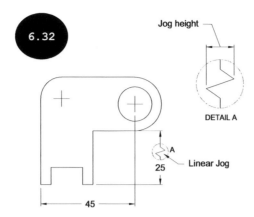

Text Tab

The options in the **Text** tab of the dialog box are used to control the dimension text style and format, see Figure 6.33. The options are as follows:

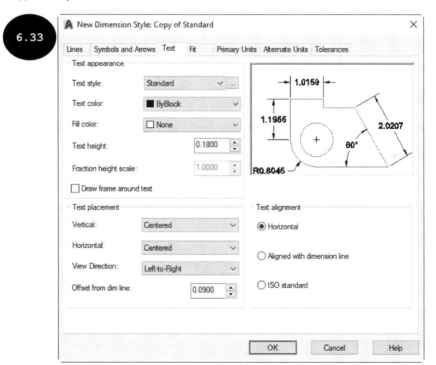

Text appearance Area

The options in the **Text appearance** area are used to control the appearance of the dimension text such as text style and color. The options are as follows:

Text style

The **Text style** drop-down list is used to select the predefined text style for dimensions. You can also modify the predefined text style and create a new text style, as required. To modify the existing text style and create a new text style, click on the [...] ⬚ button, which is available in front of the **Text style** drop-down list. The **Text Style** dialog box appears, see Figure 6.34. By using the options of this dialog box, you can modify the existing text style such as text font, font style, and height. Also, you can create new text style by using the **New** button of this dialog box. To close the dialog box, click on the **Cancel** button.

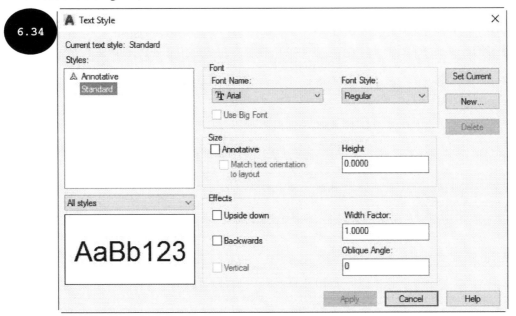

Text color
The **Text color** drop-down list is used to select the color for the dimension text.

Fill color
The **Fill color** drop-down list is used to select a fill color which appears at the background of the dimension text in a box. Figure 6.35 shows a box around the dimension text which is filled with red color.

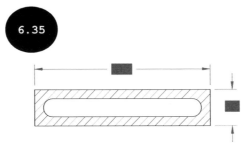

Text height
The **Text height** field is used to specify the dimension text height. Note that this field is enabled only when the text style selected in the **Text style** drop-down list has text height set to 0 (zero) in

the **Text Style** dialog box, refer to Figure 6.34. If the text height is defined or set for the selected text style then this field will not be enabled and the defined text height overrides the current text height of the dimensions.

Fraction height scale

The **Fraction height scale** field is used to specify the scale for the fraction unit format relative to the dimension text. The value specified in this field multiplies by the text height in order to calculate the height for the fraction dimensions. Note that this field is enabled only when the unit format is set to **Fractions** in the **Primary** tab of the dialog box.

Draw frame around text

On selecting the **Draw frame around text** check box, a frame box is drawn around the dimension text. By default, this check box is cleared. As a result, no frame box is drawn around a dimension text.

Text placement Area

The options in the **Text placement** area of the dialog box are used to control the dimension text placement, see Figure 6.36. The options are as follows:

Vertical

The **Vertical** drop-down list of this area is used to control the vertical placement of dimension text with respect to the dimension line. By default, the **Centered** option is selected in this drop-down list. As a result, the dimension text is placed at the center of dimension line, see Figure 6.37 (a). On selecting the **Above** option, the dimension text is placed above the dimension line, see Figure 6.37 (b). On selecting the **Outside** option, the dimension text is placed on the side of the dimension line, see Figure 6.37 (c). On selecting the **Below** option, the dimension text is placed below the dimension line, see Figure 6.37 (d). On selecting the **JIS** option, the dimension text is placed to conform to the JIS (Japanese Industrial Standards) representation.

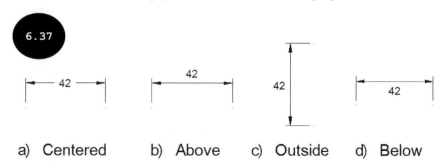

a) Centered   b) Above   c) Outside   d) Below

Horizontal

The **Horizontal** drop-down list is used to control the horizontal placement of the dimension text along the dimension line with respect to the extension lines. By default, the **Centered** option is selected in this drop-down list. As a result, the dimension text is placed at the center of extension lines along the dimension line, see Figure 6.38 (a). On selecting the **At Ext Line 1** option, the dimension text is placed near the first extension line, see Figure 6.38 (b). On selecting the **At Ext Line 2** option, the dimension text is placed near the second extension line, see Figure 6.38(c). On selecting the **Over Ext Line 1** option, the dimension text is placed over or along the first extension line, see Figure 6.38 (d). On selecting the **Over Ext Line 2** option, the dimension text is placed over or along the second extension line, see Figure 6.38 (e).

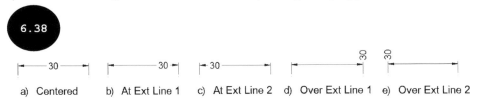

6.38

a) Centered   b) At Ext Line 1   c) At Ext Line 2   d) Over Ext Line 1   e) Over Ext Line 2

View Direction

The **View Direction** drop-down list is used to control the viewing direction of the dimension text from left to right or right to left by selecting the respective options from it.

Offset from dim line

The **Offset from dim line** field is used to specify the offset distance between the dimension text and the dimension line, see Figure 6.39.

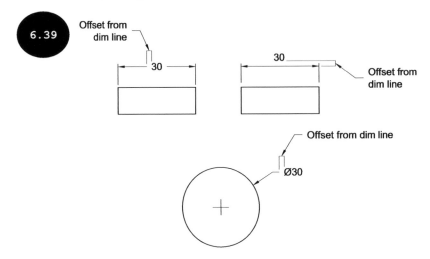

6.39

Text alignment Area

The options in the **Text alignment** area are used to control the orientation of the dimension text, see Figure 6.40. The options are as follows:

Horizontal

By default, the **Horizontal** radio button is selected. As a result, the dimension text is placed horizontally to a dimension, see Figure 6.41.

Aligned with dimension line

On selecting the **Aligned with dimension line** radio button, the dimension text aligns with the dimension line, see Figure 6.41.

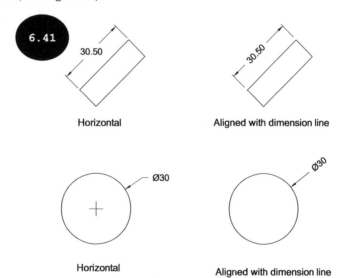

Horizontal

Aligned with dimension line

Horizontal

Aligned with dimension line

ISO standard

On selecting the **ISO standard** radio button, the dimension text aligns with the dimension line when the dimension text is placed inside the extension lines. If the dimension text is placed outside the extension lines then on selecting this radio button, the dimension text aligns horizontally.

Fit Tab

The options in the **Fit** tab of the dialog box are used to control the placement of dimension lines, arrowheads, leader lines, and scale of all dimension components/features, see Figure 6.42. The options are as follows:

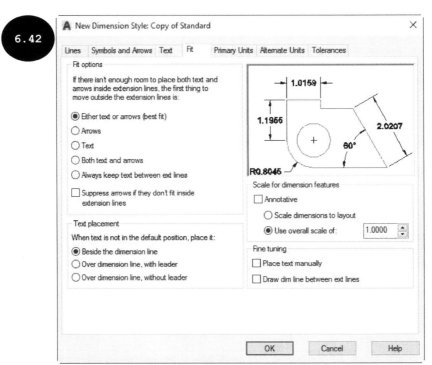

Fit options Area

The options in the **Fit options** area of the dialog box are used to control the placement of dimension text and arrowheads depending upon the availability of space between the extension lines. If the space is available for the placement then the text and arrowhead are placed between the extension lines. Whereas, if enough space is not available between the extension lines for the placement of dimension text then the dimension text and arrowheads get placed according to the fit option selected in this area. The options of the **Fit options** area are as follows:

Either text or arrows (best fit)

By default this **Either text or arrows (best fit)** radio button is selected. As a result, either the dimension text or arrowheads move outside the extension lines based on the best fit. Note that if the enough space is available between the extension lines then both text and arrowheads are placed between the extension lines. Otherwise either the text, the arrowheads, or both move outside the extension lines based on the best fit.

Arrows

On selecting the **Arrows** radio button, the arrowheads move outside the extension lines first and then the dimension text. Note that if the available space between the extension lines is available either for text or arrowheads then the arrowheads move outside the extension lines.

Text

On selecting the **Text** radio button, the dimension text moves outside the extension lines first and then the arrowheads. Note that if the available space between the extension lines is available either for text or arrowheads then the text moves outside the extension lines.

Both text and arrows

On selecting the **Both text and arrows** radio button, the dimension text and arrowheads both move outside the extension lines when the enough space is not available between the extension lines.

Always keep text between ext lines

On selecting the **Always keep text between ext lines** radio button, the dimension text is always placed between the extension lines regardless of space available between them.

Suppress arrows if they don't fit inside extension lines

On selecting the **Suppress arrows if they don't fit inside extension lines** radio button, the arrowheads get suppressed, if the enough space is not available to place them inside the extension lines.

Text placement Area

The options in the **Text placement** area of the dialog box are used to control the placement of dimension text when it is not in the default position or moved from the default position, see Figure 6.43. These options are as follows:

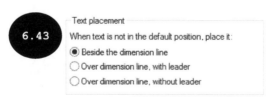

Beside the Dimension Line

The **Beside the Dimension Line** radio button is selected, by default. As a result, the dimension text is placed beside the dimension line or moves the dimension line whenever dimension text is moved.

Over the Dimension Line, with Leader

On selecting the **Over the Dimension Line, with Leader** radio button, the dimension line will not move on moving the dimension text. Whereas, on moving the dimension text away from the dimension line, a leader line is added to the dimension text which connects the dimension text to the dimension line, see Figure 6.44. Note that if the dimension text is placed very close to the dimension line then leader line can not be added.

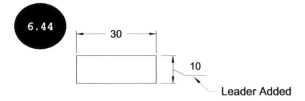

Over dimension line, without leader
On selecting the Over dimension line, without leader radio button, the dimension line will not move on moving the dimension text. However, you can move the dimension text freely or independent of the dimension line. Note that the moved dimension text will not be connected to the dimension line through a leader line if this radio button is selected.

Scale for dimension features Area
The options in the Scale for dimension features area of the dialog box are used to control the overall dimension scale value or the paper space scaling, see Figure 6.45. These options are as follows:

Annotative
The Annotative check box is used to define whether the dimension style is annotative. To make the dimension style annotative, select the Annotative check box. You will learn more about annotative dimension later in this chapter.

Scale dimensions to layout
On selecting the Scale dimensions to layout radio button, AutoCAD automatically calculates an acceptable scale factor for dimension features such as text height, arrow sizes, and so on based on the scaling between the current model space viewport and the paper space layout. You will learn more about layouts in later chapters.

Use overall scale of
On selecting the Use overall scale of radio button, the Scale field is enabled in front of it. By default, the scale value is set to 1 (one). As a result, the dimension style such as text height, arrowhead size, and all other settings that specify size, distance, or spacing are plotted at a full scale. You can specify an overall scale for controlling all dimension styles in this field, as required. Note that the scale specified in this field will not change the dimension measurement.

Fine tuning Area

The options in the **Fine tuning** area provides additional options for the placement of dimension text, see Figure 6.46. These options are as follows:

6.46

Place text manually

By default, the **Place text manually** check box is unchecked. As a result, the dimension text is placed at the middle of the dimension line, if the enough space is available. However, on selecting this check box, you can position the dimension text anywhere on the dimension line. Also, while positioning the dimension text, it ignores the horizontal justification settings, if specified.

Draw dim line between ext lines

On selecting the **Draw dim line between ext lines** check box, the dimension line is drawn between the extension lines even if the dimension text and dimension lines are placed outside the extension lines due to not having enough space.

Primary Units Tab

The options in the **Primary Units** tab are used to control the unit format, dimension precision, fraction format, measurement scale, zero suppression, and so on for linear and angular dimensions, see Figure 6.47. The options are as follows:

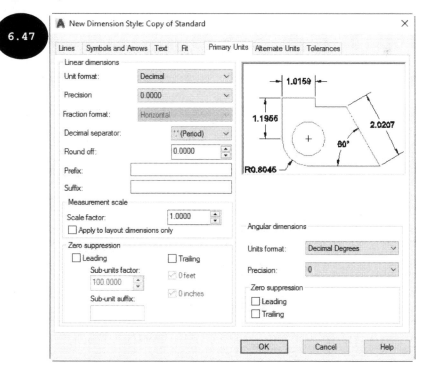

6.47

Linear dimensions Area

The options in the **Linear dimensions** area of the dialog box are used to control the unit format, precision, and so on for linear dimensions. The options of this area are as follows:

Unit format

The **Unit format** drop-down list is used to select the current unit format: Decimal, Scientific, Engineering, Architectural, Fractional, and Windows Desktop for all dimension types except angular dimensions.

Precision

The **Precision** drop-down list is used to specify the dimension precision (decimal places) for dimension text of the current/primary dimension units.

Fraction format

The **Fraction format** drop-down list is used to specify the fraction format: **Horizontal, Diagonal,** or **Not Stacked** for the fractional or architectural unit format. Note that this drop-down list is enabled only when the **Fractional** or **Architectural** unit format is selected in the **Unit format** drop-down list of this area.

Decimal separator

The **Decimal separator** drop-down list is used to specify the separator: '.'(Period), ','(Comma), ' '(Space) for decimal formats, see Figure 6.48.

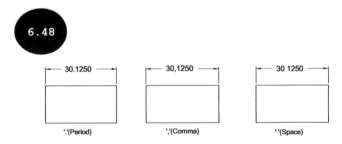

Round off

The **Round off** field is used to specify the nearest rounded value for dimension measurements of all dimension types except angular dimensions. For example, if you specify 0.5 in this field then the dimension having measurement of 30.3 gets round off to 30.5 and 30.8 gets round off to 31.0. Note that the display of number of digits after the decimal point depends on the precision setting.

Prefix

The **Prefix** field is used to specify a prefix for the dimension measurement. The prefix specified in this field is placed in front of the dimension text. You can enter text or any control code as the prefix for the dimension measurement. For example, on entering the text "Cad" as the prefix in this field, the "Cad" gets placed in front of dimension text. Also, if you enter control code "%%c" as the prefix in this field, the diameter symbol gets placed in front of dimension text.

Suffix

Similar to specifying the prefix, you can specify the suffix for the dimension measurement. The suffix specified is placed after the dimension text. You can enter text or any control code as the suffix for the dimension measurement. For example, on entering the text "mm" as the suffix, the "mm" gets placed after of the dimension text. Also, if you enter control code "%%d" as the suffix then the symbol of degree gets placed after the dimension text.

Measurement scale Area

The **Scale factor** field of this **Measurement scale** area (see Figure 6.49) is used to specify a scale factor for linear dimension measurements which also includes radii, diameters, and coordinates measurements. By default, the scale factor is specified as 1 (one) in this field. As a result, the two units segments are dimensioned as 2 units (2 X 1) only. However, if you specify 2 (two) as the scale factor in this field then the two units segments are dimensioned as 4 units (2 X 2). Note that this scale factor does not apply to angular dimensions, round off values, and to the plus or minus tolerance values.

On selecting the **Apply to layout dimension only** check box of this area (see Figure 6.49), the specified measurement scale factor applies only to the dimensions created in the layout viewports.

Zero suppression Area

The options in the **Zero suppression** area of the dialog box are used to suppress or unsuppress the leading and trailing zeros in the dimension values, see Figure 6.50.

On selecting the **Leading** check box of this area, the leading zeros in all decimal dimensions get suppressed. For example, if the dimension is 0.800 unit then on selecting this check box it becomes .800. Similarly, on selecting the **Trailing** check box, the trailing zeros in all decimal dimensions get suppressed. For example, if the dimension is 15.500 then on selecting this check box it becomes 15.5 and 15.000 becomes 15.

By default, the **0 feet** and **0 inches** check boxes of this area are not enabled. These check boxes are enabled only when the **Engineering** or **Architectural** format is selected in the **Unit format** drop-down list. If the feet and inches dimensions are less than one then on selecting the **0 feet** check box, the leading zero (feet portion) of the dimensions get suppressed. For example, if the **0 feet** check box is selected then the 0'-5 1/2" dimension becomes 5 1/2". Similarly, on selecting the **0 inches** check box, the trailing zeros (inches portion) of the feet and inches dimensions get suppressed. For example, if the **0 inches** check box is selected, the 5'-0" dimension becomes 5'.

The **Sub-units factor** field of this area is used to specify the sub unit factor for dimensions. For example, if the current dimension is in metre (2 metre) then on entering 100 as the sub-unit factor, the dimension gets converted to centimeter (2 X 100 = 200 cm). You can also enter the suffix (cm) for the sub unit in the **Sub-unit suffix** field of this area.

Angular dimensions Area

Similar to specifying the unit format, precision, and zero suppression for the linear dimensions, you can also specify the unit format, precision, and zero suppression for the angular dimensions by using the options in the **Angular dimensions** area of the dialog box, see Figure 6.51.

Alternate Units Tab

The options in the **Alternate Units** tab are used to display alternate unit for the dimension measurements and control the format and precision of the alternate unit, see Figure 6.52. The options of the **Alternate Units** tab are as follows:

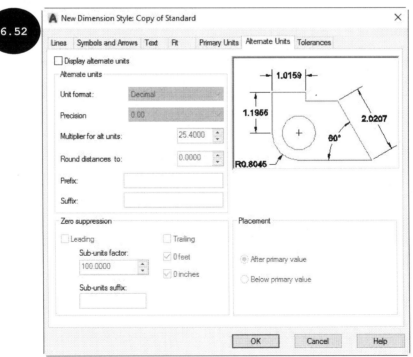

Display alternate units Check Box

By default, the **Display alternate units** check box is unchecked. As a result, the dimension measurements display only in the primary unit. To display/add alternate unit for dimension measurements in addition to the primary unit, select this **Display alternate units** check box. As soon as you select this check box, the preview area of the dialog box shows the alternate unit in bracket [ ] for all dimensions including to the primary unit. Also, the other options of the dialog box are enabled for defining the format and precision of the alternate unit. The options are as follows:

Alternate units Area

The options in the **Alternate units** area are used to specify the format and precision for the alternate unit. All these options are same as those discussed in the **Primary Units** tab except the **Multiplier for alt units** field. The **Multiplier for alt units** field of this area is used to specify the multiplier as the conversion factor for the alternate unit. For example, if the inches is specified as the current/primary unit for the dimensions and you want to add millimeter as the alternate unit for the measurements. In such case, you can enter 25.4 as the conversion factor in this **Multiplier for alt units** field. On doing so, the dimensions display inch as well as millimeter measurements, see Figure 6.53. Note that the alternate unit is not applied to the angular dimensions, round off values, or the plus or minus tolerance values.

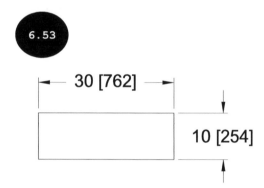

6.53

Zero suppression Area

The options in the **Zero suppression** area of the dialog box are used to suppress or unsuppress the leading and trailing zeros in the alternate dimension values, see Figure 6.54. These options are same as those discussed in the **Primary Units** tab with the only difference that these options effect the alternate dimension values.

6.54

Placement Area

The options in the **Placement** area of the dialog box are used to define the placement for the alternate unit with respect to the primary unit, see Figure 6.55.

By default, the **After primary value** radio button is selected. As a result, the alternate unit is placed after the primary unit, refer to Figure 6.53. If you select the **Below primary value** radio button then the alternate unit is placed below the primary unit.

Tolerances Tab

The options in the **Tolerances** tab of the dialog box are used to specify the parameters that control the format and display of the tolerance in the dimension text, see Figure 6.56. The options are as follows:

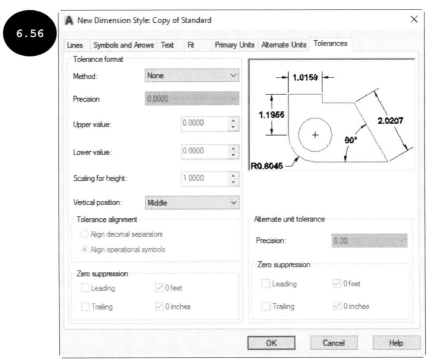

Tolerance format Area

The options in the **Tolerance format** area are used to control the tolerance format such as tolerance method, tolerance precision, scaling for height, position, and so on. The options are as follows:

Method

The **Method** drop-down list is used to select the type of tolerance: Symmetrical, Deviation, Limits, and Basic. By default, the **None** option is selected in this drop-down list. As a result, the tolerance values are not added to the dimension text. The other options of this drop-down list are as follows:

Symmetrical: On selecting the **Symmetrical** option, the symmetrical tolerances get added to the dimension texts with plus (+) and minus (-) expressions to the symmetric tolerance values, see Figure 6.57. As soon as you select this tolerance type, the other respective options of the **Tolerance format** area are enabled. You can specify the precision and tolerance values for the symmetrical tolerance in the **Precision** drop-down list and **Upper value** field of this area, respectively.

Deviation: On selecting the **Deviation** option, the deviation tolerances get added to the dimension texts with the plus (+) and minus (-) expressions to the deviation tolerance values, see Figure 6.58. You can specify the plus (+) tolerance value in the **Upper value** field and minus (-) tolerance value in the **Lower value** field of this area.

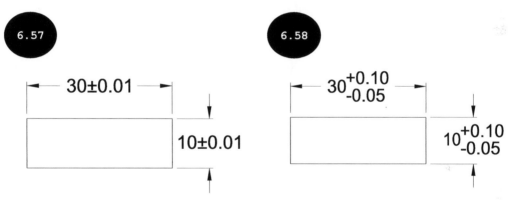

Limits: On selecting the **Limits** option, the maximum and minimum limit dimensions are applied by adding the upper limit value and subtracting the lower limit value to the actual dimension, respectively, see Figure 6.59. The maximum and minimum limit dimensions appear one above the other in the drawing area. In Figure 6.59, the maximum limit dimension is 30.10 (30 + 0.1) and the minimum limit dimension is 29.95 (30 - 0.05).

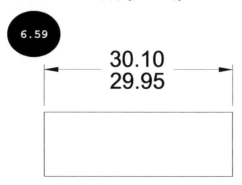

Basic: On selecting the **Basic** option, the basic dimensions are applied by drawing a box around the dimension text, see Figure 6.60. The basic dimension is also know as reference dimension.

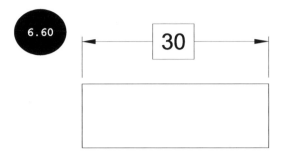

Precision, Upper value, and Lower value
The **Precision** drop-down list, **Upper value** field, and **Lower value** field are used to specify the precision, upper value, and lower value for the tolerances dimension values, respectively.

Scaling for height
The **Scaling for height** field is used to specify the scale factor for the tolerance text height with respect to the current height of the dimension text. By default, the scale factor for the tolerance text height is set to 1 (one). As a result, the height of the tolerance dimension is same as of the current dimension text height. If you want to set the tolerance dimension height as half of the current dimension text height then you need to enter 0.5 in this field.

Vertical position
The **Vertical position** drop-down is used to specify the position/text justification for the symmetrical and deviation tolerance dimension values. By default, the **Middle** option is selected in this drop-down list. As a result, the tolerance text value is aligned with the middle of the dimension text, see Figure 6.61 (a). On selecting the **Top** option, the tolerance text value gets aligned with the top of the dimension text, see Figure 6.61 (b). On selecting the **Bottom** option, the tolerance text value gets aligned with the bottom of the dimension text, see Figure 6.61 (c).

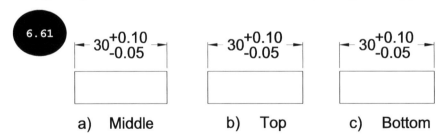

Tolerance alignment Area
The options in the **Tolerance alignment** area are used to control the alignment of upper and lower tolerance values when they are stacked. These options are available only when the **Deviation** or **Limits** tolerance type is selected. On selecting the **Align decimal separators** radio button of this area, the tolerance values get aligned vertically with respect to the decimal separators (.), see Figure 6.62 (a). However, on selecting the **Align operational symbols**, the tolerance values get aligned with respect to the operational symbols [plus (+) and minus (-)], see Figure 6.62 (b).

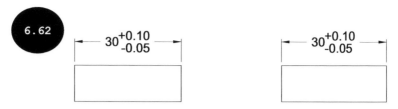

a)   Align decimal separators   b)   Align operational symbols

Zero suppression Area

The options in the Zero suppression area are used to suppress or unsuppress the leading and trailing zeros in the tolerance values, as discussed earlier.

Alternate unit tolerance Area

The options in the Alternate unit tolerance area are used to specify formats such as precision and zero suppression for the alternate tolerance units. Note that these options are enabled only when the display of alternate dimension units along with the primary dimension units are turned on.

Once you have specified all settings for creating the new dimension style, click on the OK button of the dialog box to accept the settings and to exit the New Dimension Style dialog box.

Modifying Existing Dimension Style

In addition to creating new dimension style, you can modify existing dimension styles, as required by using the Modify button of the Dimension Style Manager dialog box. To modify the settings of the existing dimension style, invoke the Dimension Style Manager dialog box by entering D in the Command Window and then pressing the ENTER key. Once the Dimension Style Manager dialog box is invoked, select the dimension style to be modified from the Styles area of the dialog box (see Figure 6.63) and then click on the Modify button. The Modify Dimension Style dialog box appears, see Figure 6.64.

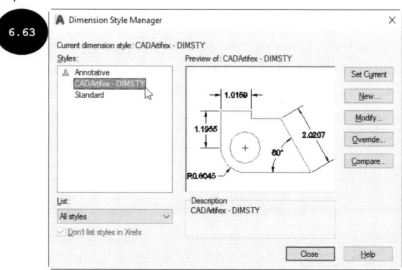

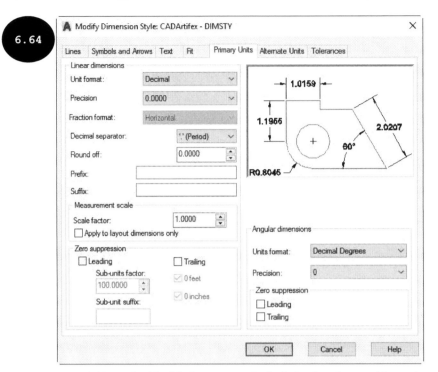

The different options available in the **Modify Dimension Style** dialog box for modifying the selected dimension style are same as those discussed earlier while creating the new dimension style. Once you have modified the dimension style settings in this dialog box, click on the **OK** button to accept the modifications and to exit the dialog box. Next, click on the **Close** button in the **Dimension Stye Manager** dialog box to close it.

Overriding Dimension Style

In addition to creating new dimension style and modifying existing dimension style, you can also define overrides or change specific parameters of an existing dimension style. Generally, most of the time we use the same dimension style throughout a drawing in order to be consistent with the style in the drawing. However, sometimes you may need to make small changes in some of the dimension parameters/settings without altering the complete dimension style. In such a case, you can use dimension style overrides. For example, you can assign different color to the extension line by overriding the color assigned to the parent dimension style. On creating a dimension style override, the sub-dimension style gets created that varies from its parent/original dimension style. When you create override for any of the dimension parameter, the original/parent dimension style will remain unchanged and the new value for color is stored in the DIMCLRE system variable. Note that all dimensions you apply includes the overrides until you delete the overrides or set another style as the current dimension style.

To create a dimension override, invoke the **Dimension Style Manager** dialog box by entering **D** in the Command Window and then pressing the ENTER key. Once the **Dimension Style Manager** dialog box is invoked, select the dimension style to be overridden from the **Styles** area of the dialog box and then click on the **Override** button. The **Override Current Style** dialog box appears, see Figure 6.65. In this dialog box, you can define overrides for the required dimension style parameters/settings.

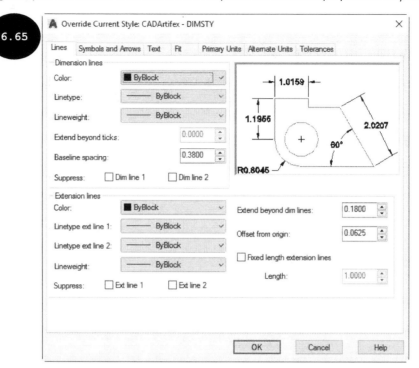

6.65

The options of the **Override Current Style** dialog box are the same as those discussed earlier while creating the new dimension style. Once you have defined overrides or changed required parameters of the existing dimension, click on the OK button. The **Override Current Style** dialog box gets closed and a sub-dimension style *<style overrides>* is created and appears under the parent dimension style in the **Styles** area of the **Dimension Style Manager** dialog box, see Figure 6.66.

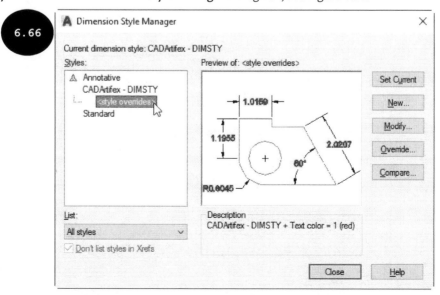

6.66

After learning about various dimension components, making a dimension style current, creating new dimension style, modifying existing dimension style, and overriding dimension style, you will now learn about applying various type of dimensions in a drawing.

Applying Dimensions

As discussed earlier, a good AutoCAD drawing is the one that has all necessary dimensions which convey the complete information about the drawing clearly and accurately, see Figure 6.67.

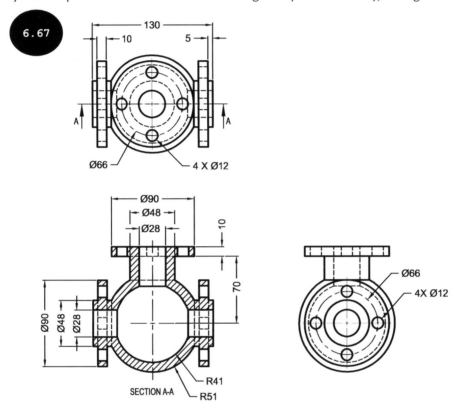

6.67

Note: When you apply dimensions in AutoCAD, a new layer named as "Defpoints" is created automatically. This "Defpoints" layer stores the dimension properties and cannot be deleted or renamed.

AutoCAD is provided with various dimensioning tools in the **Dimension** flyout of the **Annotation** panel in the **Home** tab which help you quickly and easily dimension a drawing, see Figure 6.68.

Additionally, you can access dimensioning tools from the **Dimensions** panel of the **Annotate** tab, see Figure 6.69, **Dimension** toolbar, see Figure 6.70, **Dimension** Menu Bar, see Figure 6.71, and by using the DIM command.

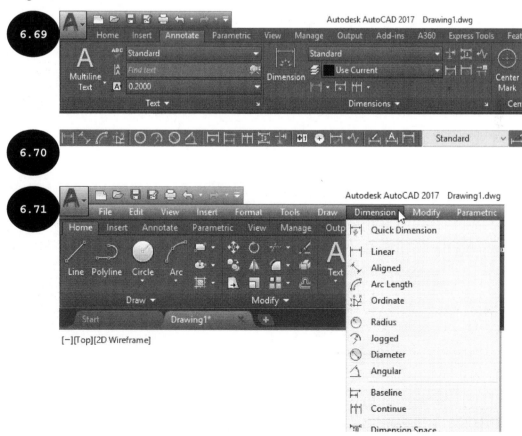

Note: By default, the display of Menu Bar and Toolbars are turned off. To turn on the display of Menu Bar, enter **MENUBAR** in the Command Window and then press ENTER. You are prompted to enter new value for MENUBAR. Enter **1** (one) to turn on the display and **0** (zero) to turn off the display of Menu Bar, respectively.

To display the **Dimension** toolbar, click on the **Tools > Toolbars > AUTOCAD > Dimension** in the Menu Bar.

You can apply different types of dimensions such as linear, aligned, angular, radius, diameter, arc length, and ordinate by using the respective dimensioning tools. Moreover, you can apply different types of dimensions by using the **Dimension** tool of the **Annotation** panel in the **Home** tab. The **Dimension** tool is a smart tool, which is used to apply dimension depending on the selected entity. For example, if you select the horizontal entity, the horizontal dimension is applied and if you select vertical entity, the vertical dimension is applied. The method of applying different types of dimensions are as follows:

Applying Linear Dimension

A linear dimension is most widely used dimension type which measures the length and width of an object. You can apply horizontal or vertical linear dimensions to horizontal, vertical, or aligned objects, by using the **Linear** tool or **Dimension** tool, see Figure 6.72. You can select two points of an object to be dimensioned or you can directly select an object.

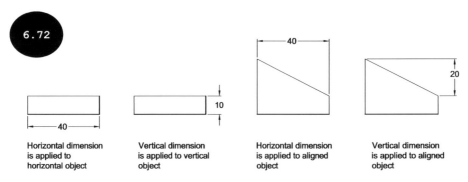

6.72

Horizontal dimension is applied to horizontal object

Vertical dimension is applied to vertical object

Horizontal dimension is applied to aligned object

Vertical dimension is applied to aligned object

Procedure for Applying Linear Dimension

1. Click on the **Dimension** tool in the **Annotation** panel in the **Home** tab. You are prompted to select objects to be dimensioned or specify origin for the first dimension extension line. Alternatively, invoke the **Dimension** flyout in the **Annotation** panel and then click on the **Linear** tool for applying the linear dimension. You can also invoke the **Linear** tool by using the DIMLINEAR command.

```
Select objects or specify first extension line origin or [Angular
Baseline Continue Ordinate aliGn Distribute Layer Undo]:
```

2. Move the cursor over the object to be dimensioned. The object gets highlighted and the preview of dimension appears in the drawing area, see Figure 6.73.

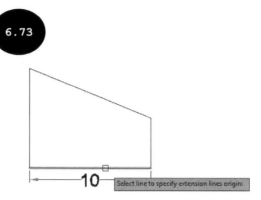

6.73

3. Click on the object to be dimensioned. The extension lines of the dimension are attached to the object and the dimension line is attached to the cursor. Also, you are prompted to specify the location for the dimension line.

```
Specify dimension line location or second line for angle [Mtext
Text text aNgle Undo]:
```

Note: To apply the vertical linear dimension to a vertical object, move the cursor over the object and then click on it. Similarly, to apply horizontal or vertical dimension to an aligned object, move the cursor over it. The preview of aligned dimension appears. Next, click the left mouse button on the aligned object and then move the cursor horizontally toward the left or right to apply the vertical dimension or move the cursor vertically upward or downward to apply the horizontal dimension.

4. Click in the drawing area to specify the location of the dimension line in the drawing area.

Note: In addition to selecting the object to be dimensioned, you can specify origin for the first and second extension line of the dimension by clicking the left mouse button on the end points (P1 and P2) one by one, see Figure 6.74. To select the end points of the object, make sure that the **Object Snap** mode is turned on.

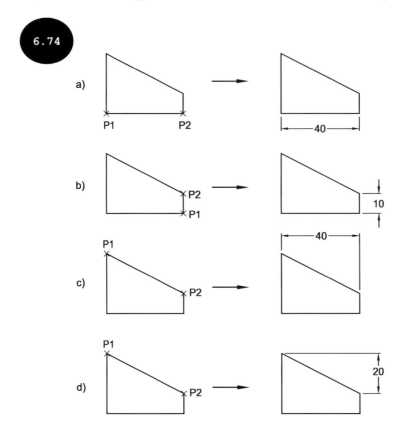

6.74

a)

b)

c)

d)

Note: If you invoke the **Linear** tool or the DIMLINEAR command for applying the linear dimension then you will be prompted to specify the origin of the first extension line "Specify first extension line origin or <select object>:". Click on the end points (P1 and P2) of the object to be dimensioned one by one (refer to Figure 6.74) as the origin of the first and second extension lines of the dimension and then specify the placement point for the dimension line. You can also select the object to be dimensioned instead of specifying the origin of the extension lines. For doing so, press the ENTER key when you are prompted to specify the origin of the first extension line.

The applied dimension parameters/settings such as dimension text, text height, text font, arrow height, and arrow style are based on the current dimension style.

Applying Aligned Dimension

An aligned dimension is used to measure the true aligned distance of an inclined object, see Figure 6.75. You can apply aligned dimension by using the **Dimension** tool, **Aligned** tool, or DIMALIGNED command. To apply the aligned dimension, you can select the object to be dimensioned or the end points of the object.

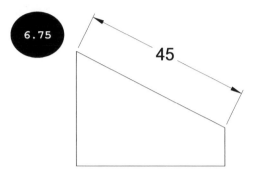

Procedure for Applying Aligned Dimension

1. Click on the **Dimension** tool in the **Annotation** panel in the **Home** tab. You are prompted to select objects to be dimensioned or specify origin for the first dimension extension line. Alternatively, invoke the **Dimension** flyout in the **Annotation** panel and then click on the **Aligned** tool for applying the aligned dimension. You can also invoke the **Aligned** tool by using the DIMALIGNED command.

```
Select objects or specify first extension line origin or [Angular
Baseline Continue Ordinate aliGn Distribute Layer Undo]:
```

2. Move the cursor over the aligned object to be dimensioned. The object is highlighted and the preview of aligned dimension appears in the drawing area, see Figure 6.76.

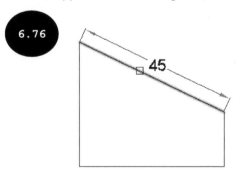

3. Click on the object to be dimensioned. The extension lines of the dimension are attached to the end points of the object and the dimension line is attached to the cursor. Also, you are prompted to specify the location for the dimension line.

```
Specify dimension line location or second line for angle [Mtext
Text text aNgle Undo]:
```

4. Press the SHIFT key and then move the cursor perpendicular to the selected object. The aligned dimension appears attached to the cursor.

5. Click in the drawing area to specify the location of the dimension line. The aligned dimension is applied.

Note: In addition to selecting the object to be dimensioned, you can specify the origin for the first and second extension line of the dimension by clicking the left mouse button on the end points (P1 and P2) of the object one by one, see Figure 6.77. To select the end points of the object, make sure that the **Object Snap** mode is turned on.

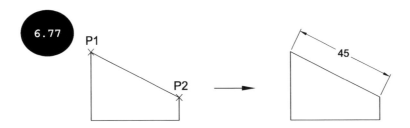

Note: If you invoke the **Aligned** tool or the DIMALIGNED command for applying the aligned dimension then you will be prompted to specify the origin of the first extension line "Specify first extension line origin or <select object>:". Click on the end points (P1 and P2) of the aligned object to be dimensioned one by one (refer to Figure 6.77) as the origin of the first and second extension lines of the dimension and then specify the placement point for the dimension line. You can also select the object to be dimensioned instead of specifying the origin of the extension lines. For doing so, press the ENTER key when you are prompted to specify the origin of the first extension line.

The applied dimension parameters/settings such as dimension text, text height, text font, arrow height, and arrow style are based on the current dimension style.

Applying Angular Dimension

An angular dimension is used to measure the angle between two non-parallel line objects, see Figure 6.78. In addition to measuring the angle between two non-parallel line objects, you can also apply angular dimensioning to an arc or a circle, see Figure 6.79. In AutoCAD, you can apply angular dimension by using the **Angular** tool.

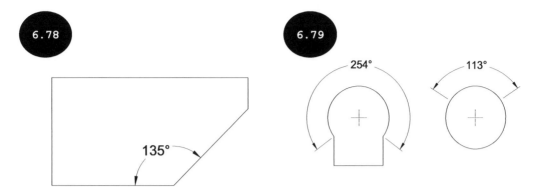

Procedure for Applying Angular Dimension between Line Objects

1. Invoke the **Dimension** flyout in the **Annotation** panel and then click on the **Angular** tool. You are prompted to select arc, circle, or line. You can also invoke the **Angular** tool by using the DIMANGULAR command.

   ```
   Select arc, circle, line, or <specify vertex>:
   ```

2. To apply angular dimension between two line objects, click on the first line object. You are prompted to select the second line object.

   ```
   Select second line:
   ```

3. Click on the second line object. The angular dimension is attached with the cursor and you are prompted to specify the location of the dimension in the drawing area.

   ```
   Specify  dimension  arc  line  location  or  [Mtext  Text  Angle
   Quadrant]:
   ```

4. Click in the drawing area to specify the location of the angular dimension. The angular dimension is applied.

Procedure for Applying Angular Dimension to an Arc

1. Click on the **Angular** tool in the **Dimension** flyout of the **Annotation** panel. You are prompted to select arc, circle, or line. Alternatively, enter DIMANGULAR in the Command Window and then press ENTER to invoke the **Angular** tool.

   ```
   Select arc, circle, line, or <specify vertex>:
   ```

2. Click on the arc to be dimensioned (P1), see Figure 6.80. The angular dimension is attached to the cursor and you are prompted to specify the location of the dimension in the drawing area.

   ```
   Specify  dimension  arc  line  location  or  [Mtext  Text  Angle
   Quadrant]:
   ```

3. Click to specify the location for the angular dimension in the drawing area (P2), see Figure 6.80. The angular dimension is applied to an arc and placed at the specified location (P2).

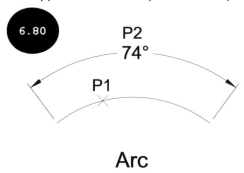

Arc

Procedure for Applying Angular Dimension to a Circle

1. Invoke the **Angular** tool. You are prompted to select arc, circle, or line.

```
Select arc, circle, line, or <specify vertex>:
```

2. Click on the circumference of the circle to be dimensioned (P1), see Figure 6.81. The specified point (P1) on the circle is used as the origin for the first extension line of the angular dimension. Also, you are prompted to specify the second angle endpoint (origin for the second extension line).

```
Specify second angle endpoint:
```

3. Click to specify a point (P2) on the circumference of the circle as the origin for the second extension line, see Figure 6.81. The angular dimension is attached with the cursor and you are prompted to specify the location of the dimension in the drawing area.

```
Specify dimension arc line location or [Mtext Text Angle
Quadrant]
```

4. Click to specify the location for the angular dimension (P3) in the drawing area, see Figure 6.81.

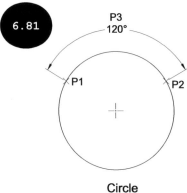

Circle

Procedure for Applying Angular Dimension by using Three Points

1. Invoke the **Angular** tool. You are prompted to select arc, circle, or line.

    ```
    Select arc, circle, line, or <specify vertex>:
    ```

2. Press the ENTER key to apply the angular dimension by using three points. You are prompted to specify the angle vertex (first point). Note that the first point is the vertex point and other two points are the endpoints of the angular dimension.

    ```
    Specify angle vertex:
    ```

3. Click to specify the angle vertex (V1), see Figure 6.82. You are prompted to specify the first angle endpoint.

    ```
    Specify first angle endpoint:
    ```

4. Click to specify the first angle endpoint (P1), see Figure 6.82. You are prompted to specify the second angle endpoint.

    ```
    Specify second angle endpoint:
    ```

5. Click to specify the second angle endpoint (P2), see Figure 6.82. The angular dimension is attached with the cursor and you are prompted to specify the location of the dimension in the drawing area.

    ```
    Specify dimension arc line location or [Mtext Text Angle Quadrant]:
    ```

6. Click to specify the location for the angular dimension in the drawing area, see Figure 6.82.

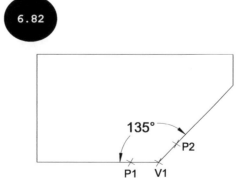

6.82

Applying Arc Length Dimension

An arc length dimension is used to measure the length of an arc or polyline arc segment, see Figure 6.83. You can apply arc length dimension by using the **Arc Length** tool of the **Dimension** flyout.

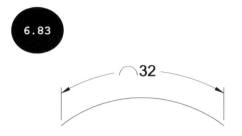

Procedure for Applying Arc Length Dimension

1. Invoke the **Dimension** flyout in the **Annotation** panel and then click on the **Arc Length** tool. You are prompted to select arc or polyline arc segment. You can also invoke this tool by using the DIMARC command.

    ```
    Select arc or polyline arc segment:
    ```

2. Click on an arc or a polyline to be dimensioned. The arc length dimension is attached with the cursor. Also, you are prompted to specify the location of the dimension in the drawing area.

    ```
    Specify  arc  length  dimension  location,  or  [Mtext  Text  Angle
    Partial]:
    ```

3. Click to specify the location for the arc length dimension in the drawing area.

Applying Radius Dimension

A radius dimension is used to measure the distance from the center to a point on the circumference of a circle/arc, see Figure 6.84. You can apply radius dimension to an arc or a circle by using the **Radius** tool of the **Dimension** flyout.

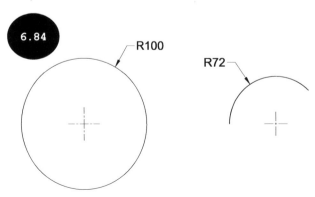

Procedure for Applying Radius Dimension

1. Invoke the **Dimension** flyout and then click on the **Radius** tool. You are prompted to select arc or circle. You can also invoke this tool by using the DIMRAD command.

    ```
    Select arc or circle:
    ```

2. Click on an arc or a circle for applying radius dimension. The radius dimension is attached with the cursor. Also, you are prompted to specify the location for the radius dimension in the drawing area.

    ```
    Specify dimension line location or [Mtext Text Angle]:
    ```

3. Click to specify the location for the radius dimension in the drawing area.

Applying Diameter Dimension

A diameter dimension is used to measure the distance from one point to another (diametrically opposite) on the circumference of a circle or an arc which passes through the center, see Figure 6.85. You can apply diameter dimension to an arc or a circle by using the **Diameter** tool.

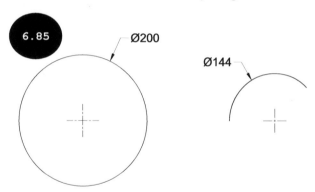

Procedure for Applying Diameter Dimension

1. Invoke the **Dimension** flyout and then click on the **Diameter** tool. You are prompted to select arc or circle. You can also invoke this tool by using the DIMDIA command.

    ```
    Select arc or circle:
    ```

2. Click on an arc or a circle for applying diameter dimension. The diameter dimension is attached with the cursor. Also, you are prompted to specify the location for the diameter dimension in the drawing area.

    ```
    Specify dimension line location or [Mtext Text Angle]:
    ```

3. Click to specify the location for the diameter dimension in the drawing area.

Applying Jogged Radius Dimension

A jogged dimension is used to apply jogged radius dimension to a circle or an arc whose center is not displayed in the drawing area or in the current viewport, see Figure 6.86. You can apply jogged radius dimension to an arc or a circle by using the **Jogged** tool.

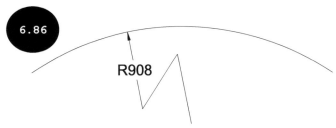

Procedure for Applying Jogged Radius Dimension

1.   Invoke the **Dimension** flyout and then click on the **Jogged** tool. You are prompted to select arc or circle. You can also invoke this tool by using the DIMJOGGED command.

```
Select arc or circle:
```

2.   Click on an arc or a circle for applying the jogged radius dimension (P1), see Figure 6.87. You are prompted to specify the override center location.

```
Specify center location override:
```

3.   Click to specify override center location (P2) for the selected object (arc or circle), see Figure 6.87. The preview of jogged dimension is attached with the cursor and you are prompted to specify the dimension line location.

```
Specify dimension line location or [Mtext Text Angle]:
```

4.   Click to specify dimension line location (P3), see Figure 6.87. You are prompted to specify jog location.

```
Specify jog location:
```

5.   Click to specify the jog location (P4), see Figure 6.87. The radius jogged dimension is applied, see Figure 6.87.

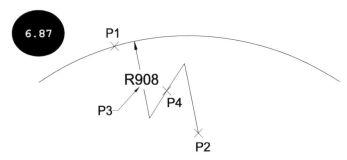

Applying Jogged Linear Dimension

A linear jogged dimension is applied to an object having high length to width ratio, see Figure 6.88. You can apply linear jogged dimension by using the **Jogged Linear** tool.

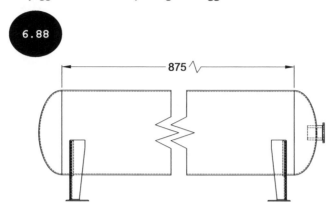

6.88

Procedure for Applying Jogged Linear Dimension

1. Invoke the **Jogged Linear** tool by clicking on the **Dimension** > **Jogged Linear** from the Menu Bar. You can also invoke this tool by using the DIMJOGLINE command. You are prompted to select the dimension to add jog.

   ```
   Select dimension to add jog or [Remove]:
   ```

2. Click on a linear dimension to add jog, see Figure 6.89. You are prompted to specify the jog location.

   ```
   Specify jog location (or press ENTER):
   ```

3. Click to specify a location for adding jog in the selected linear dimension, see Figure 6.89. The jog is added to the linear dimension at the specified location, see Figure 6.89.

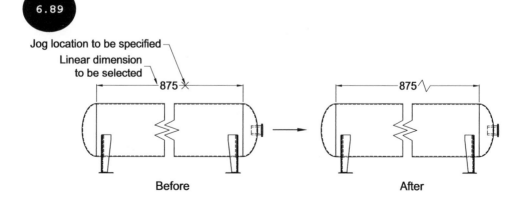

6.89

Before   After

Note: Instead of specifying the jog location, you can press ENTER to add jog in the default location of the linear dimension, automatically.

Applying Ordinate Dimension

Ordinate dimensions are used to dimension machine parts such as holes with respect to an origin for maintaining the accuracy. The ordinate dimensions measure the perpendicular distance from the specified origin and are described as X and Y ordinate dimensions, see Figure 6.90. Note that the X ordinate dimensions measure the distance from origin along the X axis and Y ordinate dimensions measure the distance from the origin along the Y axis, see Figure 6.90.

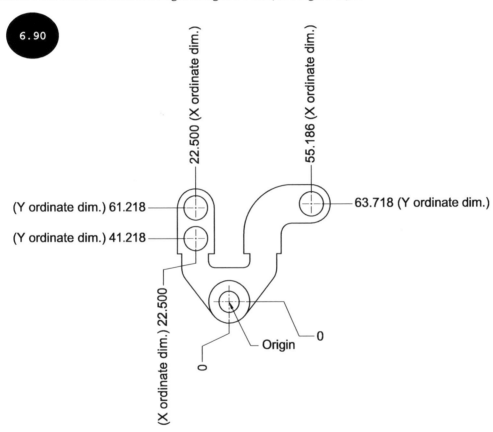

6.90

Procedure for Applying Ordinate Dimension

Before you start applying ordinate dimension, it is important to define the origin for measuring the dimensions.

1. Enter **UCS** in the Command Window and then press ENTER. You are prompted to specify the origin of the UCS.

   ```
   Specify origin of UCS or [Face NAmed OBject Previous View World X
   Y Z ZAxis] <World>: no
   ```

2. Click on the required location to specify the origin location (P1), see Figure 6.91. You can also enter coordinates (X, Y) for specifying the origin location. As soon as you specify the origin location of the UCS, you are prompted to specify a point on X-axis.

```
Specify point on X-axis or <accept>:
```

3. Click to specify a point for the X-axis of the UCS. Note that if you specify the X-axis direction of the UCS, it is recommended to turn on the **Object snap** mode. Next, press ENTER. A UCS is created at the specified origin.

   After specifying the origin location by using the UCS, you can apply the ordinate dimensions.

4. Invoke the **Dimension** flyout of the **Annotation** panel in the **Home** tab and then click on the **Ordinate** tool. You can also use the DIMORD command to invoke this tool. You are prompted to specify the feature location.

```
Specify feature location:
```

5. Click on a point/feature (P2) for applying the X or Y ordinate dimension, see Figure 6.91. You are prompted to specify the leader endpoint location.

```
Specify leader endpoint or [Xdatum Ydatum Mtext Text Angle]:
```

6. Move the cursor vertically upward and then click to specify the leader endpoint location for the X ordinate dimension in the drawing area. The X ordinate dimension is applied.

7. Similarly, invoke the **Ordinate** tool again from the **Dimension** flyout and then click on the point/feature (P2) for applying the Y ordinate dimension, see Figure 6.91.

8. Move the cursor horizontally toward the right and then click to specify the leader endpoint location for the Y ordinate dimension. The Y ordinate dimension is applied.

9. Similarly, invoke the **Ordinate** tool again and apply the remaining ordinate dimensions with respect to the specified origin (UCS), see Figure 6.91.

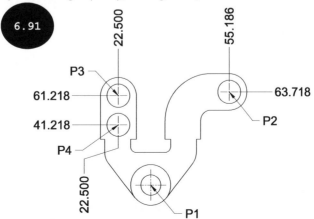

Applying Baseline Dimensions

Baseline dimensions are the series of parallel linear dimensions that share the same base point, see Figure 6.92. The baseline dimensions are used in order to eliminate cumulative errors that can occur due to the rounded dimension values between consecutive adjacent dimensions or due to the upper and lower dimension limits. In AutoCAD, you can apply baseline dimensions by using the **Baseline** tool or by using the DIMBASE command.

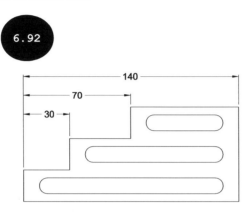

6.92

Procedure for Applying Baseline Dimensions

Before you start applying the baseline dimensions, you need to apply a linear/angular dimension which will be selected as the base dimension.

1. Apply a linear dimension in the drawing as the base dimension by using the **Linear** tool, see Figure 6.93.

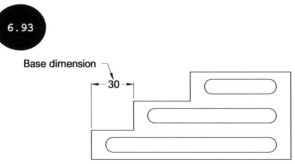

6.93

After applying the base dimension, you can apply the baseline dimensions by using the **Baseline** tool.

2. Click on the **Dimension > Baseline** from the Menu Bar. The preview of the baseline dimension appears whose origin of the first extension line is fixed at the first extension line of the base dimension and you are prompted to specify the origin of the second extension line. You can also invoke this tool by using the DIMBASE command.

```
Specify a second extension line origin or [Undo Select]
<Select>:
```

Note: If the linear, angular, or ordinate dimensions are present in the current drawing then the last applied dimension will be selected as the base dimension, automatically. Also, you are prompted to specify the origin of the second extension line. If you want to skip the automatic selection of base dimension then press the ENTER key. On doing so, you will be prompted to select the base dimension.

3. Move the cursor toward a point (P1) of the drawing which is to be selected as the origin of the second extension line, see Figure 6.94.

4. Click to specify the origin of the second extension line when the cursor snaps to the point in the drawing area. The baseline dimension is placed by maintaining the default baseline spacing, which is specified in the current dimension style. Also, the preview of another baseline dimension is attached with the cursor whose origin of the first extension line is fixed at the first extension line of the base dimension and you are prompted to specify the origin of the second extension line.

    ```
    Specify a second extension line origin or [Undo Select]
    <Select>:
    ```

Note: The default spacing between the baseline dimensions is controlled by the current dimension style parameters. You can modify the spacing between the baseline dimensions by entering the new value in the **Baseline spacing** field of the **Lines** tab in the **Modify Dimension Style** dialog box, as discussed earlier in this chapter.

5. Move the cursor toward a point (P2) in the drawing which is to be selected as the origin of the second extension line, see Figure 6.94.

6. Click to specify the origin of the second extension line when the cursor snaps to the point. The second baseline dimension is applied (see Figure 6.94) and the preview of another baseline dimension is attached with the cursor and you are prompted to specify the origin of the second extension line.

    ```
    Specify a second extension line origin or [Undo Select]
    <Select>:
    ```

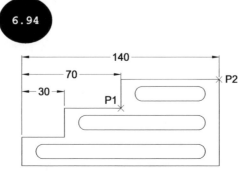

7. Similarly, you can continue to specify the origin of the second extension line and apply multiple baseline dimensions. Once you are done with applying the baseline dimensions, press the ENTER key twice to exit the tool.

Applying Continue Dimensions

Similar to applying baseline dimensions, you can apply continue dimensions in a drawing, see Figure 6.95. Continue dimensions are the chain of linear dimensions which are placed end to end (second extension line of a linear dimension is used as the first extension line for the next linear dimension). In AutoCAD, you can apply continue dimensions by using the **Continue** tool or by using the DIMCONT command.

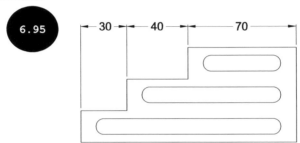

Procedure for Applying Continue Dimensions

Before you start applying the continue dimensions, you need to apply a linear/angular dimension as the base dimension.

1. Apply a linear dimension in the drawing as the base dimension by using the **Linear** tool, see Figure 6.96.

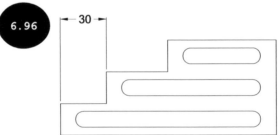

After applying the base dimension, you can apply the continue dimensions by using the **Continue** tool.

2. Click on the **Dimension > Continue** in the Menu Bar. The preview of the continue dimension is attached with the cursor whose first extension line is fixed at the second extension line of the base dimension and you are prompted to specify the origin of the second extension line. You can also invoke this tool by using the DIMCONT command.

```
Specify a second extension line origin or [Undo Select]
<Select>:
```

Note: If the linear, angular, or ordinate dimensions are present in the current drawing then the last applied dimension is selected as the base dimension, automatically. Also, you are prompted to specify the origin of the second extension line. If you want to skip the automatic selection of base dimension then press the ENTER key. On doing so, you are prompted to select the base dimension.

3. Move the cursor toward a point (P1) which is to be selected as the origin of the second extension line, see Figure 6.97.

4. Click to specify the origin of the second extension line when the cursor snaps to the point in the drawing area. The continue linear dimension is placed and the preview of another linear dimension is attached with the cursor whose origin of the first extension line is fixed at the second extension line of the previous dimension and you are prompted to specify the origin of the second extension line.

5. Move the cursor toward a point (P2) which is to be selected as the origin of the second extension line, see Figure 6.97.

6. Click to specify the origin of the second extension line when the cursor snaps to the point. The second linear dimension is applied and the preview of another linear dimension is attached with the cursor whose origin of the first extension line is fixed at the second extension line of the previous dimension and you are prompted to specify the origin of the second extension line.

```
Specify a second extension line origin or [Undo Select]
<Select>:
```

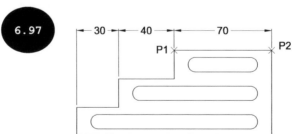

6.97

7. Similarly, you can continue to specify the origin of the second extension line and apply multiple continue linear dimensions. Once you have applied all the required continue dimensions, press the ENTER key twice to exit the tool.

Applying Multiple Dimensions

In addition to apply individual dimension one by one, as discussed, AutoCAD allows you to apply multiple dimensions together by using the **Quick Dimension** tool or QDIM command. You can apply multiple dimensions such as radius, diameter, baseline, or continue.

Procedure for Applying Multiple Dimensions

1. Click on the **Dimension > Quick Dimension** in the Menu Bar. Alternatively, enter QDIM in the Command Window and then press ENTER. You are prompted to select geometry.

    ```
    Select geometry to dimension:
    ```

2. Select geometries to be dimensioned by using the Window or Cross Window selection method, see Figure 6.98.

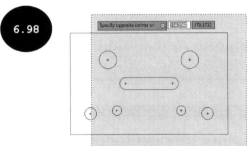

3. Once you have selected geometries to be dimensioned, press ENTER. The preview of continue dimensions are attached with the cursor and you are prompted to specify their position.

    ```
    Specify dimension line position, or [Continuous Staggered Baseline
    Ordinate Radius Diameter datumPoint Edit SeTtings] <Continuous>:
    ```

> **Note:** By default, the continue dimension is applied to the selected geometries. To apply baseline dimensions, click on the **Baseline** option in the command prompt or enter **B**. Similarly, to apply radius or diameter dimensions, click on the **Radius** or **Diameter** option in the command prompt or enter **R** or **D** in the Command Window.

4. Select the required type of dimensions to be applied by using the options available in the command prompt. For example, to apply multiple diameter dimensions, click on the **Diameter** option in the command prompt or enter **D**.

5. After specifying the type of dimensions to be applied, click to define the placement point in the drawing area. The selected type of dimensions are applied to the geometries. Figure 6.99 shows a drawing in which multiple diameter dimensions are applied.

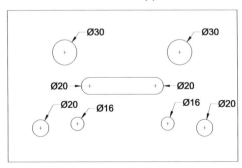

Tutorial 1

Create the drawing and apply dimensions as shown in Figure 6.100. You need to apply dimensions as per the new dimension style having following dimension parameters.

New Dimension Style Parameters	
Text font	Arial
Text font style	Regular
Text height	4.75
Text placement - Offset from dimension line	2.5
Arrowheads style	Closed filled
Arrow size	4.5
Center marks	Mark - 1
Dimension break size	3.5
Extension lines - Extend beyond dimension lines	2
Extension lines - Offset from origin	1.75
Linear dimensions - Precision	0
Angular dimensions - Precision	0

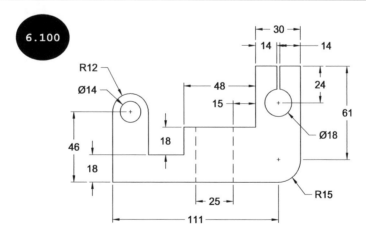

Section 1: Starting a new AutoCAD Drawing

1. Start AutoCAD and then open a new drawing file.

Section 2: Creating Drawing

1. Click on the **Line** tool in the **Draw** panel of the **Home** tab. You are prompted to specify the first point of the line. Alternatively, enter **L** in the Command Window and then press ENTER to invoke the **Line** tool.

    Specify first point:

2.   Click to specify the first/start point of the line in the drawing area. You are prompted to specify the next point of the line.

3.   Make sure that the Dynamic Input mode and the Ortho mode are turned on or activated.

4.   Follow the command sequence given below for creating the drawing.

Specify next point or [Undo]: *Move the cursor horizontally toward the right and then enter 126 in the Dynamic Input box*   (***ENTER***)

Specify next point or [Undo]: *Move the cursor vertically upward and then enter 76* (***ENTER***)

Specify next point or [Undo]: *Move the cursor horizontally toward the left and then enter 14*   (***ENTER***)

Specify next point or [Undo]: *Move the cursor vertically downwards and enter 24* (***ENTER***)

Specify next point or [Close Undo]: *Move the cursor horizontally toward the left and then enter 2*   (***ENTER***)

Specify next point or [Undo]: *Move the cursor vertically upward and then enter 24* (***ENTER***)

Specify next point or [Close Undo]: *Move the cursor horizontally toward the left and then enter 14*   (***ENTER***)

Specify next point or [Undo]: *Move the cursor vertically downward and then enter 40*   (***ENTER***)

Specify next point or [Close Undo]: *Move the cursor horizontally toward the left and then enter 48*   (***ENTER***)

Specify next point or [Close Undo]: *Move the cursor vertically downward and then enter 18*   (***ENTER***)

Specify next point or [Close Undo]: *Move the cursor horizontally toward the left and then enter 24*   (***ENTER***)

Specify next point or [Close Undo]: *Move the cursor vertically upward and then enter 28*   (***ENTER***)

Specify next point or [Close Undo]: *Move the cursor horizontally toward the left and then enter 24*   (***ENTER***)

Specify next point or [Close Undo]: *C or Close* (***ENTER***)   *(See Figure 6.101)*

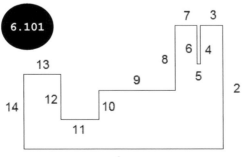

6.101

Note: In Figure 6.101, the entities are numbered for your reference to create other entities of the drawing.

After creating the line entities of the drawing, you need to create circle entities.

5. Click on the **Circle, Radius** tool in the **Circle** flyout of the **Draw** panel or enter **C** in the Command Window and then press ENTER. You are prompted to specify the center point of the circle.

```
Specify center point for circle or [3P 2P Ttr (tan tan radius)]:
```

6. Move the cursor toward the mid point of the horizontal line (13), see Figure 6.102.

7. Click to specify the center point of the circle when cursor snaps to the mid point of the horizontal line (13), see Figure 6.102. You are prompted to specify the radius of the circle.

```
Specify radius of circle or [Diameter]:
```

8. Enter **12** as the radius of the circle and then press ENTER. The circle of radius 12 units is created, see Figure 6.103.

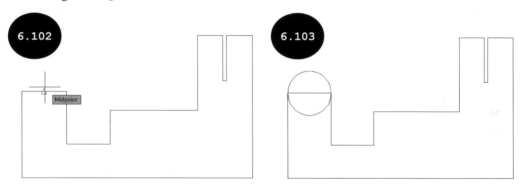

9. Similarly, create another two circles of radius 9 units and 7 units, see Figure 6.104. The center point of the circle having radius 9 units is at the mid point of line (5) and the center point of the circle having radius 7 units is at the mid point of line (13), see Figure 6.104.

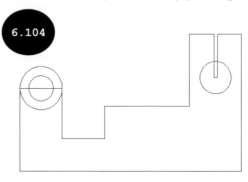

Now, you need to create a vertical line at an offset distance of 45 units from the vertical line (2).

10. Click on the **Offset** tool in the **Modify** panel of the **Home** tab or enter **O** in the Command Window and then press ENTER. You are prompted to specify the offset distance.

```
Specify offset distance or [Through Erase Layer] <Through>:
```

11. Enter **45** as the offset distance and then press ENTER. You are prompted to select object to offset.

```
Select object to offset or [Exit Undo] <Exit>:
```

12. Click on the vertical line (2) as the object to offset, refer to Figure 6.101. You are prompted to specify a point on the side to offset.

```
Specify point on side to offset or [Exit Multiple Undo] <Exit>:
```

13. Move the cursor toward left and then click to specify a point on the left side of the selected vertical line (2). The vertical line at the offset distance of 45 units is created, see Figure 6.105.

14. Press ENTER to exit the tool.

15. Similarly, create another vertical line at the offset distance of 25 units from the newly created vertical line, see Figure 6.106.

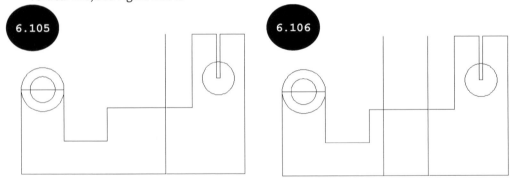

Now, you need to trim the unwanted portions of the entities.

Section 3: Trimming the Drawing Entities

1. Click on the **Trim** tool in the **Modify** panel or enter **TR** in the Command Window and then press ENTER. You are prompted to select cutting edges/boundaries.

```
Select cutting edges ...
Select objects or <select all>:
```

2. Press ENTER to skip the selection of cutting edges/boundaries. You are prompted to select object to trim.

```
Select object to trim or shift-select to extend or
[Fence Crossing Project Edge eRase Undo]:
```

3. Click on the unwanted entity (1) to be trimmed, see Figure 6.107. The selected entity is trimmed to its nearest intersection, see Figure 6.108. Also, you are prompted to select object to trim.

```
Select object to trim or shift-select to extend or
[Fence Crossing Project Edge eRase Undo]:
```

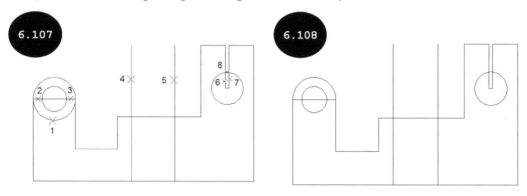

4. Similarly, click on the other unwanted entities (2, 3, 4, 5, 6, 7, and 8), see Figure 6.107. Figure 6.109 shows the drawing after trimming all the unwanted entities.

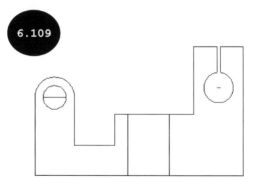

5. Once you have trimmed the entities, press the ENTER key to exit the tool.

Section 4: Deleting the Unwanted Entities

1. Click on the horizontal entities inside the circles of radius 7 units and 9 units as the entities to be deleted from the drawing area, see Figure 6.110.

2. Press the DELETE key. The selected entities are deleted, see Figure 6.111.

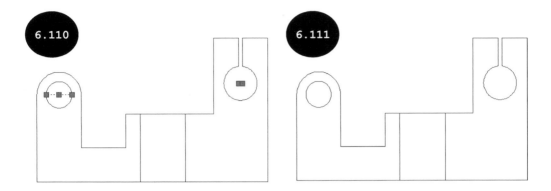

Section 5: Creating Fillet

1. Click on the **Fillet** tool in the **Modify** panel or enter **F** in the Command Window and then press ENTER. You are prompted to select the first object of the fillet.

    ```
    Select first object or [Undo Polyline Radius Trim Multiple]:
    ```

2. Click on the **Radius** option in the command prompt or enter **R** and then press ENTER. You are prompted to specify the fillet radius.

    ```
    Specify fillet radius <0.0000>:
    ```

3. Enter **15** as the fillet radius and then press ENTER. You are prompted to select the first object of the fillet.

    ```
    Select first object or [Undo Polyline Radius Trim Multiple]:
    ```

4. Click on the right most vertical line of the drawing as the first object of the fillet. You are prompted to select the second object of the fillet.

    ```
    Select second object or shift-select to apply corner or [Radius]:
    ```

5. Click on the bottom horizontal line as the second object of the fillet. The fillet of radius 15 is created, see Figure 6.112.

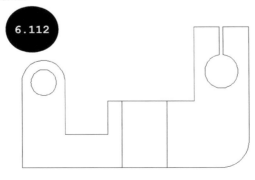

Section 6: Creating Layers

Now, you need to create layers: Object, Hidden, and Dimension. Next, assign different drawing objects to the respective layers such as hidden objects to the Hidden layer.

1. Click on the **Layer Properties** tool in the **Layers** panel of the **Home** tab or enter **LA** in the Command Window and then press ENTER. The **LAYER PROPERTIES MANAGER** appears, see Figure 6.113.

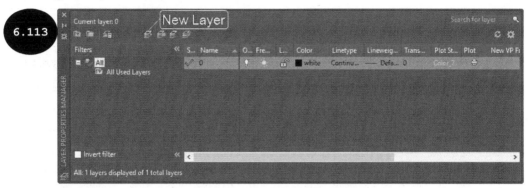

2. Click on the **New Layer** button in the **LAYER PROPERTIES MANAGER** or press ALT + N key. A new layer with default name "**Layer 1**" is created.

3. Enter **Object** as the name of the newly created layer in the **LAYER PROPERTIES MANAGER**. Accept the default parameters for the newly created Object layer.

4. Similarly, create two more layers: Hidden and Dimension. Also, assign the HIDDEN linetype to the Hidden layer and accept the default parameters for Dimension layer, see Figure 6.114.

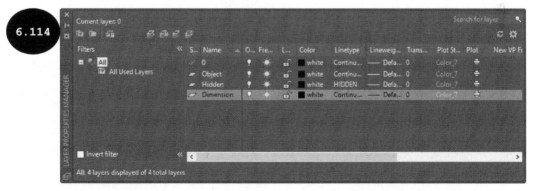

5. Once you have created all the layers, close the **LAYER PROPERTIES MANAGER**.

Section 7: Assigning Drawing Objects to the respective Layers

1. Select all the drawing objects except two vertical lines (hidden lines), see Figure 6.115.

2. Invoke the **Layer** drop-down list in the **Layers** panel of the **Home** tab, see 6.116.

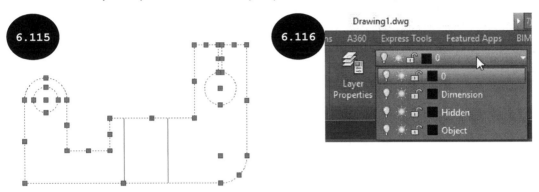

3. Move the cursor over the **Object** layer in the **Layer** drop-down list and then click on it to assign the selected objects to the **Object** layer. Next, press the ESC key to exit the selection.

4. Select two vertical lines to assign them to the Hidden layer, see Figure 6.117.

5. Invoke the **Layer** drop-down list, refer to Figure 6.116, and then click on the **Hidden** layer. The selected vertical lines are assigned to the **Hidden** layer, see Figure 6.118. Next, press the ESC key to exit the selection.

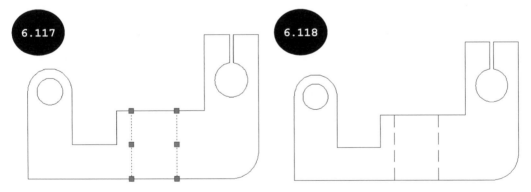

After creating the drawing, you need to apply dimensions. As mentioned in the tutorial description, you need to apply dimensions as per the new dimension style. Therefore, you need to first create a new dimension style.

Section 8: Creating New Dimension Style

1. Enter **D** in the Command Window and then press ENTER. The **Dimension Style Manager** dialog box appears, see Figure 6.119.

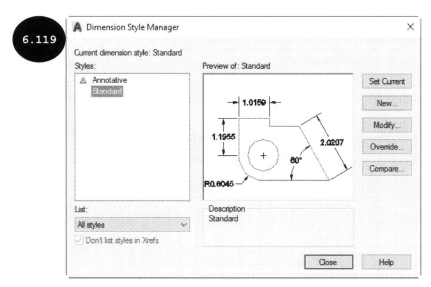

2. Click on the **Standard** dimension style in the **Styles** area of the dialog box as the base dimension style for creating the new dimension style.

3. Click on the **New** button in the **Dimension Style Manager** dialog box. The **Create New Dimension Style** dialog box appears.

4. Enter **C06_TUT** as the name of the new dimension style in the **New Style Name** field of the dialog box.

5. Click on the **Continue** button of the **Create New Dimension Style** dialog box. The **New Dimension Style** dialog box appears, see Figure 6.120.

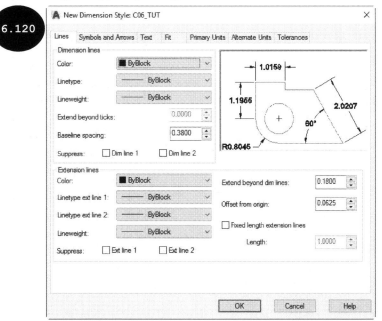

6.   Make sure that the **Text** tab is active in this dialog box.

7.   Make sure that the **Standard** option is selected in the **Text style** drop-down list.

8.   Click on the **[...]** □ button available next to the **Text style** drop-down list. The **Text Style** dialog box appears.

9.   Make sure that the **Arial** option is selected in the **Font Name** drop-down list and the **Regular** option is selected in the **Font Style** drop-down list in this **Text Style** dialog box.

10. Click on the **Cancel** button to exit the **Text Style** dialog box.

11. Enter **4.75** in the **Text height** field of the **Text appearance** area in the **Text** tab of the dialog box.

12. Enter **2.5** in the **Offset from dim line** field of the **Text placement** area in the **Text** tab.

13. Click on the **Symbols and Arrows** tab in the **New Dimension Style** dialog box.

14. Make sure that the **Closed filled** option is selected in the **First**, **Second**, and **Leader** drop-down lists of the **Arrowheads** area in the **Symbols and Arrows** tab.

15. Enter **4.5** in the **Arrow size** field of the **Arrowheads** area.

16. Make sure that the **Mark** radio button is selected in the **Center mark** area.

17. Enter **1** in the field available in front of **Mark** radio button of the **Center mark** area.

18. Enter **3.5** in the **Break size** field of the **Dimension Break** area.

19. Click on the **Lines** tab in the **New Dimension Style** dialog box.

20. Enter **2** in the **Extend beyond dim lines** field of the **Extension lines** area in the **Lines** tab.

21. Enter **1.75** in the **Offset from origin** field of the **Extension lines** area.

22. Click on the **Primary Units** tab in the dialog box.

23. Select the **0** option in the **Precision** drop-down list of the **Linear dimensions** area.

24. Select the **0** option in the **Precision** drop-down list of the **Angular dimensions** area.

25. Accept the remaining default settings and then click on the **OK** button in the **New Dimension Style** dialog box. The new dimension style named as C06_TUT is created and is listed in the **Styles** area of the **Dimension Style Manager** dialog box.

26. Click on the newly created dimension style "C06_TUT" in the **Styles** area of the **Dimension Style Manager** dialog box.

27. Click on the **Set Current** button in the dialog box to make the newly created dimension style as the current dimension style of the drawing.

28. Click on the **Close** button in the **Dimension Style Manager** dialog box to exit the dialog box.

After creating the dimension style and making it the current style of the drawing, you need to apply dimensions to the drawing.

Section 9: Applying Dimensions

1. Click on the **Linear** tool in the **Dimension** flyout of the **Annotation** panel in the **Home** tab or enter **DIMLIN** in the Command Window and then press ENTER. You are prompted to specify the origin for the first extension line.

   ```
   Specify first extension line origin or <select object>:
   ```

2. Press ENTER to directly select the object to be dimensioned. You are prompted to select the object to be dimensioned.

   ```
   Select object to dimension:
   ```

3. Click on the bottom horizontal line of the drawing. The linear dimension of the selected line is attached with the cursor. Also, you are prompted to specify the dimension line location.

   ```
   Specify dimension line location or
   [Mtext Text Angle Horizontal Vertical Rotated]:
   ```

4. Move the cursor vertically downward to a small distance and then click to specify the location for the attached dimension, see Figure 6.121.

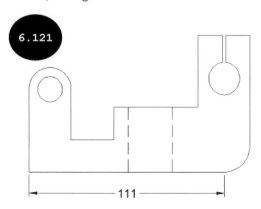

6.121

5. Click on the **Linear** tool in the **Dimension** flyout again. You are prompted to specify the origin for the first extension line.

```
Specify first extension line origin or <select object>:
```

6. Move the cursor toward the upper right corner of the drawing (P1), see Figure 6.122. Next, click on it to specify the origin of the first extension line when the cursor snaps to the point (P1). You are prompted to specify the origin of the second extension line.

```
Specify second extension line origin:
```

7. Move the cursor toward the center point of the right circle (P2), see Figure 6.122. Next, click to specify the origin of the second extension line when the cursor snaps to it. The linear dimension between the selected points (P1 and P2) is attached with the cursor. Also, you are prompted to specify the dimension location.

```
Specify dimension line location or
[Mtext Text Angle Horizontal Vertical Rotated]:
```

8. Move the cursor horizontally toward the right to a small distance and then click to specify the location for the attached dimension, see Figure 6.122.

9. Similarly, apply the remaining linear (horizontal and vertical) dimensions to other entities of the drawing, see Figure 6.123. You can apply dimension by selecting the object to be dimensioned or by selecting points. Make sure that the Object snap mode is turned on for selecting points. Figure 6.123 shows the drawing after applying all the linear dimensions.

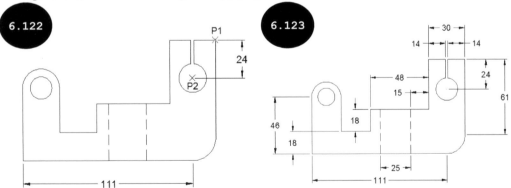

After applying the linear dimensions, you need to apply radius dimensions to the arc entities.

10. Click on the **Dimension** tool in the **Annotation** panel. You are prompted to select the object to be dimensioned. Alternatively, click on the **Radius** tool in the **Dimension** flyout of the **Annotation** panel or enter DIMRAD in the Command Window and then press ENTER.

```
Select objects or specify first extension line origin or [Angular
Baseline Continue Ordinate aliGn Distribute Layer Undo]:
```

11. Move the cursor toward the upper left arc (A1), see Figure 6.124 and then click on it. The radius dimension is attached with the cursor and you are prompted to specify the dimension location.

```
Specify dimension line location or [Mtext Text Angle]:
```

12. Click to specify the dimension location on the upper left side of the selected arc (A1). The radius dimension 12 units is applied to the arc, see Figure 6.124.

13. Similarly, apply the radius dimension to the arc (A2), see Figure 6.124.

   After applying the radius dimension to the arcs, you need to apply diameter dimension to the circle.

14. Move the cursor toward the circle (C1), see Figure 6.125 and then click on it. The diameter dimension is attached with the cursor and you are prompted to specify the dimension location.

Note: You can also apply diameter dimensions to circles by using the **Diameter** tool of the **Dimension** flyout or by using the DIMDIA command.

15. Click to specify the dimension location above the selected circle (C1). The diameter dimension is applied, see Figure 6.125.

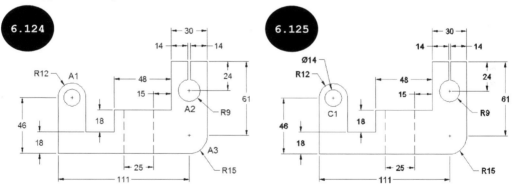

After applying all the dimensions to the drawing entities, you need to move them to the Dimension layer.

16. Select all the dimensions and then invoke the **Layer** drop-down list of the **Layers** panel in the **Home** tab. Next, click on the **Dimension** layer to assign all the selected dimensions to it.

Section 10: Saving the Drawing

After creating the drawing, you need to save it.

1. Click on the **Save** tool in the **Quick Access Toolbar**. The **Save Drawing As** dialog box appears.

2. Browse to the *AutoCAD* folder and then create a folder with the name *Chapter 6* inside the *AutoCAD* folder.

3. Enter **Tutorial 1** in the **File name** field of the dialog box and then click on the **Save** button. The drawing is saved with the name Tutorial 1 in the *Chapter 6* folder.

Hands-on Test Drive 1

Create the drawing and apply dimensions as shown in Figure 6.126. You need to modify the default dimension style "Standard" for applying the dimensions. Below are the dimension parameters to be modified in the Standard dimension style.

Dimension Style Parameters	
Text font	Arial
Text font style	Regular
Text height	4.5
Text placement - Offset from dimension line	1.75
Arrowheads style	Closed filled
Arrow size	4.25
Center marks	Mark - 1
Dimension break size	3
Extension lines - Extend beyond dimension lines	1.25
Extension lines - Offset from origin	1
Linear dimensions - Precision	0
Angular dimensions - Precision	0

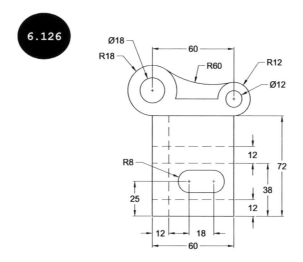

Hands-on Test Drive 2

Create the drawing and apply dimensions as shown in Figure 6.127. You need to modify the default dimension style "Standard" for applying the dimensions. The dimension parameters to be modified in the Standard dimension style are same as mentioned in the Hands-on Test Drive 1 description.

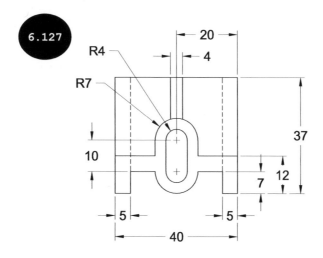

Hands-on Test Drive 3

Create the drawing and apply dimensions as shown in Figure 6.128. You need to modify the default dimension style "Standard" for applying the dimensions. The dimension parameters to be modified in the Standard dimension style are same as mentioned in the Hands-on Test Drive 1 description.

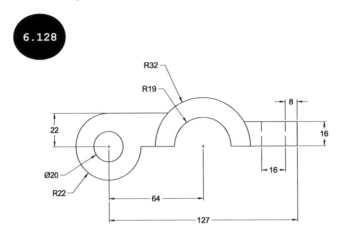

Hands-on Test Drive 4

Create the drawing and apply Continue dimensions as shown in Figure 6.129. You need to create the new dimension style for applying the Continue dimensions. The dimension parameters for creating the new dimension style are as follows.

New Dimension Style Parameters	
Text font	Arial
Text font style	Regular
Text height	2.75
Text placement - Offset from dimension line	1.5
Arrowheads style	Closed filled
Arrow size	2.5
Center marks	Mark - 1
Dimension break size	3.5
Extension lines - Extend beyond dimension lines	1.25
Extension lines - Offset from origin	1
Linear dimensions - Precision	0
Angular dimensions - Precision	0

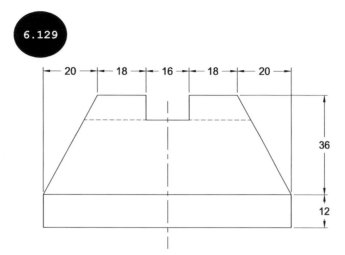

6.129

Summary

In this chapter, you have learned about various components of a dimension, how to create a new dimension style, modify existing dimension style, and override dimension style. You have also learned how to apply various types of dimensions such as linear dimension, aligned dimension, angular dimension, diameter dimension, radius dimension, jogged dimension, ordinate dimension, and baseline dimension.

Questions

- You can modify an existing dimension style or create a new dimension style, as required, by using the _____ dialog box.

- You can break dimension lines which are intersecting with other dimension or drawing object by using the _____ command.

- You can invoke the **Dimension Style Manager** dialog box by entering the _____ in the Command Window and then pressing the ENTER key.

- When you apply a dimension in AutoCAD, a new layer named as _____ is created, automatically.

- An _____ dimension is used to measure the angle between two non-parallel line objects.

- An _____ dimension is used to measure the length of an arc or a polyline arc segment.

- A _____ dimension is used to apply the jogged radius dimension to a circle or an arc whose center is not displayed in the drawing area.

- A _____ dimension is used to apply the linear dimension to an object having a high length to width ratio.

- The _____ dimensions are the series of parallel linear dimensions that share the same base point.

- AutoCAD allows you can apply multiple dimensions together by using the _____ tool or _____ command.

Editing Dimensions and Adding Text

In this chapter, you will learn the following:

- Editing dimensions using DIMEDIT command
- Editing dimensions using DIMTEDIT command
- Editing dimensions using DDEDIT command
- Editing dimensions using dimension grips
- Editing dimensions using PROPERTIES palette
- Editing dimensions using editing tools
- Adding text/notes to drawings
- Creating and modifying text style
- Adding text using the Single Line tool
- Adding text using the Multiline Text tool
- Editing Single line and Multiline Text
- Converting Single line Text to Multiline Text

In this chapter, you will learn about editing and modifying dimensions. As the drawing process involves several design revisions, the editing and modifying dimensions become very important. AutoCAD is provided with various tools/commands which make the editing and modification process faster and easy. You can edit the dimension text/value, add a prefix or suffix to the dimension value, modify dimension text format, dimension position, dimension text justification, and so on by using the DIMEDIT command, DIMTEDIT command, DDEDIT command, Dimension grips, or by using the Properties palette. Moreover, you can edit the dimensions by using the editing tools such as **Trim**, **Extend**, and **Stretch**. In addition to editing dimensions by using various tools/commands, in this chapter, you will also learn about annotating drawings.

Editing Dimensions using DIMEDIT Command

The DIMEDIT command is used to edit dimension text/value such that you can rotate, modify, restore, and specify new dimension text/value. Moreover, you can change the oblique angle of extension lines by using this command. The procedures to specify new dimension text/value, rotate and restore dimension text, change oblique angle of dimension text are as follows:

Procedure for Specifying New Dimension Text/Value

1. Enter DIMEDIT in the Command Window and then press ENTER. You are prompted to enter the editing type.

    ```
    Enter  type  of  dimension  editing  [Home  New  Rotate  Oblique]
    <Home>:
    ```

2. Click on the **New** option in the command prompt or enter **N** and then press ENTER. An edit field appears in the drawing area.

3. Enter new dimension text/value in the edit field and then click the left mouse button anywhere in the drawing area. You are prompted to select objects. You can also enter a prefix or suffix to the dimension text/value.

    ```
    Select objects:
    ```

4. Click on the dimension for specifying the new dimension text/value. Next, press ENTER. The dimension text/value of the selected dimension is changed/override to the new dimension text/value.

    Note: The newly specified/edited dimension text/value is a override dimension value, which does not effect the original size of the object.

Procedure for Rotating Dimension Text

1. Enter DIMEDIT in the Command Window and then press ENTER. You are prompted to enter the editing type.

    ```
    Enter  type  of  dimension  editing  [Home  New  Rotate  Oblique]
    <Home>:
    ```

2. Click on the **Rotate** option in the command prompt or enter **R** and then press ENTER. You are prompted to specify the rotational angle for dimension text.

    ```
    Specify angle for dimension text:
    ```

3. Enter rotational angle for dimension text and then press ENTER. You are prompted to select objects to rotate.

    ```
    Select objects:
    ```

4. Click on the dimension whose dimension text is to be rotated and then press ENTER. The dimension text of the selected dimension is rotated to a specified angle, see Figure 7.1.

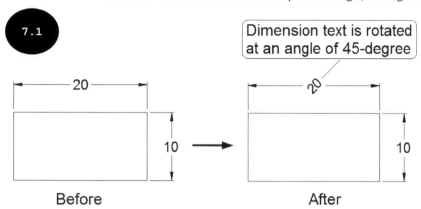

Before   After

Procedure for Restoring Dimension Text to the Original Position

1. Enter DIMEDIT in the Command Window and then press ENTER.

```
Enter type of dimension editing [Home New Rotate Oblique]
<Home>:
```

2. Click on the **Home** option in the command prompt or enter H and then press ENTER. You are prompted to select objects.

```
Select objects:
```

3. Click on the dimension whose dimension text has to be restored to its original position and then press ENTER. The dimension text of the selected dimension is restored to its default/ original position.

Procedure for Changing Oblique Angle of Extension Lines

1. Enter DIMEDIT in the Command Window and then press ENTER.

```
Enter type of dimension editing [Home New Rotate Oblique]
<Home>:
```

2. Click on the **Oblique** option in the command prompt or enter O and then press ENTER. You are prompted to select objects.

```
Select objects:
```

3. Click on dimensions whose oblique angle of extension lines have to be changed and then press ENTER. You are prompted to enter oblique angle.

```
Enter obliquing angle (press ENTER for none):
```

4.   Enter the oblique angle and then press ENTER. The oblique angle of extension lines has been changed, see Figure 7.2.

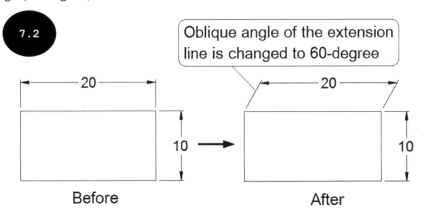

Editing Dimensions using DIMTEDIT Command

The DIMTEDIT command is used to change the dimension text justification and angle. The procedure to change dimension text justification and angle is as follows:

Procedure for Changing Dimension Text Justification and Angle

1.   Enter DIMTEDIT in the Command Window and then press ENTER. You are prompted to select dimension.

```
Select dimension:
```

2.   Click on the dimension to be edited. The dimension text is attached with the cursor and you are prompted to specify a new location for the dimension text.

```
Specify new location for dimension text or [Left Right Center Home
Angle]:
```

3.   Click on the **Left**, **Right**, or **Center** option in the command prompt for left, right, or center justification of the dimension text, respectively. Alternatively, enter **L**, **R**, or **C** in the Command Window and then press ENTER. The dimension text is placed as per the option selected, see Figure 7.3.

Note: By using the **Angle** option of the command prompt, you can change the angle/orientation of the dimension text. Also, you can restore the dimension text to the previous position or orientation by using the **Home** option of the command prompt.

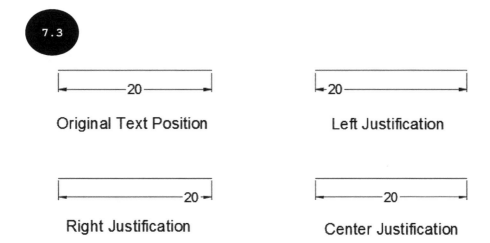

7.3

Original Text Position

Left Justification

Right Justification

Center Justification

Editing Dimensions using DDEDIT Command

The DDEDIT command is used to add a prefix or suffix to the dimension text/value or specify a new dimension value. You can also edit the single and multiline annotations of a drawing by using the DDEDIT command. You will learn about adding single and multiline annotations later in this chapter. The procedure to edit dimension text/value by using the DDEDIT command is as follows:

Procedure for Editing Dimension text/Value

1. Enter DDEDIT in the Command Window and then press ENTER. You are prompted to select an annotation object to be edited.

   ```
   Select an annotation object:
   ```

2. Click on the dimension text or annotation to be edited. The selected dimension text or annotation appears in an edit box, see Figure 7.4. You will learn about adding annotation later in this chapter.

3. Enter a new dimension text/value in the edit box. You can also add a prefix or suffix to the dimension text/value, see Figure 7.5. For example, to add a diameter symbol to a linear diameter dimension, enter '%%c' followed by a diameter value.

4. Click anywhere in the drawing area. The dimension text/value of the selected dimension is changed/override to the new dimension text/value.

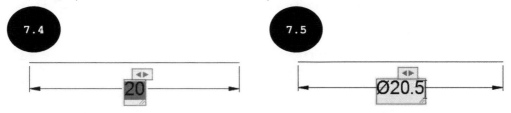

7.4

7.5

Editing Dimensions using Dimension Grips

You can also edit dimensions by using dimension grips. Grips of a dimension appear in the drawing area when you select the dimension, see Figure 7.6. By using grips of a dimension, you can change the position of the dimension text along the dimension line, change spacing between the dimension line and the object, and change the position of extension lines.

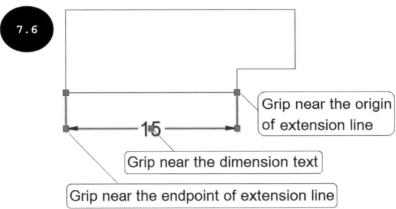

7.6

Grip near the origin of extension line

Grip near the dimension text

Grip near the endpoint of extension line

Procedure for Changing the Position of Dimension Text

1. Click on the dimension to be edited in the drawing area. The grips of the selected dimension appear in the drawing area, see Figure 7.6.

2. Click on grip near the dimension text. The dimension text with dimension line is attached with the cursor. Now, as you move the cursor, the dimension text with dimension line moves. Move the cursor along the dimension line and then click the left mouse button anywhere on the dimension line to position the dimension text.

Note: When you click on the grip near the dimension text, the dimension text with dimension line gets attached with the cursor. This is because, the default option for the movement of dimension text is set to the **Move with Dim Line** option. To change the default option or to access other options for editing the dimension text, move the cursor over the grip near the dimension text. A menu appears, see Figure 7.7. In this menu, click on the **Move Text Only** option to move only the dimension text. Now, on moving the cursor, only the dimension text moves. Next, click in the drawing area to specify the new position for the dimension text. You can specify the position of the dimension text along the dimension line or anywhere in the drawing area, as required. To move the dimension text with leader, click on the **Move with Leader** option in the menu. As soon as you click on the **Move with Leader** option, the dimension text gets attached with the cursor such that it is connected to the dimension line with a leader. Now, click to specify the position of the dimension text. The dimension text is placed to the specified position with a leader connected to the dimension line, see Figure 7.8.

To place the dimension text above the dimension line, click on the **Above Dim Line** option in the menu appeared. To move the dimension text at the center of dimension line, click on the **Center Vertically** option of this menu. To reset the text position, click on the **Reset Text Position** option.

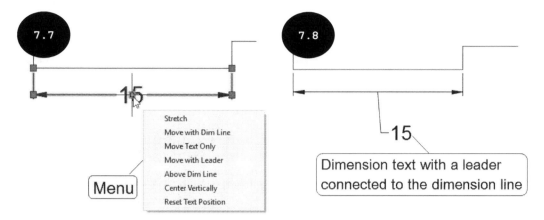

Procedure for Changing Space between Dimension Line and Object

1. Click on the dimension to be edited in the drawing area. The grips of the selected dimension appear in the drawing area, refer to Figure 7.6.

2. Click on the grip near the endpoint of extension line, refer to Figure 7.6. The dimension line is attached with the cursor. Next, move the cursor away or near the object perpendicularly. As you move the cursor, the distance between the dimension line and the object changes. Next, click on the left mouse button in the drawing area to define the new position of the dimension line.

Procedure for Changing the Position of Extension Lines

1. Click on the dimension to be edited in the drawing area. The grips of the selected dimension appear in the drawing area, refer to Figure 7.6.

2. Click on the grip near the origin of the extension line to be edited, refer to Figure 7.6. The respective extension line is attached with the cursor. Now, as you move the cursor, the extension line moves and the dimension text/value of the dimension gets modified. Next, click to specify the new position for the extension line. The position of the extension line is changed and the dimension text/value gets modified, see Figure 7.9.

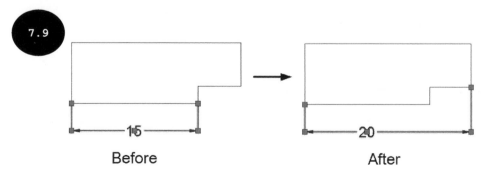

Before   After

Editing Dimensions using PROPERTIES Palette

You can also edit dimensions properties such as dimension text size, arrowhead size, linetype, lineweight, and so on by using the PROPERTIES palette. To invoke the PROPERTIES palette, click on the **View** tab in the **Ribbon**. The tools of the **View** tab appear, see Figure 7.10. Next, click on the **Properties** tool in the **Palettes** panel of the **View** tab. The PROPERTIES palette appears on the left of the drawing area, refer to Figure 7.11.

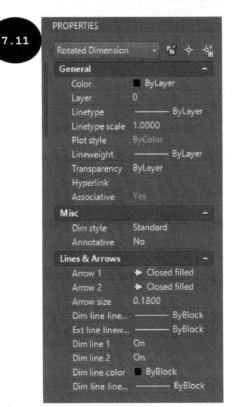

Once the PROPERTIES palette is invoked, click on the dimension to be edited. The properties of the selected dimension appear in the different categories of the PROPERTIES palette, see Figure 7.11. You can edit the properties of the selected dimension by using the options in the different categories of the PROPERTIES palette. The options are as follows:

General

The options in the **General** category of the PROPERTIES palette are used to edit the properties such as color, layer, linetype, linetype scale, lineweight, transparency, and hyperlink of the selected dimension. You can edit these properties by using the respective options available in the **General** category.

Misc

The options in the **Misc** category are used to change the dimension style and the annotative property of the selected dimension. You can change the dimension style and the annotative property by using the respective options available in this category.

Lines & Arrows

The options in the **Lines & Arrows** category are used to edit the arrowheads style, arrow size, dimension line lineweight, extension line lineweight, dimension line color, and so on. You can edit these parameters by using the respective options available in this category.

Text

The options in the **Text** category are used to edit the dimension text properties such as dimension text color, text height, text offset, text style, text horizontal position, text vertical position, text rotation, text override, and so on. You can edit these parameters by using the respective options available in this category.

Fit

The options in the **Fit** category are used to edit the fit parameters of the selected dimension such as fit dimension line between extension line on/off, position of the dimension text inside extension line on/off, text movement, overall dimension scale, and so on. You can edit the fit parameters by using the respective options available in this category.

Primary Units

The options in the **Primary Units** category are used to edit the unit format, dimension precision, dimension prefix/suffix, dimension scale factor, zero suppression, and so on for the selected dimension.

Alternate Units

The options in the **Alternate Units** category are used to edit the alternate unit format, alternate unit precision, prefix/suffix of alternate unit, alternate unit scale factor, and so on. Note that the options of this category are not enabled by default. To enable the options of this category, select the **On** option in the **Alt enabled** drop-down list.

Tolerances

The options in the **Tolerances** category are used to edit parameters that control the format and display of the tolerance in the dimension text.

Editing Dimensions using Editing Tools

You can also edit the dimensions by using the editing tools such as Trim, Extend, and Stretch. The procedures to edit dimension using the editing tools are as follows:

Procedure for Editing Dimensions using Trim Tool

1. Click on the **Trim** tool in the **Modify** panel of the **Home** tab. You are prompted to select cutting edges/boundaries objects. Alternatively, enter **TR** in the Command Window and then press ENTER.

    ```
    Select cutting edges ...
    Select objects or <select all>:
    ```

2. Click on the object/entity as the cutting edge to trim the dimension, see Figure 7.12. Next, press ENTER. You are prompted to select objects to be trimmed.

    ```
    Select object to trim or shift-select to extend or
    [Fence Crossing Project Edge eRase Undo]:
    ```

3. Click on the dimension to be trimmed, see Figure 7.12. The portion of the selected dimension is trimmed and the dimension value of the dimension is modified accordingly, see Figure 7.13.

4. Press ENTER to exit the tool.

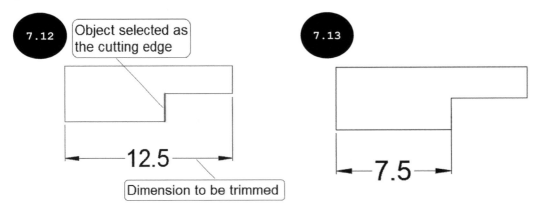

Procedure for Editing Dimensions using Extend Tool

1. Click on the down arrow next to the **Trim** tool in the **Modify** panel. A flyout appears. In this flyout, click on the **Extend** tool. You are prompted to select boundary edges objects. Alternatively, enter **EX** in the Command Window and then press ENTER to invoke the **Extend** tool.

    ```
    Select boundary edges ...
    Select objects or <select all>:
    ```

2. Click on the object as the boundary edge for extending dimension, see Figure 7.14. Next, press ENTER. You are prompted to select objects to be extended.

```
Select object to extend or shift-select to trim or
[Fence Crossing Project Edge Undo]:
```

3. Click on the dimension to be extended, see Figure 7.14. Next, press ENTER. The selected dimension is extended upto the boundary edge and the dimension value of the dimension is modified, see Figure 7.15.

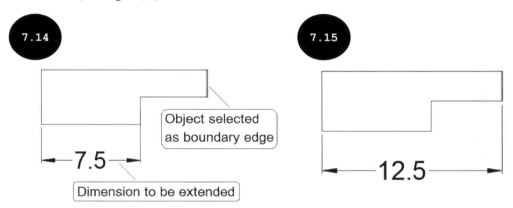

Procedure for Editing Dimensions using Stretch Tool

1. Click on the **Stretch** tool in the **Modify** panel or enter **S** in the Command Window and then press ENTER. You are prompted to select objects to be stretched.

```
Select objects:
```

2. Draw a cross window by defining first and second corner points around the objects to be stretched such that the Cross Window encloses the objects partially, see Figure 7.16. You can select the objects to be stretched by using the Cross Window or Cross Polygon selection method.

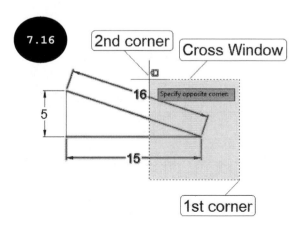

3. Press ENTER. You are prompted to specify the base point for stretching the objects.

   ```
   Specify base point or [Displacement] <Displacement>:
   ```

4. Click to specify the base point in the drawing area, see Figure 7.17. Next, move the cursor in the drawing area. The selected objects get stretched, dynamically. Also, the dimension value of the dimensions get modified, dynamically. You are prompted to specify the second point.

   ```
   Specify second point or <use first point as displacement>:
   ```

5. Click to specify the second point in the drawing area as the placement point for the objects. The objects get stretched and dimensions are modified, see Figure 7.18.

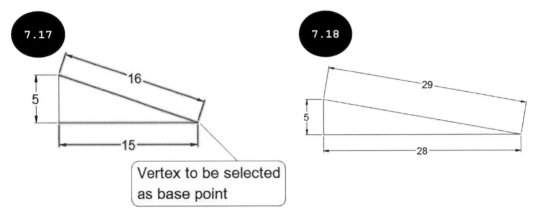

Adding Text/Notes to Drawings

Text/notes are used in drawings in order to convey additional information that are not available in drawings. In AutoCAD, you can add text by using the **Single Line** and **Multiline Text** tools. Before you learn about adding text in drawings, it is important to understand about setting up a text style. A text style stores all information about text such as text height and font. When you open a new AutoCAD drawing file with default template, the Annotative and Standard text styles are available, by default. You can edit the default text styles or create a new text style as per the requirement. Creating a new text style and adding text to a drawing are discussed next.

Creating and Modifying Text Style

To create a new text style, enter ST in the Command Window and then press ENTER. The **Text Style** dialog box appears, see Figure 7.19. Alternatively, expand the **Annotation** panel of the **Home** tab and then click on the **Text Style** tool to invoke the **Text Style** dialog box, see Figure 7.20.

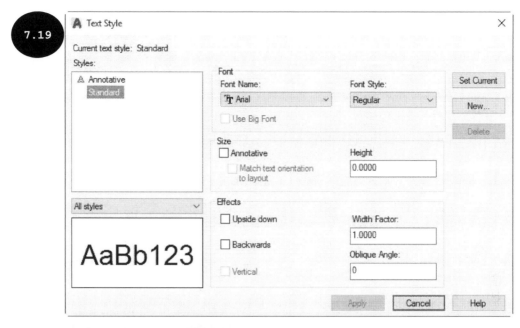

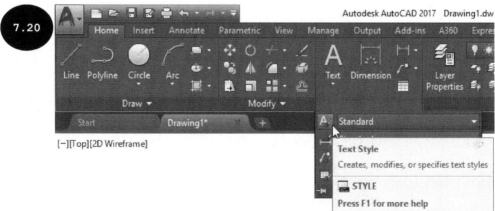

In the **Text Style** dialog box, click on the **New** button. The **New Text Style** window appears, see Figure 7.21.

In this window, enter the name of the text style to be created and then click on the **OK** button. A new style is created and its name is listed in the **Styles** area of the **Text Style** dialog box. Make sure that the newly created text style is selected in the **Styles** area of the dialog box. Next, specify the text font in the **Font Name** drop-down list, font style in the **Font Style** drop-down list, text height in the **Height** field, and so on for the text style. After specifying the properties for the text style, click on the **Apply** button and then click on the **Set Current** button in the dialog box to make the newly added text style as the current text style for the drawing. Next, click on the **Close** button to exit the dialog box.

Similar to creating a new text style, you can modify the existing text style parameters as per the requirement. To modify the existing text style, invoke the **Text Style** dialog box using the **ST** command. Next, select the text style to be modified in the **Styles** area of the **Text Style** dialog box. The parameters of the selected text style appear on the right of the dialog box. You can modify the parameters such as text font, font style, and text height of the text style by using the respective options of the dialog box. Once you have made the changes, click on the **Apply** button of the dialog box and then click on the **Close** button to exit the dialog box.

After creating a new text style or modifying the existing text style, you can start with adding text/note in the drawing area. You can add text/notes in a drawing by using the **Single Line** and **Multiline Text** tools. Both these tools are as follows:

Adding Text using the Single Line Tool

The **Single Line** tool is used for adding single line text such as labels and notes in a drawing. You can add one or more lines of text by using the **Single Line** tool, where each text line is an independent object which can be moved, formatted or modified individually. The procedure to add a single line text is as follows:

Procedure for Adding Single Line Text

1. Invoke the **Text** flyout in the **Annotation** panel of the **Home** tab, see Figure 7.22. Next, click on the **Single Line** tool in the **Text** flyout, see Figure 7.22. Alternatively, enter **TEXT** in the Command Window and then press ENTER to invoke the **Single Line** tool. You are prompted to specify the start point of text.

```
Specify start point of text or [Justify Style]:
```

Note: You can also specify the justification and style for the text to be added. To specify the text justification, click on the **Justify** option in the command prompt when you are prompted to 'Specify start point of text or [Justify Style]:'. Next, select the required text justification such as left, center, right, or middle in the command prompt. Similarly, to specify the text style, click on the **Style** option in the command prompt and then enter the name of the style in the Command Window and then press ENTER.

2. Click in the drawing area to specify the start point of text, see Figure 7.23. You are prompted to specify text height.

   ```
   Specify height <0.2000>:
   ```

3. Enter value of the text height, see Figure 7.23 and then press ENTER. Alternatively, click in the drawing area to specify the text height. You are prompted to specify the rotation angle of text.

   ```
   Specify rotation angle of text <0>:
   ```

4. Enter the rotation angle of text, see Figure 7.23 and then press ENTER. A blinking cursor appears in a text window and you are prompted to write the text in the drawing area.

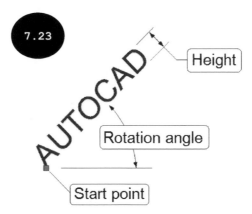

5. Write text in the text window, as required. To add multiple text lines, press ENTER at the end of each line. Figure 7.24 shows the text window with multiple text lines written. After writing the text, click anywhere in the drawing area and then press the ESC key to exit the tool.

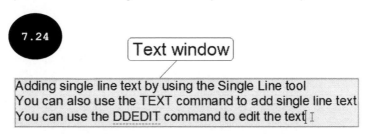

Note: The multiple text lines written by using the **Single Line** tool/**TEXT** command act as independent objects which can be selected, moved, formatted, or edited individually.

Adding Text using the Multiline Text Tool

The **Multiline Text** tool is used to add multiline text such as a paragraph of information, a block of text, and longer notes in a paragraph form in a drawing. In AutoCAD, writing multiline text is similar to writing text in a word document, where you can select words and change their properties such as height, color, and font. The procedure to add multiline text is as follows:

Procedure for Adding Multiline Text

1.   Invoke the **Text** flyout in the **Annotation** panel of the **Home** tab, refer to Figure 7.22. Next, click on the **Multiline Text** tool in the **Text** flyout. Alternatively, enter **MTEXT** in the Command Window and then press ENTER to invoke the **Multiline Text** tool. You are prompted to specify the first corner of the text window.

```
Specify first corner:
```

2.   Click to specify the first corner of the text window in the drawing area, see Figure 7.25. You are prompted to specify the opposite corner of the text window.

```
Specify opposite corner or [Height Justify Line spacing Rotation
Style Width Columns]:
```

Note: You can change the default text height by using the **Height** option of the command prompt, text justification by using the **Justify** option, text style by using the **Style** options of the command prompt, and so on. For example, to change the default text height, click on the **Height** option in the command prompt when you are prompted to specify the opposite corner. You can also enter **H** in the Command Window and then press ENTER to change the default text height. Next, enter new text height and then press ENTER.

3.   Click to specify the opposite corner of the text window in the drawing area, see Figure 7.25. The **Text Editor** tab appears in the **Ribbon**, see Figure 7.26. Also, the **In-Place Text Editor** window appears with the tab and indent ruler in the drawing area for writing the text, see Figure 7.27.

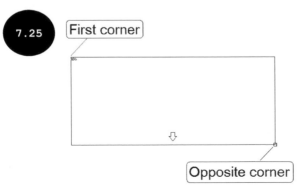

7.25   First corner

Opposite corner

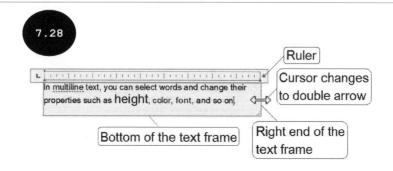

Note: The options in the **Text Editor** tab are used to control the text parameters such as text style, text height, text font, layer, bold, italic, underline, text justification, bullets and numbering, columns, symbol, and so on. The **Text Editor** allows you to control the text parameters similar to a word document.

4. Write text in the text window, as required, see Figure 7.27. Next, click anywhere in the drawing area. The text appears in the area which is defined by specifying the corners of the text window.

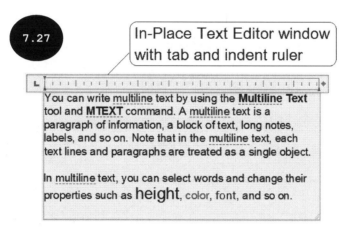

Note: You can change the width and height of the **In-Place Text Editor** window. To change the width of the window, move the cursor either over the right end of the text frame or the ruler until the cursor changes to a double arrow, see Figure 7.28. Next, drag the cursor to adjust the width. Similarly, to change the height, move the cursor over the bottom of the text frame and then drag the cursor to adjust the height of the window.

Editing Single Line and Multiline Text

You can edit the single line and multiline text by using the DDEDIT command. To edit text, enter DDEDIT in the Command Window and then press ENTER. Alternatively, double-click on the text to be edited in the drawing area. You are prompted to select an annotation object to be edited.

```
Select an annotation object:
```

Next, click on the text/annotation in the drawing area. The **In-Place Text Editor** window appears. Now, you can edit the text, as required. Once you have made the necessary modifications, click anywhere in the drawing area to exit the command.

Converting Single line Text to Multiline Text

In a drawing, you may need to combine several individual single line text objects into a single multiline text object. You can convert one or more than one single line text objects to a multiline text object by using the TXT2MTXT command. To convert a single line text to a multiline text, enter **TXT2MTXT** in the Command Window and then press ENTER. You are prompted to select the objects to be converted into multiline text object. Alternatively, click on the **Convert to Mtext** tool in the **Text** panel of the **Express Tools** tab of the **Ribbon** to invoke this command.

```
Select objects:
```

Click on the single line text objects to be converted into a multiline text one by one in the drawing area. Next, press ENTER. All the selected single line text objects are converted into a single multiline text object.

Tutorial 1

Create the drawing shown in Figure 7.29. Apply dimensions as shown in the figure. You need to edit the linear diameter dimensions of the drawing to add diameter symbols as a prefix to them, see Figure 7.29.

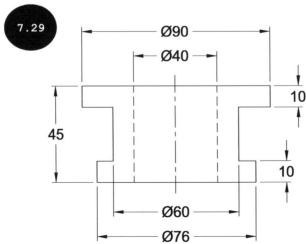

Section 1: Starting AutoCAD

1. Start AutoCAD and then open a new drawing file.

Section 2: Creating Drawing

1. Click on the **Line** tool in the **Draw** panel of the **Home** tab. You are prompted to specify first point of the line. Alternatively, enter **L** in the Command Window and then press ENTER.

```
Specify first point:
```

2. Click to specify the first point of the line in the drawing area. You are prompted to specify the next point of the line.

3. Make sure that the dynamic input mode and the Ortho mode is turned on or activated.

4. Follow the command sequence given below for creating the drawing.

```
Specify next point or [Undo]:
```
*Move the cursor horizontally toward the right and then enter **76** in the Dynamic Input box   (**ENTER**)*
```
Specify next point or [Undo]:
```
*Move the cursor vertically upward and then enter **10** (**ENTER**)*
```
Specify next point or [Undo]:
```
*Move the cursor horizontally toward the left and then enter **8** (**ENTER**)*
```
Specify next point or [Undo]:
```
*Move the cursor vertically upward and then enter **25** (**ENTER**)*
```
Specify next point or [Close Undo]:
```
*Move the cursor horizontally toward the right and then enter **15** (**ENTER**)*
```
Specify next point or [Undo]:
```
*Move the cursor vertically upward and then enter **10** (**ENTER**)*
```
Specify next point or [Close Undo]:
```
*Move the cursor horizontally toward the left and then enter **90** (**ENTER**)*
```
Specify next point or [Undo]:
```
*Move the cursor vertically downward and then enter **10** (**ENTER**)*
```
Specify next point or [Close Undo]:
```
*Move the cursor horizontally toward the right and the enter **15** (**ENTER**)*
```
Specify next point or [Close Undo]:
```
*Move the cursor vertically downward and then enter **25** (**ENTER**)*
```
Specify next point or [Close Undo]:
```
*Move the cursor horizontally toward the right and then enter **8** (**ENTER**)*
```
Specify next point or [Close Undo]:
```
*C or **Close** (**ENTER**) (See Figure 7.30)*

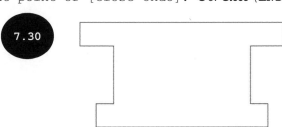

7.30

After creating the line entities of the drawing, you need to create hidden and centerline entities.

5. Click on the **Offset** tool in the **Modify** panel. You are prompted to specify the offset distance. Alternatively, enter O in the Command Window and then press ENTER.

    ```
    Specify offset distance or [Through Erase Layer] <Through>:
    ```

6. Enter **10** as the offset distance and then press ENTER. You are prompted to select object to offset.

    ```
    Select object to offset or [Exit Undo] <Exit>:
    ```

7. Click on the left middle vertical line as the object to offset, see Figure 7.31. You are prompted to specify a point on side to offset.

    ```
    Specify point on side to offset or [Exit Multiple Undo] <Exit>:
    ```

8. Click the left mouse button on the right of the vertical line selected. The offset entity is created, see Figure 7.31. You are prompted to select the object to offset again.

    ```
    Select object to offset or [Exit Undo] <Exit>:
    ```

9. Click on the right middle vertical line as the object to offset, see Figure 7.32. Next, click on the left of the vertical line selected. The offset entity is created, see Figure 7.32.

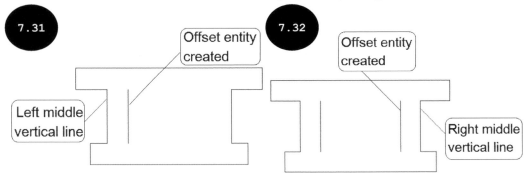

10. Press ENTER to exit the **Offset** tool.

    Now, you need to extend the offset entities upto their next intersection.

11. Enter **EX** in the Command Window and then press ENTER. The **Extend** tool is invoked and you are prompted to select boundary edges. Alternatively, click on the **Extend** tool in the **Modify** panel of the **Home** tab.

    ```
    Select boundary edges ...
    Select objects or <select all>:
    ```

12. Press ENTER to skip the selection of boundary edges. You are prompted to select the object to be extended.

```
Select object to extend or shift-select to trim or
[Fence Crossing Project Edge Undo]:
```

13. Click on the upper side of the left offset entity in the drawing area. The upper side of the offset entity gets extended upto the next intersection, see Figure 7.33. Next, click on the lower side of the left offset entity. The lower side of the entity gets extended, see Figure 7.34.

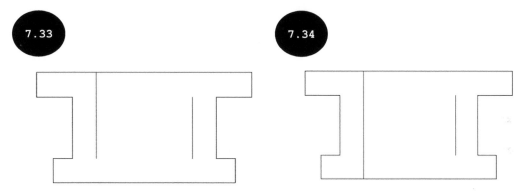

7.33

7.34

14. Similarly, click on both sides of the right offset entity to extend one by one. Figure 7.35 shows the drawing after extending the entities. Next, press ENTER to exit the **Extend** tool.

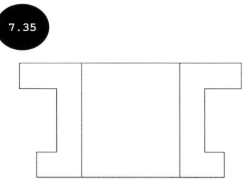

7.35

Now, you need to draw centerline of the drawing.

15. Click on the **Line** tool in the **Draw** panel or enter L and then press ENTER. The **Line** tool is invoked and you are prompted to specify the first point of the line.

```
Specify first point:
```

16. Make sure that the Object Snap mode is activated.

17. Move the cursor to the midpoint of the upper horizontal line and when cursor snaps to the midpoint, see Figure 7.36 move the cursor vertically upward to a small distance. Next, click the left mouse button to specify the first point of the line. You are prompted to specify the next point of the line.

```
Specify next point or [Undo]:
```

18. Move the cursor vertically downward and click to specify the end point of the line outside the bottom horizontal line of the drawing. The line is created, see Figure 7.37. Next, press ENTER to exit the **Line** tool.

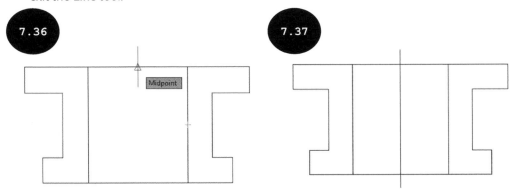

Section 3: Creating Layers and Assigning Objects to Layers

1. Click on the **Layer Properties** tool in the **Layers** panel of the **Home** tab. The **LAYER PROPERTIES MANAGER** appears.

2. Create three layers with the name Object, Hidden, and Center in the **LAYER PROPERTIES MANAGER**, see Figure 7.38.

3. Assign the hidden linetype to the Hidden layer, the center linetype to Center layer, and accept the remaining default properties of the layer, see Figure 7.38. Next, exit the **LAYER PROPERTIES MANAGER**.

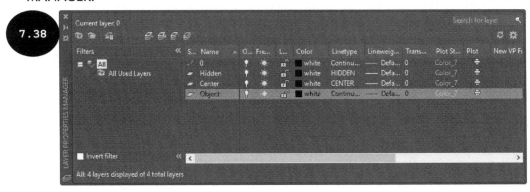

4. Assign the hidden line entities to the Hidden layer, centerline entity to the Center layer, and remaining line entities of the drawing to the Object layer. Figure 7.39 shows the drawing after assigning the drawing entities to the respective layers.

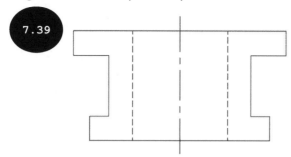

7.39

> **Note:** If the hidden lines and centerline of the drawing appear as continuous/solid lines in the drawing area then you need to change the linetype scale of the entities. To change the linetype scale of entities, enter **PR** in the Command Window and then press ENTER. The **PROPERTIES** palette appears. Alternatively, click on the **Properties** tool in the **Palettes** panel of the **View** tab to invoke the **PROPERTIES** palette. Next, select the entity whose scale has to be changed. The current properties of the selected entity appear in the **PROPERTIES** palette. Next, enter new linetype scale for the selected entity in the **Linetype** field of the palette. You can try with different scale values to match your requirement.

Section 4: Applying Dimensions

1. Apply dimensions to the drawing by using the **Dimension** tool of the **Annotation** panel in the **Home** tab, see Figure 7.40.

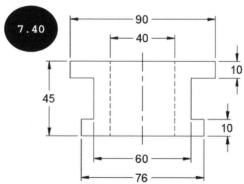

7.40

> **Note:** By default, dimensions appear as per the default dimension style properties, which may not fit the requirement and dimensions may appear either very small or large relative to the drawing size. In such a case, you may need to create a new dimension style or edit the existing dimension style to match the dimension properties as per the requirement. You can create a new dimension style or edit an existing dimension style by using the **Dimension Style Manager** dialog box. You can invoke this dialog box by using the **D** command.

Section 5: Editing Dimensions

Now, you need to edit the linear diameter dimensions of the drawing to add diameter symbols as refix to them.

1. Enter **DDEDIT** in the Command Window and then press ENTER. You are prompted to select an annotation object to be edited. Alternatively, double-click on the dimension to be edited. You can also use the DIMEDIT command to edit a dimension text.

   ```
   You are prompted to select an annotation object:
   ```

2. Click on the dimension measuring 76 units in the drawing area. The dimension text of the selected dimension appears in an edit box, see Figure 7.41.

3. Enter '**%%c**' as the prefix to the dimension text '76 units' in the edit box to add the diameter symbol. Next, click anywhere in the drawing area. The diameter symbol is added to the selected dimension, see Figure 7.42.

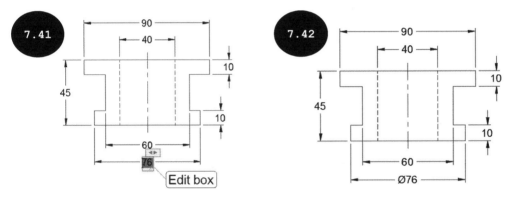

4. Similarly, add the diameter symbol to other linear diameter dimensions of the drawing. Figure 7.43 shows the final drawing.

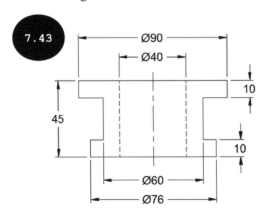

Section 6: Saving the Drawing

After creating the drawing, you need to save it.

1. Click on the **Save** tool in the **Quick Access Toolbar**. The **Save Drawing As** dialog box appears.

2. Browse to the *AutoCAD* folder and then create a folder with the name *Chapter 7* inside the *AutoCAD* folder.

3. Enter **Tutorial 1** in the **File name** field of the dialog box and then click on the **Save** button. The drawing is saved with the name Tutorial 1 in the *Chapter 7* folder.

Tutorial 2

Create the drawing shown in Figure 7.44. Apply dimensions as shown in the figure. You need to add labels in the different areas of the drawing, see Figure 7.44.

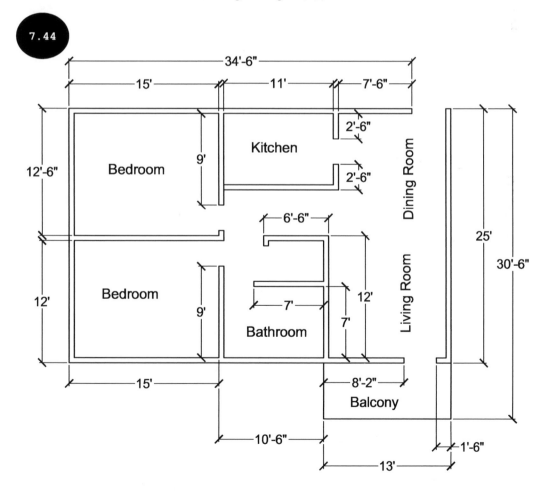

Section 1: Starting AutoCAD

1.   Start AutoCAD and then open a new drawing file.

Section 2: Specifying Unit System

You need to change the default unit system to the Architectural unit system.

1.   Enter **UN** in the Command Window and then press ENTER. The **Drawing Units** dialog box appears.

2.   Select the **Architectural** unit system in the **Type** drop-down list of the **Length** area in the **Drawing Units** dialog box.

3.   Make sure that the **0'-0 1/16"** option is selected in the **Precision** drop-down list of the **Length** area in the dialog box.

4.   Click on the **OK** button to accept the change and to exit the dialog box. The Architectural unit system has been set for the current drawing.

Section 3: Creating Drawing

1.   Create the drawing as shown in Figure 7.45. To create the drawing, you can use various drawing tools such as **Line**, **Offset**, **Trim**, and **Extend**. Also, refer to Figure 7.44 for dimensions.

Note: To enter feet dimension values, use the single quote (') and to enter inches values, use the double quotes (") as the suffix to the dimension values. You can specify the inches values with or without double quotes ("). For example, 15 feet is specified as 15' and 10 feet 6 inches is specified either as 10'6" or 10'6.

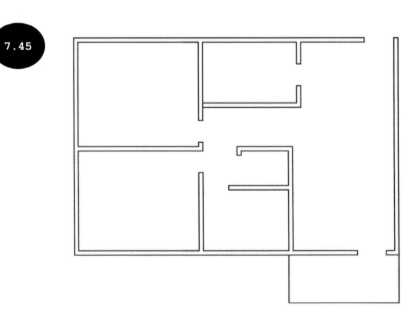

7.45

Section 4: Editing Dimension Style and Applying Dimensions

Now, you need to edit the dimension style of the drawing.

1. Enter **D** in the Command Window and then press ENTER. The **Dimension Style Manager** dialog box appears.

2. Select the **Standard** dimension style in the **Styles** area of the dialog box and then click on the **Modify** button. The **Modify Dimension Style** dialog box appears.

3. Click on the **Symbols and Arrows** tab in the dialog box. Next, select the **Architectural tick** option in the **First** and **Second** drop-down lists of the **Arrowheads** area in the dialog box.

4. Specify the other dimension properties such as arrow size, text height, offset from dimension line, extend beyond dimension lines, and offset from origin in the respective fields.

5. Click on the **OK** button to accept the change and to exit the **Modify Dimension Style** dialog box. Next, click on the **Close** button in the **Dimension Style Manager** dialog box.

    After modifying the dimension style as per the requirement, you can apply dimensions in the drawing area.

6. Apply dimensions to the drawing by using the **Linear** tool of the **Dimension** flyout in the **Annotation** panel, see Figure 7.46.

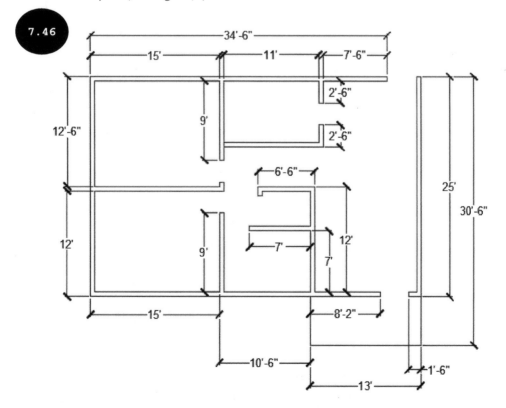

7.46

Section 5: Adding Annotation/Text

1.   Enter **TEXT** in the Command Window and then press ENTER. The **Single Line** text tool is invoked and you are prompted to specify the start point of the text. Alternatively, click on the **Single Line** tool in the **Text** flyout of the **Annotation** panel in the **Home** tab.

```
Specify start point of text or [Justify Style]:
```

2.   Click in the kitchen area of the drawing to specify the start point of the text. You are prompted to specify the height of the text.

```
Specify height <1'0">:
```

3.   Enter **1'** as the height of the text and then press ENTER.

```
Specify rotation angle of text <0>:
```

4.   Enter **0** as the rotation angle of the text and then press ENTER. A blinking cursor appears in a text window and you are prompted to enter text in the drawing area.

5.   Enter **Kitchen** in the text window and then click anywhere in the drawing area. Next, press ESC key. The Kitchen label is added to the kitchen area of the drawing, see Figure 7.47.

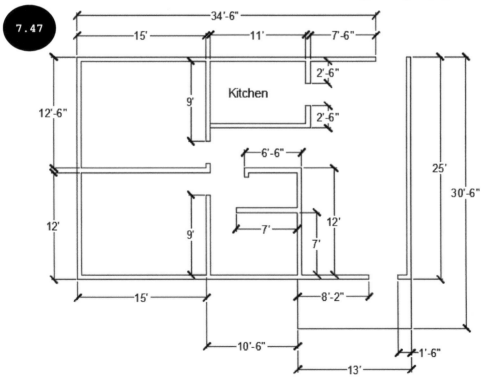

6.   Similarly, add labels to the other area of the drawing. Figure 7.48 shows the final drawing after adding all the labels/text to the drawing.

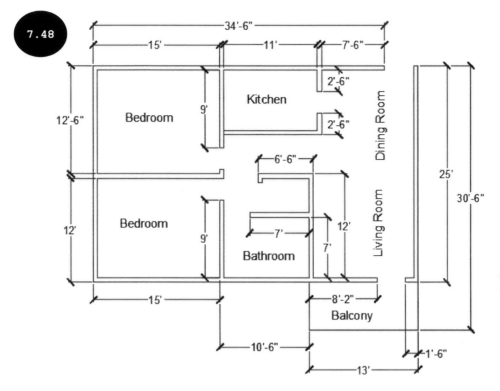

7.48

Section 6: Saving the Drawing
1. Save the drawing with the name Tutorial 2 inside the *Chapter 7* folder.

Hands-on Test Drive 1

Create the drawing and add multiline text to the drawing, see Figure 7.49.

7.49

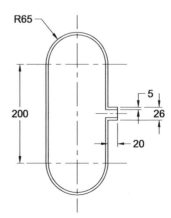

DESIGN SPECIFICATION
Design pressure = 800 psi
Design temperature = 700 F
Material:
     Shell SA-516 Gr. 70
     Head SA-181 Class 70
     Nozzle SA-106 Gr. B
Weld efficiency factor = 1.0 = E
(Full radiographic examination)

Summary

In this chapter, you have learned to edit dimensions by using the DIMEDIT command, DIMTEDIT command, DDEDIT command, dimension grips, **Properties** palette, and editing tools such as **Trim**, **Extend**, and **Stretch**. You have also learned about adding text/notes to drawings, creating and modifying text style, and adding text by using the **Single Line** and **Multiline Text** tools. In addition, in this chapter, you have learned about editing single line and multiline texts, and to convert single line text to multiline text.

Questions

- The _____ command is used to edit the dimension text/value such that you can rotate, modify, restore, and specify a new dimension text/value.

- The _____ command is used to change the dimension text justification and angle.

- The _____ command is used to add a prefix or suffix to the dimension text/value or specify a new dimension value.

- By using the _____ of a dimension, you can change the position of the dimension text along the dimension line, spacing between the dimension line and the object, and the position of extension lines.

- In AutoCAD, you can add text by using the _____ and _____ tools.

- The _____ command is used to invoke the **Text Style** dialog box.

- The _____ tool is used for adding single line text such as labels and notes in a drawing.

- The _____ tool is used to add multiline text such as a paragraph of information and a block of text.

- You can convert one or more than one single line text objects to a multiline text object by using the _____ command.

Modifying and Editing Drawings - II

In this chapter, you will learn the following:

- Editing objects by using Grips
- Editing objects by using PROPERTIES palette
- Matching properties of objects
- Identifying coordinates of a point

In Chapter 5, you have learned about various editing operations such as trim, extend, mirror, array, move, and rotate. In this chapter, you will learn about some advance editing operations such as editing objects by using grips, editing objects properties, matching objects properties, and so on.

Editing Objects by using Grips

In AutoCAD, all objects have grips, which appear when you select objects in the drawing area, see Figure 8.1. A grip is a small square blue symbol. The number of grips vary object to object. For example, a line object has three grips, an arc object has four grips, and a circle object has five grips, see Figure 8.1. By using these grips, you can perform various editing operations such as stretch, move, rotate, scale, and mirror. Different editing operations using the grips are as follows:

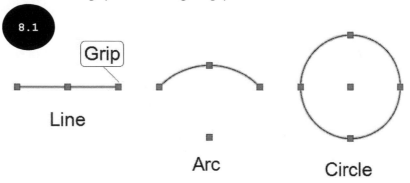

8.1

Grip

Line

Arc

Circle

Stretching Objects by using Grips

To stretch objects by using grips, select them. The grips of the selected objects appear in the drawing area, see Figure 8.2. In this figure, the horizontal and inclined lines of the drawing are selected. Next, click on a grip as the base point to stretch objects, see Figure 8.2. As soon as you click on a grip, the **Stretch** command is activated, automatically. Next, move the cursor to a required distance in the drawing area. As you move the cursor, the objects stretch, dynamically. Next, click to specify the placement point for the objects in the drawing area. The objects get stretched, see Figure 8.3.

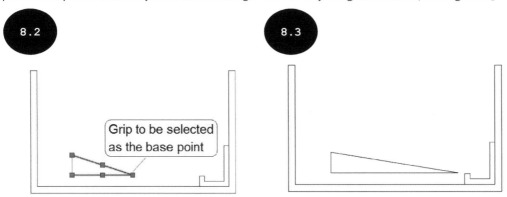

You can select one or more than one grip together to stretch multiple objects, simultaneously. To select multiple grips, press the SHIFT key and then click on the grips one by one to select them. After selecting the grips, release the SHIFT key and then click on a grip as the base point to stretch objects, simultaneously. Next, move the cursor to a required distance and then click to specify the placement point. The selected objects get stretched. Figure 8.4 shows six objects and four grips selected to be stretched. Figure 8.5 shows the resultant drawing after stretching the objects.

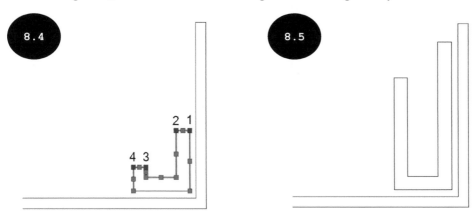

Moving Objects by using Grips

To move objects by using grips, select them. The grips of the selected objects appear in the drawing area, see Figure 8.6. Next, click on a grip as the base point to move objects, see Figure 8.6. The **Stretch** command is activated, by default. Press ENTER or SPACEBAR to activate the **Move** command. Alternatively, right-click to invoke a shortcut menu and then click on the **Move** option to invoke the **Move** command. Next, move the cursor in the drawing area. As you move the cursor, the objects move, dynamically. Next, click to specify the placement point in the drawing area, see Figure 8.6. The objects are moved to the new specified location, see Figure 8.7. Next, press the ESC key to exit the selection of objects.

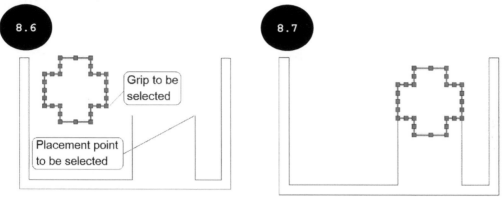

Note: By pressing the ENTER or SPACEBAR key after selecting a grip, you can cycle through the **Stretch**, **Move**, **Rotate**, **Scale**, and **Mirror** commands.

Tip: If you press and hold the CTRL key and then specify the placement point, a copy of the selected objects will be created in the new specified location.

Rotating Objects by using Grips

To rotate objects by using grips, select them. The grips of the selected objects appear in the drawing area, see Figure 8.8. Next, click on a grip as the base point to rotate objects, see Figure 8.8. The **Stretch** command gets activated, by default. Press the ENTER or SPACEBAR key twice to activate the **Rotate** command. You can cycle through the **Stretch**, **Move**, **Rotate**, **Scale**, and **Mirror** commands by pressing the ENTER key. Alternatively, right-click to invoke a shortcut menu and then click on the **Rotate** option to invoke the **Rotate** command. Next, enter the value of the rotation angle and then press ENTER. You can also click in the drawing area to specify the rotation angle. The selected objects is rotated around the base point at the specified rotation angle, see Figure 8.9. Next, press the ESC key to exit the selection of objects.

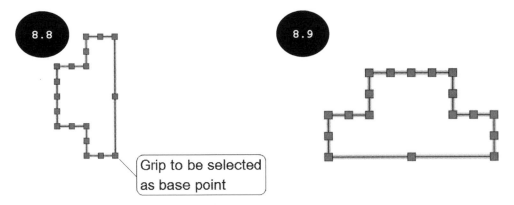

Scaling Objects by using Grips

To scale objects by using grips, select them. The grips of the selected objects appear in the drawing area, see Figure 8.10. Next, click on a grip as the base point to scale objects, see Figure 8.10. The **Stretch** command gets activated, by default. Press the ENTER key until the **Scale** command gets activated. Next, enter the scale factor and then press ENTER. The selected objects is scaled with respect to the base point and the scale factor specified, see Figure 8.11. Note that to enlarge the selected objects, you need to enter scale factor greater than 1 and to shrink them, you need to enter scale factor smaller than 1. Next, press the ESC key to exit the selection of objects.

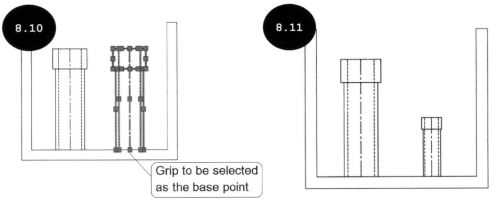

Mirroring Objects by using Grips

To mirror objects by using grips, select them. The grips of the selected objects appear in the drawing area, see Figure 8.12. Next, click on a grip as the start point of the mirroring line, see Figure 8.12. The **Stretch** command gets activated, by default. Press the ENTER key until the **Mirror** command gets activated and the command prompt appears "`Specify second point or [Base point Copy Undo eXit]:`". Next, click on the **Copy** option in the command prompt to keep the original or source objects in the resultant drawing. Next, click in the drawing area to specify the second point of the mirroring line. The selected objects is mirrored and the original or source objects are retained in the drawing area, see Figure 8.13. If you do not want to keep or retain the original or source objects then you can skip the selection of **Copy** option in the command prompt and directly specify the second point of the mirroring line. Once the objects have been mirrored, press the ESC key to exit the selection.

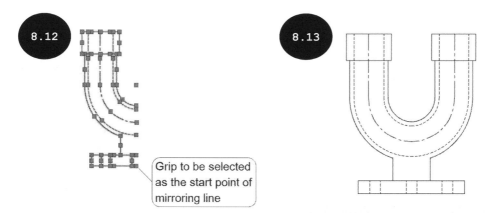

Grip to be selected as the start point of mirroring line

Editing Objects by using PROPERTIES Palette

You can edit object properties such as color, linetype, lineweight, layer, angle, and coordinates by using the PROPERTIES palette. To invoke the PROPERTIES palette, enter PR in the Command Window and then press ENTER. Alternatively, click on the Properties tool in the Palettes panel of the View tab in the Ribbon. The PROPERTIES palette appears on the left of the drawing area. Next, select the object whose properties are to be edited. The current properties of the selected object appears in the PROPERTIES palette, see Figure 8.14. Next, change the properties of the selected object as required by using the respective fields or drop-down lists. For example, to change the color of the selected object, click on the Color field, see Figure 8.15. An arrow appears. Next, click on the arrow. The Color drop-down list appears, see Figure 8.15. In this drop-down list, you can select the required color for the selected object. Similarly, to edit the linetype scale, click on the Linetype scale field of the palette and then enter the new linetype scale value in it.

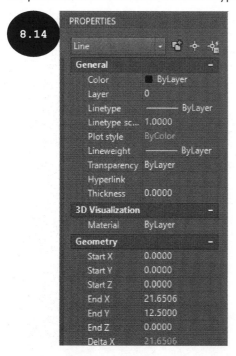

Color field

Color drop-down list

Note: By using the PROPERTIES palette, you can also edit the properties of the text/annotation, dimensions, and so on. Also, the availability options in the PROPERTIES palette depend upon the type of object selected.

Matching Properties of Objects

In AutoCAD, you can match or copy the properties such as color, linetype, linetype scale, lineweight, and layer of an object to another objects by using the **Match Properties** tool. For example, if you have assigned a particular set of properties such as color, linetype, linetype scale, lineweight to an object of a drawing then you can transfer the exact properties of this object to the another objects of the drawing. You can also control the settings of match properties such that only a specific set of properties of the source object should transferred or copied to another objects. The procedure to match properties and control the setting of the match properties is as follows:

Procedure for Matching Properties and Controlling Setting

1. Click on the **Match Properties** tool in the **Properties** panel of the **Home** tab. The **Match Properties** tool gets invoked and you are prompted to select the source object. Alternatively, enter **MA** in the Command Window and then press ENTER to invoke the **Match Properties** tool.

    ```
    Select source object:
    ```

2. Click on the source object whose properties are to be transferred to the desired objects of the drawing. You are prompted to select the destination objects.

    ```
    Select destination object(s) or [Settings]:
    ```

3. Click on an object as the destination object to transfer the properties of the source object. The properties of the source object is transferred to the destination object selected.

4. Similarly, click on other objects as the destination objects to match the properties one by one. You can also select destination objects by using the Window or Cross Window selection method. Next, press ENTER to exit the **Match Properties** tool.

Note: To change the settings of match properties, click on the **Settings** option in the command prompt when you are prompted to select destination objects "Select destination object(s) or [Settings]:". Alternatively, enter **S** and then press ENTER. The **Property Settings** dialog box appears, see Figure 8.16. In this dialog box, select the check boxes for the properties which you want to transfer and uncheck the remaining check boxes. Next, click on the **OK** button of the dialog box. The settings of the match properties get changed.

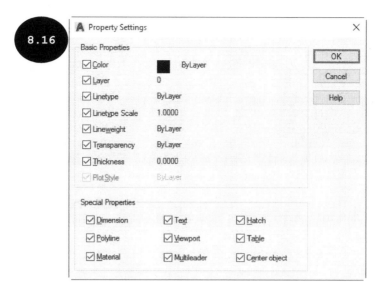

8.16

Identifying Coordinates of a Point

In AutoCAD, you can identify location/coordinates of a point in a drawing by using the **ID Point** tool. To identify coordinates/location of a point, click on the **ID Point** tool in the expanded **Utilities** panel of the **Home** tab, see Figure 8.17. Alternatively, enter **ID** and then press ENTER to invoke this tool.

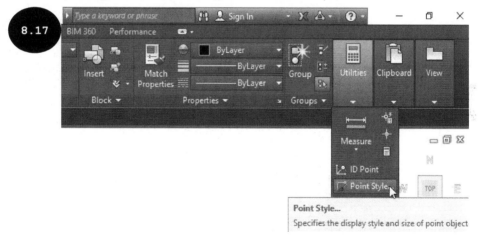

8.17

Once the **ID Point** tool has been invoked, you are prompted to specify a point. Click on the point whose coordinates are to be identified. The coordinates (X, Y, Z) of the specified point appears on the screen as well as in the command prompt.

Note: The identified coordinates of the point are stored in the LASTPOINT system variable, which can be used as the start point for creating new entities of the drawing by entering @ in the Command Window and then pressing ENTER. For example, while creating a line by using the **Line** tool when you are prompted to specify the start point of the line, enter @ in the Command Window and then press ENTER. The start point of the line is specified at the last identified point in the drawing area.

Tutorial 1

Create the drawing shown in the Figure 8.18. In this tutorial, you need to set the dimension properties for a dimension and then use the **Match Properties** tool to transfer the specified properties to another dimensions of the drawing.

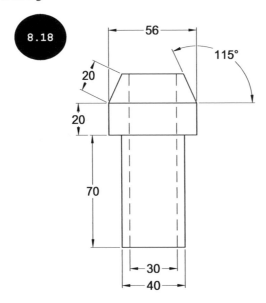

Section 1: Starting AutoCAD
1.   Start AutoCAD and then open a new drawing file.

Section 2: Creating Drawing
1.   Create a drawing by using the **Line** tool as shown in Figure 8.19.

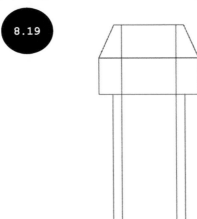

Section 3: Assigning Properties to Hidden Lines

Now, you need to assign the Hidden linetype to the hidden lines of the drawing by using the PROPERTIES palette. However, you first need to load the Hidden linetype in the drawing.

1. Click on the **Layer Properties** tool in the **Layers** panel of the **Home** tab. The **LAYER PROPERTIES MANAGER** window appears, see Figure 8.20.

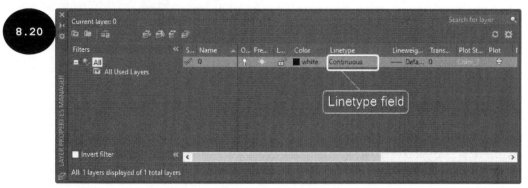

2. Click on the **Linetype** field of the **0** layer, see Figure 8.20. The **Select Linetype** dialog box appears.

3. In the **Select Linetype** dialog box, click on the **Load** button. The **Load or Reload Linetype** dialog box appears.

4. Select the **Hidden** linetype in the **Load or Reload Linetype** dialog box and then click **OK**. The Hidden linetype is loaded in the dialog box.

5. Click on the **Cancel** button in the **Select Linetype** dialog box and then close the **LAYER PROPERTIES MANAGER** window.

   After loading the Hidden linetype in the drawing, you need to assign it to the hidden lines of the drawing by using the **PROPERTIES** palette.

6. Enter **PR** in the Command Window and then press ENTER. The **PROPERTIES** palette appears. Alternatively, click on the **Properties** tool in the **Palettes** panel of the **View** tab in the **Ribbon**.

7. Click on the left vertical line of the drawing to be converted into the hidden line, see Figure 8.21. The current properties of the selected line appears in the **PROPERTIES** palette.

8. Click on the **Linetype** field of the **PROPERTIES** palette. An arrow appears. Next, click on the arrow. The **Linetype** drop-down list appears, see Figure 8.22.

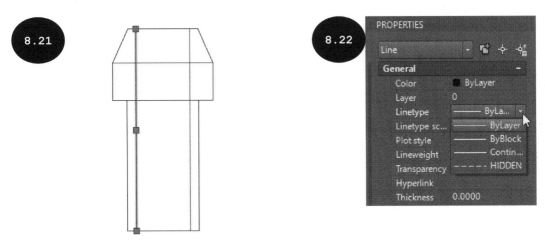

9.   Click on the **HIDDEN** linetype in the **Linetype** drop-down list. The Hidden linetype is assigned to the selected line of the drawing.

10. Click on the **Linetype scale** field of the **PROPERTIES** palette and then enter **10** as the linetype scale of the selected line. The selected line appears similar to the one shown in Figure 8.23. Next, press the ESC key to exit the selection of line in the drawing area.

Section 4: Matching Properties of Hidden Lines

Now, you need to match the properties of left hidden line to the right hidden line of drawing.

1.   Click on the **Match Properties** tool in the **Properties** panel of the **Home** tab. You are prompted to select the source object.

```
Select source object:
```

2.   Click on the left hidden line of the drawing as the source object. You are prompted to select the destination objects.

```
Select destination object(s) or [Settings]:
```

3. Click on the right vertical line of the drawing to be converted into hidden line. The properties of the selected line are matched with the source object, see Figure 8.24.

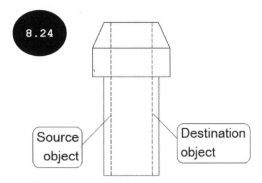

8.24

Source object

Destination object

Section 5: Applying Dimensions

Now, you need to apply dimensions in the drawing and then set the dimension properties by using the **PROPERTIES** palette.

1. Click on the **Dimension** tool in the **Annotation** panel of the **Home** tab. You are prompted to select the object to be dimensioned.

    ```
    Select object or specify first extension line origin or [Angular
    Baseline Continue Ordinate aliGn Distribute Layer Undo]:
    ```

2. Move the cursor over the lower horizontal line of the drawing and then click on the line when it highlights in the drawing area. The linear dimension is attached with the cursor.

3. Move the cursor vertically downward and then click to specify the placement point for the dimension in the drawing area. The linear dimension is applied and placed in the specified location, see Figure 8.25. Note that the dimension text of the applied dimension may appear very small relative to the drawing size because of the dimension properties of the current dimension style, see Figure 8.25. You will modify the dimension properties later in this tutorial.

4. Similarly, apply the remaining dimensions of the drawing, see Figure 8.26.

8.25

Linear dimension applied

8.26

Section 6: Assigning and Matching Dimension Properties

Now, you need to assign the dimension properties to a dimension of the drawing by using the **PROPERTIES** palette and then match these properties to another dimensions of the drawing.

1. Click on the dimension of the bottom horizontal line and then invoke the **PROPERTIES** palette.

2. Click on the **Arrow size** field in the **PROPERTIES** palette and then enter **5** as the arrow size of the dimension.

3. Similarly, enter **5.5** as the text height in the **Text height** field, **1.5** in the **Ext line ext** field, **1.5** in the **Ext line offset**, and **1.5** in the **Text offset** field of the **PROPERTIES** palette. The selected dimension appears similar to the one shown in Figure 8.27.

    Now, you need to set the precision value of the dimension to 0.

4. Right-click on the dimension of the bottom horizontal line. A shortcut menu appears. In this shortcut menu, click on the **Precision < 0** to set the precision for the selected dimension. Next, press the ESC key. The dimension properties of the dimension are modified, see Figure 8.28.

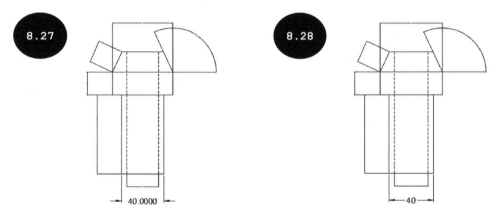

Now, you need to match the properties of the modified dimension properties to another dimensions of the drawing.

5. Click on the **Match Properties** tool in the **Properties** panel of the **Home** tab. You are prompted to select the source object.

    `Select source object:`

6. Click on the dimension of the bottom horizontal line as the source object. You are prompted to select the destination objects.

    `Select destination object(s) or [Settings]:`

7. Click on the dimensions of the drawing one by one to match with the properties of the source dimension. Figure 8.29 shows the drawing after matching all the dimension properties.

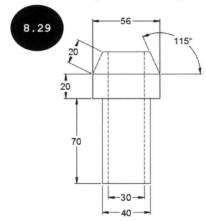

Section 7: Saving the Drawing

After creating the drawing, you need to save it.

1. Click on the **Save** tool in the **Quick Access Toolbar**. The **Save Drawing As** dialog box appears.

2. Browse to the *AutoCAD* folder and then create a folder with the name *Chapter 8* inside the *AutoCAD* folder.

3. Enter **Tutorial 1** in the **File name** field of the dialog box and then click on the **Save** button. The drawing is saved with the name Tutorial 1 in the *Chapter 8* folder.

Hands-on Test Drive 1

Create the drawing shown in the Figure 8.30. Modify dimension properties of the dimension style and then apply dimensions to the drawing. You can assume the values of dimension properties such as dimension height and arrow size.

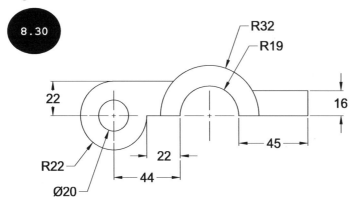

Hands-on Test Drive 2

Create the drawing shown in the Figure 8.31. Modify dimension properties of the dimension style and then apply dimensions to the drawing. You can assume the values of dimension properties.

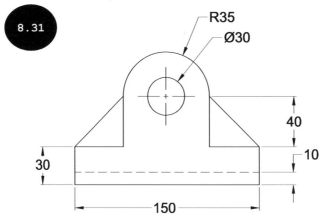

Hands-on Test Drive 3

Create the drawing shown in the Figure 8.32. Modify dimension properties of the dimension style and then apply dimensions to the drawing. You can assume the values of dimension properties such as dimension height and arrow size.

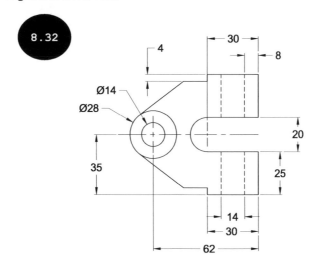

Summary

In this chapter, you have learned how to edit drawing objects/entities by using the grips and the Properties palette. You have also learned about matching the properties of an object/entity with the other drawing objects/entities. In addition, in this chapter, you have learned how to identify coordinates of a point in a drawing.

Questions

*   A line object has _____ number of grips and an arc object has _____ number of grips.

*   After selecting a grip of an object, when you press the _____ or _____ key, you cycle through the **Stretch**, **Move**, **Rotate**, **Scale**, and **Mirror** commands.

*   When you click on a grip of an object, the _____ command gets activated, by default.

*   Click on a grip of an object and then press the ENTER or SPACEBAR key twice to activate the _____ command.

- You can edit object properties such as color, linetype, lineweight, layer, angle, and coordinates by using the _____ palette.

- To invoke the PROPERTIES palette, enter _____ in the Command Window and then press ENTER.

- The _____ tool is used to match or copy the properties of an object such as color, linetype, linetype scale, lineweight, and layer with other objects of a drawing.

- The _____ tool is used to identify the location/coordinates of a point in a drawing.

Hatching and Gradients

In this chapter, you will learn the following:

- Creating Hatches
- Creating Gradients

In mechanical drawings, hatches are generally used to represent the cross-sectional shape and material of components. The cross-sectional shape of a component is created by cutting the component by using an imaginary cutting plane and then viewing it from the direction normal to the cutting plane, see Figure 9.1. Note that the view that represents the cross-sectional shape of a component is known as section view.

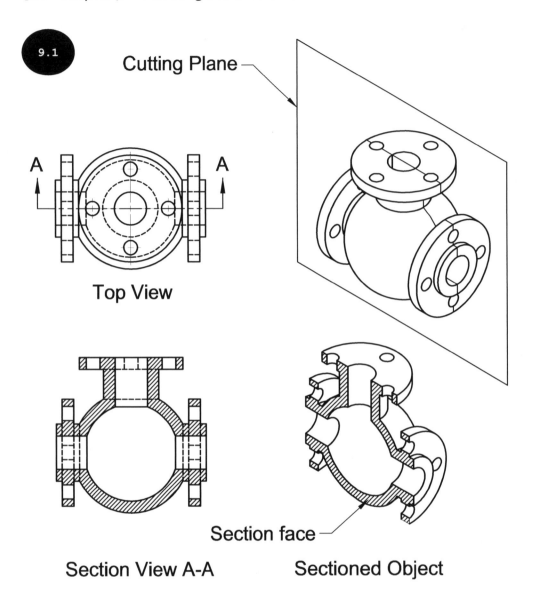

9.1

Cutting Plane

Top View

Section View A-A

Section face

Sectioned Object

It is evident from the above figure that hatching is created by filling enclosed areas of drawing views with hatch patterns. A hatch pattern is composed of hatch lines or solid fill. AutoCAD is provided with various hatch patterns that can be used to represent the cross-sectional shape and material of components. In architectural drawings, hatches are generally used to represent the type of material such as brick, stone, wood, and sand. Figure 9.2 shows some of the hatch patters in AutoCAD.

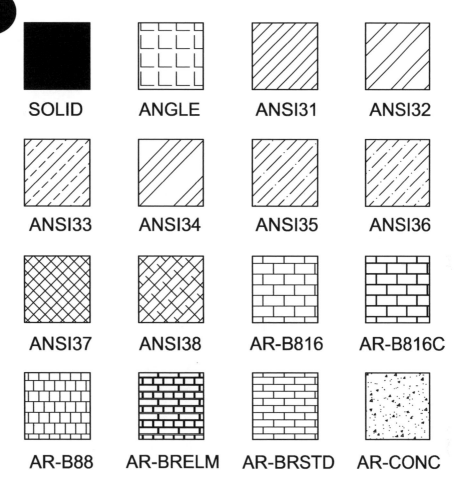

9.2

SOLID	ANGLE	ANSI31	ANSI32
ANSI33	ANSI34	ANSI35	ANSI36
ANSI37	ANSI38	AR-B816	AR-B816C
AR-B88	AR-BRELM	AR-BRSTD	AR-CONC

Creating Hatches

You can create hatching in an enclosed area of a view by using the **Hatch** tool or HATCH command. To create hatch, click on the **Hatch** tool in the **Draw** panel of the **Home** tab. The **Hatch Creation** tab appears in **Ribbon**, see Figure 9.3. Also, you are prompted to pick the internal point. Alternatively, enter **H** in the Command Window and then press ENTER to invoke this tool.

```
Pick internal point or [Select object Undo seTtings]:
```

9.3

In the **Hatch Creation** tab, you can specify the pattern type and pattern properties such as pattern angle, scale, and transparency. Click on the pattern to be created in the **Pattern** panel and then specify the pattern properties in the respective fields of the **Properties** panel of the **Hatch Creation** tab. Next, click on a close area of the drawing view to create hatch pattern. The hatch pattern is created in the specified enclosed area of the drawing view, see Figure 9.4. Next, press the ESC key to exit the creation of hatch pattern. The options of the **Hatch Creation** tab are as follows:

9.4

Boundaries Panel

The options in the **Boundaries** panel of the **Hatch Creation** tab are used to defined enclosed areas of drawing views to create hatch patterns, see Figure 9.5. The options are as follows:

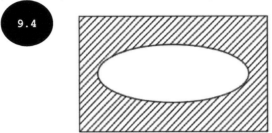

9.5

Pick Points

The **Pick Points** tool is used to select a pick point in an enclosed area of a view to create the hatch pattern. By default, this tool is activated. As a result, you are prompted to specify the pick point. Click to specify a pick point in an enclosed area of a drawing view. The hatch pattern is created such that the enclosed area, which is defined by the pick point is filled with hatch pattern, see Figure 9.6. You can specify multiple pick points in a drawing to create hatch patterns.

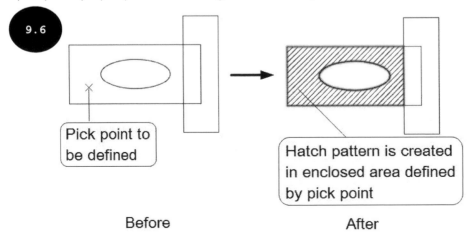

9.6

Pick point to be defined

Hatch pattern is created in enclosed area defined by pick point

Before   After

Select

The **Select** tool of the **Boundaries** panel is used to select the object for creating hatch pattern. When you click on the **Select** tool in the **Boundaries** panel, you are prompted to select objects for creating the hatch pattern. Click on an enclosed object of a drawing. The enclosed area of the selected object is filled with hatch pattern, see Figure 9.7. You can select multiple enclosed objects of a drawing to create hatch pattern.

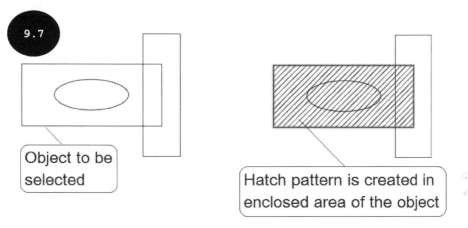

Remove

The **Remove** tool is used to remove the previously selected boundary/object for removing the hatch pattern created in it.

Pattern Panel

The options in the **Pattern** panel are used to select the type of hatch pattern to be created. AutoCAD is provided with various hatch patterns. Figure 9.8 shows the expanded **Pattern** panel. You can expand the **Pattern** panel by clicking on the down arrow on the lower right of the panel to display additional hatch patterns.

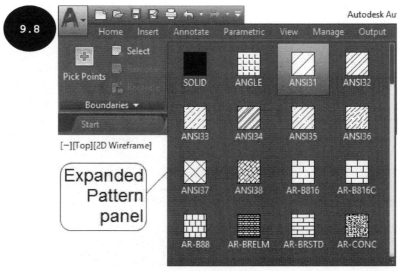

Properties Panel

The **Properties** panel is used to specify the hatch pattern properties such as hatch pattern color, hatch background color, hatch transparency, hatch angle, and hatch scale in the respective fields of the panel, see Figure 9.9.

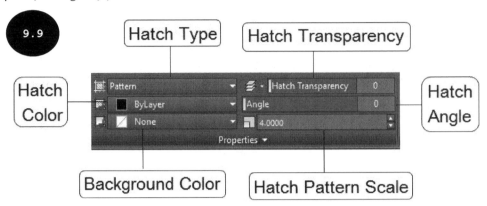

Options Panel

The **Associative** tool of the **Options** panel is used to make the hatch pattern associative to the object/ boundary. An associative hatch pattern is updated automatically on modifying its object/boundary. To create an associative hatch pattern, click on the **Associative** tool in the **Options** panel and then create hatch patterns on enclosed objects. The **Annotative** tool is used to make the hatch pattern annotative such that the scale of the hatch pattern adjusts automatically with respect to the scale of the viewport.

After specifying the hatch pattern properties, click to specify an enclosed area or object to create the hatch pattern. The hatch pattern is created.

Creating Gradients

Similar to creating hatches by filling the boundary or enclosed area of a view with hatch patterns, you can also fill boundaries or enclosed areas with gradient having one or more gradient color, see Figure 9.10. Applying gradients are very useful to make the drawing presentable and give a realistic appearance to the drawing views. Gradients are also used to represent the section area and distinguish between two or more objects or enclosed areas of drawing views.

To apply gradient to an enclosed area of a drawing view, click on the down arrow next to the **Hatch** tool in the **Draw** panel. A flyout appears, see Figure 9.11. In this flyout, click on the **Gradient** tool. The **Hatch Creation** tab appears, see Figure 9.12. Also, you are prompted to pick an internal point.

```
Pick internal point or [Select object Undo seTtings]:
```

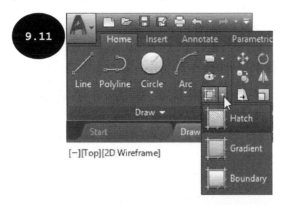

9.11

9.12

The options in **Hatch Creation** tab are used to specify the gradient pattern and its properties. All these options are same as those discussed earlier while creating the hatch patterns. Select the gradient pattern to be created in the **Pattern** panel and then specify the pattern properties such as gradient color 1 and gradient color 2 in the respective fields of the **Properties** panel of the **Hatch Creation** tab. Next, click on a close area of a drawing view to create a gradient pattern. The gradient pattern is created in the specified enclosed area of the drawing view, see Figure 9.13. You can specify multiple enclosed areas one by one to create gradient patterns. Next, press the ESC key to exit the creation of hatch pattern.

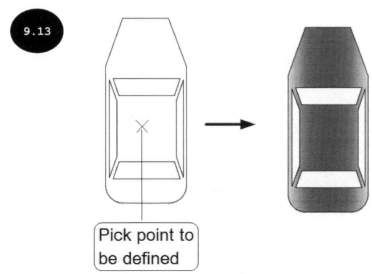

9.13

Pick point to be defined

Tutorial 1

Create the drawing shown in the Figure 9.14. You need to apply ANSI31 hatches to the drawing at different hatch angles as shown in the Figure 9.14.

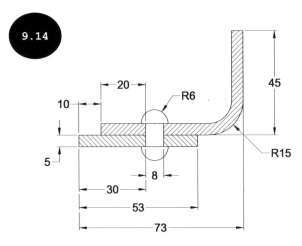

Section 1: Starting AutoCAD

1.   Start AutoCAD and then open a new drawing file.

Section 2: Creating Drawing and Applying Dimensions

1.   Create a drawing as shown in Figure 9.15.

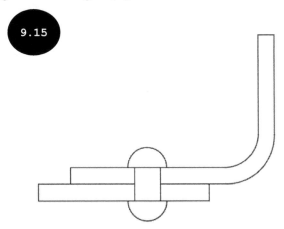

2.   Invoke the **Modify Dimension Style** dialog box and then modify the Standard dimension style: Text height = 3.5, Offset from dim line = 1, Arrow size = 3.25, Extend beyond dim lines = 1, Offset from origin = 1, and Precision = 0. To invoke this dialog box, enter **D** in the Command Window and then press ENTER.

3. Apply dimensions to the drawing by using the dimension tools, see Figure 9.16.

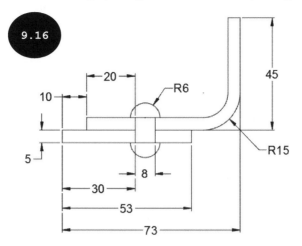

Section 3: Creating Hatches

1. Click on the **Hatch** tool in the **Draw** panel of the **Home** tab, see Figure 9.17. The **Hatch Creation** tab appears in the **Ribbon**. Also, you are prompted to pick an internal point. Alternatively, enter H in the Command Window and then press ENTER.

```
Pick internal point or [Select objects Undo seTtings]:
```

2. Click on the upper left enclosed area of the drawing, see Figure 9.18. The hatching is created, see Figure 9.18.

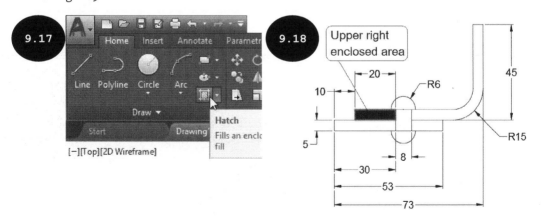

3. Make sure that the ANSI31 is selected as the hatch pattern in the **Pattern** panel of the **Hatch Creation** tab in the **Ribbon**.

    It is evident from the Figure 9.18 that the scale of the hatch pattern is very small. Therefore, you need to change the scale of the hatch pattern.

4.   Enter **12** in the **Hatch Pattern Scale** field of the **Properties** panel of the **Hatch Creation** tab and then press ENTER. The scale of the hatch pattern changes, see Figure 9.19.

5.   Click on the right enclosed area of the upper part of the drawing. The hatch is created, see Figure 9.20.

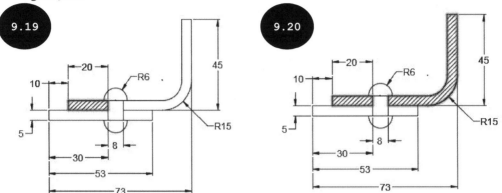

6.   Press ENTER to exit the creation of Hatch. The hatch is created on the upper part of the drawing.

Now, you need to create the hatch on the lower part of the drawing.

7.   Click on the **Hatch** tool in the **Draw** panel of the **Home** tab again. The **Hatch Creation** tab appears. Also, you are prompted to pick an internal point. Alternatively, enter H in the Command Window and then press ENTER.

```
Pick internal point or [Select objects Undo seTtings]:
```

8.   Click on the lower left enclosed area of the drawing, see Figure 9.21. The hatching is created, see Figure 9.21. Make sure that the scale of the hatch is specified as 12 in the **Hatch Pattern Scale** field of the **Properties** panel. Now, you need to change the angle of hatch pattern.

9.   Enter **90** as the angle of hatch pattern in the **Angle** field of the **Properties** panel of the **Hatch Creation** tab. The angle of the hatch pattern is changed, see Figure 9.22.

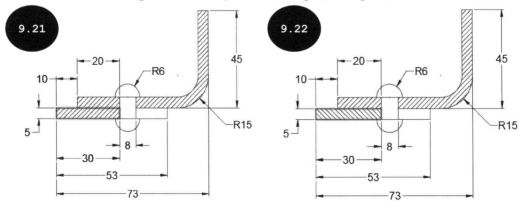

10. Click on the right enclosed area of the lower part of the drawing. The hatch pattern is created, see Figure 9.23. Next, press ENTER. Figure 9.23 shows the final drawing after creating the hatch pattern.

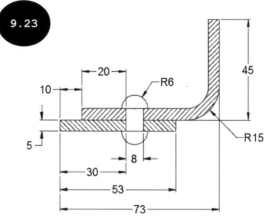

9.23

Section 4: Saving the Drawing

1. Click on the **Save** tool in the **Quick Access Toolbar**. The **Save Drawing As** dialog box appears.

2. Browse to the *AutoCAD* folder and then create a folder with the name *Chapter 9* inside the *AutoCAD* folder. Next, enter **Tutorial 1** in the **File name** field of the dialog box.

3. Click on the **Save** button. The drawing is saved with the name Tutorial 1 in the *Chapter 9* folder.

Hands-on Test Drive 1

Create the drawing shown in the Figure 9.24. You need to apply ANSI31 hatches to the drawing at different hatch angles as shown in the Figure 9.24.

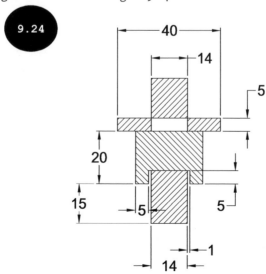

9.24

Hands-on Test Drive 2

Create the drawing shown in the Figure 9.25. You need to apply ANSI35 hatches to the drawing at different hatch angles as shown in the Figure 9.25.

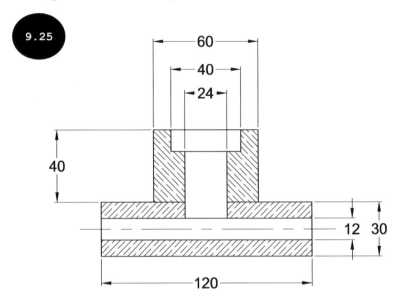

Summary

In this chapter, you have learned how to create different types of hatch patterns and gradients in enclosed areas of a drawing.

Questions

*   A drawing view which represents the cross-section of a part is known as _____ .

*   You can create hatching in an enclosed area of a drawing view by using the _____ tool or the _____ command.

*   The _____ tool is used to select a pick point in an enclosed area of a drawing view to create hatch pattern.

*   The _____ tool is used to remove the previously selected boundary/object for removing the hatch pattern created.

*   The _____ tool is used to make the hatch pattern associative to the object/boundary.

*   The _____ tool is used to create gradient in an enclosed area of a drawing view.

Working with Blocks and Xrefs

In this chapter, you will learn the following:

- Creating Block
- Inserting Block in drawing
- Creating WBlock
- Inserting WBlock in drawings
- Editing Blocks
- Making dynamic Blocks
- Working with external references (Xrefs)

Block is a very powerful feature of AutoCAD, which helps designers to speed up the creation of a design, increases efficiency, and saves time. For example, in a drawing, you often find some repetitive objects such as symbols and fasteners. Instead of creating the same objects again and again, you can create its block and use it several times in a drawing. A block is a collection of objects that are combined together and act as a single object. Figure 10.1 shows a geometry having multiple objects and Figure 10.2 shows the same geometry after converting into a block, in which all objects are treated as a single object.

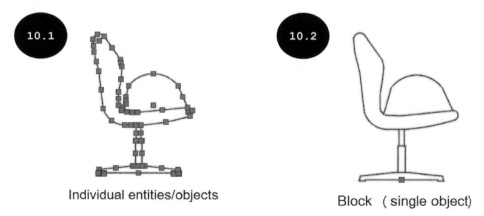

Individual entities/objects

Block (single object)

In AutoCAD, you can create two types of blocks: internal block (Block) and external block (WBlock). An internal block is a group of objects that can be saved internally in the drawing and used several times within the drawing. The internal block is created by using the BLOCK command and known as Block. Whereas the external block is a group of objects or entire drawing that can be saved as an external file and used in any drawing file. The external block is created by using the WBLOCK command and know as WBlock.

Creating Block

In AutoCAD, you can create block either by using the **Create Block** tool or the BLOCK command. To create a block, click on the **Create Block** tool in the **Block Definition** panel of the **Insert** tab, see Figure 10.3. The **Block Definition** dialog box appears, see Figure 10.4. Alternatively, enter B, shortcut of BLOCK command, in the Command Window and then press ENTER. The options in the **Block Definition** dialog box are used to define the block definition such as block name, insertion/base point, and objects to be converted into block. The options are as follows:

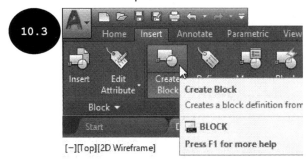

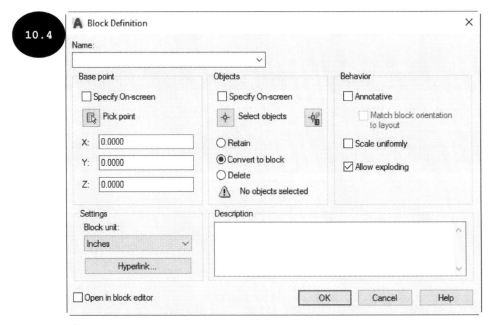

Name

The **Name** field of the dialog box is used to specify the name of the block. You can write up to 255 characters in a block name, which includes letters, numbers, blank spaces, any special characters that are not used by the operating system. Note that all the existing blocks or blocks created in the current drawing are listed in the **Name** drop-down list of this dialog box. To display the **Name** drop-down list, click on the arrow in the **Name** field of the dialog box, see Figure 10.5.

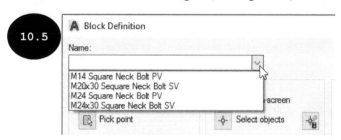

Base Point

The **Base point** area of the dialog box is used to specify a base/insertion point of a block. A base point of a block is used as a reference point while inserting the block in a drawing. Note that blocks are inserted into a drawing with respect to the specified base point. Therefore, base point of a block has to be defined very carefully. You can define base point by picking/specifying a point in the drawing area or by entering the coordinates (X, Y, and Z). To define a base point by picking/specifying a point in the drawing area, click on the **Pick point** button in the **Base point** area. The **Block Definition** dialog box gets closed and you are prompted to specify the insertion base point.

```
_block Specify insertion base point:
```

Click to specify a point in the drawing area as the base/insertion point of a block, see Figure 10.6. Generally, a corner point or a center point of the block is specified as a base point. As soon as you specify the base point of a block, the **Block Definition** dialog box appears again and the X, Y, and Z coordinate values of the selected base point are displayed automatically in the X, Y, and Z fields of the **Base point** area of the dialog box, respectively. Alternatively, you can enter the X, Y, and Z coordinates of the base point in the respective fields of the **Base point** area of the dialog box.

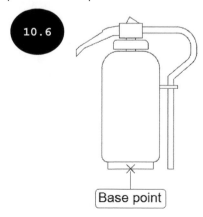

Note: If you do not specify the base point for a block then the origin point (0,0,0) is used as the base/insertion point of the block, by default.

Objects

The **Objects** area of the dialog box is used for selecting the objects of the drawing to be converted into a block. To select objects, click on the **Select objects** button in the **Objects** area. The **Block Definition** dialog box gets closed and you are prompted to select objects to be converted into block.

```
Select objects:
```

Select objects of the drawing to be converted into a block, see Figure 10.7. You can select the objects by clicking the left mouse button or by using the Window selection or Cross Window selection method. After selecting the objects, press ENTER. The **Block Definition** dialog box appears again and displays the information about the number of objects selected at the bottom of the **Objects** area in the dialog box, see Figure 10.8. The remaining options of the **Objects** area of the dialog box are as follows:

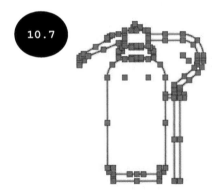

10.7

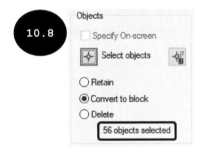

10.8

Retain

On selecting the **Retain** radio button of the **Objects** area, the objects selected for converting into block are retained in the drawing area as an individual entities and a new block is created, which gets saved internally in the drawing, automatically.

Convert to block

By default, the **Convert to block** radio button is selected in the dialog box. As a result, the objects selected get converted into a block in the drawing area and treated as a single object. Also, a copy of block gets saved internally in the drawing.

Delete

On selecting the **Delete** radio button, the objects selected for converting into block get deleted in the drawing area and a new block is created, which gets saved internally in the drawing.

Behavior

The options in the **Behavior** area of the dialog box are used for define the behavior of the block, see Figure 10.9. The options are as follows:

Annotative

On selecting the **Annotative** check box, the selected objects are converted into an annotative block. An annotative block can be used several times with different scales in a drawing. Also, the size/scale of an annotative block is adjusted to the appropriate scale of the viewport.

Match block orientation to layout

The **Match block orientation to layout** check box is enabled only if the **Annotative** check box is selected. On selecting this check box, the orientation of the block in the paper space viewports matches to the orientation of the layout.

Scale uniformly

On selecting the **Scale uniformly** check box, the block maintains uniform scale such that it can stretch in all directions/axes uniformly. When this check box is unchecked, the block can be stretched in any of the axes with different scales.

Allow exploding

By default, the **Allow exploding** check box is selected. As a result, you can explode the block objects into individual objects.

Settings

The options in the **Settings** area of the dialog box are used to specify settings for the block, see Figure 10.10. The options are as follows:

Block unit

The **Block unit** drop-down list is used to specify the insertion unit for the block. When you insert a block in a drawing, the block will be scaled as per the insertion unit specified in this drop-down list. The current unit of the drawing is used as the insertion unit for the block and is selected in this drop-down list, by default.

Hyperlink

The **Hyperlink** button is used to assign a hyperlink to the block. When you click on the **Hyperlink** button, the **Insert Hyperlink** dialog box appears. In this dialog box, you can select the file or specify a web page address (URL) to be Hyperlinked with the block.

Description

The **Description** area of the dialog box is used add a brief description about the block.

Open in block editor

On selecting the **Open in block editor** check box, the block is created as per the specified block definitions and get opened in the Block Editor when you click on the **OK** button in the dialog box. The Block Editor is used to edit the block definitions. You will learn about editing blocks by using the Block Editor later in this chapter.

After specifying the block definitions such as block name, insertion/base point, and objects to be converted into block, click on the **OK** button of the dialog box. The block is created and saved internally in the current drawing file for further use in the drawing.

Procedure for Creating Block

1. Click on the **Create Block** tool in the **Block Definition** panel of the **Insert** tab. The **Block Definition** dialog box appears. Alternatively, enter **B** in the Command Window and then press ENTER.

2. Click on the **Pick point** button in the **Base point** area of the dialog box. The **Block Definition** dialog box gets closed and you are prompted to specify the insertion base point. Note the **Pick point** button is enabled only when the **Specify On-screen** check box is unchecked in the **Base point** area of the dialog box.

    ```
    Specify insertion base point:
    ```

3. Click to specify a insertion base point for the block in the drawing area. The **Block Definition** dialog box appears again and the base point is specified.

4. Click on the **Select objects** button in the **Objects** area of the dialog box. The **Block Definition** dialog box gets closed and you are prompted to select objects.

    ```
    Select objects:
    ```

5. Select objects to be converted in a block. The **Block Definition** dialog box appears again and the objects are selected.

6. Specify remaining block definitions such as annotative, block unit, hyperlink, and allow exploding by using the respective options of the dialog box. You can also accept the default specified definitions and skip this step.

7. Click on the **OK** button. The block is created and saved internally in the current drawing.

Inserting Block in Drawing

The blocks created in the current drawing can be inserted in the drawing several times by using the **Insert** tool of the **Block** panel in the **Insert** tab. To insert a block in the drawing, click on the **Insert** tool in the **Block** panel of the **Insert** tab. The **Insert** flyout appears, see Figure 10.11. This flyout contains a list of all the blocks created in the current drawing. In this flyout, click on the block to be inserted in the drawing. The selected block gets attached with the cursor such that the base/insertion point specified while creating the block is attached to the cursor tip. Also, you are prompted to specify the insertion point in the drawing area for placing the attached block.

```
Specify insertion point or [Basepoint Scale X Y Z Rotate]:
```

Click in the drawing area to specify the insertion point for the block. The attached block is inserted at the specified location in the drawing. You can also control the block parameters such as scale and angle of rotation before specifying the insertion point by using the options available in the command prompt or by using the **Insert** dialog box. The **Insert** dialog box provides additional options for controlling the block parameters. To invoke the **Insert** dialog box, click on the **More Options** button in the **Insert** flyout, refer to Figure 10.11.

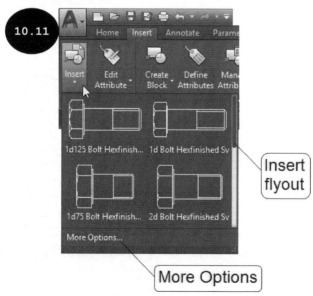

As soon as you click on the **More Options** button, the **Insert** dialog box appears, see Figure 10.12. Alternatively, enter **I** in the Command Window and then press ENTER to invoke the **Insert** dialog box. The options in the **Insert** dialog box are used to select the block to be inserted in the drawing area and other parameters for the block such as scale, angle of rotation, and insertion point. The options are as follows:

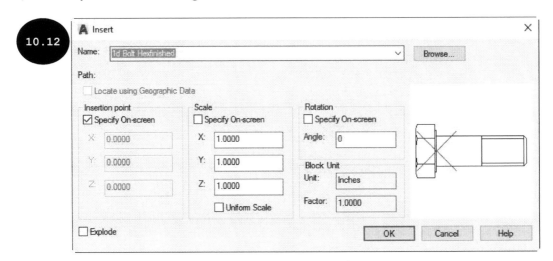

Name

The **Name** drop-down list of the **Insert** dialog box is used to select the block to be inserted in the drawing. To invoke the **Name** drop-down list, click on the down arrow, see Figure 10.13. The **Name** drop-down list displays a list of all the blocks created or available in the current drawing. You can also enter the name of the block to be inserted in the drawing here.

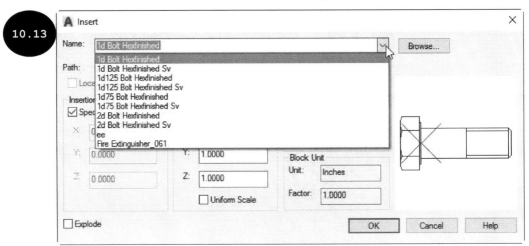

Insertion point

By default, the **Specify On-screen** check box is selected in the **Insertion point** area. As a result, you can specify insertion point in the drawing area. To specify insertion point in the drawing area, select the **Specify On-screen** check box and then click on the **OK** button. You are prompted to specify the insertion point. Click to specify the insertion point in the drawing. The selected block is inserted in the drawing area and placed in the specified insertion point location.

If you uncheck the **Specify On-screen** check box, the X, Y, and Z fields of the **Insertion point** area are enabled. In these fields, you can specify the X, Y, and Z coordinates of the insertion point.

Scale

The **Scale** area of the dialog box is used to specify the scale for the block. By default, the 1 value is specified as the scale value in the **X**, **Y**, and **Z** fields. As a result, the block gets inserted in the drawing in its original size. You can specify scale in the X, Y, and Z axes of the block in the respective fields. On selecting the **Uniform Scale** check box, the block can be scaled uniformly in all axes. On selecting the **Specify On-screen** check box, you are prompted to specify scale for the block in the drawing area when you exit the dialog box by clicking on the **OK** button.

Rotation

The **Rotation** area of the dialog box is used to specify the rotational angle for the block. By default, **0** is specified in the **Angle** field of the **Rotation** area. In the **Angle** field, you can specify the rotational angle for the block, as required. You can also specify the rotational angle for the block in the drawing area by selecting the **Specify On-screen** check box.

After specifying all the parameters for inserting the block, click on the **OK** button in the dialog box. The selected block gets attached with the cursor such that the base/insertion point specified while creating the block is attached to the cursor tip, see Figure 10.14. Also, you are prompted to specify the insertion point in the drawing area. Click to specify an insertion point for the block. The block is inserted at the specified insertion point, see Figure 10.15. In this figure, the block has been inserted by specifying the insertion point at the location 1 as marked in the Figure 10.14. Similarly, you can insert the same block several times in the drawing. Figure 10.16 shows the drawing in which 6 instances of the block have been inserted in the drawing.

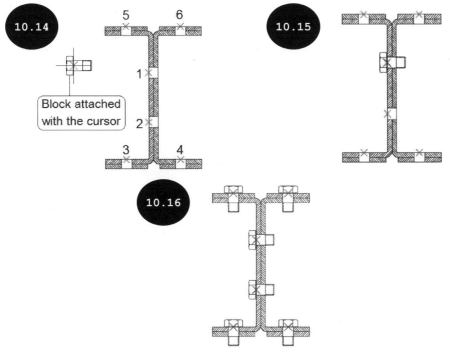

Creating WBlock

A WBlock is a group of objects or entire drawing that is saved as external file and acts as a single object. In AutoCAD, WBlocks are same as Blocks with the difference that WBlocks are saved as external files and can be inserted several times in any drawing whereas Blocks can only be inserted in the current drawing in which they are created. You can create a WBlock either by using the **Write Block** tool or by using the WBLOCK command. To create a WBlock, click on the **Write Block** tool in the **Block** flyout of the **Block Definition** panel in the **Insert** tab, see Figure 10.17. The **Write Block** dialog box appears, see Figure 10.18. Alternatively, enter **W**, shortcut of WBLOCK command, in the Command Window and then press ENTER. The **Write Block** dialog box has two areas: **Source** and **Destination**. The options of both these areas are as follows:

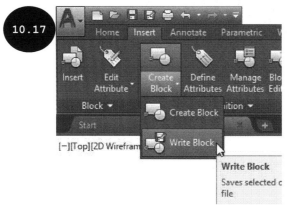

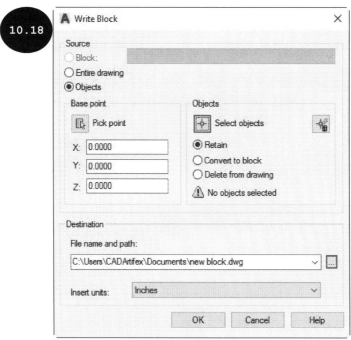

Source

The options in the **Source** area of the dialog box are used to specify whether the block, entire drawing, or objects of the drawing are to be converted into a WBlock. The options are as follows:

Block

The **Block** radio button is used to select an existing block for converting into a WBlock. On selecting the **Block** radio button, the **Block** drop-down list is enabled in front of this radio button. In the **Block** drop-down list, select the required Block to be converted into a WBlock. Note that the **Block** radio button is enabled only when the current drawing has existing Blocks available.

Entire drawing

The **Entire drawing** radio button is used to convert the entire drawing into a WBlock.

Objects

The **Objects** radio button is used to select a group of objects of the drawing for converting into a WBlock. The **Objects** radio button is selected by default. Note that when this radio button is selected, the options in the **Base point** area and the **Objects** area of the dialog box are enabled, see Figure 10.19. The options of the **Base point** area and the **Objects** area are as follows:

Base Point

The options of the **Base point** area are used to select a base point for the WBlock. You can specify the base point either by specifying a point in the drawing area or by entering X, Y, and Z coordinates of the base point in the **X, Y,** and **Z** fields, respectively. To specify a base point, click on the **Pick point** button in the **Base point** area of the dialog box. The **Write Block** dialog box is closed and you are prompted to specify an insertion base point. Click in the drawing area to specify the base point. The **Write Block** dialog box appears again and the base point is specified.

Objects

The options of the **Objects** area are used to select a group of objects to be converted into a WBlock. To select objects, click on the **Select objects** button of this area. The **Write Block** dialog box gets closed and you are prompted to select objects. Select objects in the drawing area by clicking the left mouse button or by using the Window/Cross Window selection method. After selecting the objects, press ENTER. The **Write Block** dialog box appears again and the information about the number of objects selected appears at the bottom of this area, see Figure 10.19. Similar to this, the other options such as **Retain, Convert to block,** and **Delete from drawing** of this area are same as those discussed earlier while creating Blocks using the **Create Block** tool.

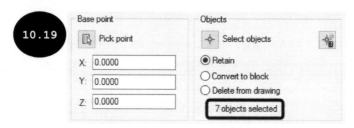

10.19

Destination

After specifying the source (block, entire drawing, or objects) for creating a WBlock, you need to define the name and the destination/location where you want to save the WBlock. You can specify a name and the destination for the WBlock by using the options of the **Destination** area. The options area as follows:

File name and path

The **File name and path** field is used to specify a name and location where the WBlock will be saved. To specify a name and location for the WBlock, click on the [...] button ☐ on the right of this field. The **Browse for Drawing File** dialog box appears. In this dialog box, browse to the location where you want to save the WBlock and then enter a new name for the WBlock in the **File name** field of this dialog box. Next, click on the **Save** button. The **Browse for Drawing File** dialog box gets closed and the specified location and the name appears in the **File name and path** field of the **Write Block** dialog box.

Insert units

The **Insert units** drop-down list is used to select the unit for the WBlock.

After specifying the source and destination, click on the **OK** button. The **Write Block** gets closed and the WBlock is saved in the specified location.

Inserting WBlock in Drawings

You can insert a WBlock in any drawing by using the **Insert** tool of the **Block** panel in the **Insert** tab or by using the INSERT command. To insert a WBlock in a drawing, enter I in the Command Window and then press ENTER. The **Insert** dialog box appears, see Figure 10.20. Alternatively, you can use the **Insert** tool of the **Block** panel in the **Insert** tab to invoke the **Insert** dialog box.

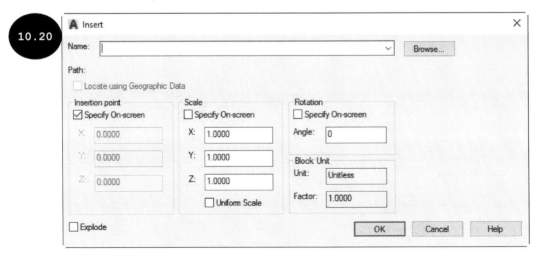

10.20

In the **Insert** dialog box, click on the **Browse** button. The **Select Drawing File** dialog box appears. In this dialog box, browse to the location where the WBlock has been saved and then click on the WBlock to be inserted. Next, click on the **Open** button in the dialog box. The **Select Drawing File** dialog box gets closed and the name of the selected WBlock appears in the **Name** field of the **Insert** dialog box. Next, specify other parameters such as scale and angle of rotation in the respective fields of the **Insert** dialog box. The options in the **Insert** dialog box are the same as those discussed earlier. Next, click on the **OK** button. The selected WBlock gets attached with the cursor such that the base point specified while creating the WBlock is attached to the cursor tip. Next, click to specify the insertion point in the drawing area. The WBlock gets inserted at the specified insertion point. Similarly, you can insert a WBlock several times in a drawing.

Editing Blocks

In a drawing, you may need to edit or modify existing blocks. In AutoCAD, you can edit the existing blocks either by using the **Block Editor** tool or BEDIT command. To edit a block, click on the **Block Editor** tool in the **Block Definition** panel of the **Insert** tab, see Figure 10.21. The **Edit Block Definition** dialog box appears, see Figure 10.22. It displays a list of all the blocks available in the current drawing. Alternatively, enter **BE** in the Command Window and then press ENTER (BE is shortcut of BEDIT command).

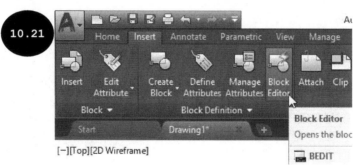

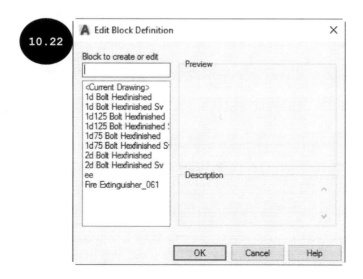

Click on the block to be edited in the **Edit Block Definition** dialog box. The preview of the selected block appears in the **Preview** area of the dialog box. Next, click on the **OK** button. The selected block is opened in the Block Editor and the **Block Editor** tab appears in the **Ribbon**, see Figure 10.23. Now, you can make the changes in the block such as add new entities, delete existing entities, stretch, rotate, and so on by using the respective tools in the **Home** tab of the **Ribbon**. The tools in the **Block Editor** tab are used to make the block dynamic. You will learn more about making dynamic block later in this chapter. After making the necessary changes in the block, click on the **Save Block** tool in the **Open/Save** panel of the **Block Editor** tab. The changes made in the block are saved. Next, click on the **Close Block Editor** tool in the **Close** panel of the **Block Editor** tab to close the Block Editor. Note that if you have not saved the block after making the changes then on clicking the **Close Block Editor** tool, the **Block - Changes Not Saved** window appears, see Figure 10.24.

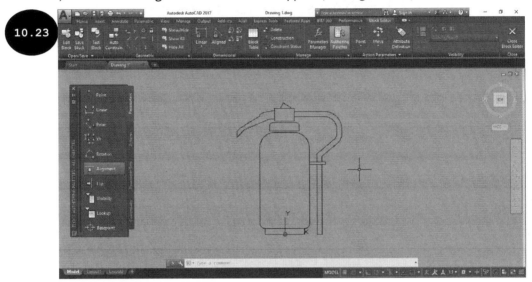

In the **Block - Changes Not Saved** window, click on **Save the changes to *name of the block*** to save the changes made in the Block Editor. To discard the changes made, click on **Discard the changes and close the Block Editor**.

Making Dynamic Blocks

A dynamic block is a block that can be modified dynamically in the drawing area. You can make a block dynamic by specifying the required parameters and actions using the tools in the **Block Editor** tab. To make a dynamic block, click on the **Block Editor** tool in the **Block Definition** panel of the **Insert** tab, see Figure 10.25. The **Edit Block Definition** dialog box appears. Alternatively, enter **BE** in the Command Window and then press ENTER (BE is shortcut of BEDIT command).

In the **Edit Block Definition** dialog box, select the block to be edited or converted into dynamic block and then click on the **OK** button. The selected block gets opened in the Block Editor and the **Block Editor** tab appears in the **Ribbon**, see Figure 10.26. In this figure, a rectangular block representing a table appears in the Block Editor.

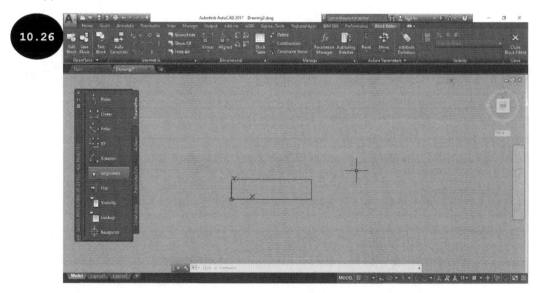

Once the block has been opened in the Block Editor, you can make the block dynamic by specifying required parameters and actions. To specify parameters for creating a dynamic block, click on the **Parameters** tab in the **BLOCK AUTHORING PALETTES**. The tools to specify parameters appear, see Figure 10.27. By using the tools of the **Parameters** tab, you can specify the parameters for the dynamic block.

For example, to specify a linear parameter, click on the **Linear** tool in the **Parameters** tab. You are prompted to specify the start point.

```
Specify start point or [Name Label Chain Description Base Palette
Value set]:
```

Next, click to specify the start point for the linear parameter, see Figure 10.28. In this figure, the midpoint of the upper horizontal line of the rectangle is specified as the start point. As soon as you specify the start point, a label is attached with the cursor and you are prompted to specify the endpoint, see Figure 10.28.

```
Specify endpoint:
```

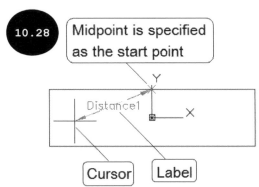

Next, click to specify the endpoint of the label, see Figure 10.29. You are prompted to specify the label location.

```
Specify label location:
```

Click to specify the label location. The label is placed in the specified location and the linear parameter is defined. Also, the grips appear at the specified midpoints, see Figure 10.30. The linear parameter allows you to modify the block in a linear fashion dynamically by using the grips in the drawing area. However, only specifying the linear parameter does not make the block dynamic. You also need to specify the action such as stretch, scale, or move for the linear parameter.

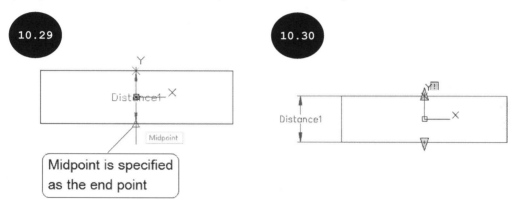

To specify the action for the parameter, click on the **Actions** tab in the **BLOCK AUTHORING PALETTES**. The tools to specify actions for the parameter appear in the **Actions** tab, see Figure 10.31.

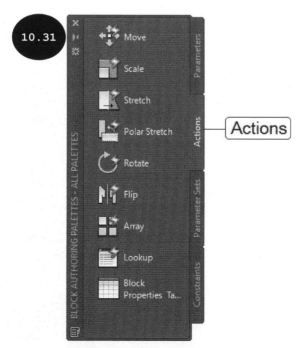

For example, to specify a stretch action for the linear parameter, click on the **Stretch** tool in the **Actions** tab of the BLOCK AUTHORING PALETTES. You are prompted to select a parameter for the specifying action.

```
Select parameter:
```

Click on the parameter (linear parameter) for specifying action to it. You can click on the label of the parameter to select it. As soon as you select the parameter (linear parameter), you are prompted to specify the parameter point to associate the action.

```
Specify parameter point to associate with action or enter [sTart
point Second point] <Second>:
```

Move the cursor over the grip, which is displayed at the midpoint of the upper horizontal line, see Figure 10.32. The cursor snaps to the midpoint and a circle with cross mark appears, see Figure 10.32. Next, click on the midpoint of the upper horizontal line as the parameter point to associate the action. You are prompted to specify the first corner of the stretch frame. Note that the stretch frame is used to define objects to be stretched by using the grip selected. You can create stretch frame by specifying two opposite corners of the Cross Window.

```
Specify first corner of stretch frame or [CPolygon]:
```

Click to specify the first corner of the stretch frame, see Figure 10.33. You are prompted to specify the opposite corner of the stretch frame.

```
Specify opposite corner:
```

Move the cursor diagonally opposite to the first corner and then click to specify the second corner of the stretch frame, see Figure 10.33. You are prompted to select objects to be stretched.

```
Select objects:
```

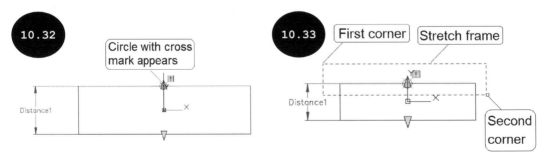

Click on the rectangle as the object to be stretched. Next, press ENTER. The stretch action is assigned to the upper selected grip of the rectangle. Similarly, assign the stretch action to the grip, which appears at the midpoint of the lower horizontal line of the block (rectangle). After assigning the parameter and the required action to it, click on the **Close Block Editor** tool in the **Close** panel of the **Block Editor** tab. The **Block - Changes Not Saved** window appears, see Figure 10.34. Click on **Save the changes to** *name of the block* in the **Block - Changes Not Saved** window. The changes made in the Block Editor are saved and the Block Editor is closed. Also, the block becomes a dynamic block.

Now, if you select the block (dynamic block) in drawing area, the grips appears in the block, see Figure 10.35. By using these grips you can stretch the block dynamically in the drawing.

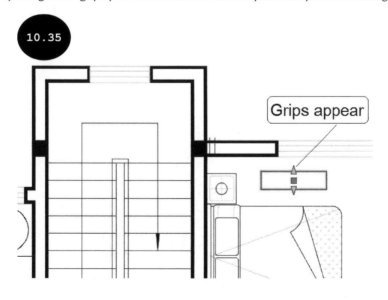

Working with External References (Xrefs)

In AutoCAD, external references are also known as Xrefs, which are linked/attached to the current drawing. External references (Xrefs) are not the permanent part of the drawing and are attached externally to the drawing. However, the external references update automatically every time when you open the current drawing. The external references (Xrefs) are most widely used in large assembly drawings, which have multiple parts. You can create drawings of all parts as individual drawings and then assemble them in a main drawing as external references (Xrefs). External references also allows multiple users (CAD Engineers/Operators) to work on a single project (drawing) and then assemble all the drawings created by different users as external references to a drawing. You can attach external references to a drawing by using the **EXTERNAL REFERENCES** Palette. To invoke the **EXTERNAL REFERENCES** Palette, click on the **External References Palette** tool in the **Palettes** panel of the **View** tab, see Figure 10.36. The **EXTERNAL REFERENCES** Palette appears, see Figure 10.37. Alternatively, enter **XREF** in the Command Window and then press ENTER to invoke this palette.

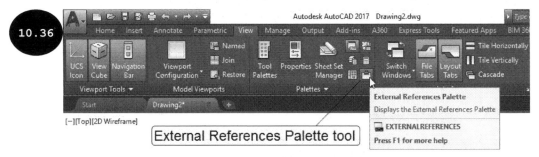

External References Palette tool

The **EXTERNAL REFERENCES** Palette is used to attach new Xref, detach existing Xref, unload the attached Xref, reload the unload Xref, and so on. Also, the EXTERNAL REFERENCES Palette displays the current status of each Xref attached in the current drawing.

To attach a Xref in the current drawing, click on the arrow in the **Attach** tool of the **EXTERNAL REFERENCES** Palette. The **Attach** flyout appears, see Figure 10.38. By using the tools of this flyout you can attach DWG, Image, DWF, DGF, PDF, Point Cloud, and Coordinate Model files. For example, to attach a DWG file, click on the **Attach DWG** tool in the **Attach** flyout. The **Select Reference File** dialog box appears. In this dialog box, browse to the location where the file to be attached is saved. Next, select the DWG file and then click on the **Open** button. The **Attach External Reference** dialog box appears, see Figure 10.39.

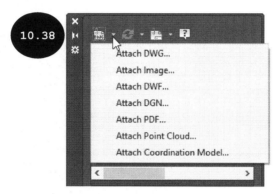

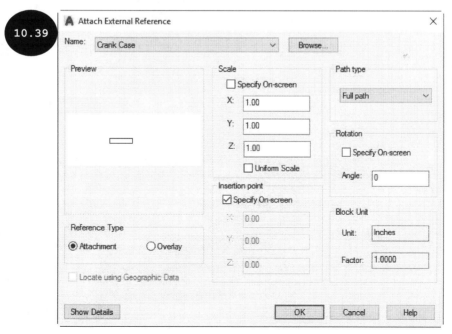

In the **Attach External Reference** dialog box, specify the parameters such as scale, insertion point, reference type, and rotation for attaching the external reference. Next, click on the **OK** button. The selected DWG file is attached with the cursor at its base point and you are prompted to specify the insertion point.

```
Specify insertion point or [Scale X Y Z Rotate PScale PX PY PZ
PRotate]:
```

Click to specify the insertion point in the drawing area. The selected drawing (DWG) is attached to the current drawing and is placed at the specified insertion point. Also, the name of the attached drawing is listed in the **EXTERNAL REFERENCES** Palette. Similarly, you can attach multiple files to the current drawing.

To detach an existing Xref, unload the attached Xref, reload the unload Xref, and so on, click on the Xref in the **EXTERNAL REFERENCES** Palette and then right-click. A shortcut menu appears, see Figure 10.40. In this shortcut menu, click on the required option. For example, if you want to unload an existing Xref, click on the **Unload** option. The selected field gets unloaded and is disappeared from the current drawing. Also, a symbol of cross mark appears in front of the file name in the **EXTERNAL REFERENCES** Palette. You can reload the unloaded file. To reload the unloaded file, click on the name of the drawing file to be reloaded in the current drawing and then right-click. A shortcut menu appears. In this shortcut menu, click on the **Reload** option. The file gets reloaded and is visible in the drawing area. Similarly, you can detach the existing Xrefs, change the Xref type, and so on. The **Details** area of the **EXTERNAL REFERENCES** Palette displays the status of the selected Xref.

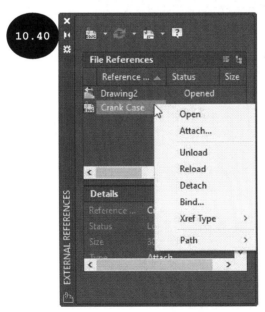

Tutorial 1

Create the objects: arrow, condenser, exchanger, boiler, pump, Flux drum, and valve (see Figure 10.41) and then convert them into blocks. After creating the blocks, create the process flow diagram and insert the blocks in it, see Figure 10.42. Do not apply dimensions in the blocks. Also, you can assume the missing dimensions. You also need to add multiline text in the flow diagram, see Figure 10.42.

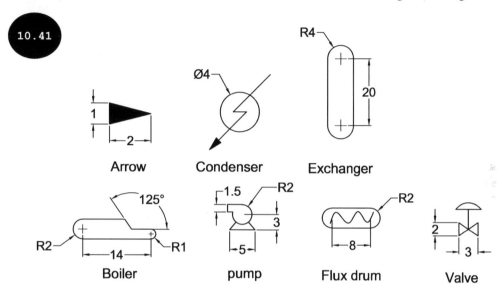

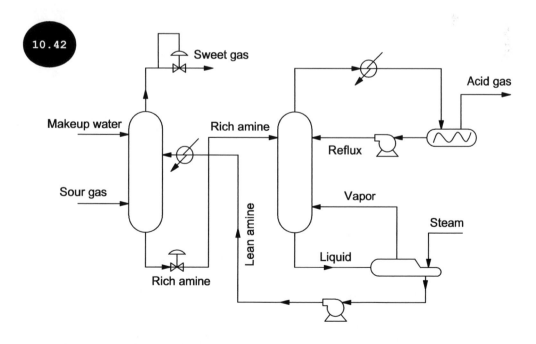

Section 1: Starting AutoCAD

1. Start AutoCAD and then open a new drawing file.

Section 2: Creating Blocks

1. Create the drawing of an arrow as shown in Figure 10.43 by using the **Line** tool. For overall size of the arrow, refer to Figure 10.41.

2. Fill the enclosed area of the arrow with the solid pattern by using the **Hatch** tool, see Figure 10.44.

After creating the drawing of the arrow, you can convert it into block.

3. Click on the **Insert** tab in the **Ribbon**. The tools of the **Insert** tab of the **Ribbon** appears, see Figure 10.45.

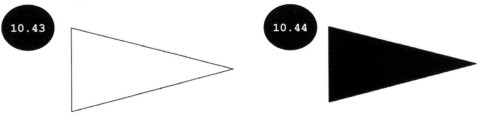

4. Click on the **Create Block** tool in the **Block Definition** panel of the **Insert** tab. The **Block Definition** dialog box appears, see Figure 10.46.

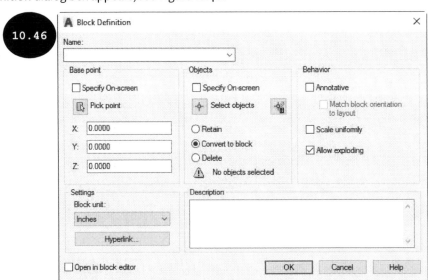

5. Enter **Arrow** as the name of the block in the **Name** field of the dialog box.

6. Click on the **Pick point** button in the **Base point** area of the dialog box. The dialog box disappears and you are prompted to specify the insertion base point.

```
_block specify insertion base point:
```

7. Click on the tip of the arrow as the insertion base point of the block, see Figure 10.47. The base point has been defined and the **Block Definition** dialog box appears again.

8. Click on the **Select objects** button in the **Objects** area of the dialog box. The dialog box disappears and you are prompted to select objects.

```
Select objects:
```

9. Select the arrow object created in the drawing area by using the Window selection method, see Figure 10.48.

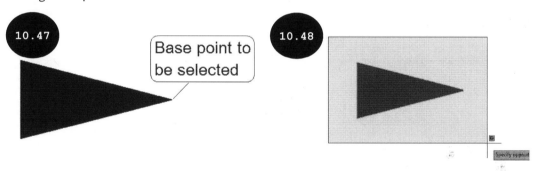

10. Press ENTER. The arrow object has been selected and the **Block Definition** dialog box appears again.

11. Select the **Delete** radio button in the **Objects** area of the dialog box to delete the selected object (arrow) in the drawing area and to create a block in the drawing.

12. Click on the **OK** button in the **Block Definition** dialog box. The block is created and saved internally in the drawing. Also, the selected object (arrow) is deleted in the drawing area.

13. Similarly, create the remaining objects: condenser, exchanger, boiler, pump, flux drum, and valve and then convert them into blocks, see Figure 10.49. In this figure, the cross mark indicates the base point of the objects.

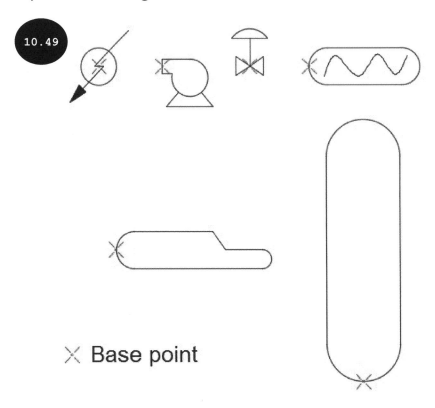

10.49

× Base point

After creating the blocks, you can create the drawing (flow diagram) and insert the blocks.

Section 3: Creating Drawing and Inserting Blocks

1. Click on the **Insert** tab in the **Ribbon**. The tools of the **Insert** tab of the **Ribbon** appears.

2. Click on the **Insert** tool in the **Block** panel of the **Insert** tab. The **Block** flyout appears with the display of all the blocks created in the drawing, see Figure 10.50. In this flyout, you may need to scroll the block list to select the required block.

10.50

3. Click on the Exchanger block in the flyout appeared. The Exchanger block is attached with the cursor at its specified base point. Also, you are prompted to specify the insertion point.

```
Specify insertion point or [Basepoint Scale X Y Z Rotate]:
```

4. Click anywhere in the drawing area to specify the insertion point of the Exchanger block. The Exchanger block is placed at the specified location in the drawing area.

5. Similarly, insert another instance of the Exchanger block in the drawing area, see Figure 10.51. Note that you need to place the second instance of the Exchanger block inline with the first inserted Exchanger block, see Figure 10.51.

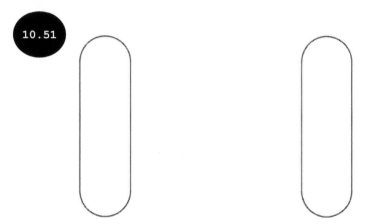

6. Invoke the **Line** tool and then create the line entities of the drawing as shown in Figure 10.52. You can assume the length of the lines. In the figure, the cross marks (P1 to P6) indicate the insertion points for the blocks in the drawing and are for your reference only.

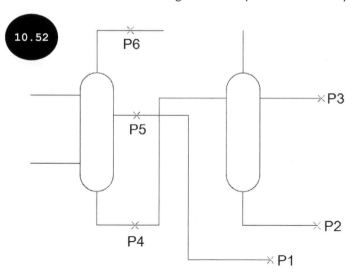

7. Click on the **Insert** tool in the **Block** panel of the **Insert** tab. The **Block** flyout appears. In this flyout, click on the Pump block. The Pump block is attached with the cursor at its specified base point. Also, you are prompted to specify insertion point.

```
Specify insertion point or [Basepoint Scale X Y Z Rotate]:
```

8. Move the cursor toward the insertion point "P1" in the drawing, refer to Figure 10.52. Next, click to specify the insertion point for the Pump block. The Pump block is placed at the specified insertion point in the drawing area, see Figure 10.53.

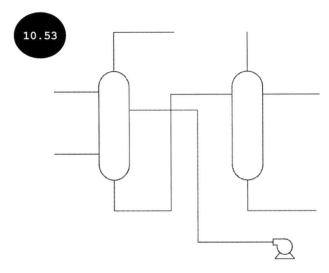

10.53

9. Similarly, insert a Boiler block at the insertion point "P2", a Pump block at the insertion point P3, a Valve block at the insertion point P4, a Condenser block at the insertion point P5, and a Valve block at the insertion point P6, see Figure 10.54.

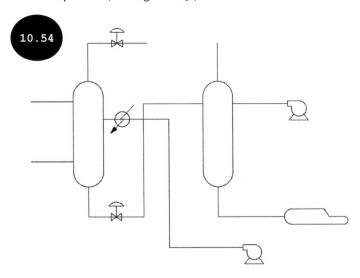

10.54

10. Create the line entities (L1 through L10) of the drawing by using the **Line** tool, see Figure 10.55. You can assume the length of the lines. Note that the Figure 10.55 is numbered for your reference only.

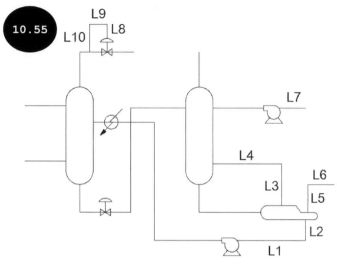

11. Insert the Flux drum block at the end point of the line "L7", see Figure 10.56.

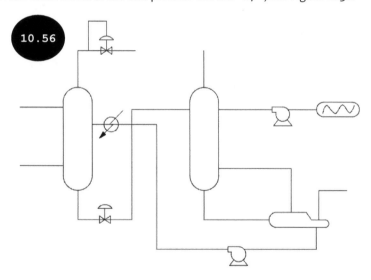

12. Create the line entities (L11 through L14) of the drawing by using the **Line** tool, see Figure 10.57. You can assume the length of the lines. Note that the Figure 10.57 is numbered for your reference only.

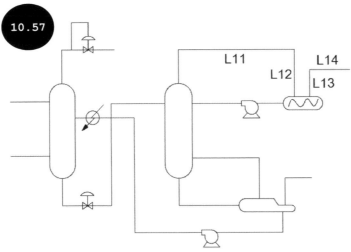

13. Insert the Condenser block at the mid point of the Line "L11", see Figure 10.58.

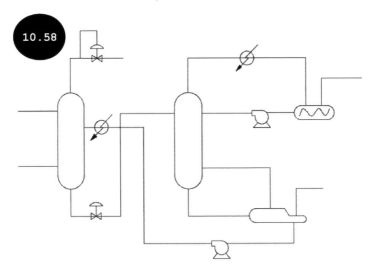

Now, you need to insert the Arrow blocks in the drawing to define the flow of the process in the drawing.

14. Click on the **Insert** tool in the **Block** panel of the **Insert** tab. The **Block** flyout appears. In this flyout, click on the Arrow block. The Arrow block gets attached with the cursor at its base point. Also, you are prompted to specify the insertion point.

```
Specify insertion point or [Basepoint Scale X Y Z Rotate]:
```

15. Move the cursor to the end point of the line "L14", refer to Figure 10.57. Next, click to specify the insertion point of the Arrow block when the cursor snaps to the end point of the line. The Arrow block is inserted and placed at the specified insertion point, see Figure 10.59.

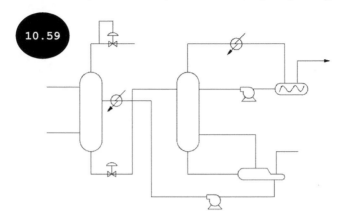

10.59

16. Again, invoke the **Block** flyout and then click on the Arrow block. The Arrow block gets attached with the cursor at its specified base point. Also, you are prompted to specify the insertion point.

```
Specify insertion point or [Basepoint Scale X Y Z Rotate]:
```

17. Click on the **Rotate** option in the command prompt. You are prompted to specify the rotation angle. Alternatively, enter **R** in the Command Window and then press ENTER.

```
Specify rotation angle <0>:
```

18. Enter **-90** in the Command Window and then press ENTER. The rotation angle of the attached Arrow block has been changed.

19. Move the cursor to the end point of the Line "L12", refer to Figure 10.57. Next, click to specify the insertion point of the Arrow block when the cursor snaps to the end point of the line. The Arrow block is inserted and placed at the specified insertion point, see Figure 10.60.

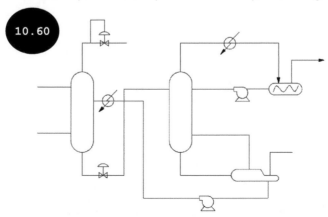

10.60

20. Similarly, insert the Arrow blocks at the remaining required locations of the drawing, see Figure 10.61.

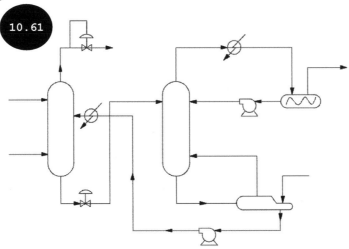

Section 4: Adding Single Line Text

1. Add the single line text in the drawing area by using the **Single Line** tool, see Figure 10.62.

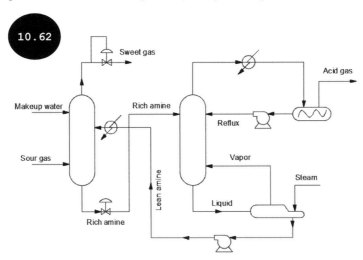

Section 5: Saving the Drawing

1. Click on the **Save** tool in the **Quick Access Toolbar**. The **Save Drawing As** dialog box appears.

2. Browse to the *AutoCAD* folder and then create a folder with the name *Chapter 10* inside the *AutoCAD* folder. Next, enter **Tutorial 1** in the **File name** field of the dialog box.

3. Click on the **Save** button. The drawing is saved with the name Tutorial 1 in the *Chapter 10* folder.

Hands-on Test Drive 1

Create the drawing template, as shown in Figure 10.63 and then convert it into WBlock (external block) by using the WBLOCK command so that you can insert the drawing template in any drawing as a block. Dimensions are for your reference only. You can assume the missing dimensions.

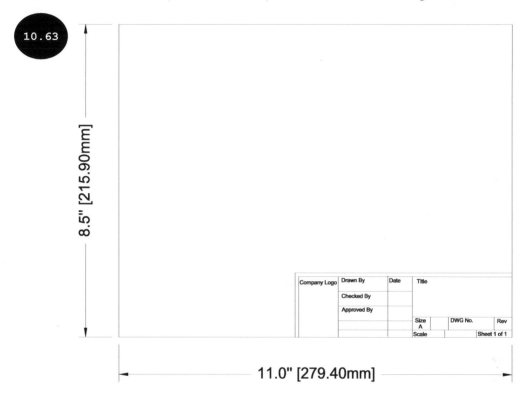

Summary

In this chapter, you have learned how to create and insert Block and WBlock. You have also learned how to edit Blocks and make dynamic Blocks. In addition, you have learned how to work with external reference files (Xrefs).

Questions

*   In AutoCAD, you can create a Block either by using the _____ tool or _____ command.

*   The _____ is the shortcut of the BLOCK command.

- The blocks created in the current drawing can be inserted in the drawing several times by using the _____ tool.

- You can create a WBlock either by using the _____ tool or _____ command.

- In AutoCAD, you can edit existing blocks either by using the _____ tool or _____ command.

- A _____ block can be modified dynamically in the drawing area.

- In AutoCAD, external references are also known as _____ .

- You can attach external references to a drawing by using the _____ palette.

- To invoke the EXTERNAL REFERENCES Palette, click on the _____ tool.

Working with Layouts

In this chapter, you will learn the following:

- Getting started with Paper space/layout
- Understanding different components of a layout
- Setting up the sheet/paper size of a layout
- Adding/renaming/deleting a layout
- Working with viewports
- Accessing Model space within a viewport
- Clipping existing viewports
- Locking the object scale in a viewport
- Controlling the display of objects of a viewport
- Controlling layers properties for viewports
- Switching to Model space
- Creating viewports in Model space

So far in this textbook you have learned about creating drawings in Model space. AutoCAD is provided with two distinct working environments: Model space and Paper space. By default, when you start AutoCAD, the Model space is the activated environment for creating drawings. You can create drawings in the Model space. The drawing created in Model space is in 1:1 scale. Also, it represents the real world size of the model. Whereas the Paper space is generally used for plotting drawings and generating different drawing views. In Paper space, you can create multiple viewports, which represent different drawing views with different or same scale. Paper space is nothing but a sheet of paper on which the final drawing is printed or plotted. Paper space is also known as layout. You can switch between the Model space and Paper space by using the tabs: **Model**, **Layout1**, and **Layout2** available at the lower left corner of the drawing area, see Figure 11.1. By default, two layouts: **Layout1** and **Layout2** are provided as Paper space. By using these layouts, you can prepare your drawing for plotting and generate different drawing views. In addition to the default layouts (Layout1 and Layout2), you can add multiple layouts as required. You will learn about adding layouts later in this chapter.

11.1

Model · Layout1 · Layout2 · +

Getting Started with Paper Space/Layout

As discussed, the Paper space is a sheet of paper, which is used to prepare drawing for plotting and printing. Drawings are used to fully and clearly communicate the requirement for manufacturing the end product. It is a language that communicates ideas and information about the end product with each other. You can either take the print out of the drawing on paper or create an electronic file to communicate the information about the end product. The Design Web Format (DWF) is the most commonly used electronic file format to communicate the information about the end product. In AutoCAD, you can plot a drawing in both the working environments: Model space and Paper space (layout). However, it is recommended to use Paper space (layout) for plotting a drawing. This is because, Paper space/layout gives you more flexibility to control the drawing for printing and allows you to generate different drawing views with different scales. Also, it gives the same appearance of the drawing as it is on the sheet of paper. By default, two layouts: **Layout1** and **Layout2** are provided as Paper space for plotting a drawing. In addition to the default layouts, you can add multiple layouts to generate different drawing views of an object on different layouts. In AutoCAD, each layout represents a sheet of paper having a standard size. You will learn about adding layouts later in this chapter.

To activate the Paper space, click on the **Layout1** tab in the lower left corner of the drawing area, see Figure 11.2. The Paper space gets activated and the drawing created in the Model space appears in a default viewport. Also, the **Layout** tab appears in the **Ribbon**. You can create multiple viewports, delete the existing viewports, and modify the viewports in a layout. However, before you learn about creating, deleting, and editing viewports, it is important to understand the different components of a layout and setting up the sheet size for a layout.

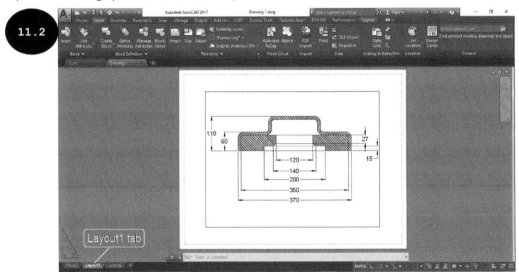

11.2

Understanding Different Components of a Layout

In AutoCAD, a layout has several components such as paper, plot area, viewports, and layout icon, see Figure 11.3. The paper of a layout has a standard size. By default, the paper size of a layout1 is 8.5" X 11.0", which is ISO A4 sheet. You can define the sheet size as required. You will learn about setting up the sheet size later in this chapter. The plot area of a layout is the maximum area of printing the drawing, represented by dotted lines. The viewports of a layout are used to create different drawing views of a model. You can create multiple viewports in a layout. You will learn about creating viewports later in this chapter.

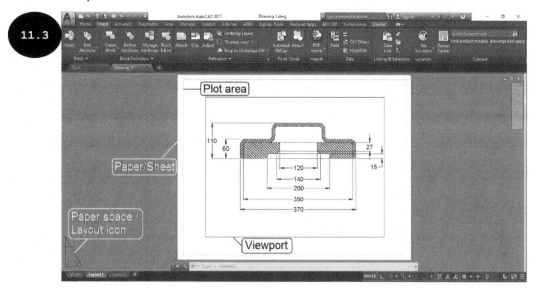

Setting up the Sheet/Paper Size of a Layout

In AutoCAD, the default layouts (Layout1 and Layout2) have default paper/sheet size assigned. You can change the default paper/sheet size of a layout, as per the requirement. To change the default paper/sheet size, activate the layout whose paper/sheet size is to be changed by clicking on its tab available at the lower right corner of the drawing area. Next, right-click on the activated layout tab. A flyout appears, see Figure 11.4. In this flyout, click on the **Page Setup Manager** option. The **Page Setup Manager** dialog box appears, see Figure 11.5. Alternatively, click on the **Page Setup** tool in the **Layout** panel of the **Layout** tab in the **Ribbon**. Note that the **Layout** tab appears in the **Ribbon** only when a layout/Paper space is activated.

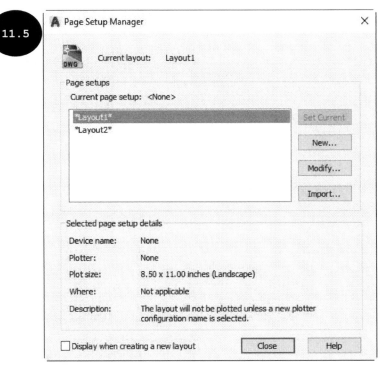

In the **Page Setup Manager** dialog box, the current activated layout is selected in the **Current pager setup** area. Also, the details of the selected layout such as plot size and description of the layout is displayed in the **Selected page setup details** area of the dialog box. Click on the **Modify** button in the dialog box to modify the default page size of the selected layout. The **Page Setup** dialog box appears, see Figure 11.6.

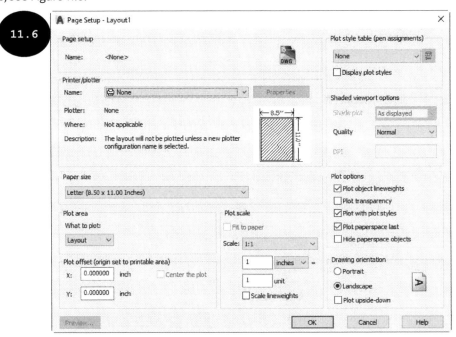

By using the **Paper size** drop-down list of the **Page Setup** dialog box, you can select the required paper size for the layout. You can also select the orientation of the sheet: portrait or landscape by using the respective radio buttons in the **Drawing orientation** area of the dialog box. Once you have selected the required paper/page size and orientation of the layout, click on the OK button in the dialog box. The page/sheet size for the selected layout has been set. Now, you can close the **Page Setup Manager** dialog box by clicking in the **Close** button of the dialog box.

Adding/Renaming/Deleting a Layout

As discussed, by default, two layouts: **Layout1** and **Layout2** are provided as Paper space to prepare the drawing for plotting and printing. Each layout is represent a sheet of paper. However, in some of the drawing, these two layouts are not enough, you may need to add additional layouts for generating different drawing views of a drawing in different layouts. In AutoCAD, you can add multiple layouts for a drawing as required. To add additional layouts, right-click on the layout tab in the lower left corner of the drawing area. A flyout appears, see Figure 11.7. In this flyout, click on the **New Layout** option, see Figure 11.7. A new layout with a default name gets added, see Figure 11.8. In this figure, **Layout3** is the newly added layout. Alternatively, you can click on the +sign available on the right of the last layout tab to add an additional layout in a drawing, see Figure 11.8. You can also click on the **New** tool in the **Layout** panel of the **Layout** tab in the **Ribbon** to add an additional layout, see Figure 11.9.

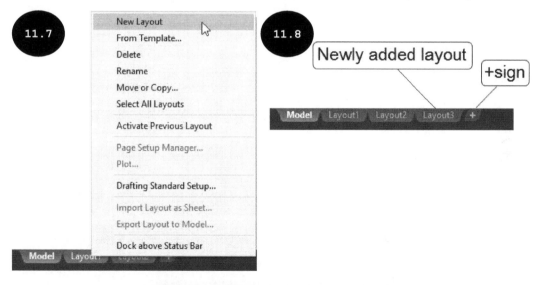

As discussed, on adding a layout, a default name is assigned to the newly added layout such as Layout3, Layout4, or Layout5. You can change the default assigned name of the newly added or existing layouts of a drawing. To assign a name to a layout, right-click on the layout tab whose name has to be renamed. A flyout appears, refer to the Figure 11.7. In this flyout, click on the **Rename** option. The default name of the selected layout appears in an edit field, see Figure 11.10. In this edit field, enter the new name for the layout as required and then press ENTER. The newly specified name for the layout has been assigned.

You can also delete a layout which was added by mistake or is no longer required to be the part of a drawing. To delete a layout, right-click on the layout tab which is to be deleted. A flyout appears. In this flyout, click on the **Delete** option. The selected layout gets deleted and is no longer the part of the current drawing.

Working with Viewports

When you activate a layout by clicking on its respective tab (Layout1 or Layout2) available at the lower left corner of the drawing area, the drawing created in the Model space appears in a default viewport, see Figure 11.11. A viewport is a rectangular area which displays the drawing of an object created in the Model space. You can fit the entire drawing in a single viewport or create multiple viewports in a layout for displaying different views of an object/model at different scales. Also, you can perform various editing operations on a viewport such as move, copy, rotate, scale, and stretch. Moreover, you can also delete an existing viewport of a drawing. The method of editing, deleting, and creating viewports are as follows:

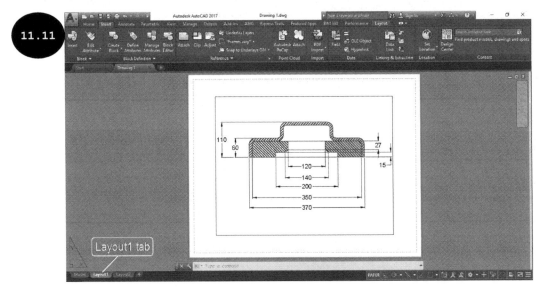

Editing a Viewport

In AutoCAD, similar to performing various editing operations on an entity such as line, rectangle, and circle, you can perform editing operations such as move, copy, rotate, scale, and stretch on a viewport of a layout. For example, to stretch a viewport, click on the viewport boundary to be stretched. The viewport boundary gets highlighted with the display of grips, see Figure 11.12. Now, by using the grips of the highlighted viewport boundary, you can stretch the viewport as required. Alternatively, you can also used the **Stretch** tool. Figure 11.13 shows a shrink view of the viewport after stretching it. Note that in this figure, after shrinking or stretching the viewport, the drawing view is not displayed completely inside the viewport or not completely fitted inside the viewport. In such cases, you can access the model space within the viewport of a layout to zoom or pan the drawing such that it fits inside the viewport. You will learn about accessing the model space within the viewport of a layout later in this chapter.

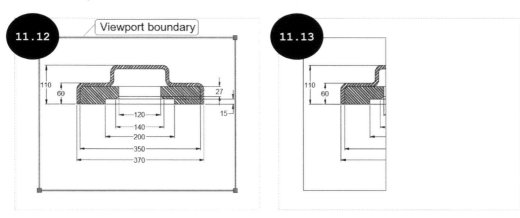

Deleting a Viewport

In AutoCAD, similar to deleting an entity such as line, rectangle, and circle, you can delete a viewport of a layout. To delete a viewport, click on it. Its boundary is highlighted with the display of grips, refer to Figure 11.12. Next, press the DELETE key. The selected viewport gets deleted.

Creating Viewports

In addition to the default viewports, you can create multiple viewports in a layout for displaying different views of an object/model, see Figure 11.14. The viewports created in a layout are known as floating viewports. This is because, you can create the viewports of any shape and size. Moreover, the viewports in a layout can be overlapped and edit.

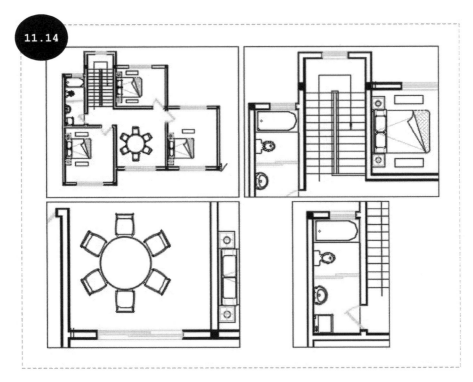

11.14

The tools to create viewports are in the **Layout Viewports** panel of the **Layout** tab in the **Ribbon**, see Figure 11.15. You can create different types of viewports by using these tools. The method of creating viewports are as follows:

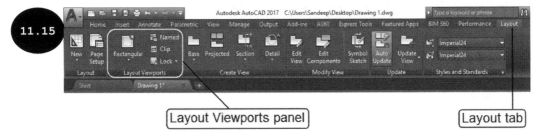

11.15

Layout Viewports panel

Layout tab

Creating Rectangular Viewports

To create a rectangular shape viewport, click on the **Rectangular** tool in the **Layout Viewports** panel of the **Layout** tab, refer to Figure 11.15. You are prompted to specify the first corner of the viewport. Alternatively, enter **-VPORTS** in the Command Window and then press ENTER to create a rectangular viewport.

```
Specify corner of viewport or [ON OFF Fit Shadeplot Lock Object
Polygonal Restore LAyer 2 3 4] <Fit>:
```

Click to specify a corner of the viewport in the paper area of the layout, see Figure 11.16. You are prompted to specify the opposite corner of the viewport.

```
Specify opposite corner:
```

Click to specify the diagonally opposite corner of the viewport, see Figure 11.16. A rectangular viewport is created and the drawing created in the Model space fits completely inside the viewport created, see Figure 11.16. Similarly, you can create multiple rectangular viewports in a layout. You can zoom, pan, or change the scale of the drawing view in a viewport by accessing the model space within the viewport of a layout. You will learn about accessing the model space within the viewport of a layout later in this chapter.

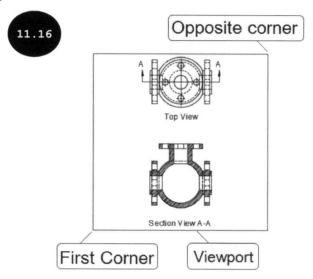

Note: You can also create rectangular viewports by using the MVIEW command. To create rectangular viewports by using the MVIEW command, enter **MV** in the Command Window and then press ENTER. You are prompted to specify the first corner of the viewport. Specify the first and second/opposite corner of the viewport in a layout. A rectangular viewport is created. You can also create two, three, or four viewports together. To create two, three, or four viewports, enter 2, 3, or 4, respectively and then press ENTER when you are prompted to specify the first corner of the viewport. You are prompted to specify the arrangement of the viewports "Enter viewport arrangement [Horizontal Vertical Above Below Left Right] <Right>:" Specify the arrangement for the viewports by clicking on their respective option in the command prompt. Next, specify the first and second/opposite corner that defines the overall area/boundary for the viewports. The respective viewports are created.

Creating Polygonal Viewports
To create a polygonal viewport, click on the **Layout** tab in the **Ribbon** and then click on the down arrow in the **Rectangular** tool of the **Layout Viewports** panel, see Figure 11.17. The **Viewport** flyout appears, see Figure 11.17. In the **Viewport** flyout, click on the **Polygonal** tool. You are prompted to

specify the start point. Alternatively, enter -VPORTS in the Command Window and then click on the **Polygonal** option in the command prompt.

```
Specify start point:
```

Click to specify the start point of the polygonal viewport in the paper/sheet area of the layout, see Figure 11.18. You are prompted to specify the next point for creating the polygonal viewport.

```
Specify next point or [Arc Length Undo]:
```

Click to specify the second point of the polygonal viewport, see Figure 11.18. You can also specify the length of the line or coordinates (X, Y) of the end point. As soon as you specify the second point, you are prompted to specify the third point for creating the polygonal viewport.

```
Specify next point or [Arc Close Length Undo]:
```

Similarly, you can continue to specify points in the paper/sheet area of the layout for creating a polygonal viewport. To close the viewport, either click on the **Close** option in the command prompt or enter C and then press ENTER. The closed polygonal viewport is created and the drawing views created in the Model space appear in the viewport, see Figure 11.18. Note that the drawings views created in the Model space may not fit completely inside the viewport. You can fit the drawings views in the viewport as well as zoom, pan, or change the scale by accessing the model space within the viewport. You will learn about accessing the Model space within the viewport later in this chapter.

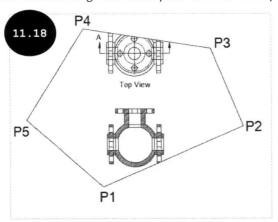

You can create a polygonal viewport having line entities or the combination of line and arc entities. To create a polygonal viewport having arc entities, you need to activate the arc mode either by clicking on the **Arc** option in the command prompt or by entering **A** in the Command Window and then pressing ENTER. Note that once the arc mode has been activated, you can create a chain of arc entities by specifying the arc end points. To activate the line mode again, either click on the **Line** option in the command prompt or enter **L** and then press ENTER. Figure 11.19 shows the polygonal viewport created by line and arc entities.

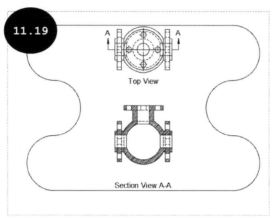

Creating Viewports from Closed Object/Geometry

In addition to creating rectangular and polygonal viewports, you can convert an existing closed geometry into a viewport. Note the all entities of the closed geometry to be converted into a viewport must act as a single entity. You can convert a rectangle created by using the **Rectangle** tool, a circle, an ellipse, a closed spline, or a group of closed polyline entities created by using the **Polyline** tool into a viewport. Note that the polylines entities must be closed by using the **Close** option of the command prompt to convert into a viewport. Figure 11.20 shows a closed spline and a group of polyline entities.

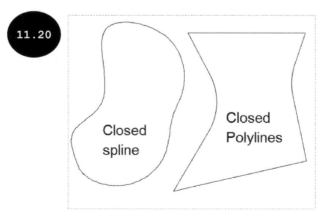

To convert a closed geometry into a viewport, click on the **Layout** tab in the **Ribbon** and then click on the down arrow in the **Rectangular** tool of the **Layout Viewports** panel, see Figure 11.21. The **Viewport** flyout appears, see Figure 11.21. In this flyout, click on the **Object** tool. You are prompted to select object to be converted into a viewport. Alternatively, enter **-VPORTS** in the Command Window and then click on the **Object** option in the command prompt.

```
Specify corner of viewport or [ON OFF Fit Shadeplot Lock Object
Polygonal Restore LAyer 2 3 4] <Fit>:_o Select object to clip
viewport:
```

Click on the object to be converted into a viewport. The selected object is converted into a viewport and the drawing views created in the Model space appear inside the viewport, see Figure 11.22. Similarly, you can again invoke the **Object** tool and convert another closed object into a viewport, see Figure 11.23.

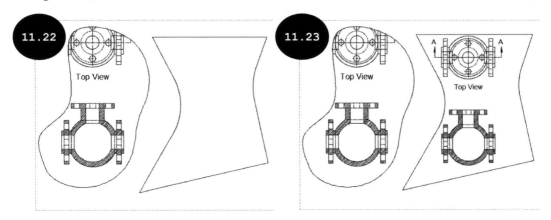

Creating Pre-Define Standard Viewports

You can create standard viewports in a layout by using the **Named** tool of the **Layout Viewports** panel in the **Layout** tab. To create standard viewports, click on the **Named** tool in the **Layout Viewports** panel of the **Layout** tab, see Figure 11.24. The **Viewports** dialog box appears. In this dialog box, click on the **New Viewports** tab to display the list of standard viewports, see Figure 11.25. Alternatively, enter **+VPORTS** in the Command Window and then press ENTER twice to invoke the **Viewports** dialog box.

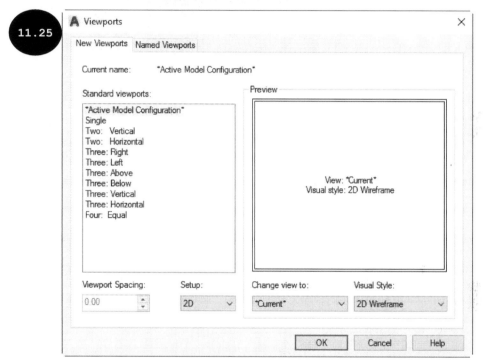

In the **Standard viewports** area of the dialog box, you can select the required standard viewports to be created. For example to create four rectangular viewports of equal sizes, select the **Four: Equal** option in the **Standard viewports** area. The preview of the selected standard viewports appears in the **Preview** area of the dialog box. After selecting the required standard viewports, click on the **OK** button in the dialog box. You are prompted to specify the first corner of a window which encloses/ fits the viewports.

```
Specify first corner or [Fit] <Fit>:
```

Click to specify the first corner of the window in the paper area of the layout, see Figure 11.26. You are prompted to specify the opposite corner of the window.

```
Specify opposite corner:
```

Click to specify the diagonally opposite corner of the window, see Figure 11.26. The viewports are created, see Figure 11.26. In this figure, four viewports of equal sizes are created.

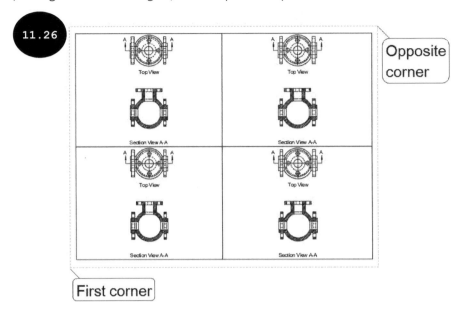

11.26

Opposite corner

First corner

Accessing Model Space within a Viewport

In AutoCAD, you can access Model space within a viewport of a layout to perform the editing operations and change the drawing display. Generally, accessing model space within a viewport is used to zoom, pan, fit the drawing view, or change the scale of the drawing view within the viewport. To access the model space within a viewport of a layout, double-click inside the viewport. The Model space gets activated and the UCS icon appears inside the viewport, which indicates that the Model space has been activated, see Figure 11.27.

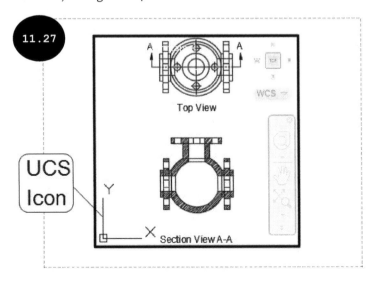

11.27

UCS Icon

Once the Model space has been accessed, you can zoom or pan the drawing to fit the drawing view inside the viewport. Also, you can change the scale of the drawing view by using the **Scale of the selected viewport** drop-down list in the Status Bar. To invoke the **Scale of the selected viewport** drop-down list, click on the **Scale of the selected viewport** button in the Status Bar, see Figure 11.28. Moreover, you can edit the properties of the drawing entities such as linetype scale, lineweight, and linetype in the Model space.

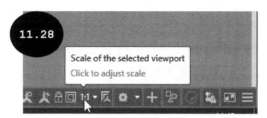

Alternatively, you can also access the Model space within a viewport by clicking on the **Paper** button in the Status Bar (see Figure 11.29) or by using the MSPACE command. Note that if only one viewport is available in the layout then on clicking the **Paper** button or by entering the MSPACE command, the Model space gets activated within the available viewport. However, if more than one viewports are available in the layout then the Model space gets activated within the last created or activated viewport of the layout. In such a case, you can click on the required viewport of the layout to access the Model space in it.

Once you have made the necessary changes in the display of drawing view in the Model space, you need to switch back to the Paper space. To switch back to the Paper space, double-click anywhere outside the viewport. Alternatively, click on the **Model** button in the Status Bar (see Figure 11.30) or enter PSPACE and then press ENTER.

Clipping Existing Viewports

You can clip the existing viewports of a layout by using the **Clip** tool of the **Layout Viewports** panel in the **Layout** tab. Note that you need to first create a closed object as the clipping object for clipping the viewport. The object that can be used as clipping includes a rectangle created by using the **Rectangle** tool, a circle, an ellipse, a closed spline, or a group of closed polyline entities created by using the **Polyline** tool (the polylines entities must be closed by using the **Close** option of the command prompt).

To clip a viewport, click on the **Clip** tool in the **Layout Viewports** panel in the **Layout** tab, see Figure 11.31. You are prompted to select the viewport to be clipped. Alternatively, enter VPCLIP in the Command Window and then press ENTER to invoke the **Clip** tool.

```
Select viewport to clip:
```

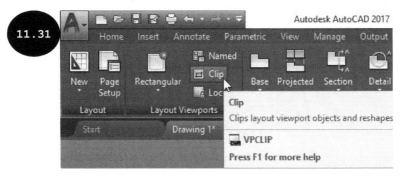

Click on the viewport to be clipped, see Figure 11.32. You are prompted to select a clipping object.

```
Select clipping object or [Polygonal] <Polygonal>:
```

Click on the clipping object, see Figure 11.32. The selected viewport gets clipped, see Figure 11.33.

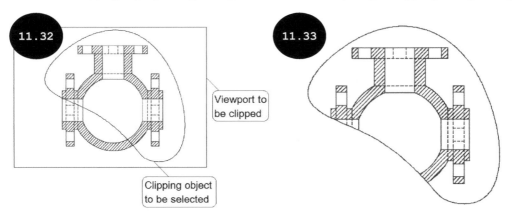

Note: You can create a group of closed polyline entities by using the **Polyline** tool as the clipping object before or after invoking the **Clip** tool. To create a clipping object by using the **Polyline** tool after invoking the **Clip** tool, press ENTER when you are prompted to select the clipping object in the command prompt. As soon as you press ENTER, you are prompted to specify the start point of the polylines. After specifying all the points of the polylines, click on the **Close** option in the command prompt to create a closed loop of polylines. The selected viewport gets clipped with respect to the object created.

Locking the Object Scale in a Viewport

In AutoCAD, you can lock or unlock the display (scale) of objects in a viewport by using the **Lock** or **Unlock** tool of the **Layout Viewports** panel in the **Layout** tab, respectively. Note that once the objects of a viewport are locked, you cannot perform operations such as zoom and pan after accessing the Model space in the layout. Locking the display (scale) of objects is very useful if you want to prevent any modification by mistake.

To lock the display (scale) of objects in a viewport, click on the **Lock** tool in the **Layout Viewports** panel of the **Layout** tab, see Figure 11.34. You are prompted to select objects to be locked.

```
Select objects:
```

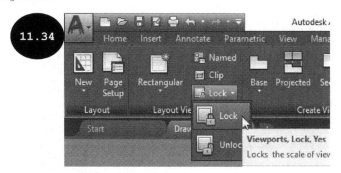

Click on the viewport whose objects/drawing views is to be locked. You can select multiple viewports one by one to be locked. Next, press ENTER. The display of the objects of the selected viewport is locked. Note that you can access the Model space within the locked viewport but cannot modify the display/scale of the objects. However, you can edit the properties of the object entities such as linetype scale, linetype, and lineweight. You can add or delete the entities. To unlock the viewport, click on the arrow in the **Lock** tool of the **Layout Viewports** panel. A flyout appears, refer to Figure 11.34. In this flyout, click on the **Unlock** tool. Next, click on the viewport to be unlocked.

Alternatively, to lock the display of objects of a viewport, click on the viewport to be locked and then right-click. A shortcut menu appears. In this shortcut menu, click on the **Display Locked > Yes**. Similarly, click on the **Display Locked > No** to unlock the display of objects of the selected viewport.

Controlling the Display of Objects of a Viewport

You can turn on or off the display of objects in a viewport. To turn off the display of objects in a viewport, click on the viewport and then right-click. A shortcut menu appears. In this shortcut menu, click on the **Display Viewport Objects > No**. The display of objects of the selected viewport turns off. To turn on the display of objects again, click on the viewport and then right-click. Next, click on the **Display Viewport Objects > Yes** in the shortcut menu appeared.

Controlling Layers Properties for Viewports

In AutoCAD, you can control the layer properties for viewports such as freeze/thaw the newly created viewports, freeze all viewports, viewport color, viewport linetype, and viewport lineweight by using the **LAYER PROPERTIES MANAGER**. The concept of layers has been discussed in chapter 3.

To control the layer properties for a viewport, double-click inside the viewport to access the Model space or to activate the viewport. Next, invoke the **LAYER PROPERTIES MANAGER** either by clicking on the **Layer Properties** tool in the **Layers** panel of the **Home** tab or by entering the **LA** in the Command Window, see Figure 11.35. Most of the options of the **LAYER PROPERTIES MANAGER** have been discussed in chapter 3. The options that are not discussed in chapter 3 are as follows:

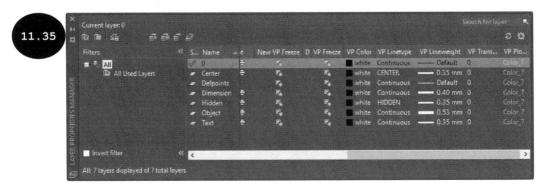

Viewport Freeze

The **Viewport Freeze** field of the **LAYER PROPERTIES MANAGER** is used to freeze the objects of the current viewport. To freeze objects of the current viewport, click on the **VP Freeze** field of the layer, see Figure 11.36. The layer gets frozen and the objects assigned to the frozen layer become invisible in the current active viewport. For example, if you click on the **VP Freeze** field of the Dimension layer (see Figure 11.36) then the Dimension layer gets frozen and all dimensions assigned to the layer become invisible in the current active viewport.

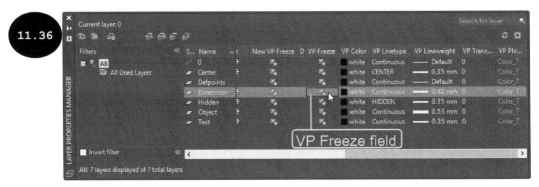

Viewport Color

You can change the color of the objects in the current viewport by using the **VP Color** field of a layer. To change the objects color in the current viewport, click on the **VP Color** field of a layer, see Figure 11.37. The **Select Color** dialog box appears. In this dialog box, select the required color to be assigned to the respective objects of the layer. Next, click on the **OK** button to accept the change and to close the dialog box. The color of the objects of the selected layer gets changed in the current viewport. For example, to change the color of the hidden lines in the current viewport, click on the **VP Color** field of the Hidden layer (see Figure 11.37) and then select the required color in the **Select Color** dialog box appeared. Next, click **OK** in the **Select Color** dialog box. The color of the hidden lines assigned to the Hidden layer gets changed in the current viewport.

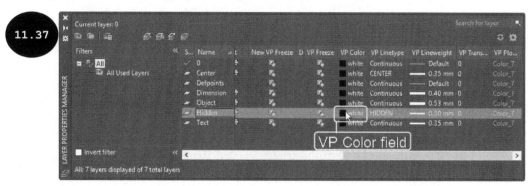

Similarly, you can change the linetype, lineweight, and transparency of the objects of the current viewport by using the VP Linetype, VP Lineweight, and VP Transparency fields of the LAYER PROPERTIES MANAGER, respectively.

Note: If none of the viewports is activated then on changing the viewport color, viewport linetype, viewport lineweight, and so on, only the boundary of the viewports in the layout gets effected by the change.

Switching to Model Space

As discussed, you can switch between the Model space and Paper space (layout) any time by using the tabs (**Model**, **Layout1**, and **Layout2**) available at the lower left corner of the drawing area, see Figure 11.38. The **Model** tab represent the model space and **Layout** tab represent the paper space (layout).

Creating Viewports in Model Space

In AutoCAD, you can also create viewports in the Model space. The viewports created in Model space are known as Tiled viewports. By default, when you start AutoCAD, a single viewport is displayed in the Model space. You can create multiple viewports in the Model space to display the different drawing views of an object. Creating viewports in Model space is same as dividing the work/drawing area into multiple area/viewports. You can only create rectangular space viewports in the Model space by using the tools available in the **Model Viewports** panel of the **View** tab in the **Ribbon**, see Figure 11.39. The tools are as follows:

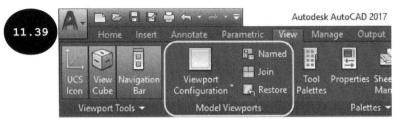

Viewport Configuration

The **Viewport Configuration** drop-down list of the **Model Viewports** panel of the **View** tab is used to select the pre-defined tiled viewport configurations, see Figure 11.40. You can select the required tiled viewport configuration in this drop-down list such as **Two: Vertical, Two: Horizontal, Three: Right, Three: Left**, and **Four: Equal**. Depending upon the viewport configuration selected, the drawing area gets divided and the drawing appears in all viewports.

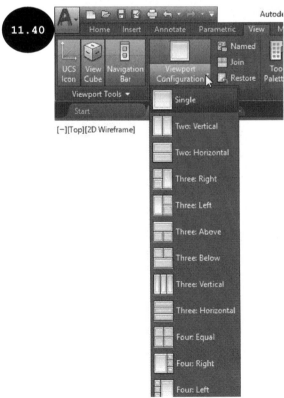

Similarly, you can create viewports in the Model space by using the **Named** tool in the **Model Viewports** panel of the **View** tab.

Joining Two Viewports

You can also merge or join two viewports by using the **Join** tool of the **Model Viewports** panel in the **View** tab. To join two viewports, click on the **Join** tool in the **Model Viewports** panel. You are prompted to select the dominant viewport.

```
Select dominant viewport <current viewport>:
```

Click on a viewport as the dominant viewport in the drawing area. You are prompted to select the viewport to be joined to the dominant viewport selected.

```
Select viewport to join:
```

Click on the viewport to be joined. The selected viewport is joined with the selected dominant viewport.

Restoring Viewports

You can restore the multiple viewport configuration to the default single viewport in the Model space by using the **Restore** tool of the **Model Viewports** panel in the **View** tab. The **Restore** tool is used to toggle between a single viewport and the last multiple viewport configuration.

Tutorial 1

Create the drawing in the Model space, see Figure 11.41. After creating the drawing, create an elliptical viewport in a layout and set the drawing scale in the viewport to 1:40, see Figure 11.42. The major axis of the ellipse is 8 inches (203.20 mm) and minor axis of the ellipse is 5 inches (127 mm) for your reference.

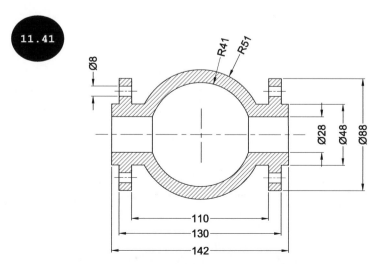

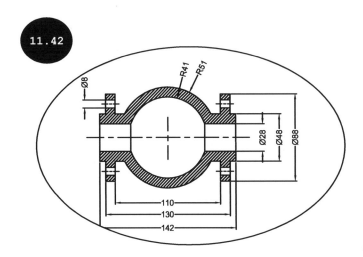

11.42

Section 1: Starting AutoCAD

1.   Start AutoCAD and then open a new drawing file.

Section 2: Creating Drawing and Applying Dimensions

1.   Create the drawing as shown in Figure 11.43. You can refer to Figure 11.41 or 11.42 for dimensions. Also, you can assume the missing dimensions.

2.   Apply the ANSI31 hatch pattern in the required enclosed areas of the drawing by using the **Hatch** tool in the **Draw** panel of the **Home** tab, see Figure 11.44. Note that you may need to adjust the hatch pattern scale so that the pattern appears similar to the one shown in Figure 11.44.

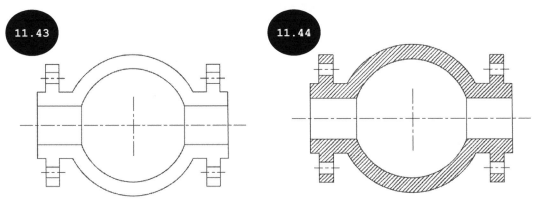

11.43

11.44

3. Apply dimensions to the drawing by using the dimension tools, see Figure 11.45. Note that you need to modify the dimension style properties such as text height, arrow size, extend beyond dimension lines, and offset from origin by using the DIMSTYLE command.

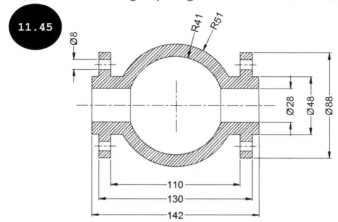

Section 3: Creating Elliptical Shaped Viewport in a Layout

1. Click on the **Layout1** tab in the lower left corner of the drawing area. The **Layout1** is activated and the drawing created in the Model space appears in a default viewport, see Figure 11.46.

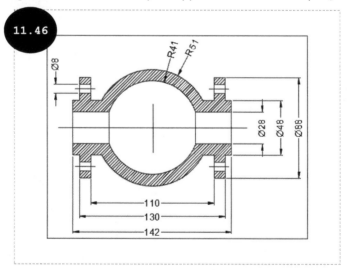

2. Click on the rectangular boundary of the viewport and then press the DELETE key to delete the default viewport.

Now, you need to draw an ellipse as the boundary of the viewport.

3. Create an ellipse having major axis of 8 inches (203.20 mm) and minor axis of 5 inches (127 mm) on the sheet, see Figure 11.47. You can create an ellipse by using the **Center** tool of the **Ellipse** flyout in the **Draw** panel of the **Home** tab, see Figure 11.48 or by entering **EL** in the Command Window. The EL is the short form of ELLIPSE command.

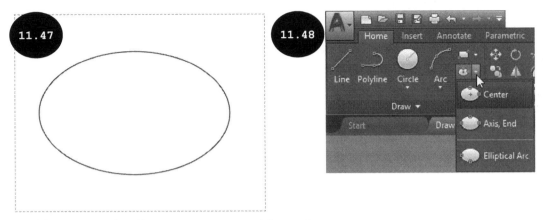

After creating the ellipse, you can convert it into a viewport.

4.   Click on the **Layout** tab in the **Ribbon** to display the tools and panels of the **Layout** tab.

5.   Click on the down arrow in the **Rectangular** tool of the **Layout Viewports** panel in the **Layout** tab, see Figure 11.49. The **Viewport** flyout appears, see Figure 11.49. In this flyout, click on the **Object** tool. You are prompted to select the object to be converted into a viewport. Alternatively, enter **-VPORTS** in the Command Window and then click on the **Object** option in the command prompt.

```
Specify corner of viewport or [ON OFF Fit Shadeplot Lock Object
Polygonal Restore LAyer 2 3 4] <Fit>: o Select object to clip
viewport:
```

6.   Click on the ellipse drawn in the sheet as the object to be converted into viewport. The ellipse is converted into a viewport and the drawing created in the Model space is displayed inside it with the default scale, see Figure 11.50.

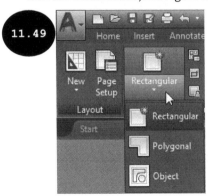

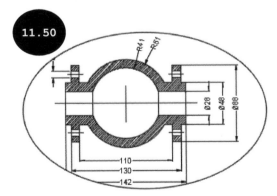

7.   Double-click inside the elliptical viewport to access the Model space in the Layout. Next, select the **1:40** as the scale of the viewport in the drop-down list which appears on clicking the **Scale of the selected viewport** tool in the **Status Bar**, see Figure 11.51.

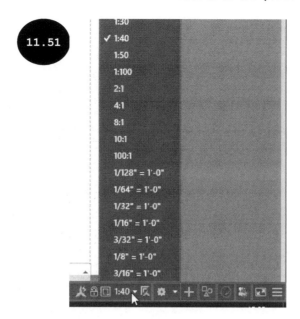

8. Double-click anywhere outside the elliptical viewport to switch back to the Paper space (layout). The scale of the selected viewport has been changed to 1:40, see Figure 11.52.

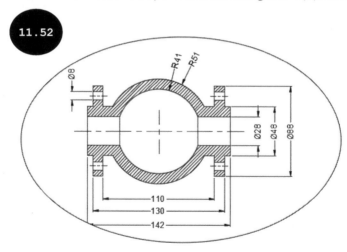

Section 4: Saving the Drawing

1. Click on the **Save** tool in the **Quick Access Toolbar**. The **Save Drawing As** dialog box appears.

2. Browse to the *AutoCAD* folder and then create a folder with the name *Chapter 11* inside the *AutoCAD* folder. Next, enter **Tutorial 1** in the **File name** field of the dialog box.

3. Click on the **Save** button. The drawing is saved with the name Tutorial 1 in the *Chapter 11* folder.

Hands-on Test Drive 1

Create the drawing in the Model space, see Figure 11.53. After creating the drawing, create two rectangular viewports in a layout, see Figure 11.54. In the first viewport, fit the drawing completely inside the viewport, see Figure 11.54 (a). In the second viewport, zoom the object such that it appears similar to the one shown in the Figure 11.54 (b).

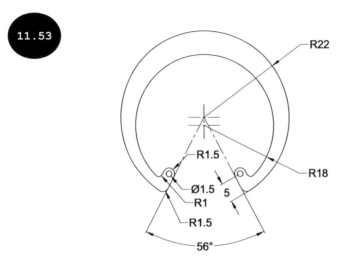

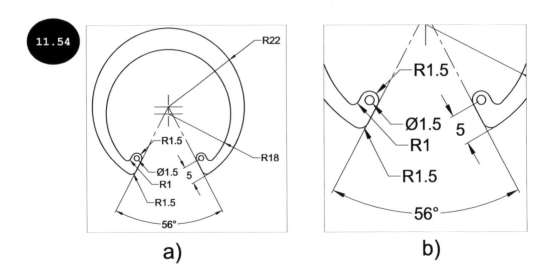

a)   b)

Hands-on Test Drive 2

Open the drawing created in Tutorial 2 of Chapter 7 and then create four rectangular viewports of equal sizes in a layout, see Figure 11.55. In these four viewports, adjust the drawing similar to the one shown in Figure 11.55.

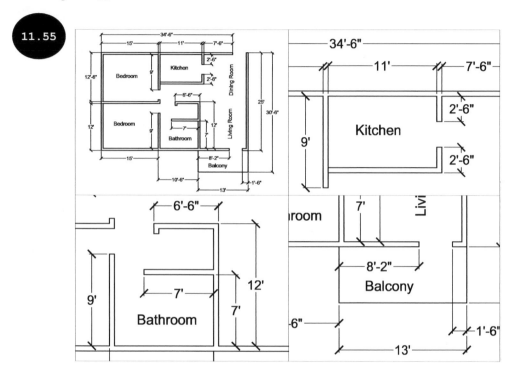

11.55

Summary

In this chapter, you have learned how to start with Paper space/layout and different components of a layout (Paper space). You have also learned how to set up sheet/paper size of a layout and how to add, rename, and delete a layout. In addition, you have learned how to work with viewports, access model space within a viewport, clip an existing viewport, lock the object scale in a viewport, control the display of objects in a viewport, and control layer properties of a viewport. Moreover, you have learned how to switch between Model space and Paper space (layout), and how to create viewports in the Model space.

Questions

• AutoCAD is provided with two distinct working environments: _____ and _____ .

• The _____ working environment of AutoCAD is generally used for plotting/printing drawings and generating different drawing views.

• The _____ tool in the **Layout** panel of the **Layout** tab is used to invoke the **Page Setup Manager** dialog box.

• A viewport created in a layout is known as _____ viewport.

• The _____ tool is used to create rectangular viewports in a layout.

• The _____ tool is used to create polygonal viewports in a layout.

• The _____ tool is used to convert a closed geometry/object into a viewport.

• The _____ tool is used to clip the existing viewports of a layout.

• The _____ and _____ tools are used to lock and unlock the display (scale) of objects in a viewport, respectively.

• The viewports created in the Model space are known as _____ viewports.

• The _____ tool is used to merge or join two viewports in the Model space.

Printing and Plotting

In this chapter, you will learn the following:

- Configuring plotter (output) devices
- Creating plot style
- Setting up default plot style
- Plotting drawings

Printing/plotting is a process of getting hard-copy output of a drawing. The hard-copy of a drawing is very important to communicate ideas and information about the end product/model store in the drawing to the engineers working on site. However, before you learn about plotting/printing a drawing in AutoCAD, it is important to understand how to configure a plotter (output device) and to setup a plot style.

Configuring Plotter (Output) Devices

AutoCAD plotter is used to send the output information to the system printer for getting the hard-copy of a drawing. To configure a plotter, click on the **Plotter Manager** tool in the **Plot** panel of the **Output** tab, see Figure 12.1. The **Plotters** system window appears, which displays the list of AutoCAD plotters, see Figure 12.2. Alternatively, enter **PLOTTERMANAGER** in the Command Window and then press ENTER.

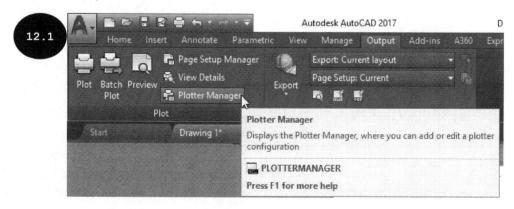

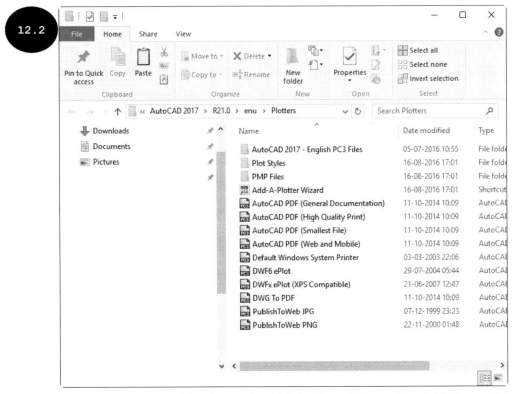

In the **Plotters** system window, double-click on the **Add-A-Plotter Wizard**. The **Add Plotter** dialog box is displayed with the **Introduction Page**, see Figure 12.3.

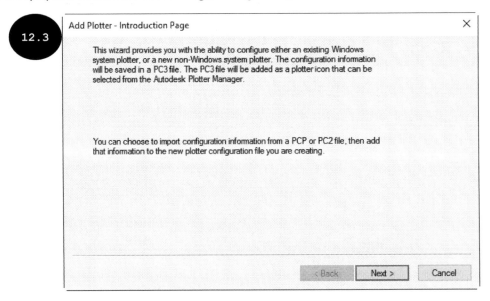

Click on the **Next** button in the dialog box, the **Begin** page of the **Add Plotter** dialog box appears, see Figure 12.4.

In the **Begin** page of the **Add Plotter** dialog box, select the **System Printer** radio button and then click on the **Next** button. The **System Printer** page of the **Add Plotter** dialog box appears, which displays the list of system printer installed in your system, see Figure 12.5. In Figure 12.5, the **HP Deskjet 1510 series** is displayed as the system printer installed in the system. In your case, the listed printers may differ depending on which printer drivers have been installed in your system. Note that if none of the printers are installed in your computer, you need to first install the printer to add plotter and to take the print out of the drawing. Select the system printer from the list of printers in the dialog box and then click on the **Next** button. The **Import Pcp or Pc2** page of the dialog box appears. This page is used to import a legacy PCP or PC2 file from older versions of AutoCAD.

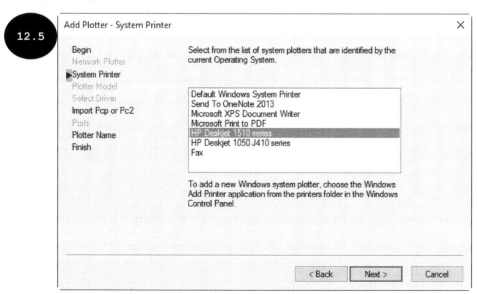

Click on the **Next** button in the **Import Pcp or Pc2** page of the dialog box. The **Plotter Name** page of the dialog box appears, see Figure 12.6. Enter the name for the plotter in the **Plotter Name** field of the **Plotter Name** page. By default, the name of the printer selected appears in this field. You can accept the default name or enter a new name for the plotter in this field. After entering the name of the plotter, click on the **Next** button. The **Finish** page of the **Add Plotter** dialog box appears. This page of the dialog box informs you that the plotter has been installed successfully with the default configuration settings. You can modify the default configuration settings of the installed plotter by using the **Edit Plotter Configuration** button of this page. Accept the default configuration settings for the plotter and then click on the **Finish** button in the dialog box. The dialog box is closed and the plotter has been installed.

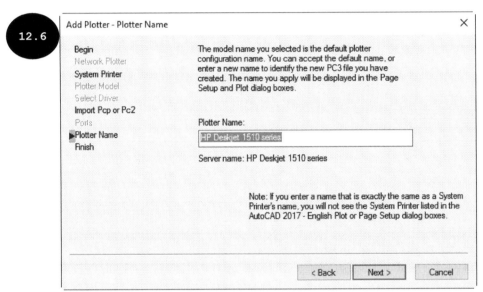

After adding the plotter and connecting the system printer with your computer through USB or wifi, you can take the print out of the drawing. However, before you start taking the print out it is important to understand how to create plot styles for plotting drawings.

Creating Plot Style

A plot style is used to define the appearance of drawing objects which includes color, linetype, lineweight, line end style, and so on. Note that the plot style overrides the layer properties of the drawing objects. For example, if the red color is assigned to a layer and the plot style has assigned blue color to the objects then on plotting, the objects will be plotted in blue color. However, if no plot style has been assigned then the objects will be plotted in red color, which is assigned to the layer.

To create a plot style, enter **STYLESMANAGER** in the Command Window and then press ENTER. The **Plot Styles** system window appears, which displays the list of predefined plot style files, see Figure 12.7.

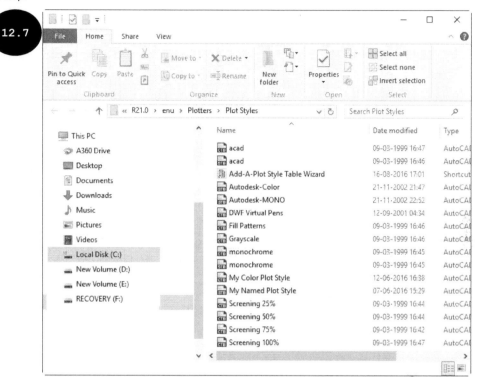

In this **Plot Styles** system window, double-click on the **Add-A-Plot Style Table Wizard**. The **Add Plot Style Table** dialog box appears, see Figure 12.8. Read the information and then click on the **Next** button in the **Add Plot Style Table** dialog box. The **Begin** page of the **Add Plot Style Table** dialog box appears, see Figure 12.9.

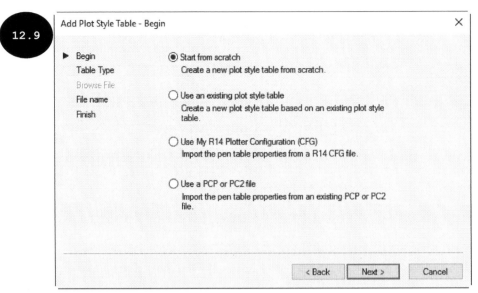

In the **Begin** page of the **Add Plot Style Table** dialog box, the **Start from scratch** radio button is selected by default. This radio button is used to create a new plot style from scratch. On selecting the **Use an existing plot style table** radio button, you can select an existing plot style as the base style to create the new plot style. On selecting the **Use My R14 Plotter Configuration (CFG)** radio button, the Release 14 *acad.cfg* (R14 CFG) file is used as the base style to create the new plot style. On selecting the **Use a PCP or PC2** radio button, the Release 14 PCP or PC2 file is used as the base style to create the new plot style. Select the **Start from scratch** radio button in the dialog box and then click on the **Next** button. The **Pick Plot Style Table** page of the dialog box appears, see Figure 12.10.

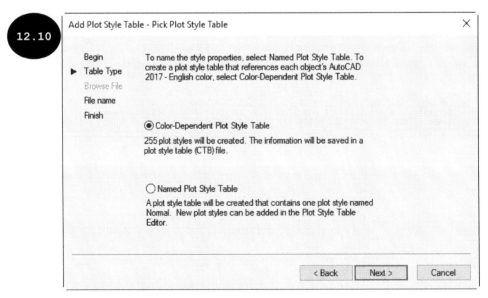

The **Pick Plot Style Table** page of the dialog box is used to select the type of plot style to be created. You can create two types of plot style: color-dependent and named by selecting the respective radio buttons in the dialog box. The color-dependent plot style allows you to assign plot styles to the individual AutoCAD colors. For example, you can assign 0.5 mm width to the red objects of the drawing and 0.75 mm width to the blue objects of the drawing. In such a case, all red objects get plotted with 0.5 mm width (pen) and blue objects get plotted with 0.75 mm width (pen). The color-dependent plot style is similar to the older method of highlighting the drawing objects with specific physical pen whereas, the named plot style allows you to assign plot style directly to objects or layers of the drawing instead of color only.

Select the required type of plot style in the dialog box by selecting the respective radio button (**Color-Dependent Plot Style Table** or **Named Plot Style Table**) and then click on the **Next** button. The **File name** page of the dialog box appears. Enter the name of the plot style in the **File name** field of the dialog box and then click on the **Next** button. The **Finish** page of the **Add Plot Style Table** dialog box appears, see Figure 12.11. Note that the **Finish** page of the dialog box appears based on the type of plot style selected in the **Pick Plot Style Table** page of the dialog box. Figure 12.11 shows the **Finish** page when the **Color-Dependent Plot Style Table** radio button is selected as the plot style. The **Finish** page of the dialog box informs you that the plot style has been created with default settings. You can edit the default settings of the added plot style by using the **Plot Style Table Editor** button of the **Finish** page. When you click on the **Plot Style Table Editor** button, the **Plot Style Table Editor** dialog box appears. Note that the display of the **Plot Style Table Editor** dialog box depends on the type of plot style selected. Figure 12.12 shows the **Plot Style Table Editor** dialog box when the color-dependent plot style is selected and Figure 12.13 shows the **Plot Style Table Editor** dialog box when the named plot style is selected.

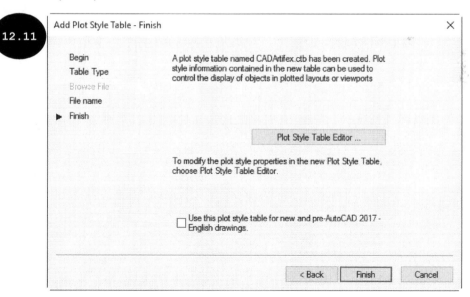

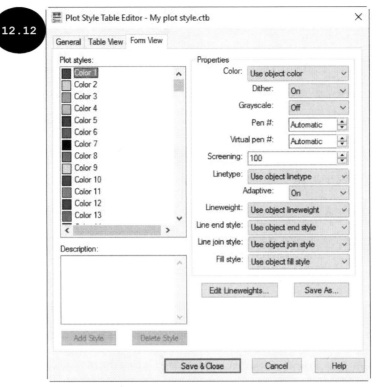

The **Plot Style Table Editor** dialog box has three tabs: **General**, **Table View**, and **Form View**. By using these tabs, you can edit all the properties of the plot style. The **General** tab of the dialog box displays the information such as the name, path, scale factor, and description of the plot style. In this tab, all the provided information are read only except the description.

The **Table View** tab of the dialog box displays all existing styles created in the plot style with their properties. In case of a color-dependent plot style, the different color styles (**Color 1**, **Color 2**, **Color 3**, …. and **Color 255**) are displayed in different columns of the **Table View** tab in the dialog box. You can edit the properties of color styles by using the respective fields or drop-down lists of the **Table View** tab of the dialog box. Whereas, in case of a named plot style, the Normal style is the default created style and is displayed in the **Table View** tab of the dialog box. You can edit the default style or add new styles by using the **Add Style** button of the dialog box, refer to Figure 12.13. On clicking the **Add Style** button in the **Table View** tab of the dialog box, a new column with the default style name "**Style 1**" is added in the dialog box. By using the fields or drop-down lists of the newly added column (style), you can change the style name, edit the style properties such as object color, linetype, lineweight, screening, and line end style.

The **Form View** tab of the **Plot Style Table Editor** dialog box displays the list of all the available styles in one form. The available styles are displayed in the **Plot Styles** area of the dialog box and the properties of the selected style are displayed in the **Properties** area of the dialog box. You can select any style in the **Plot Styles** area and then edit its properties in the **Properties** area of the dialog box.

After editing the properties of the existing styles and creating new styles for a plot style in the **Plot Style Table Editor** dialog box, click on the **Save & Close** button to save the changes made and to close the dialog box. Next, click on the **Finish** button in the **Add Plot Style Table** dialog box. The plot style has been created and saved as *.ctb* or *.stb* file in the **Plot Styles** directory of the local drive of your system. Note that the color-dependent plot style is saved with *.ctb* file extension whereas the named plot style is saved with *.stb* file extension.

Setting up Default Plot Style

After creating the plot style: color-dependent or named, you need to add the plot style in drawings for plotting. You can add plot style by using the **Option** dialog box. To add plot style for plotting drawings, enter **OP** in the Command Window and then press ENTER. The **Options** dialog box appears, see Figure 12.14. In the **Options** dialog box, click on the **Plot and Publish** tab. The options related to plot and publish drawings appear in the dialog box, see Figure 12.14. Next, click on the **Plot Style Table Settings** button in the lower right of the dialog box. The **Plot Style Table Settings** dialog box appears, see Figure 12.15.

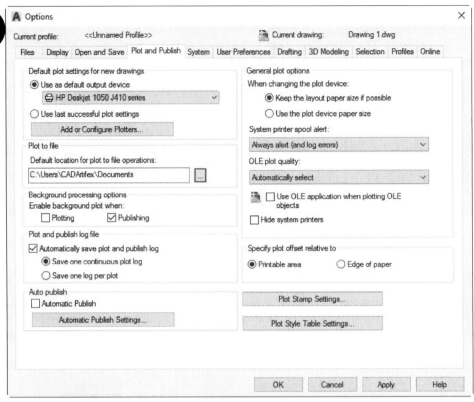

In the **Plot Style Table Settings** dialog box, the **Use color dependent plot styles** radio button is selected in the **Default plot style behavior for new drawings** area and the **acad.ctb** style is selected in the **Default plot style table settings** drop-down list, by default. As a result, the **acad.ctb** color-dependent style is used as the default plot style for plotting drawings. You can select any other color-dependent plot style in the **Default plot style table settings** drop-down list as the default plot style. To define the named plot style as the default plot style, select the **Use named plot styles** radio button in the **Default plot style behavior for new drawings** area of the dialog box. Next, select the required named plot style in the **Default plot style table** drop-down list as the default plot style for plotting drawings. Also, you can select the default style for the objects of layer o in the **Default plot style for layer o** drop-down list and the default style for the objects in the **Default plot style for objects** drop-down list of the dialog box. Once you have specified the default plot style (color-dependent or named), click on the OK button in the **Plot Style Table Settings** dialog box and then click on the OK button in the **Options** dialog box. The default plot style has been specified. Note that the changes made for setting the default plot style in the **Plot Style Table Settings** dialog box is reflected in the new drawing only (not in the current drawing).

Plotting Drawings

After adding the plotter and creating the plot style, as required, you can plot the drawing on a sheet of paper. You can plot drawings in the Model space as well as in the Paper space (layout). Plotting drawings in Model space is usually done to create test plot. Whereas, the Paper space (layout) is the recommended environment for plotting drawings where you can display multiple scaled drawing views in different viewports. The method of plotting drawing in both the environments (Model space and Paper space) are same.

To plot a drawing, activate the required environment (Model space or Paper space) for plotting the drawing. To activate the Model space, click on the **Model** tab. To activate the Paper space, click on the required layout tab (**Layout1**, **Layout2**, ...) in the lower left corner of the drawing area. Next, click on the **Plot** tool in the **Plot** panel of the **Output** tab, see Figure 12.16. The **Plot** dialog box appears, see Figure 12.17. Alternatively, press CLRL + P to invoke the **Plot** dialog box. You can also right-click on the active **Model** tab or an active layout tab. A shortcut menu appears. In this shortcut menu, click on the **Plot** option to invoke the **Plot** dialog box.

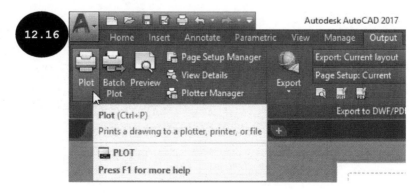

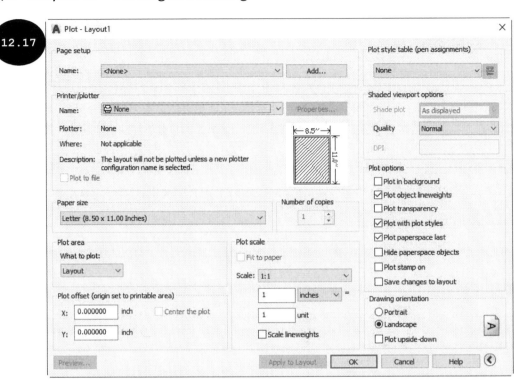

The options in the **Plot** dialog box are used to specify plot settings such as plotter, page size, plot area, plot scale, plot style, and drawing orientation. Some of the options of the **Plot** dialog box are as follows:

Page setup Area

The **Page setup** area of the dialog box is used to select an already saved page setup. A page setup consists of plot settings such as plotter, page size, plot area, plot scale, plot style, and drawing orientation. You can select an already saved page setup in the **Name** drop-down list of this area. You can also add a new page setup in the drawing by using the **Add** button of this area. To add a new page setup, first specify the plot settings such as plotter, page size, plot area, and plot scale in the dialog box and then click on the **Add** button. The **Add Page Setup** dialog box appears, see Figure 12.18. In this dialog box, enter the name of the page setup and then click on the **OK** button. The new page setup with the specified plot settings gets added and is selected in the **Name** drop-down list of the dialog box.

Printer/plotter Area

The **Name** drop-down list of the **Printer/plotter** area is used to select a configured plotting device for plotting the drawing. Select the plotter in the **Name** drop-down list of the **Printer/plotter** area. For example, you can also edit or review the properties of the configured plotter. To edit or review the properties, click on the **Properties** button in the **Printer/plotter** area of the dialog box. The **Plotter Configuration Editor** dialog box appears. This dialog box displays the information about the selected plotter. You can edit the plotter properties by using the options in the **Device and Document Settings** tab of the dialog box. Next, click on the **OK** button to exit the dialog box.

By default, the **Plot to file** check of the **Printer/plotter** area is unchecked. As a result, the drawing gets printed/plotted by using the configured plotter. On selecting the **Plot to file** check box, the output is plotted to a file such as .dwf, .plt, .jpg, or .png format depending upon the plotter selected. You can also plot the output to a .pdf file. To plot the output to a .pdf file, select the **Microsoft Print to PDF** option in the **Name** drop-down list of the **Printer/plotter** area and then specify the remaining plot settings such as paper size, plot area, and plot scale. The options to specify the plot settings are discussed next.

Paper size

The **Paper size** drop-down list is used to select the standard paper size for the selected plotter. This drop-down list displays the list of standard paper sizes that are available for the selected plotter in the **Name** drop-down list of the **Printer/plotter** area of the dialog box. If the **None** option is selected in the **Name** drop-down list of the **Printer/plotter** area then all the standard paper sizes are listed in the **Paper size** drop-down list.

Number of copies

The **Number of copies** field is used to specify the number of copies to be printed. Note that if the **Plot to file** check box is selected in the **Printer/plotter** area then this **Number of copies** field is not enabled.

Plot area

The options in the **What to plot** drop-down list of the **Plot area** are used to specify the portion of the drawing to be plotted. The options in the **What to plot** drop-down list are displayed depending upon whether you are plotting in Model space or in Paper space (layout). Figure 12.19 shows the **What to plot** drop-down list when you are in Model space and Figure 12.20 shows the **What to plot** drop-down list when you are in Paper space (layout). The options are as follows:

Display

The **Display** option of the **What to plot** drop-down list is used to plot the portion of the drawing that is currently displayed on the screen.

Extend

The **Extend** option is used to plot the portion of the drawing that contains drawing objects. By using this option, you can plot the complete drawing even if some of its objects are not currently displayed on the screen. On adding or removing objects in the drawing, the drawing gets regenerated such that the extent of the drawing is recalculated in order to include all drawing objects in the plot.

Limits

The **Limits** option is used to plot the complete area that is defined by the drawing limits. Note that this option is available only if you are plotting the drawing in the Model space.

Layout

The **Layout** option is used to plot the drawing that lies within the printable area of the selected paper size in the active layout. Note that this option is available only if you are plotting the drawing in the Paper space (in a layout).

Window

The **Window** option is used to define a window around the area/portion of the drawing to be plotted. On selecting the **Window** option, the **Plot** dialog box disappears and you are prompted to specify the first corner of the window. Click to specify the first corner. You are prompted to specify the opposite corner of the window. Click to specify the opposite corner. The area to be plotted has been defined by the window drawn and the **Plot** dialog box appears again.

Plot offset (origin set to printable area)

The options in the **Plot offset (origin set to printable area)** area are used to specify offset distances from the origin (0,0) to define the lower left corner of the printable area. By default, the origin (0,0) is defined as the lower left corner of the printable area (plot origin), see Figure 12.21. You can specify the X and Y offset distances from the origin (0,0) to define the lower left corner of the printable area in the X and Y fields of this area, respectively.

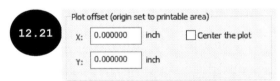

On selecting the **Center the plot** check box, AutoCAD automatically calculates the X and Y offset values to center the plot on the paper. Note that the **Center the plot** check box is not enabled when the **Layout** option is selected in the **What to plot** drop-down list of the **Plot** area.

Plot scale

The options in the **Plot scale** area are used to control the scale of the drawing relative to the plot area. By default, the scale is set to 1:1 in the **Scale** drop-down list for plotting the drawing in a layout, see Figure 12.22. You can specify a scale for the plot by using the **Scale** drop-down list, as per the requirement. The **Fit to paper** check box is selected as the default scale for plotting the drawing in the Model space, see Figure 12.23. When the **Fit to paper** check box is selected, AutoCAD automatically, fits the entire drawing on the paper. Note that the **Fit to paper** check box is enabled only when you are plotting in the Model space.

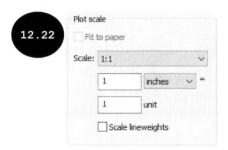

On selecting the **Scale lineweights** check box of this area, the lineweights of the objects to be plotted get scaled in proportion to the specified plot scale. Note that this **Scale lineweights** check box is not enabled when you are plotting in the Model space.

Plot style table (pen assignments)

The **Plot style table (pen assignments)** area is used to select the plot style of plotting the drawing. The **Plot style table** drop-down list in this area displays the list of already created plot styles. You can select the required ploy style from this drop-down list. By default, the **None** option is selected in the **Plot style table** drop-down list. As a result, no plot style is used for plotting the drawing and the drawing gets plotted as per the layers properties of the drawing objects. As discussed, a plot style overrides the layer properties of the drawing objects.

Note: If you are working with default drawing template (*acad.dwt*) then the **Plot style table** drop-down list of the **Plot style table (pen assignments)** area displays the list of color-dependent plot styles. To display the default plot styles: named or color-dependent specified in the **Plot Style Table Settings** dialog box, you need to open the drawing without default template. The **Plot Style Table Settings** dialog box is displayed on clicking the **Plot Style Table Settings** button in the **Plot and Publish** tab of the **Options** dialog box. To open the drawing without default template, click on the **New** tool in the **Quick Access Toolbar**. The **Select template** dialog box appears, see Figure 12.24. In this dialog box, select the **acad.dwt** template file and then click on the arrow next to the **Open** button in the dialog box. A flyout appears, see Figure 12.24. In this flyout, either click on the **Open with no Template - Imperial** or the **Open with no Template - Metric** option, as required. The new drawing file with no default template is opened.

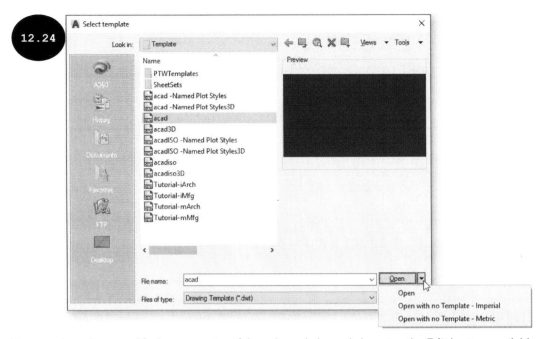

You can also edit or modify the properties of the selected plot style by using the **Edit** button available next to the **Plot style table** drop-down list in the **Plot style table (pen assignments)** area of the **Plot** dialog box. On clicking the **Edit** button, the **Plot Style Table Editor** dialog box appears, which is used to edit the properties of the selected plot style. After making the changes in the selected plot style, you can click on the **Save & Close** button in the **Plot Style Table Editor** dialog box to save the changes made and to exit the dialog box.

Shaded viewport options

The options in the **Shaded viewport options** area of the dialog box are used to plot a shaded or a rendered image of the drawing. By default, the **As displayed** option is selected in the **Shade plot** drop-down list, see Figure 12.25. As a result, the drawing objects are plotted as they appear on the screen. Note that the **Shade plot** drop-down list of this area is enabled only if you are plotting the drawing in Model space.

On selecting the **Legacy wireframe** option in the **Shade plot** drop-down list, the drawing gets plotted in wireframe. On selecting the **Legacy hidden** option, the drawing gets plotted with hidden lines removed display style. On selecting the **Conceptual** option, the drawing objects get plotted with the conceptual visual style. On selecting the **Hidden** option, the drawing objects get plotted with hidden lines removed display style. On selecting the **Realistic** option, the drawing objects get plotted with the realistic visual style. On selecting the **Shaded** option, the drawing objects get plotted with the shaded visual style. On selecting the **Shaded with edges** option, the drawing objects get plotted with shaded with edges visual style. On selecting the **Shades of Gray** option, the drawing objects get plotted with the shades of gray visual style. On selecting the **Sketchy** option, the drawing objects get plotted with the sketchy visual style. On selecting the **Wireframe** option, the drawing objects get plotted in wireframe. On selecting the **X-Ray** option, the drawing objects get plotted with the x-ray visual style. On selecting the **Rendered** option, the drawing objects get plotted as rendered.

The options in the **Quality** drop-down list of the **Shaded viewport options** area are used to select the printing quality/resolution at which shaded and rendered drawing objects are to be plotted. You can select the **Draft, Preview, Normal, Presentation, Maximum,** or **Custom** option in the drop-down list as the plot quality of the drawing objects.

Plot options

The **Plot options** area is provided with additional options to control the display of drawing objects in the print, see Figure 12.26. The options are as follows:

Plot in background
On selecting the **Plot in background** check box, the process of plotting the drawing take place in the background only. By default, this check box is unchecked. As a result, the process of plotting the drawing does not take place in the background.

Plot object lineweights
By default, the **Plot object lineweights** check box is selected. As a result, the objects are plotted as per the lineweights assigned to the objects and layers.

Plot transparency
On selecting the **Plot transparency** check box, the objects are plotted with specified transparency.

Plot with plot styles
By default, the **Plot with plot styles** check box is selected. As a result, the objects are plotted with the specified plot style.

Plot paperspace last

The **Plot paperspace last** check box is enabled only if you are plotting the drawing in a layout. By default, this check box is selected. As a result, the Model space geometry is plotted first followed by the Paper space geometry.

Hide Paperspace Objects

The **Hide Paperspace Objects** check box is enabled only if you are working in a layout. On selecting the **Hide Paperspace Objects** check box, the 3D model drawn in a layout is plotted with hidden lines removed display style. You can copy and paste the 3D model drawn in Model space to a layout.

Plot stamp on

On selecting the **Plot stamp on** check box, the display of plot stamp is turned on in the plot. The plot stamp settings are specified in the **Plot Stamp** dialog box. A plot stamp is used to add logo or additional information about the current drawing such as drawing name, layout name, date and time, and paper size. To invoke the **Plot Stamp** dialog box, click on the **Plot stamp on** check box. The **Plot Stamp Settings** button appears next to the check box, see Figure 12.27. Alternatively, you can invoke the **Plot Stamp** dialog box for specifying the plot stamp settings by clicking on the **Plot Stamp Settings** button in the **Plot and Publish** tab of the **Options** dialog box.

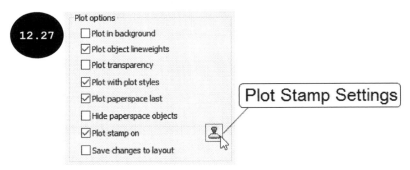

Save changes to layout

On selecting the **Save changes to layout** check box, the changes made in the **Plot** dialog box get saved with the current layout.

Drawing orientation

The options in the **Drawing orientation** area are used to specify the orientation (portrait or landscape) of the drawing on the paper, see Figure 12.28. You can select the **Portrait** or **Landscape** radio button as per the requirement to specify the orientation of the drawing. The **Plot upside-down** check box is used to flip the orientation of the plot upside down depending upon whether the **Portrait** or **Landscape** radio button is selected.

OK

After specifying all the plot settings/parameters in the **Plot** dialog box, click on the OK button. The **Plot Job Progress** window appears, which indicates that the process of plotting the drawing in the file or plotters as specified has been started. Once the process of plotting is done, the **Plot Job Progress** window is closed and you get the plotter output of the drawing.

Tutorial 1

Create the drawing in the Model space, see Figure 12.29. After creating the drawing, take the printout of the drawing in a sheet of paper with the default settings.

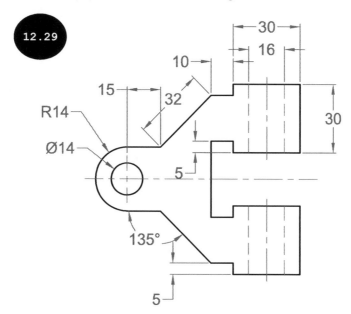

Section 1: Starting AutoCAD
1. Start AutoCAD and then open a new drawing file.

Section 2: Creating Drawing
1. Create the drawing and apply dimensions, see Figure 12.30. For creating the drawing, you need to create different layers for hidden lines, centerlines, object entities, and dimensions. Also, for dimensions, you need to change the dimension settings such that the dimension text, dimension arrow, and so on are visible clearly in the drawing area. You can control the dimension settings either by creating the new dimension style or by editing the existing dimension style. You can create or edit the dimension style by using the **Dimension Style Manager** dialog box as discussed in earlier chapters.

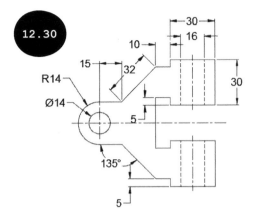

Section 3: Configuring/Adding Plotter

1. Make sure that a plotter is configured in your system. Before configuring a plotter, make sure that the system printer (output device) is installed in your computer.

To configure a plotter, enter **PLOTTERMANAGER** in the Command Window and then press ENTER. The **Plotters** system window appears. Alternatively, click on the **Plotter Manager** tool in the **Plot** panel of the **Output** tab in the **Ribbon**. Next, double-click on **Add-A-Plotter Wizard** in the **Plotters** system window. The **Introduction Page** of the **Add Plotter** dialog box appears, see Figure 12.31.

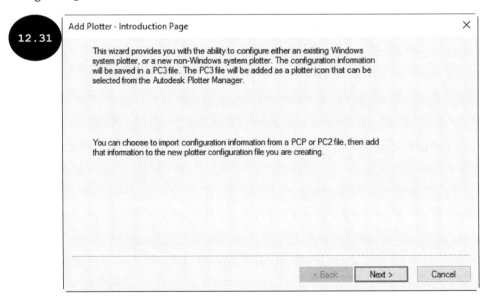

Read the information given in the **Introduction Page** of the **Add Plotter** dialog box and then click on the **Next** button. The **Begin** page of the dialog box appears. In the **Begin** page, select the **System Printer** radio button and then click on the **Next** button. The **System Printer** page of the dialog box appears. In this page, select the system printer. If the system printer is not listed in this page then you need to first install the printer drivers in your system. After selecting the system printer, click on the **Next** button. The **Import Pcp or Pc2** page appears. Click on the

Next button in the **Import Pcp or Pc2** page. The **Plotter Name** page appears. Enter the name of the plotter in this page and then click on the **Next** button. The **Finish** page of the dialog box appears. Next, click on the **Finish** button. The plotter is configured in the system.

2.   Make sure that the system printer is connected with your computer through USB or wifi.

Section 4: Plotting/Printing Drawing

1.   Click on the **Layout1** tab in the lower left corner of the drawing area. The **Layout1** tab gets activated and the drawing created in the Model space appears in the default viewport in the layout, see Figure 12.32. You can also delete the default viewport and create a new viewport as per your requirement by using the MV command or by using the tools in the **Layout Viewports** panel of the **Layout** tab in the **Ribbon**.

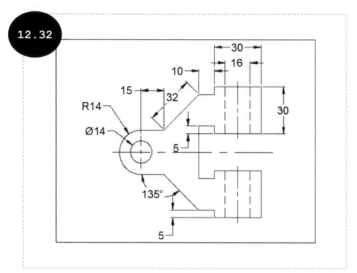

2.   Click on the **Plot** tool in the **Plot** panel of the **Output** tab in the **Ribbon**. The **Plot** dialog box appears, see Figure 12.33. Alternatively, press the CTRL + P to invoke the **Plot** dialog box. Note that if the multiple drawings/layouts are opened in the current session of AutoCAD then on clicking the **Plot** tool, the **Batch Plot** window appears. In this window, click on the **Continue to plot a single sheet** button to invoke the **Plot** dialog box.

3.   Select the plotter from the **Name** drop-down list of the **Printer/plotter** area of the dialog box, see Figure 12.33. In this figure, **HP Deskjet 1510 series** potter is selected.

4.   Select the **A4** in the **Paper size** drop-down list of the dialog box.

5.   Select the **Window** option in the **What to plot** drop-down list of the **Plot area** in the dialog box. The **Plot** dialog box disappears and you are prompted to specify the first corner of the plot window.

```
Specify first corner:
```

6.   Click to specify the first corner of the plot window. Note that the plot window defines the area of the drawing to be plotted. You are prompted to specify the opposite corner of the window.

```
Specify first corner: <Osnap off> Specify opposite corner:
```

7.   Click to specify the opposite corner of the plot window. The plot window has been defined and the **Plot** dialog box appears again.

12.33

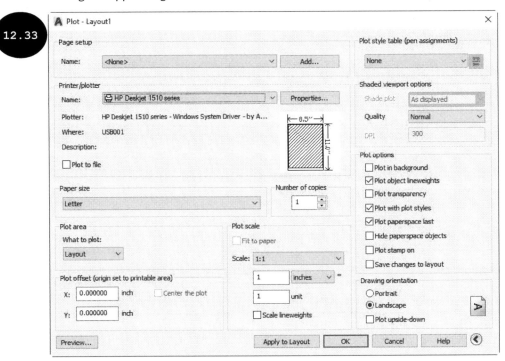

8.   Make sure that the **Center the plot** and **Fit to paper** check boxes of the dialog box are selected.

9.   Accept the remaining default plot settings in the dialog box and then click on the **OK** button. The **Plot Job Progress** window appears and the process of plotting starts. Once the process of plotting the drawing has been done, the **Plot Job Progress** window disappears and the drawing is plotted on a sheet of paper. Make sure that your printer device is connected with your computer through USB or wifi before taking the printout of the drawing. If you want to view the preview of the plot before plotting the drawing, click on the **Preview** button of the dialog box.

Tutorial 2

Create the drawing in the Model space, see Figure 12.34. You need to assign red color to the centerline, blue color to hidden lines, magenta color to dimensions, and black color to objects entities of the drawing. You can assign these different colors to drawing entities by creating different layers. After creating the drawing with different colors, you need to take a printout of the drawing by creating a color-dependent plot style (My Color Plot Style) such that all drawing entities are printed in black color in a sheet of paper. Also, assign the 0.8 mm lineweight to the object entities, 0.65 mm lineweight of the dimensions, 0.53 mm lineweight to hidden lines, 0.5 mm lineweight to centerlines in the color-dependent plot style for taking the printout of the drawing.

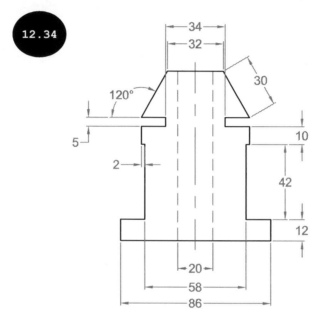

Section 1: Starting AutoCAD

1.   Start AutoCAD and then open a new drawing file.

Section 2: Creating Layers

1.   Invoke the **LAYER PROPERTIES MANAGER** by clicking on the **Layer Properties** tool in the **Layers** panel of the **Home** tab.

2.   Create four layers with the names: **Object**, **Dimension**, **Hidden**, and **Centerline**. Next, assign the magenta color to **Dimension** layer, blue color to **Hidden** layer, and red color to **Centerline** layer. Also, assign **Center** linetype to **Centerline** layer, **Hidden** linetype to **Hidden** layer, and accept the remaining default parameters of the layers, see Figure 12.35.

3. Double-click on the **Object** layer to make it the current layer of the drawing. A green color tick mark appears in front of the name of the **Object** layer in the **LAYER PROPERTIES MANAGER**, which indicates that the **Object** layer is now the current layer of the drawing, see Figure 12.35.

4. Close the **LAYER PROPERTIES MANAGER**.

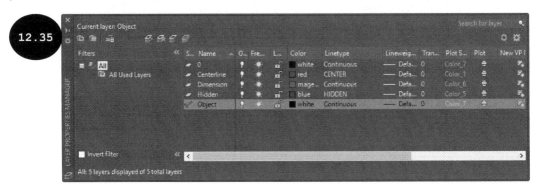

12.35

After creating the layers and assigning the required layer properties, you can create the drawing.

Section 3: Creating Drawing

1. Create the object entities of the drawing by using the **Line** tool, see Figure 12.36.

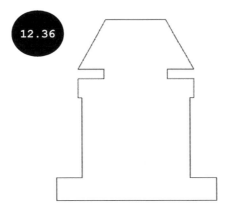

12.36

After creating the object entities of the drawing, you need to create hidden lines, centerline, and apply dimensions to the drawing.

2. Make the **Hidden** layer as the current layer of the drawing and then draw the hidden lines, see Figure 12.37.

3. Make the **Centerline** layer as the current layer of the drawing and then draw the centerline, see Figure 12.38.

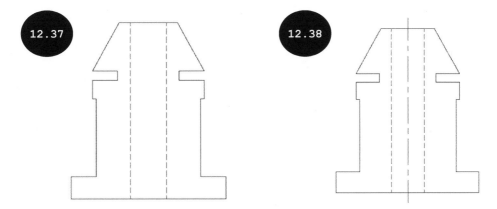

4. Make the **Dimension** layer as the current layer of the drawing and then apply dimensions to the drawing, see Figure 12.39. Note that you need to change the dimension settings such that the dimension text, dimension arrow, and other dimension components are visible clearly in the drawing area either by creating the new dimension style or by editing the existing dimension style. You can create or edit the dimension style by using the **Dimension Style Manager** dialog box as discussed in earlier chapters.

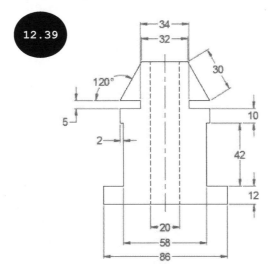

Section 4: Configuring/Adding Plotter

1. Make sure that a plotter is configured in your system. Before configuring plotter, you need to make sure that the system printer (output device) is installed in your computer.

   To configure a plotter, enter **PLOTTERMANAGER** in the Command Window and then press ENTER. The **Plotters** system window appears. Alternatively, click on the **Plotter Manager** tool in the **Plot** panel of the **Output** tab in the **Ribbon**. Next, double-click on **Add-A-Plotter Wizard** in the **Plotters** system window. The **Introduction Page** of the **Add Plotter** dialog box appears, see Figure 12.40.

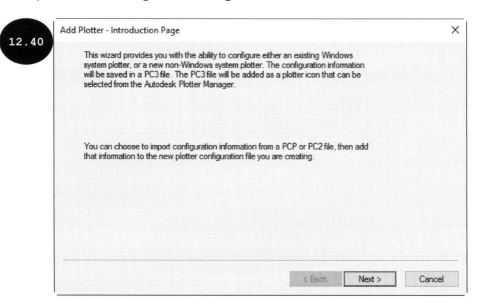

Read the information given in the **Introduction Page** of the **Add Plotter** dialog box and then click on the **Next** button. The **Begin** page of the dialog box appears. In the **Begin** page, select the **System Printer** radio button and then click on the **Next** button. The **System Printer** page of the dialog box appears. In this page, select the system printer. If the system printer is not listed in this page then you need to first install the printer drivers in your system. After selecting the system printer, click on the **Next** button. The **Import Pcp or Pc2** page appears. Click on the **Next** button in the **Import Pcp or Pc2** page. The **Plotter Name** page appears. Enter the name of the plotter in this page and then click on the **Next** button. The **Finish** page of the dialog box appears. Next, click on the **Finish** button. The plotter is configured in the system.

2.   Make sure that the system printer is connected with your computer through USB or wifi.

Section 5: Creating Color-Dependent Plot Style

1.   Enter **STYLESMANAGER** in the Command Window and then press ENTER. The **Plot Styles** system window appears, which displays the list of predefined plot style files.

2.   Double-click on **Add-A-Plot Style Table Wizard** in the **Plot Styles** system window. The **Add Plot Style Table** dialog box appears. Read the information on this page and then click on the **Next** button. The **Begin** page of the **Add Plot Style Table** dialog box appears, see Figure 12.41.

3.   Make sure that the **Start from scratch** radio button is selected in the **Begin** page of the dialog box, see Figure 12.41. Next, click on the **Next** button. The **Pick Plot Style Table** page of the dialog box appears.

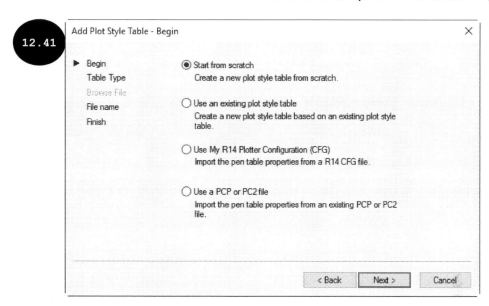

4. Make sure that the **Color-Dependent Plot Style Table** radio button is selected in the **Pick Plot Style Table** page of the dialog box. Next, click on the **Next** button. The **File name** page of the dialog box appears, see Figure 12.42.

5. Enter **My Color Plot Style** in the **File name** field as the name of the plot style, see Figure 12.42. Next, click on the **Next** button. The **Finish** page of the dialog box appears.

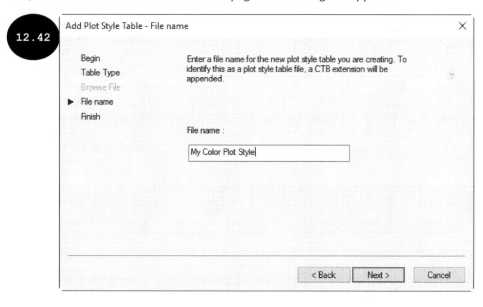

6.   Click on the **Plot Style Table Editor** button in the **Finish** page of the dialog box. The **Plot Style Table Editor** dialog box appears, see Figure 12.43.

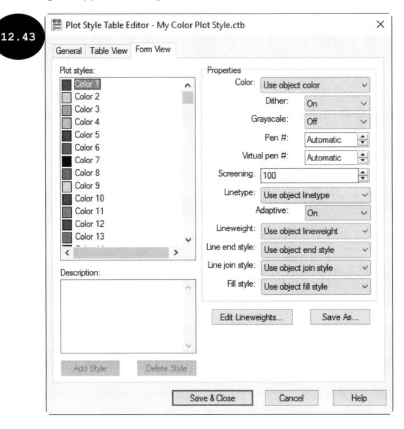

12.43

7.   Make sure that the **Form View** tab of the **Plot Style Table Editor** dialog box is activated, see Figure 12.43.

8.   Click on the **Color 1** (red color) in the **Plot styles** area of the dialog box. All the properties of the **Color 1** plot style appears in the **Properties** area of the dialog box, see Figure 12.43.

9.   Select the **Black** color in the **Color** drop-down list of the **Properties** area of the dialog box, see Figure 12.44.

10. Select the **0.5000 mm** in the **Lineweight** drop-down list of the **Properties** area, see Figure 12.44.

11. Select the **Color 5** (blue color) in the **Plot styles** area of the dialog box. All the properties of the **Color 5** plot style appears in the **Properties** area of the dialog box, see Figure 12.45.

12. Select the **Black** color in the **Color** drop-down list and the **0.5300 mm** in the **Lineweight** drop-down list of the **Properties** area of the dialog box, see Figure 12.45.

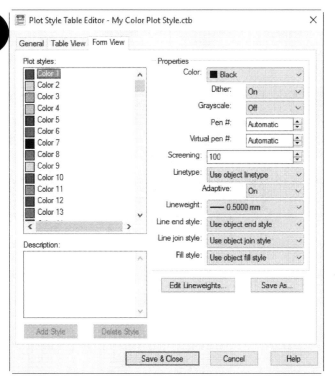

12.44

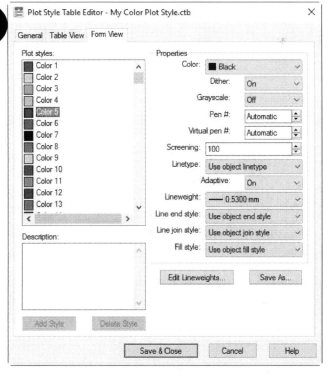

12.45

13. Similarly, change the properties of the **Color 6** (magenta color) and **Color 7** (black color) plot styles. For the **Color 6** plot style, select the black color as the print color of the objects and the 0.65 mm as the print lineweight of the objects. For **Color 7** (black color), select the black color as the print color of the objects and the 0.8 mm as the print lineweight of the objects.

14. After editing the plot style properties, click on the **Save & Close** button of the **Plot Style Table Editor** dialog box. The dialog box gets closed and the plot style properties are modified.

15. Click on the **Finish** button in the **Add Plot Style Table** dialog box. The color-dependent plot style with the name **My Color Plot Style** is created and saved.

After creating the plot style, you can print the drawing as per the newly created plot style.

Section 6: Plotting/Printing Drawing

1. Click on the **Layout1** tab in the lower left corner of the drawing area. The **Layout1** tab gets activated and the drawing created in the Model space appears in the default viewport in the layout, see Figure 12.46.

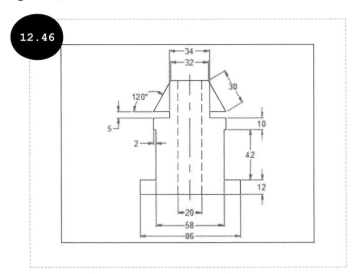

12.46

2. Click on the **Plot** tool in the **Plot** panel of the **Output** tab in the **Ribbon**. The **Plot** dialog box appears, see Figure 12.47. Alternatively, press the CTRL + P to invoke the **Plot** dialog box. Note that if the multiple drawings/layouts are opened in the current session of AutoCAD then on clicking the **Plot** tool, the **Batch Plot** window appears. In this window, click on the **Continue to plot a single sheet** button to invoke the **Plot** dialog box.

3. Select the plotter from the **Name** drop-down list of the **Printer/plotter** area of the dialog box, see Figure 12.47. In this figure **HP Deskjet 1510 series** potter is selected.

4. Make sure that the **Letter** option is selected in the **Paper size** drop-down list and the **Layout** option is selected in the **What to plot** drop-down list of the **Plot** area in the dialog box, see Figure 12.47.

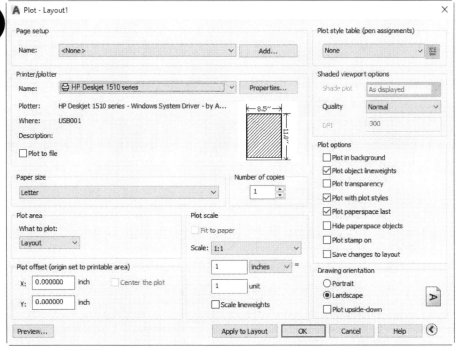

5. Select the *My Color Plot Style.ctb* plot style in the **Plot style table** drop-down list of the **Plot style table (pen assignments)** area.

6. Make sure that the **Plot with plot styles** check box is selected in the **Plot options** area of the dialog box.

7. Accept the remaining default settings and then click on the **OK** button. Next, click on the **Preview** button in the dialog box. The plot preview of the drawing appears in the **Preview** window, see Figure 12.48.

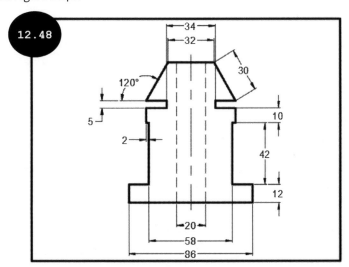

8. Right-click in the **Preview** window. A shortcut menu appears. In this shortcut menu, click on the **Plot** option. The **Plot Job Progress** window appears and the process of plotting gets started. Once the process of plotting the drawing has been done, the **Plot Job Progress** window disappears and the drawing is plotted on a sheet of paper. Make sure that your printer device is connected with your computer through USB or wifi before taking the printout of the drawing.

Section 7: Saving the Drawing

1. Click on the **Save** tool in the **Quick Access Toolbar**. The **Save Drawing As** dialog box appears.

2. Browse to the *AutoCAD* folder and then create a folder with the name *Chapter 12* inside the *AutoCAD* folder.

3. Enter **Tutorial 2** in the **File name** field of the dialog box and then click on the **Save** button. The drawing is saved with the name Tutorial 2 in the *Chapter 12* folder.

Hands-on Test Drive 1

Open the drawing created in the Hands-on Test Drive 1 of Chapter 8, see Figure 12.49 and the take 2 copies of printout on the A4 size sheets .

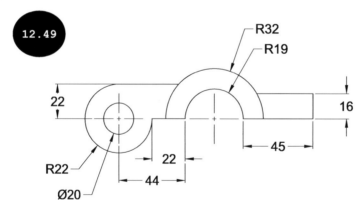

Hands-on Test Drive 2

Open the drawing created in Tutorial 1 of Chapter 9, see Figure 12.50 and the take the printout of the drawing in the Model space.

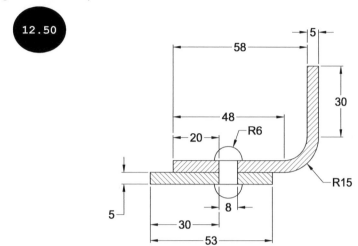

12.50

Summary

In this chapter, you have learned how to configure plotter (output) device in AutoCAD, how to create plot style and set up default plot style for plotting/printing. In addition, you have also learned how to plot/print drawings in AutoCAD.

Questions

• The _____ tool and the _____ command are used to invoke the **Plotters** system window for configuring a plotter in AutoCAD.

• The _____ command is used to invoke the **Plot Styles** system window for creating a plot style.

• In AutoCAD, you can create two types of plot style: _____ and _____ .

• The _____ tool is used to invoke the **Plot** dialog box for plotting/printing a drawing.

• The options in the _____ drop-down list of the **Plot** area in the **Plot** dialog box are used to specify the portion of the drawing to be plotted.

- The _____ option is used to plot the portion of the drawing that is currently displayed on the screen.

- The _____ option is used to define a window around the portion of the drawing to be plotted.

- The _____ style is used to override the layer properties of the drawing objects while plotting/printing.

- The _____ radio button in the **Begin** page of the **Add Plot Style Table** dialog box is used to create a new plot style from scratch.

- The _____ plot style allows you to assign plot styles to the individual AutoCAD colors.

- The _____ plot style allows you to assign plot style directly to objects or layers of a drawing.

- The _____ dialog box is used to setup the default plot style for plotting/printing a drawing.

INDEX